THE BUILDER'S COMPLETE GUIDE TO CONSTRUCTION BUSINESS SUCCESS

Laurence E. Reiner, M.E.,P.E.

THE BUILDER'S COMPLETE GUIDE TO CONSTRUCTION BUSINESS SUCCESS

McGraw-Hill Book Company

New York   St. Louis   San Francisco   Auckland   Bogotá
Düsseldorf   Johannesburg   London   Madrid   Mexico
Montreal   New Delhi   Panama   Paris   São Paulo
Singapore   Sydney   Tokyo   Toronto

Library of Congress Cataloging in Publication Data

Reiner, Laurence E
    The builder's complete guide to construction business
success.

    Includes index.
      1. Building.   2. Construction industry.
I. Title.
TH145.R44   690   77-10333
ISBN 0-07-051837-8

1234567890   KPKP   787654321098

The editors for this book were Jeremy Robinson and
Lester Strong, the designer was Elliot Epstein, and
the production supervisor was Teresa F. Leaden. It
was set in Baskerville by University Graphics, Inc.

Printed and bound by The Kingsport Press.

CONTENTS

Part Two
THE SPECULATIVE BUILDER

PREFACE

The purpose of this book is to guide the small builder from the inception of his venture through the steps of practical construction to the point where he can manage a successful and profitable business of his own. In addition to other related topics the text covers such subjects as finance, cost accounting, job progress planning, and legal matters.

In more than 40 years in the building business the writer has known many small and large builders—some very large. He is convinced that, while undoubtedly many builders are familiar with some or even all of the material, very few organize this knowledge into its maximum potential benefit.

Diligent study of the contents of this guide will accomplish this objective.

The book is divided into two separate portions. The first part deals with the fundamentals of the building business. This portion should be required reading for the person who, while experienced in construction, wishes to enter into the business of construction contracting on his own. The second part of the book deals with speculative building. The foreword to this second part explains its purpose.

GENERAL NOTE

This book has been written essentially for the General Contractor who performs a good part or all of the work himself or with his own employees. In almost any job of any consequence, however, some subcontractors must be used (possibly excavators, masons, electricians, plumbers, roofers, tile setters, resilient-floor layers, and painters among others).

But the words "General Contractor" or "contractor" or "builder" as used here always mean the General Contractor or the Prime Contractor. He is the one who is responsible for the proper completion of the job and he is the one who must be sure that his subcontractors understand what the job is about.

One last point—the use of masculine pronouns within this book should be taken in a purely generic sense, in no way meant to deny the role women already play in the construction industry or their increasing importance to the field. "He" and "his" have been employed solely to avoid the grammatical awkwardness of the "he or she" or "his/her" types of phrasing.

Acknowledgments

I would like to express my appreciation to the various federal agencies that have published energy standards for the use of builders and building managers, and to the Small Business Administration for its booklet on the financing of small business enterprises.

I also want to thank the Darien Library for its help in obtaining reference works; my proofreader for helping to keep my grammar and thoughts in order; and Karin, my wife, who typed the manuscript and to whom this book is dedicated.

ONE

FUNDAMENTALS
OF THE
BUILDING BUSINESS

1

ORGANIZATION OF A SMALL BUILDING BUSINESS

1.1. THE AREAS OF KNOWLEDGE THAT ARE REQUIRED

The building contractor who wishes to succeed in his business must organize that business properly. To "organize," he does not need to employ other people, but he must arrange his business so that he gets the most out of his own time and knowledge.

To start with, there are areas of knowledge of which the builder himself should be aware; if he is not, he should seek help in familiarizing himself with them. This is approximately the order in which they occur in a building business:

Expert reading of plans and specifications
Estimating and bidding procedures
Construction contracts
Purchasing
Progress scheduling
Cost control and accounting
Insurance and bonding
Legal aspects of construction
Financial planning
Field superintendence
Construction unions
Building and zoning codes
Licensing laws

This looks like a formidable list—and it is—but anyone who wants to start a building business or is already in the business has a general working knowledge of most of these items or can get information about them from people who do know. With charts and illustrations, this book will define the basic information the builder should have in order to perform most of the work himself—particularly when his business is small.

1.2. THE ORGANIZATION OF A BUILDER'S OFFICE

It is strongly recommended that the contractor have an office or a working space of his own if he cannot justify an office away from his home. It is presumed that the building business is his livelihood, so he must be able to concentrate. Plans and specifications need to be spread out, papers must be kept in orderly arrangement, a telephone* should be immediately available for outgoing and incoming calls, and there should be some privacy.

If the builder has an office of his own it must be organized in certain ways. First, there should be a large, flat, well-lighted table where plans can be kept or spread out and examined. Second, a safe space should be provided for files and account books. (Incidentally, it does not take much time to keep orderly files and to keep them up to date. This is most important and should be done daily.) Third, if possible, there should be space for more than one desk. There will be occasions when others must work in the office, and, of course, in time the business will grow and require more help. Fourth, the working area must provide space for all the functions called for in the sample work charts that follow.

1.3. SAMPLE ORGANIZATION CHARTS

Work that must be done on a current basis:

CHART A

Contractor

Estimating
    Contractor's own work
    Subcontractors

Record keeping
    Material control
    Cost control
    Inventory

Field organization
    Site planning
    Job progress
    Labor control
    Subcontractors
    Safety

Purchasing and labor
    Material lists and quantities
    Subcontractors
    Labor pay rates

Bookkeeping
    Payroll
    Income and expenses

New work
    Travel and interviewing
      prospects
    Planning

*A private telephone is most important. Prospective clients or business associates must not be kept waiting while a 12-year-old offspring does homework on the telephone.

All items on Chart A must get close attention—some daily. It must be made clear right now that none of this work can be done on a "when I have time" basis. It must be done on time. The importance of this cannot be overemphasized.

There are some things that need not be done on a current basis but which do require attention at the proper time:

CHART B

Contractor

Financial
    Banks or other financial
      institutions
    Forward planning

Public authority
    Permits
    Building codes
    Zoning codes
    Licensing laws
    Labor laws
    OSHA regulations

Insurance
    Workmen's compensation
    Public liability
    Bonding

Legal
    Contracts
    Liens
    Labor unions

Taxes
    Real estate
    Income
    Sales
    Improvement

1.4. DIVIDING THE WORK LOAD

The foregoing lists and organizational charts show what has to be done in a successful building contractor's office and in the field. The question now is how best to perform these tasks. The contractor should know how many of these things he can do himself. At the very start of a business he may want to perform some of the actual field work himself and hire temporary labor as he needs it, but this should be stopped as soon as possible. *It is only through the effective management of outside field and office labor that a contractor can hope to earn a reasonable income over and above a day's pay.*

At this point the contractor should make up a schedule or chart of what he thinks he can do himself and the work he should get others to do. A suggested form follows. The amount of time to be spent on each item can be corrected after sufficient experience. Of course there are many variables here. The time he spends on each item will depend on whether he does a number of small jobs which call for constant estimating, purchasing, etc., builds complete houses, does major alteration work, or works on a mixed bag of all of these. The figures shown in Table 1-1 represent a general average.

These activities make a 60-hr week. The contractor can make cuts in this schedule but he must give priorities to the profit-making activities.

TABLE 1-1   TIME CHART FOR AVERAGE CONTRACTOR

Kind of Work	Who Does and How Many Hours a Week
Estimating	Myself. Quantity takeoffs. Labor costs. Bids from materials dealers and subcontractors. Estimate of overhead and profit. Assembling bid. 10 hr
Purchasing	Myself. Negotiating with material dealers and subcontractors after contract is signed. Negotiating for field labor. 5 hrs
Field supervision	Myself and Joe Jones (working carpenter foreman). Keep J.J. on large jobs; I will take care of all others. Visit all jobs daily. Own time: 15 hr
Look for new work	Myself. 5 hr
Record keeping	Myself and Mary Smith, part time (high-school business student). Purchase orders, delivery slips, time records, inventory records. Own time: 10 hr
Bookkeeping	Mary Smith or Mrs. Contractor. Make up payrolls. Send bills. Pay bills. Keep records of income and expense on each job. Distribute overhead charges. Work with Tax auditor. Own time: 5 hr
Financial	Myself. Bank. Mortgage payouts. Loans. Forward planning. 5 hr
Public authorities, insurance, legal, taxes	Myself with insurance broker, attorney, accountant. 5 hr

1.5. THE ORGANIZATION OF THE CONTRACTOR'S OWN TIME

Now that the contractor has made an educated guess on how much time he feels he should spend on each item of work, the next step is to keep an hour-by-hour record of his time. Figure 1-1 shows the possible work load of a small but active contractor. It may seem like a waste of time to keep such a record, but the few minutes that it takes will repay the contractor many times over. An entry can be made on the log after each item of work is completed.

At the end of each work day such a complete daily log will give the contractor an overall picture of what he did and where his time went. It enables him to analyze his work load and to see whether he is using his time to the best possible advantage. Although all parts of his work are important, there are some things that must take priority: tight and careful estimating, negotiating prices for materials and with subcontractors, guidance and supervision of field labor, dealing with clients and banks, and following up new work are priority items. An analysis of the sample daily log breaks down as follows:

Expediting subcontractors	¼ hr
Estimating	2 hr
Field supervision	2¼ hr
Job progress	¼ hr
Public authority	¾ hr
Looking for new work	¾ hr
Financial planning	¾ hr
Client relations	¼ hr
Forward planning	½ hr
Traveling	2½ hr

It is interesting to compare these analyses with the time table or chart which the contractor has made for himself and which to his mind represents the best use of his own time and knowledge.

Contractor's Weekly Chart	As Estimated, hr (Table 1-1)	Actual Daily Log, hr
Estimating and subcontractors	10	2
Purchasing	5	None
Field supervision	15	2
Look for new work	5	1
Record keeping	10	None
Bookkeeping	5	None
Financial, forward planning	5	1¼
Public authority, etc.	5	¾
Traveling		2¼

No time has been spent on purchasing, record keeping, or bookkeeping. These tasks will have to be done after the contractor has spent over a 10 hr day, and it is imperative that it be done on a daily basis. Travel has taken over 20 percent of the working day. This is a waste of time and money. Not enough time has been spent on field supervision. There has been almost no time spent on client relations. The contractor has not had time to carefully examine his records to find how closely he is keeping to his cost estimate and progress schedules. The conclusion is that he has tried to do too many things and has spent too much time traveling.

1.5A. Current Planning

In order to make the most efficient use of his time and to make sure that the important things are done, the contractor must do some planning. Once a week, at least, he should take time to write down all the things he must do in

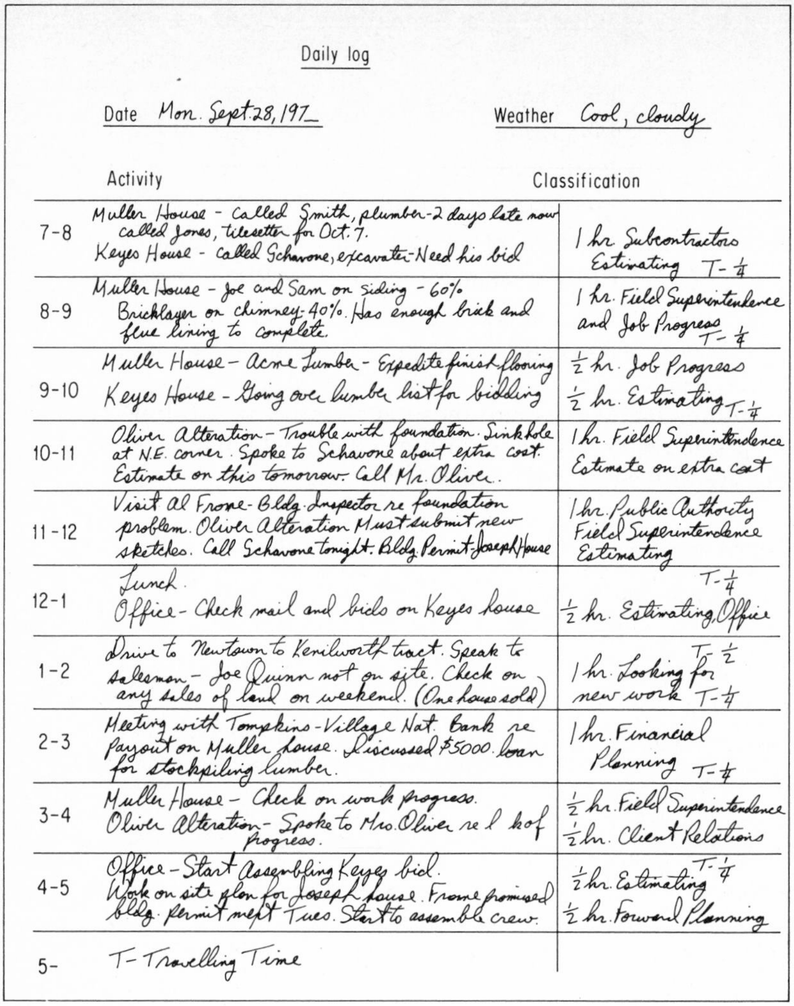

Daily log

Date Mon. Sept. 28, 197_ Weather Cool, cloudy

	Activity	Classification
7-8	Muller House - Called Smith, plumber-2 days late now called Jones, tilesetter for Oct. 7. Keyes House - called Schavone, excavater-Need his bid	1 hr. Subcontractors Estimating T-¼
8-9	Muller House - Joe and Sam on siding - 60% Bricklayer on chimney-40%. Has enough brick and flue lining to complete.	1 hr. Field Superintendence and Job Progress T-¼
9-10	Muller House - Acme Lumber - Expedite finish flooring Keyes House - Going over lumber list for bidding	½ hr. Job Progress ½ hr. Estimating T-¼
10-11	Oliver Alteration - Trouble with foundation. Sink hole at N.E. corner. Spoke to Schavone about extra cost. Estimate on this tomorrow. Call Mr. Oliver.	1 hr. Field Superintendence Estimate on extra cost
11-12	Visit Al Frone-Bldg. Inspector re foundation problem. Oliver Alteration Must submit new sketches. Call Schavone tonight. Bldg. Permit-Joseph House	1 hr. Public Authority Field Superintendence Estimating
12-1	Lunch. Office - Check mail and bids on Keyes house	T-¼ ½ hr. Estimating, Office
1-2	Drive to Newtown to Kenilworth tract. Speak to salesman - Joe Quinn not on site. Check on any sales of land on weekend. (One house sold)	T-½ 1 hr. Looking for new work T-¼
2-3	Meeting with Tompkins-Village Nat. Bank re payout on Muller house. Discussed $5000. loan for stockpiling lumber.	1 hr. Financial Planning T-¼
3-4	Muller House - Check on work progress. Oliver Alteration - Spoke to Mrs. Oliver re l kof progress.	½ hr. Field Superintendence ½ hr. Client Relations
4-5	Office - Start assembling Keyes bid. Work on site plan for Joseph house. Frone promised bldg. permit mept Tues. Start to assemble crew.	T-¼ ½ hr. Estimating ½ hr. Forward Planning
5-	T - Travelling Time	

Figure 1-1

the next few days (and allow some leeway for emergencies, which are always arising in the building business). He should be sure that the people he wants to see will be there when he wants to see them. Bankers, clients, architects, building inspectors, and attorneys all like to be seen by appointment and are impressed by those who make one. Time should be allowed for the things which contribute most to a profitable business.

To repeat some of these items, there should be follow-up for new work, tight inventory and cost control, material control (especially in these days of sudden spot shortages), and labor control. If he thinks it through carefully, the contractor can make up a list of how he can spend his time most profitably.

A daily log for a contractor who actually performs some of his own field labor would of course show an entirely different distribution of time. This is a good way of starting in the business, but it also takes careful forward planning. The following questions must be answered:

- How many jobs can the contractor himself handle at any one time? This includes labor, obtaining material, financing, record keeping.

- If he is asked to estimate on a job, can the contractor say within a few days when he can start? This is very important. Angry customers make poor advertising.

- How much time can the contractor devote to paper work? He must know how he comes out on each job so that he can estimate the next one accurately.

- Can he get reliable part-time field help so that he can handle more than one job at a time?

Many reputations are lost because a contractor takes on too many jobs and tries to do them without adequate help. The result is dissatisfied customers and the possible drying up of all new work. Reliable workmanship and on-time performance are most important for a growing contracting business.

1.6. OVERHEAD

No chapter about the organization of a building contractor's business can be complete without an explanation of overhead expenses—how to estimate them and how to distribute them. Overhead expense is a part of the cost of doing business which is not chargeable to any particular piece of work. Here is a list of some of the expenses which make up overhead. (The individual contractor can add some of his own or deduct those that do not apply.)

- Office rent
- Light, heat, and power (if not included in rent)
- Telephone not including job phones; answering service
- Stationery and printing
- Office supplies
- Insurance (other than that directly chargeable to jobs)
- Bonding
- Office salaries

- Field salaries (not directly chargeable to any single job)
- Accounting fees
- Legal fees
- Travel expenses including automobile
- Depreciation of office furniture and equipment
- Subscriptions
- Association dues
- Rental of storage yard or, if yard is owned, taxes, mortgage interest, and interest on own investment
- Depreciation of working equipment

The contractor new in the business would be well advised to look at each item in the list mentioned above that applies to him and attempt to estimate its cost. Some items such as rent, utilities, travel expenses, and salaries are easily determined, but items such as legal, accounting, and insurance charges should be checked with experts in these respective fields. The total amount may come as something of a surprise. It is better, however, to be aware of the final cost of these items so that the unnecessary expenses may be reduced or eliminated before they are incurred. Even the experienced contractor should look closely and constantly at his overhead expense. Overhead has a way of eating into profits.

Overhead expenses should be listed in a permanent record and entries should be made on a daily, weekly, or monthly basis as the expenses occur. In this way the contractor knows at any time what his overhead cost is and can use the record to estimate his future cost. This will be of incalculable help to him when he estimates on new work. Chapter 8 will show a sample of how such entries could be made.

Note that the contractor's own salary or profit is not included. This amount should be calculated by the contractor as he makes up each bid or estimate after he allows for labor, material, and all other out-of-pocket job expense.

1.7. EQUIPMENT

In addition to having an office or working space, the contractor must also have some basic equipment and a place to store it. At first the equipment need only be the family automobile, but any amount of business will necessitate much more. For instance:

- A small truck which can be used to transport material of all kinds to a job, so that there is no need for waiting for the lumberyard or hardware dealer to deliver it. Work may be held up for an hour because someone forgot to order a keg of six-penny nails.

- Power tools such as saws and drills.

- Tarpaulins to cover work in progress against bad weather.

- A surveying instrument for laying out foundations, lining up corners, and shooting levels.

- Hand tools (depending on what the contractor intends to do himself).

Many of these items can be purchased second hand and their cost can be written off as depreciation on the overhead cost. However, the contractor must be aware of this in estimating his cost of starting and continuing in business. An example of an equipment inventory record will be shown in Chap. 9.

1.8. FINDING NEW WORK

Finding new work is of paramount importance. The contractor must make every effort to ensure a constant flow of work to keep himself and his workers busy. It is only in this way that he can gain the confidence of good craftsmen, material dealers, and others. He must spend a significant part of his time in this activity.

Some of the potential sources of new construction work are listed below. All should be explored.

1. Local architect. The contractor can introduce himself and leave a card. He should also write, giving his experience and mentioning references, to ask the architect to keep him in mind when asking for bids or when negotiating a contract without competitive bidding. Many smaller contracts (and some large ones) are consummated in this way. If the contractor can mention satisfied customers it will help.

2. Local building inspector. This official is always worth cultivating. He is usually well informed and often knows who is planning to build or alter. Very often homeowners come in for advice before altering or plot owners come in to ask about zoning or other matters.

3. Local zoning official. (This can be the building inspector.) This person will know what subdivisions are being planned and who the land developers are. He also knows who is asking for a zoning variance, which means a new house or an addition to an existing structure.

4. Advertising. This can be done in a local newspaper or by direct mail. The newspaper advertisement can be in the class-

ified section under "business services" or "construction" or whatever the newspaper uses as a heading. The advertisement should be at least 2 in. long and preferably 3 in. It can say: "John Jones, builder. Lowest prices for excellent work. Alterations and new construction. Call for an estimate 421-1234." The direct-mail folder can be a typed sheet with possibly a small pen-and-ink sketch of a house under construction. The cost for offset printing 2000 sheets is less than $100. Addresses can be obtained from the town voters' list or tax list.

5. Local material dealers. These people are often asked about reliable contractors. The contractor should try to purchase all of his material from a local dealer. He not only is likely to obtain better service and a better price on quantity, but he becomes known to the dealer. He should make it known to the material dealer that he is looking for new work. New work for the contractor means business for the dealer. Some dealers have bulletin boards for posting contractor's cards, but word of mouth is better.

6. Real estate broker. When selling a house, brokers often find that the new owner wishes to add a room or two or to finish a second floor or otherwise add to or alter a house. The builder is sure to meet brokers or real estate salesmen in the course of his business. He can make it known that any business referred to him will be treated on a quid pro quo basis. This is, of course, also true in the sale of vacant land.

7. Local bank or other mortgage lender. People who intend to build or make alterations on their property will visit a local financial institution to discuss mortgage money or a short-term loan. The contractor should be sure that he is known to the lending official in the event that the owner asks for names of builders.

8. Land developers. Many land developers also build all of the houses on their tracts, but others will just build some houses and then confine themselves to the sale of building lots. The contractor should know where such developments are, how they are being developed, and the identities of the people who are in a position to recommend a builder. He can also, through the town land records or the local newspaper, find who has purchased vacant land.

9. Local business association. There are many local associations of business people which meet regularly and where a local builder can become known and gain information regarding proposed building activities.

10. Local insurance broker. The local broker will be the first (after the fire department) to know of a fire or other damage. Many times the insurance carrier has its own adjuster but there are general adjustment bureaus in all larger towns. (Telephone yellow pages under "adjusters.") A call on these people can do no harm (they often ask a local contractor to give them an estimate of the damage). A call on the owner of the damaged house and an offer of an estimate may result in business. Repairing fire damage can be a profitable source of income.

11. Word of mouth. Just doing a good job on time for a client can result in a surprising amount of new business.

There are more ways than those listed above to gain new business, but in all cases the contractor's reputation for reliability and good organization will persuade people to mention his name or to recommend him.

1.9. CUSTOMER RELATIONS

The acquisition of new business through the various sources mentioned in Sec. 1.8 will only continue if the builder maintains good customer relations. The local material dealer, broker, or banker who may mention the contractor's name to a prospective client will very soon find out if he has made a mistake. The unhappy client will soon tell him. The builder must be very careful to:

- Keep his appointments or telephone if he cannot.

- Start a job when he has said he would.

- Not abandon a job for a number of days while he is busy elsewhere. If he is that busy he should keep the client informed as to when he will be back.

- Provide the best quality of construction he is capable of.

- Complete the job on time.

- Always answer telephone calls from his clients.

Small builders are business people, They should act like responsible business people if they want to continue in business.

1.10. FINANCING A CONSTRUCTION BUSINESS

The financing of a construction business will be explored in a later chapter, but it is well to mention it here in connection with the organizing of the business. Anyone who is starting or is in the early stages of the contracting business knows that it is a risk business. The risk can be cut down, however, by careful planning. The risk is the smallest in alteration work. Here the contractor need only carry himself with a small line of credit from the local material dealer until he is paid by the owner. If it is an entire house, then he must carry all his expenses with credit from material dealers and subcontractors until a payment is made by the bank. Such payouts occur at certain stages of construction and the contractor must plan for them (Chap. 11). The builder must in the meantime be able to meet his weekly payroll and to pay for utilities, permits, etc., on which no credit is granted.

Although the general matter of financing is the same for all custom construction, each contractor's personal need for cash is different and each contractor must be sure that he has enough liquid funds on hand to carry through the job.

Speculative building is an altogether different problem and will be discussed under its own heading.

2

THE PLANS AND SPECIFICATIONS

2.1. THE MEANING OF PLANS AND SPECIFICATIONS

The plans and specifications for any piece of construction work should tell the contractor exactly what he is to do, what materials he is to use, how he is to put them together, and how the finished structure is to look. They can range anywhere from a dimensioned sketch by the owner in the case of a small alteration, to a set of architectural, structural, mechanical, and electrical plans by an architect/engineer. In all instances, however, the contractor must be certain that he understands exactly what he is to do.

In a small alteration, if there is no professional drawing, it is well to go over the sketch with the owner and to describe to him exactly what he is to get. Amateurs are likely to forget or they do not mention important electrical or mechanical changes that may be necessary. They often have only a vague idea of what the finished product will look like or how an alteration may change a roof line or the exterior appearance. If the owner does not employ an architect or other professional, then the builder must perform this service. If the job is worth the effort, an hour or two spent in describing to the owner how it will look and what materials will be used will be well worthwhile.

Most communities require a building permit for other than minor alterations, and in order to obtain such a permit, a plan must be filed. It is sad but true, however, that many of these plans leave too much to the imagination, and unfortunately it is usually the contractor who is blamed for any shortcoming. There are many cases where a contractor is called in only to find that no plans have been prepared, the owner simply describing several changes or additions to be made with no idea of the work involved. Should there be any difference between the builder's intent and the owner's expectations, it is strongly suggested that a memorandum be made in the form of notations and small sketches which can be initialed by the owner and the contractor. The small amount of time thus spent can save many hours of bickering, held-up payments, and possible lawsuits. (See Fig. 2-1.)

15

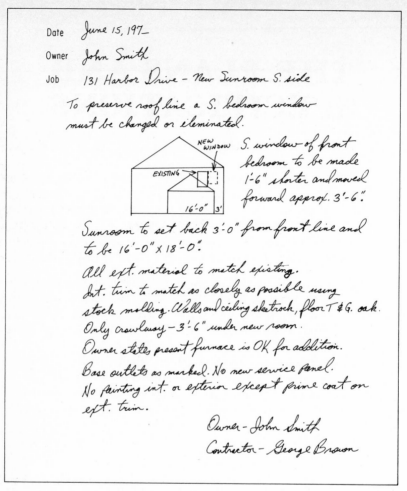

Date June 15, 197_

Owner John Smith

Job 131 Harbor Drive - New Sunroom S. side

To preserve roof line a S. bedroom window must be changed or eliminated.

S. window of front bedroom to be made 1'-6" shorter and moved forward approx. 3'-6".

Sunroom to set back 3'-0" from front line and to be 16'-0" X 18'-0".

All ext. material to match existing.
Int. trim to match as closely as possible using stock molding. Walls and ceiling sheetrock, floor T & G. oak.
Only crawlway - 3'-6" under new room.
Owner states present furnace is OK for addition.
Base outlets as marked. No new service panel.
No painting int. or exterior except prime coat on ext. trim.

Owner - John Smith
Contractor - George Brown

Figure 2-1   Suggested form of memorandum prior to construction.

Even when a full set of plans and specifications has been drawn up by a professional, the builder is still advised to take nothing for granted. Plans and specifications are intended to complement each other and any work that is mentioned in either one has the same effect as if mentioned in both. That is why the builder should have both documents spread before him so that he can compare them and become aware of the full extent of the work he is to do.

The specifications, in addition to detailing materials and quality of workmanship, also include a section known as "General Conditions," which are subsequently discussed in detail.

2.2. THE GENERAL CONDITIONS

The "General Conditions" of a construction contract mean exactly what the words say. This document stipulates the provisions which are applicable to every part of the contract and specifies the obligations of the architect/ engineer, the owner, and the contractor.

Many smaller builders have never been exposed to a set of general conditions and it would be a waste of time to have such a document for a small alteration. As jobs get bigger, however, and when an architect is involved, there are always general conditions which become a part of the contract. But even in the smallest construction job there are implied general conditions. For instance, the contractor has the obligation to carry proper insurance, to be familiar with the building code and other applicable regulations, to be responsible for carrying out and satisfactorily completing the job on time and to the owner's satisfaction. The owner has the obligation to furnish the contractor with necessary surveys, to give the contractor all necessary information so that the work can be properly performed, to carry his proper portion of the insurance, to make payments for the work as such payments become due. The owner also has every right to believe that when he employs a professional builder, the builder is familiar with code requirements, insurance requirements, etc., and that he will call the owner's attention to inferior materials or noncomplying aspects.

2.2A. The Basic Provisions of the General Conditions

The following discussion of the basic provisions will be valuable for all contractors who perform jobs large enough to warrant the inclusion of a general conditions document (this would include almost every job in which plans are drawn by a professional).

There are many forms of general conditions but certain requirements are common to them all.

2.2A1. DEFINITION OF THE CONTRACT DOCUMENTS

The contract itself is only a portion of the contract documents. The contractor must know that the entire contract under which he is obligated to perform consists also of the drawings, the specifications, the general conditions, any supplementary conditions, the agreed-upon alternates, any agreed-upon modifications to the contract, any agreed-upon addenda to the specifications.

2.2A2. CORRELATION OF THE PLANS AND SPECIFICATIONS

As previously mentioned, the plans and specifications are complementary. The best way to illustrate this extremely important point is to quote from an actual document: "The drawings and specifications are intended to be complementary. Anything mentioned in the specifications and not shown on the drawings, or shown on the drawings and not mentioned in the specifications shall be of like effect as if shown or mentioned in both. Generally the specifications describe work which cannot be readily indicated on the drawings . . . nor [is it possible] to show on the drawings all the items of work described or required by the specifications. . . ." The contractor must therefore become thoroughly familiar with both these documents.

2.2A3. THE OBLIGATION OF THE OWNER

It is always the owner's responsibility to provide a correct survey showing exactly where the property lies. (Builders have been known to alter or build structures or even demolish structures on the wrong lot.) He must also provide information on easements where necessary and all other information that will aid the contractor to perform his functions properly. The owner must also carry fire and extended-coverage insurance to cover materials on the site and as they are built into the structure itself. (And of course he must pay for the work and pay on time.)

2.2A4. THE OBLIGATION OF THE ARCHITECT/ENGINEER

Unless otherwise specifically stated, the architect is considered the representative of the owner and assumes the duty to see to it that the work is carried out in accordance with his plans and specifications. The architect determines when payments for the work are due and in what amount. The architect may also reject work that does not meet the quality as specified, and he must approve change orders which in almost all cases mean an increase in the cost of construction. (Change orders will be discussed in Chap. 8.) The architect also interprets the plans and specifications in the event of a dispute between the owner and the contractor.

2.2A5. THE OBLIGATIONS OF THE GENERAL CONTRACTOR

The first duty of the contractor is to carefully evaluate the intent of the plans and specifications. The general conditions always say that "the contractor is deemed to have examined the site . . . and will be deemed to be satisfied as to the conditions under which he, (the contractor) will be obliged to operate in performing the work." They also mention that the builder must comply with all codes, labor laws, insurance provisions, and any and all regulations set forth by any public authority having jurisdiction. This is a very interesting catchall provision and has often resulted in cost overruns and delays for the unwary contractor. Presumably the architect is familiar with all the rules, regulations, and laws that apply. In the great majority of jobs this is true, but there is always the one where there has been a recent change in code, for example, or where an old regulation has become more strictly enforced. It is in these instances that the language of the general conditions or specifications—which state that the contractor must serve notice on the architect of noncompliance with codes, etc., and that his failure to do so will make him completely responsible—can result in serious loss. This seems fair to the contractor and to an extent it is. But the contractor and his subcontractors should be aware of changes in codes and uses of material.

If the contractor finds conditions on the site unsatisfactory or some of the specified material or methods noncomplying or hard to obtain, he should speak up.

The contractor also has the obligation to pay for all labor, material, equipment, tools, temporary water, heat and utilities, transportation, and any other facilities necessary for the proper completion of the work. The contractor has to pay all sales and consumer taxes and has to secure and pay for all building permits, licenses and other government fees.

The contractor is responsible for proper superintendence of the work, for preparing and living up to a progress schedule, for the proper use and maintenance of the construction site and obtaining all required highway permits, for performing all necessary cutting and patching so that all parts of the work fit together properly, and finally for cleaning up the building and site when completed and ready for occupancy. Although the foregoing seems like a lot of words the contractor is advised to read it carefully and to take it seriously. After all, that is what a contractor's job is all about!

2.2A6. SUBCONTRACTORS

The subcontractor clause of the general conditions is not often observed (except in very large jobs), and yet it provides a certain amount of coverage for the general contractor. It states that "The general contractor agrees to deliver to every subcontractor a copy of these general conditions ..." and then goes on to say "Every Subcontractor having knowledge of these General Conditions shall be deemed to be bound by them, whether or not so agreeing." This clause means that even on the smallest job in which subcontractors are involved, the general contractor has the right to assume that the plumber, electrician, excavator, etc., are familiar with the various codes and regulations referring to their work, and that these subcontractors have the proper licenses and permits to carry on their work just as the owner looks to the general contractor for such knowledge. The general contractor, however, is advised not to assume anything.

2.2A7. INSURANCE

All General Conditions spell out in detail the kind and amount of insurance that must be carried and who is to carry it. The general contractor must carry insurance to cover himself and the owner. Such insurance usually consists of:

> Workmen's compensation
> Employer's liability
> Comprehensive general liability
> Comprehensive automobile liability

The owner carries fire and extended-coverage insurance to cover the structure as well as all material stored on the site that is to be built into the structure. (For detailed information on insurance see Chap. 10.)

2.2A8. MISCELLANEOUS CLAUSES

To name the more important ones, there are clauses on liens, arbitration, payments and completion, owner's right to complete the work (in case of default), guarantees, owner's right to occupy, payments, etc. These clauses should be studied but, the clauses detailed in Sections 2.2A1 through 2.2A7 are the ones that most directly affect the actual construction progress and are the ones that most directly concern profit and loss.

2.2B. Supplementary General Conditions

As the title indicates, this contract document is in addition to the General Conditions and, unlike the latter document, usually relates to the conditions of a particular job. Items included may be a job telephone, protection of trees and shrubs on the site, cold weather protection, temporary toilet facilities, and insurance over and above that normally carried.

Before his final estimate is submitted, the contractor should read the Supplementary Conditions very carefully.

2.3. PLANS AND SPECIFICATIONS FOR AN ALTERATION

In Fig. 2-1 there is a sample of a memorandum between a contractor and an owner when there is no formal specification or plan. The builder, however, should become familiar with such formal specifications. If this alteration were designed by a professional, and if regular specifications were written, they would be about as follows*:

> A. *General and Special Conditions.* The contractor is to furnish all labor, material, equipment, tools, transportation and any other facilities necessary to complete the project in accordance with the plans and

---

*The reader is to note that nowhere in these sample specifications are any manufacturers or brand names mentioned. The actual specifications will of course have such names and other specific identifications.

specifications. The contractor is to pay for all permits, fees, licenses, etc. to carry on the work and in accordance with all applicable codes and regulations of any governmental authority having jurisdiction. The contractor is to be responsible for obtaining a final certificate of occupancy where required. Contractor is to remove all rubbish from site and to leave premises broom-clean.

B. *Excavation and Foundations.* General excavation is to go down to a depth of 3'-6" below the bottom of the floor joists. Top soil to be piled to be used later. Excavation for the footings is to go down at least 3'-6" below finish grade but in any case to firm undisturbed ground. Leave only enough excavated material for backfill. All other to be removed.

Footings to be of 1:2:4 concrete* to be 16" wide by 8" deep as shown on plan and to have 2½" deformed reinforcing rods as shown, running their entire length. Footings to be keyed into existing footings by the insertion of the reinforcing rods into these footings and by the cutting of niches into them so that the concrete can be poured into these niches and around the rods. (See Fig. 2-2.)

Foundation walls to be of 8-in. wide concrete block with the top course to be solidly filled with mortar and to contain ½ in. holding down bolts at 6'-0" intervals. Every other block is to be keyed into existing wall for a depth of at least 4".

C. *Framing.* To be done in best workmanlike manner using kiln-dried Southern pine or Douglas fir (no hemlock). Sills to be treated with wood preservative and contractor to furnish and apply metal termite shield as shown. Studs to be on 16" centers and to be doubled at

*1:2:4 concrete consists of 1 part cement, 2 parts sand, 4 parts stone and not more than 7½ gal water per bag of cement. This will develop a strength of approximately 2500 psi after 28 days. All proportions are by weight.

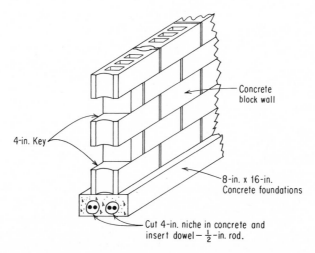

Figure 2-2 Example of keying of existing footings and foundation to new wall.

windows and tripled at corners. Rafters to be on 16″ centers and fastened with collar beams. Lintels to be of sizes as shown. Joists to be of sizes shown and spaced as shown and to be solidly bridged at two equidistant spaces in their length.

Contractor to cut and remove siding from present house where this structure abuts it and to cut and frame a doorway as shown. Contractor is also to solidly attach the framing of the addition to the existing framing.

Floor to be of ½″ plywood nailed over 15-lb tarred building paper and select red oak T & G strip flooring to match existing floors.

Walls and ceiling to be ½″ gypsum board nailed securely over 4″ thick rock or glass wool bats with vapor barrier fastened between exterior studs. Contractor to lay 4″ bats over ceiling boards before or after ceiling boards are in place. Taping of gypsum board to be omitted.

D. *Roofing and Sheet Metal.* Roof to be of 235-lb asphalt shingles over heavy metal-reinforced fibered paper and is to match color of existing roof. Flashing to be of 16-oz soft-rolled copper; leaders and gutters as shown to be of 16 oz hard-rolled copper and to match existing work. Contractor must very carefully step-flash all joints between existing house and this new work.

E. *Millwork.* Trim to match existing. Windows to be double hung of sizes as shown with built-in weatherstripping by J. J. Jones or equal. Windows to match existing. Install foil backing behind recessed radiators and trim around them.

Alternate for Millwork: Furnish and install combination aluminum storm and screen windows to match existing.

F. *Finishes.* Contractor to sand floors and to apply one coat filler and one coat filler and wax in color selected by owner.

G. *Alternate for Finishes.* Contractor to quote alternates as follows:

To tape all joints in gypsum board walls and ceilings using three-coat process, carefully feathered and sanded, and to paint with two coats latex-base flat paint in color to be selected.

To paint exterior walls and trim using one coat primer and one coat exterior-grade oil-base paint, color to match existing.

H. *Heating.* Contractor to furnish and install recessed radiators to match design of existing and to be of size and capacity to maintain interior temperature at 70°F. when exterior temperature is 0°F. Contractor is to check and to assure owner that the boiler and oil burner are of sufficient capacity to handle this additional space.

I. *Electrical.* Furnish and install base outlets as shown on plan. One outlet as shown to be controlled by switch located just inside doorway. Contractor is to check and assure owner that there is sufficient panel capacity to connect the additional circuit.

The above specification can be considered average for a good-quality job. With some additions this could be a model specification for a typical small house. When he is dealing with an owner only, and without formal documents, the contractor would be well advised to still maintain the quality.

2.4. PLANS AND SPECIFICATIONS FOR A PRIVATE RESIDENCE

This study is of an actual set of plans and specifications from which a private residence has been built. It is a large house (five bedrooms, four baths) and the specifications have been prepared by an architect/engineer. Each section will be explained in detail. It is to be carefully noted that the specifications are for a specific house in a specific location and cannot be used for just any house anywhere, except in their general sense. The actual specification will be identified and an explanation will follow.

2.4A. Addendum No. 1

Addenda are very often placed at the beginning to make sure they are not missed. This addendum consists of three parts:

1. Because this house is in open country, the first part describes in great detail exactly where the building lot is located. The description is reinforced by the first sheet of the drawings which show a survey and contour lines in small scale and the location of the house on the lot. The survey is explicit—it gives directions, distances between stakes, and fixed landmarks. The first sheet also shows the house outline scale with reference to the survey lines.

2. This is a clarification of the site work which follows in another section. It states that the contractor need only remove those trees on the actual house site.

3. Again a clarification of the site work. It states that the contractor is not to include the driveway in his bid but is to quote it as an alternate.

2.4B. Instructions to Bidders

In this section the bidder is asked to:

1. Submit the bid at a fixed place, and on a certain day and hour.

2. Quote a lump sum for the job, including allowances, subcontractors' costs, overhead, and profit.

3. Quote on a list of named alternates.

4. Give an estimated time of completion in working days.

5. Quote on the unit cost for rock and trench excavation.

Up to this point the directions are clear enough and require only that the contractor read them carefully and do what they say. Failure to do so can result in a bid being thrown out after the contractor has spent days in preparing it. (It happens time and time again that bids are thrown out because they are not in the proper form.)

2.4C. General and Special Conditions

This section summarizes in architect's language what is expected of the contractor over and above the actual construction. It is a repeat of what has been said here before, but it is important enough to warrant repetition. The contractor must take account of these items in his estimate. They all cost money.

1. It is stated that the General Conditions—Standard Form of the American Institute of Architects* is to apply.

2. There is a clause that states that "All work shall be of the best quality and in conformance with all applicable codes." This is a catchall.

3. There are a number of clauses that tell the contractor what he has to pay for: all permits and certificates; temporary electricity and telephone during construction; temporary toilet; glass breakage and breakage of materials stored on site; broom-cleaning house and cleaning windows; waxing floors where shown; cold weather protection; protection of designated trees, shrubs, and fences; protection against weather at any time. This is a longer list than usual and the contractor who does not read and account for all these items is in trouble right at the start.

4. This clause repeats that it is the contractor's responsibility to call to the architect's attention any discrepancies in the plans and specifications and to request an interpretation before proceeding. It also states that if there is a conflict between these documents and the contractor has not called attention to it, then he must perform the work in the best and most expensive way.

---

*It is suggested that the contractor obtain a copy of this form (AIA Document A201) by writing to the American Institute of Architects, 1735 New York Ave., N.W., Washington, D.C. 20006. There will be a charge (unspecified here because prices keep changing).

5. The contractor is told he must guarantee workmanship and materials for a period of 1 year from date of final acceptance unless a longer guarantee is asked for specific items.

2.4D. Allowances, Items Furnished by Others, Alternates

There are many items of construction, especially those used for finishing, which are difficult for a contractor to estimate because they depend on the owner's choice. To overcome this, the specification usually calls for allowances for these items. In the case of smaller jobs or where the owner does not know what he wants, it is up to the contractor to state in his estimate what allowances he has made. Following are the allowances asked for in this particular specification:

> Bath accessories and hardware $\quad$ \$_____
> Sliding glass doors $\qquad$ _____
> Kitchen and laundry cabinets $\qquad$ _____
> (Lighting fixtures are not mentioned here)

The contractor has to include the installation of all of these but he has no risk so far as the cost of the material is concerned. He also has to install the refrigerator, stove, dishwasher, and dryer, which will be furnished by the owner.

In the case of items furnished and installed by others there are:

Overhead power and telephone lines
Septic system
Water supply system
Asphalt driveway and turnaround
Finish grading, seeding, and planting

The contractor is asked only to coordinate his work with these various contractors.

Some alternates are asked for:

Finishing a certain spare room with walls, floors, and ceiling
Adding cabinets as shown in a certain room
Adding skylights to certain bathrooms
Running electric and telephone service underground from end of
  pole line

The contractor must be sure to add profit and overhead to each of these prices. The contractor is warned, however, not to "kill the goose" with excessive prices or too small a deduction for work omitted. Contracts are often lost because of costly alternates. The contractor should know that the accepted alternates are added to the base price before a contract is awarded. This holds for even the smallest job. In such a case the contractor may be asked how much more (or less) he will charge if one type of hardware or window or door is used or if he adds or deducts the painting.

2.4E. Excavation and Sitework

SECTION 3—EXCAVATION AND SITEWORK

3.0   The General Conditions and Special Conditions shall apply to this Section of the Specifications.

3.1   Stake out accurately the foundations under supervision of the Architect, establishing floor elevations under supervision.

3.2   Protect against damage: All precaution shall be taken to prevent unreasonable and unnecessary damage to trees, shrubs, stone walls, etc. Cut trees, brush, etc. in immediate area as directed. Cut trees to two foot lengths and store on site. Remove brush.

3.3   Contractor shall strip topsoil as directed and stockpile redistributing as directed on completion of work. Rock shall be exposed and lines shall be indicated on their surfaces, marking areas to be blasted. Payments for rock excavation shall be as follows: (The quantity of rock excavation to be paid for will be the number of cubic yards exposed and measured in its original position in presence of the Architect.)

   a.   Pipes—Space at bottom of trench 2'-0" wider than outside diameter of pipe or conduit, side surfaces vertical, and 6" below bottom of pipe.

   b.   Foundation walls, piers, footing, etc.—1'-0" outside line of structure vertically, to bottom of footing.

   c.   Below floor slabs—6" below bottom of concrete slab.

3.4   Clearing and removal of stumps and roots on area to be stripped of topsoil and elsewhere as indicated or required; pile to one side and remove from site.

3.5   Remove topsoil to its full depth on areas that require change of contours; foundations, footing, piers; foundation drains; trenches; sewer line; water line; driveway; parking area and turn-around.

3.6   Execute general exterior grading, cutting, filling, etc. required to transform existing grades to final grades shown on Drawings: and for all items noted in paragraph 5 above.

3.7   Solid bearing under the foundation walls shall be provided by using undisturbed earth, or solid rock. Exterior wall footing shall be to 3'-6" below grade or to solid rock.

3.8   Backfilling against foundation walls shall be done carefully to prevent damage to walls.

3.9   Footing drains of 4″ Terra Cotta or perforated Orangeburg pipe shall be properly sized, trenched and pitched and graded to provide adequate drainage. Footing drains shall have a backfill of 18″ of 1½″ crushed stone, a layer of salt hay, and bank run gravel to within 6″ of finished grade for a width of 2′-0″ from the building wall.

3.10   Establish sub grades 4″ below interior slabs, backfilling with well tamped bank run gravel if required.

3.11   Excavate and backfill for all trades as shown or required, including water line, electric service, house sewer, roof drains, etc.

3.12   Run leader drains as shown of 4″ or 6″ solid Orangeburg pipe to grade.

3.13   Rough grading of driveway and turn-arounds is included in this Contract. Driveway and turn-arounds to receive a sub base of 8″ bank run gravel, to limits shown.

3.14   Fill under concrete slabs with 4″ crushed stone.

3.15   Any additional fill, above and beyond that obtained on the site from excavation work required to bring grades to those shown on the drawings and as required for Driveway and turn-arounds, shall be supplied and distributed by the General Contractor.

3.16   Remove all stumps, brush and debris from site on completion of work.

3.17   Rough grade distributing topsoil on completion of work, establishing grades as shown. Excess rock to be disposed of on site where directed.

Commentary. It is to be noted that this section and all succeeding sections have an opening clause which states "The General and Special Conditions are a part of this Section of the Specifications," or words to that effect. This clause serves to alert every subcontractor to be sure that he understands and allows for these conditions in his part of the work.

This is the first section of the specifications to describe the actual construction work. It now goes from the general to the specific. The comments that follow this and other sections are intended to point out the items in specifications that the builder might miss and which could cause considerable extra expense or trouble.

Paragraph 3.1. This paragraph calls for the contractor to stake out the foundation and the elevations. This is a large site and such work requires a knowledge of field surveying. It is suggested that the contractor employ the original surveyor to do this work.

Paragraph 3.2. Cutting, clearing, and removal of brush is normal but the cutting of trees into 2-ft lengths is to be noted.

Paragraph 3.3. Rock excavation is very expensive and the quantity is almost always a cause of dispute. The contractor is warned not to touch any rock until the exact quantity has been measured and certified by the architect (or owner). If subsequently the contractor uncovers rock that has not been measured he must call it to the attention of the architect *before* he removes it.

Paragraphs 3.5 and 3.6. These paragraphs require a knowledge of the quantity of material that must be moved. The services of a surveyor may be required before a bid can be made.

Paragraph 3.15. This paragraph may require the hauling of extra fill, which is expensive. The comments on Paragraphs 3.5 and 3.6 apply here.

2.4F. Concrete and Masonry

SECTION 4—CONCRETE AND MASONRY

4.0   The General and Special Conditions shall apply to this Section of the Specifications.

4.1   Footings shall be accurately laid out according to plan. Where loose rock or earth material is found, same shall be removed to sound rock or earth. Where ledge is encountered, such surfaces shall be scraped clean and shall be "stepped", if angle is found to be more than 45°. All trenches and ledge surfaces shall be kept clean of falling soil material until pouring is done. Footings for walls shall be of stone concrete mix 1:2:4.

4.2   Walls shall be of concrete block of sizes as noted on Drawings. Top course of concrete block at beam bearing points and concrete block piers shall be filled solid with concrete.

4.3   Materials: Mortar shall be cement lime mortar; 1 part "Portland Cement", 1 part lime putty, 4½ parts sand. Mortar shall be mixed by volume, and no mortar that has stood for more than one hour shall be retempered and used. Use of approved premixed mortars is permitted.

4.4   Fill solid under sills and steel bearing locations and extend anchor bolts at least 2 courses, at every 8'-0" on center, and 2'-0" from corners.

4.5   Terra cotta flues, thimbles and chimneys shall be built as detailed. Flue pipes shall be free of cracks, chips or distortion.

4.6   Slab at stoop to pitch as indicated on Drawings and receive a wood float finish for tile. Max. variation in slab surface ¼"—in 10'-0". (This is not to be confused with pitch of slab).

4.7 Apply a dustproof troweled finish on garage, storage, and heater room floors. Use Ladidolith as manufactured by Sonneborn Co.

4.8 Supply and install aluminum screened vents with closing louver.

4.9 All concrete shall be mixed to obtain 3000 PSI strength in accordance with American Concrete Institute specifications, properly placed and cured. All slabs to be reinforced with 6" × 6", #10 wire mesh and placed on Moistop vapor barriers lapped 12". Anchor all ductwork to prevent floating and encase entirely in concrete.

4.10 Chimneys to be brick set in running bond. Brick to be approved by Architect. Allow $90 per thousand for brick.

4.11 Apply ½" parging to all exterior concrete block foundation walls to top of footing. Damp-proof below grade with two coats of asphaltic mopping. Apply one coat of asphaltic mopping on *inside* of block walls west side of Rooms 107 and 109, before furring. Parge outside of this wall and south wall, Room 111 and apply two coats of asphaltic mopping.

4.12 Supply and install C.I. cleanout doors at Heater Room and Bedroom chimnies, and ash drop.

4.13 Build chimney with sand plaster finished hood as detailed. (See Section 10 for furring and lathing specifications).

Commentary. *Paragraph* 4.1.A "stepped foundation" is mentioned as one to be used where necessary. Stepped foundations are expensive and must be cut with care. The *diagram* in Fig. 2-3 shows such a foundation. Extra money must be allowed for this work.

Paragraph 4.7. This calls for a top admixture for troweled surfaces. The

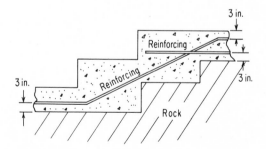

Figure 2-3 Stepped footing for use on sloping rock or sloping ground. Width and depth of footing depend on load and capacity of soil. Design is responsibility of architect/engineer.

contractor is cautioned in general to watch concrete specifications for admixtures. They can be quite expensive.

Paragraph 4.9. The 3000 psi (3000 lb/sq in. in compression) concrete can best be obtained by ready-mix truck with a certificate from the dealer. If the site is remote from a ready-mix plant and is too expensive to truck, the contractor can mix his own. Engineering handbooks give the proper mixtures, but the following mixtures are suggested.

For a strength of 2500 psi after 28 days, the mixture is 1 part of portland cement, 2 parts of sand, and 4 parts of stone to be dry mixed. Then not more than 7½ gal of water per bag of cement is added and thoroughly mixed. The strength of concrete is determined by the water-cement ratio. If the dry mixture above is mixed with only 6 gal of water per bag of cement, the strength will go up to 3200 psi in 28 days.

The contractor is cautioned that these suggested mixtures hold only for normal above-freezing temperatures, with clean ingredients and water and proper mixing and placing of the concrete.

Paragraph 4.11. The contractor is to note the asphaltic mopping and parging of the foundation walls. The mopping requires hot pitch. Who will do this?

2.4G. Carpentry and Millwork

SECTION 5—CARPENTRY AND MILL WORK

5.0   The General and Special Conditions shall be a part of this Section of the Specifications.

5.1   All work shall be of the highest quality, in conformance with all codes, manufacturers' directions, and trade standards.

5.2   The following is a list of some, but not necessarily all, materials to be furnished and installed under this Section.

    a.   All sills in contact with masonry shall be Wolmanized.
    b.   Framing: Kiln-dried 1500 #PS1 Southern Pine or Douglas Fir, dry and straight. (Hemlock not permitted).
    c.   Flat roof and wall sheathing ½" Plyscord with exterior glue secured with coated nails.
    d.   Sub floor—⅝" Plyscord with exterior glue secured with coated nails.
    e.   Interior stair treads, rails, stringers, nosings, clear red oak.
    f.   Exposed interior trim, self edging on Novaply Board, etc.— clear Ponderosa Pine.
    g.   Furring strips—spruce.
    h.   Siding: "D" and better resawn face Western red cedar of section shown.
    i.   Decking: 5/4" × 4" clear vertical grain Douglas Fir. Secure with galvanized finishing nails. Decking to be square edged.

j. Closet shelving—¾″ Novaply Board, medium density, edged with clear Ponderosa Pine.

k. Exterior trim—to be clear solid red cedar.

l. Insulation:
1. Between studs thermal type batt insulation.
2. Between studs sound insulation, rock mineral wool.
3. Perimeter—Styrofoam.

m. Exterior siding nails—aluminum Stronghold by Independent Nail Corporation Ringed type. All other exterior fastenings to be galvanized.

n. Caulking—To be Butyl Rubber type, color selected by Architect.

o. Sheetrock—½″ tapered edges with galvanized corner beads and 200-B casing beads where sheetrock meets other materials, etc.

p. Screening—on edge ventilation and screen porch—fiberglass insect screening.

q. Building paper—15# felt on side walls and rosin sized paper under flooring.

r. Soffits and porch and entry stoop ceiling—½″ Duraply.

s. Underlayment—½″ plyscord, with waterproof glue, plugged and touch sanded.

t. Roof decking to be: Size shown, 6″ nominal, Potlatch Lock Deck, *Select Douglas Fir face side,* laid random length continuous. COMBINATION OF DECK-DOUGLAS FIR/LARCH Laminated beams to be: Potlatch, Electro-Lam, E = 1.8 Architectural Grade, Douglas Fir.

u. Oak strip flooring 25/32″ × 2¼″ select, best grade oak.

v. Doors:
1. Garage—Flush masonite overhead type, Overhead Door Co., with automatic control and two transmitters.
2. All interior passage doors, except passage door to Garage and passage door to Heater Room to be 1⅜″ solid core paint grade birch.
3. Interor passage doors to Garage and Heater Room to be 1¾″ solid core paint grade Red Birch.
4. Exterior doors 1¾″ solid core paint grade Birch.
5. Closet doors 1⅜″ hollow core paint grade Birch.

w. Roof shingles—Elmco Co., black color wind seal shingles, 235# per square. Exposure 5″ and secured with 4 nails per shingle.

5.3 Weatherstripping—All exterior wood passage doors and all doors from Garage to House—interlocking zinc with aluminum saddle and door hook strip by Zero.

5.4 All sills to be Wolmanized. Sleepers under decking to be Wolmanized.

5.5 Install all bath accessories and finished hardware, misc. metal, etc. included under other Sections.

5.6   Cut and provide blocking for all trades. Coordinate framing for ductwork, lights, etc. with heating and electrical Contractor.

5.7   All framing shall be carefully done providing all hangers, wood 1 × 3 bridging, etc. Double frame at all openings and provide double joists under all partitions. Provide all necessary headers and blocking for all trades as required for size of opening. Bearing 4 × 4 members shall be treated on lower ends and rest on solid masonry. Reinforce all framing as shown or as required to build structure.

5.8   Provide all rough hardware and misc. fastenings as required.

5.9   Furnish and install shop fabricated bathroom vanities made of full overlay construction of Novaply construction. Doors and drawer fronts shall be flush and encased on edges, faces and backs with formica. Tops to be formica clad, self edged with back and side splashes, cut for sinks and tops are to receive a formica backing material on underside. Hardware included in hardware allowance.

5.10 Sheetrock shall be applied under this Section, along with corner beads and casing beads.. Sheetrock shall be carefully cut around all openings, light fixtures, etc. Sheetrock shall be applied in as large pieces as possible, minimizing joints, Sheetrock to be a taped, 3 coat job using Perf-A-Tape joint system unless otherwise noted.

    a.   Sheetrock at Garage and Heater Room to be $5/8''$ firecode sheetrock.
    b.   Sound proof walls as shown.
    c. $1/2''$ sheetrock at all other locations.

5.11 Provide oak or marble saddles where different floor materials meet as indicated on drawings.

5.12 Oak flooring on slabs to be installed as shown on treated 1 × 2 spruce furring members set in mastic strip and secured to concrete slab. Polyethylene shall be continuous and lapped on top of furring members. Sand and finish sanding with 1.0 paper. Refer to Section 9 for finishing.

5.13 Apply transite to Heater Room side of Heater Room and Garage doors if required by code.

5.14 Roof decking to be laid random length continuous observing the following:

    a.   Distance between joints in adjacent rows of decking must be at least 2 feet.
    b.   Joints in rows not directly adjacent must be separated by one row of decking and one foot measured along the axis of the plank, or by *two* rows of decking.
    c.   In any section of a deck less than one foot in length the number of end joints must not exceed one third of decking courses.

5.15　Porch floor—Use ¾" exterior plywood A-C grade, with blocking under all joints or two layer method, first layer to be ⅝" plyscord with exterior glue and second layer to be ½" exterior plywood A-C or A-D facing. Use aluminum ringed nails for nailing.

Commentary. This is a high-quality and expensive specification. The normal house will not use materials of this quality. Note solid red cedar, solid core doors, special nails, etc.

Paragraph 5.2l. No thickness is mentioned for sound or weather insulation. Sound insulation is not ordinarily specified.

Paragraph 5.2o and *Paragraph* 5.10. If possible, the contractor should employ a subcontractor who specializes in wallboarding and taping. Excellent prices and faster construction can be obtained. All fair-sized cities have such contractors.

Paragraph 5.1w. The carpentry contractor is called upon to do the roof shingling.

Paragraph 5.5. The carpentry contractor is responsible for the installation of bathroom accessories which have been purchased under an allowance.

Paragraph 5.6. The contractor must watch this provision carefully and allow for it. Mechanical and electrical subcontractors often cut holes wherever it is convenient for them, sometimes leaving one inch of a stud or two or three inches of a supporting joist or girder. Framing holes is also expensive.

Paragraph 5.9. The carpentry contractor furnishes and installs bathroom vanities. These can be quite expensive. The contractor should purchase these under an allowance. The specifications are not clear about this. The contractor must find out.

General note: There are some rather complicated framing details on the plan. If the contractor is in doubt he should have the architect explain.

Because this is a large house, the doors and windows are shown on a separate schedule.

2.4H. Roofing, Sheet Metal, and Skylights

SECTION 6—ROOFING, SHEET METAL AND SKYLIGHTS

6.0　The General and special conditions are a part of this Section of the Specifications.

6.1　All copper work shall comply with the Standard Specifications for Sheet Copper Work of the Copper and Brass Research Association.

6.2　All counter flashing, drips, etc. shall be of 16 ounce cold-rolled copper. All chimney flashings, step flashing, etc. shall be of 16 ounce soft copper. Cap and base flashing shall overlap 6" min. Embed flashing into roofing felts 4" min. Flashing of chimney shall be thru flashing to flues.

6.3 Leaders shall be of the plain round type, 3" round. Provide outlet strainer at all leader openings.

6.4 All copper work including gravel stops, drips, counter flashings, gutters, step flashings, etc. shall be preformed in the shop.

6.5 All flat roofs to be five ply tar and gravel. Use white limestone chips. Roof shall comply with Johns Manville Specifications #800, 20 year bonded type.

6.6 All vents and skylights shall be flashed in accordance with manufacturer's recommendations.

6.7 Provide 1" *Polyurethane* foam type insulation under asphalt shingle roof. First provide sheathing paper (5#/100 sq. ft.) lapped 2" nailed. Starting at low point of roof lay one ply Vaporbar by Barrett Co., lapping 4" over next sheet and 6" on ends. (Nail only enough to hold in place until shingles are nailed, through the insulation into the wood deck).

6.8 Furnish and set Josam roof drains to be connected up by Plumbing Contractor. Drains to be Josam #413, 3".

6.9 Skylights to be double dome type as manufactured by Wasco Co. with integral 4" curb. Wasco A1-2828. Outer dome to be clear, inner dome to be white translucent. Install according to manufacturer's direction, including flashing and insulation.

6.10 Gutters to be preformed of 16 ounce cold-rolled copper in the shop. As detailed on drawings.

6.11 Apply General Electric Co. Silicone Traffic Topping to Porch floor plywood. Apply Primer first and trowel on Traffic Topping all in accordance with direction of the manufacturer, $\frac{3}{32}$" thickness coating in color selected by Architect. Turn up at sidewalls and over edges as required. Guarantee work for 2 years.

Commentary. Paragraphs 6.2, 6.3, and 6.4. Note that all roof metal is copper.
Paragraph 6.5. Note five-ply tar and gravel roof.
Paragraph 6.7. The roofing contractor is to provide and install sheathing paper, vapor barrier, and then 1-in. polyurethane, but the asphalt shingle roofing is in the carpentry specification. It is suggested that the roofing subcontractor be given the entire roofing job including the final shingling so that he can be held solely responsible.
Paragraph 6.11. The special "traffic topping" that is called for should be investigated for price and practicability. Who guarantees for 2 years?

2.4I. Slate Flooring and Ceramic Tile

SECTION 7—SLATE FLOORING AND CERAMIC TILE

7.0 The General Conditions and Special Conditions are a part of this Section of the Specifications.

7.1   All slate tile to be 9″ × 9″ gauged Buckingham Black slate, set by the thin-set method in Pecora A-135 mastic with ¼″ trowel over underlayment or on slab. Tile to be natural cleft.

7.2   Grout for slate tile shall be premixed similar to L&M Surco Co. Acid R, Black in color. Throughly clean on completion of job ready for sealing by others. Use Latex additive in grout over wood joists.

7.3   Bathroom wall tile to be by Romany Spartan Co. 2″ × 2″ size. Bathroom 109 tile to be Matte Glaze 2873 Spice White. Bath 211 to be 2081, Crinkle Tan. Set in lath and plaster base and provide combination soap and grab at each tub. Use mildew resistant grout. Protect fixtures during cleaning. Supply and install white marble saddles where indicated on Drawings.

Commentary. This specification calls for 2 × 2-in. ceramic wall tile and mentions colors and types of glaze. The bathroom floors are of slate set in mastic.

This is not a usual specification. In a great majority of houses the bathroom floors are of random-pattern ceramic tile or of vinyl and the walls are 4½ × 4½-in. cushion type (that is with bullnose on all four sides).

The contractor must be sure that the colors and glaze called for are available. If the colors and glaze are not in stock and have to be put on order, it can take 12 to 16 weeks for delivery.

The specification also calls for built-in tile accessories. Again the contractor must check to see if the colors and styles are available. Tiling is a very tricky item. The final completion may be held up for months because of the unavailability of certain tile or of the subcontractor himself.

2.4J. Glass and Glazing

SECTION 8—GLASS AND GLAZING

8.0   The General and Special Conditions are a part of this Section of the Specifications.

8.1   Work shall be confined to glazing of glass in wood frames and mirrors. (Aluminum sliding glass doors to be glazed by others).

8.2   Door and glass stops to be finished before glazing.

8.3   All window glass to be $7/32$″ heavy sheet "A" quality Glass set in a full bed of glazing compound.

8.4   Mirrors to be ¼″ polished plate, copper backed with ground edges set with mastic and plain chrome clips.

8.5   Provide 20″ × 60″ door mirror mounted on door where indicated by Owner.

Commentary. In the case of a private residence, small office building, etc., this section of a specification should hold no surprises. This particular one, because of larger-than-normal glass areas, calls for $\frac{7}{32}$-in. heavy sheet "A" quality glass. It also calls for $\frac{1}{4}$-in. polished plate copper-backed mirrors. Normally window sash comes ready-glazed with "A" quality double-thick glass, from the millwork dealer.

2.4K. Painting and Finishing

SECTION 9—PAINTING AND FINISHING

9.0   The General and Special Conditions are a part of this Section of the Specifications.

9.1   Included in this work shall be all exterior trim, spackling and taping of sheetrock which shall be done in the three coat method, in the best manner, according to manufacturer's directions, painting of interior walls, trim, shelving, etc.

9.2   All surfaces shall be spackled and sanded before finishing. Wood surfaces shall be sanded between coats and sheetrock surfaces shall be touched up with spackle and sanded as required between coats.

9.3   The following is a general schedule for finishing: See schedules for rooms not to be finished. Paints and varnishes shall be by Pratt & Lambert Co.; wood stains by Samuel Cabot: wood floor finish materials by Duraseal. All colors as selected by Architect.

    a.   Interior walls and ceiling (except walls in Kitchen and Bathrooms—2 coats latex base flat wall paint.

    b.   Walls in Kitchen and Bathrooms and interior wood trim—2 coats primer, one coat semi-gloss enamel.

    c.   Exterior and interior galvanized steel pipe rails—one coat metal primer, one coat enamel. Rails shall be shop primed with one coat zinc chromate primer.

    d.   Exterior wood doors, and Garage door—2 coats primer, one coat satin enamel.

    e.   Interior and trim—two coats primer, one coat satin enamel.

    f.   Exterior of house—one coat Cabots stain as directed by Architect.

    g.   Hardwood floors—shall be carefully sanded and finished with 2 coats of Duraseal and one coat of Durafinish all as made by International Chemical Co. Color to be selected by Architect.

    h.   Closet shelving—Three coats clear varnish.

    i.   Wood decks—2 coats clear Woodlife before assembly, and after cutting.

    j.   Interior slate—seal with clear Duraseal on completion of grouting, in accordaince with manufacturer's directions. Finish with coat of Durafinish.

9.4   Prepare samples of all work as requested before starting finishing.

9.5   Backprime exterior decking with clear Woodlife before installation. Cut ends shall be treated.

9.6   Finish door tops and bottoms and edges *after* they have been fitted.

9.7   One year from acceptance of building by Owner, painting Contractor shall repair any nail pops, ridging, etc.

Commentary. Paragraph 9.1. The taping and spackling of wallboard is in this specification. If the general contractor can get the erecting and taping of wallboard done by a single contractor as mentioned in Sec. 2.4F, he will get a better, faster, and less expensive job. If not, then the erection of wallboard by the carpenter and the taping by the painter is the best that can be done.

Paragraph 9.3. The schedule of finishes is better than normal for interior walls and ceilings—two coats latex-base flat paint, bathrooms, and kitchen, and interior wood trim—two coats primer, one coat semigloss enamel (usually one coat primer); exterior doors—two coats primer, one coat satin enamel (usually one coat primer). Exterior trim in this case is redwood, but the usual pine exterior finish is one coat primer and one coat oil-base semigloss exterior grade paint. Exterior walls get one coat extra-heavy-bodied shingle stain. Hardwood floors get two coats sealer, one coat finish (wax). (Usually hardwood floors get one coat sealer.)

This specification is for an expensive house. In the smaller house or alteration where there is no formal specification and where the contractor is asked to do the painting and to make recommendations, he could very easily frighten off a prospective customer by quoting such standards. A good-quality job can be obtained by eliminating one coat of primer in many cases. A painting job consisting of one coat of good-quality, well-applied primer and one coat of a good-quality, well-brushed-on finish will last for several years with full satisfaction to the owner. Good-quality paint that is well applied is something that the owner sees for years. The contractor is advised to get the best. The difference in cost is very little.

2.4L. Miscellaneous

SECTION 10—MISCELLANEOUS

10.0   The General Conditions and Special Conditions shall be a part of this Section of the Specifications.

10.1   All structural steel to be type A-36 shop fabricated to AISC specifications, primed with Rust-O-Leum or equal paint.

10.2   Baseboards to 4″ high vinyl, cove type on slate floors and wood floors and square edge on carpeted floors. Color as selected by Architect.

10.3   Furring and lathing—Provide galvanized furring and lathing with casing and corner beads for fireplace chimney hood. Work shall be done by an experienced furring and lathing Contractor.

10.4 Connect prefab fireplace (to be furnished by Owner) with damper controls, black smoke pipe.

10.5 Furnish and install metal deck rail to be fabricated of black iron pipe, welded, shop drilled and primed. Use galvanized lag bolts for securing.

10.6 Provide ventilating ductwork and wall caps for kitchen hood, bath fans, and clothes dryer.

Commentary. This section is a catch-all for the miscellaneous items of construction that do not warrant a full section. Nevertheless there are some expensive items involved.

Paragraph 10.1. The steel should be ordered as soon as possible from a structural iron and steel fabricator. If the sizes are not in stock it may take a while to get them.

Paragraph 10.2. Note the 4-in. vinyl base. This is an expensive item.

Paragraph 10.3. Note the furring and lathing. This is an additional trade unless the mason contractor can do it.

Paragraph 10.5. The rail can probably be obtained from the iron fabricator.

Paragraph 10.6. The air-conditioning sheet metal installer can do this.

2.4M. Plumbing

SECTION 11—PLUMBING

11.0 The General Conditions and Special Conditions shall be a part of this Section of the Specifications.

11.1 Work shall conform to all local, state and federal codes, and be done in the best workmanlike manner by skilled mechanics. Contractor shall cooperate with other trades to prevent delays in the work and shall do all necessary cutting and patching.

11.2 This system shall consist of soil, waste, drain, vent, and hot and cold water supply lines. House sewer shall be carried a minimum of 10 ft. beyond building line to septic tank.

11.3 Water supply system to be complete as shown on drawings, and as indicated herein. Provide valves at each fixture so that each may be isolated without shutting off system. Run 3/4" cold water lines to each plumbing area and size all lines so that water supply at one location will not be reduced when another is in use. Provide water hammer arrestors at each fixture. Insulate cold water lines in ceilings with fiberglass insulation. Copper soils 4" and copper vents 2" type L to meet the codes.

11.4   Materials

   a.   Water and waste inside, above grade, to be type "L" hard temper copper.
   b.   Waste lines, below grade, cast iron.
   c.   Water lines, below grade to be type "K" soft copper tubing, to be wrapped with 30# felt roofing jacket and coated with two coats asphaltam.
   d.   Trim—chrome plated brass.

11.5   Plumbing fixtures: All in white by American Standard unless otherwise indicated.

   1.   Bath 109

      a.   Lavatory—Ovalyn—$21\frac{1}{4}$ × $17\frac{1}{4}$ F470 with stainless frame and N 2101-8 Heritage fittings.
      b.   Tub—Spectra 70P-2605R with Heritage trim #1303.015 pop-up drain, and 1611.052, five foot rod.
      c.   Water Closet—Elongated Cadet F2109-11 with white Church seat.

   2.   Bath 211

      a.   Tub—Kohler tub—Bradford K-805-S white in color, with Heritage trim #1303.015 (less shower head). Eurotherm #4002 to replace shower head.
      b.   Water Closet—Elongated Cadet F2109-11 with white Church seat.

   3.   Shower 212

      a.   Swan Circle Shower with integral door and *light,* white color model #64KD, and #1204.015 Heritage shower fittings.

   4.   Lavatory 213

      a.   Lavatory—Ovalyn—$21\frac{1}{4}$ × $17\frac{1}{4}$ F470 with stainless frame and N 2101-8 Heritage fittings.
      b.   Water Closet—Elongated Cadet F 2109-11 with white Church seat.

   5.   Kitchen 203

      a.   Sink—stainless steel, Elkay LWR 3722-L with LK99 and LK221.

   6.   Mechanical 103

      a.   Two (2) Fiat—Serva-Sink wall hung white color L-1 with American Standard Laundry Sink faucets similar to #8363.012.

11.6   Connect appliances furnished by others including disposal, dishwasher, clothes washer, and ice maker.

11.7 Connect humidifiers supplied and installed by Heating Contractor.

11.8 Supply and install a complete hot water system with a A. W. Smith Co. 120 gal. quick recovery round electric hot water heater (10 year guarantee) with all safety devices, glass lined tank.

11.9 Install frost proof (non freeze) hose bibbs.

11.10 Perform all tests on all water supply and waste lines before structure is closed up.

11.11 General Contractor to provide excavation and backfill for sewer line from tank to the house.

11.12 Well with pump and storage tank is to be supplied by others and Plumbing Contractor will connect water supply system to house plumbing. Septic tank to be by others, and Plumbing Contractor to connect cast iron sewer to septic tank.

11.13 Connect and install roof drain furnished by roofing Contractor and connect to outside drain lines, furnished by excavating Contractor.

Commentary. This specification is for a high-quality plumbing system. The fixtures named are above average. New houses for the average purchaser use plastic pipe for waste lines instead of copper and cast iron. Note the stainless steel sink. Note the specification for the shower.

Paragraph 11.6. All appliances to be connected under this contract.

Paragraph 11.7. Humidifiers to be connected under this contract.

Paragraph 11.8. Note hot water system with 120-gal tank.

Paragraph 11.12. Note well connection. How far is well from house connection? From Paragraph 11.4 the water line is copper wrapped with 50-lb felt roofing jacket and coated with two coats of asphaltum.

Paragraph 11.13. Note connection of roof drain to outside drain lines.

2.4N. Electrical

SECTION 12—ELECTRICAL

12.1 The General Conditions and Special Conditions shall be a part of this Section of the Specifications.

12.2 The Electrical Contractor shall be responsible for all wiring in the house, including running the service line from the last pole to the house (note alternate for underground service) and the wiring of the entire system, including the lighting, appliances (furnished by Owner), the heating and air conditioning system, light fixtures, etc. The Electrical Contractor shall supply all devices required for this work, including mounting boards, coordinating his work with the General Contractor and the utility company. Work shall conform with all applicable codes. All wiring devices shall be U.L. approved.

12.3 Arrange and pay for the running of the telephone line from the street to the house.

12.4 Furnish all light fixtures with bulbs indicated. Furnish and install completely all bathroom fans.

12.5 Electric service shall be 120/240 volt, 400 ampere, single phase, running from the last pole to the house. Panel board to be Square 'D' circuit breaker type with at least 6 blank breakers.

12.6 Appliances to be double self cleaning oven and hood, cook top, disposal, dishwasher, clothes washer, clothes dryer. Wire hot water heater and any devices furnished by other Contractors.

12.7 Provide typewritten marking of circuit breaker panel box with all circuits marked.

12.8 Materials and wiring devices:

    a. Switch gear to be Westinghouse, Bulldog or approved equal.
    b. Switches and receptacles to be Arrow Hart #2891-W, 2892-W, etc. white in color.
    c. Cover plates—Arrow Hart, white, smooth design.
    d. Floor outlets—Arrow Hart #5797.
    e. Waterproof outlets—Arrow Hart, #5797.
    f. Dimmers—by Hunt of required capacity.

12.9 Door buzzer and bell—by Edwards Co. complete with transformer. Buttons to be Edwards #620, polished chrome. Buzzer and bell type and location to be approved by Architect.

Commentary. Paragraph 12.2. The only departure from the standard wording is the responsibility of the electrical contractor for running the service from the pole line to the house. This is usually done by the power company.

Paragraph 12.3. This subcontractor is also obligated to pay for running the telephone line from the nearest pole line to the house.

Paragraph 12.4. This paragraph calls for the subcontractor to furnish lighting fixtures. There is no allowance mentioned for lighting fixtures, although there is a schedule of fixtures by manufacturer and catalog number. Their cost should be established.

Paragraph 12.5. Note that 400-ampere service is mentioned. Most medium-sized private residences have 100-ampere service.

Paragraph 12.8(f). Note that certain of the lights are to be controlled by dimmers.

2.40. Heating and Air Conditioning

SECTION 13—HEATING AND AIR CONDITIONING

13.1   The General Conditions and Special Conditions shall be a part of this Section of the Specifications.

13.2   All work shall be in conformance with the Standards of the American Society of Heating and Ventilating Engineers as well as all applicable codes.

13.3   Air conditioning unit shall be Trane No. 8 Climate Changer with capacity for handling 3,000 CFM against 1¼″ E.S.P. and incorporating: Two (2) circuit DX 4 row cooling coil, with each circuit rated at 40 MBH (A.R.I. standards); throw-away filter section with one set of spare filters; blower section with 2 H.P. motor drive and guard assembly; fully insulated and vapr-proofed casings with drain pan under coil section; rail type vibration isolators; spray assembly for winter humidity control. Run air condensate to nearest indirect waste or drain. Pipe water to humidifier.

13.4   Duct electric heating coils shall be Inoeeco, complete with all required fan prooving switches, limit devices, contactors, etc. bearing U.L. label on complete assembly.

13.5   Duct Heaters:

    a. Zone I—   15KW @ 5 stages
        Living Room
        Dining Room

    b. Zone II—   1⅓KW @ 2 stages
        Study

    c. Zone III—   6⅓KW @ 2 stages
        Master Bedroom
        Bedroom 108
        Storgae 111

    d. Zone IV—   None (Baseboard)
        Entry

    e. Zone V—   6⅓KW @ 2 stages
        Kitchen
        Breakfast
        Storage 204

    f. Zone VI—   10KW @ 4 stages
        Mechanical
        Bedroom 105
        Hall 106
        Bedroom 107

13.6   Baseboard electric heaters shall be as indicated.

13.7   Temperature controls (Barber-Colman):

    a. Zone I shall incorporate room thermostat TP5131 acting on

SP408 program switch with 2 stages of cooling and 5 stages of heating and control thru holding coil circuits of the 2 condensing units and the electric duct heater the needs for Heating Zone I and the entire house cooling.

b. Zones II, III and V shall incorporate 2 stage heating stats controlling respective electric duct heaters thru holding coils.

c. Zone VI shall be the same as Zone I, except no cooling controls and 4 stage SP 404 on holding coils of electric duct heater.

d. Zone IV is heated by baseboard electric heaters.

e. All baseboard electric heaters shall incorporate integral factory installed 2 stage thermostats and disconnect switches and be U.L. listed.

f. Condensing units shall incorporate integral controls and limit devices.

g. Smoke detector on return side of main duct to air conditioner shall shut down unit and sound audible alarm.

h. Humidistat in Zone I shall control spray assembly motor operated valve at air conditioning unit.

i. Electrostatic air filter shall incorporate fully automatic timed cleaning and drying cycles.

13.8 Electrostatic air filter shall be Electro-Aire with capacity to handle 3,000 CFM and be fully automated. Run drain water to nearest drains.

13.9 Condensing units shall be located where shown on plans and be piped to air conditioning unit coil with Type I copper tubing with Sil-Fos silver soldered connections to wrought copper sweat fittings. Each unit shall be Trane Climate Changer RAUA35 air cooled condensing, assembly rated at 40 MBH @ A.R.I. standard conditions. The two (2) units shall be mounted on raised concrete pad where shown on plans

13.10 Sheet metal work, including code required fire dampers, shall conform to minimum ASHRAE standards. All elbows shall incorporate turning vanes, all zone and branch ducts set dampers.

13.11 Grilles and diffusers shall be Tuttle and Bailey Imperialine floor type and double deflection wall type with finishes as approved by Architect and incorporate opposed blade key operated dampers and all aluminum construction.

13.12 System air balance shall be performed by the James Brennan Co., Stamford, Conn. or approved equal.

13.13 Insulation:

a. All ductwork in Mechanical Room and that portion running over or under unconditioned spaces shall be insulated with 1″ thick glass fiber with vinyl coated vapor barrier stapled and taped at all joints and punctures or tears

     b.   Refrigerant and water piping shall be insulated with ½″ thick Armaflex.

Commentary. This is a large house and the specification calls for a single central unit to heat and air-condition by forced air.

The specification is not unlike that for a small office building. It gives the size and capacity of the central unit, the capacity of the reheat units, a layout of the zone controls, the size and capacity of the condenser units, etc.

The smaller contractor will not usually encounter this type of specification. If he does so when he bids for larger jobs he should obtain bids from experienced HVAC (heating, ventilating, and air conditioning) firms, which have the engineering know-how to properly evaluate and bid on such work. These contractors furnish and install the duct work, the controls, and the central units, and leave only the wiring for the electrical contractor.

In the smaller private residence or in alteration work, the specification may state "The heating system is to be a hot water system using Jones Co. type X recessed radiators (or baseboard radiators) in locations as shown. The heating plant is to be as manufactured by Smith Co. and is to be oil (or gas) fired. The system is to be thermostatically controlled from location (or locations) as shown. Each thermostat is to control a separate circulating pump. [Here the specification must show which area is serviced by each pump system.] The entire system is to be designed to maintain interior temperature at 70°F when outside temperature is 0°F." (This can be − 10° or + 10° or whatever depending on the weather in the particular area.)

Neither the designer or owner of a small house or alteration nor the contractor who performs such work is expected to calculate heating loads or boiler sizes. The heating and the plumbing contractors are usually the same person for such small houses. This contractor purchases his supplies from a wholesaler who will supply the engineering service to figure the heating load, radiator sizes, pipe sizes, pump sizes and boiler capacity.

2.5. DETAILED STUDY OF THE PLANS AND SPECIFICATIONS FOR A SMALL OFFICE BUILDING

This section (like Section 2.4 for a residence) is the study of a set of plans and specifications from which a small office building was built. This is a two-story office building in a small town. Its dimensions are approximately 50 by 60 ft, or 3000 sq ft. It is on a lot covering an area of over 10,000 sq ft located in a business area that is immediately adjacent to a residential area. Because of this, the zoning requirements for parking, buffer strips, and planting strips are so strict that the building could only cover 30 percent of the land area. (Chapter 13 of this book will discuss zoning codes.) Because the building is of a certain size and height it can be semifireproof and therefore the second floor is supported on steel girders and wood joists. (See Chap. 14 on building codes.)

The specification contains the following sections. Some of the following material contains the actual wording and is followed by explanations and comments.

2.5A. Addendum No. 1

Contains changes and corrections which resulted from discussions with the building inspector and a restudy of the completed drawings. First, a stairway that was the secondary means of egress is located and a sketch is attached. Second, an alternate price is requested if the first floor is built with wood joists and steel girders (like the second floor), instead of having it as a concrete slab on the ground. (There is no cellar.) The alternate price is to include a 2-ft, 6-in. crawl space under the floor, to be paved with 2 in. of concrete over a vapor barrier. Third, an alternate is asked for, one using flush hollow metal doors and frames instead of wood as shown.

2.5B. Addendum No. 2

This is an excellent example of what can lie in wait for a contractor. Because test borings were made it was found that the upper 5 to 6 ft of the land was of sand mixed with organic silt. It was feared that this relatively unstable earth could not properly support the 3000 sq ft first-floor concrete slab unless the top layer of earth was excavated down to a depth of 5 or 6 ft and filled with stable compacted fill. Therefore this part of the addendum calls for an alternate to the floor slab (see Sec. 2.5A). A wise contractor will attempt by price or other means to convince the owner and architect that it is best to be safe by building an independent floor structure supported on spread footings. In this case there were test borings. There are, however, many small buildings that go out for bid without test borings. The contractor must always cover himself in his bid.

2.5C. The General and Special Conditions

These are, in general, a repetition of those previously discussed for a private residence, except that, since the job is larger, some provisions become more strict.

The insurance clause names higher amounts of coverage and calls for owners' contingent liability as well as the other coverage previously named (Chap. 10, Insurance and Bonding).

The only allowance mentioned is for that of hardware and toilet accessories.

The contractor's attention is specifically called to the test boring results which become a part of the specification.

2.5D. Sitework and Excavation (Office Building)

SECTION 2—SITEWORK

1. The General and Special Conditions shall apply to this Section of the Specifications.

2. This contractor shall supply and install all site work including excavation, backfill, rough and finish grading, additional fill, drainage lines, retaining wall, manholes, curbs, sidewalks, paving, seeding, etc. *The septic system and planting of trees will be by others.*

3. Before any work is begun the Contractor shall stake out the lines of the building and driveway-parking areas, and shall set sufficent grade stakes to indicate all important finished grades. This contractor shall remove any obstructions on the site which conflict with new work and general grading operations. Trees shall not be removed unless removal is approved by the architect.

4. Topsoil shall be removed and stockpiled for the full depth encountered in all areas upon which construction occurs in cut and fill except that where to do so would injure existing trees to remain. Excess topsoil shall remain the property of owner.

5. Exising septic tank shall be pumped out and filled with sand or otherwise disposed of in accordance with the town authorities.

6. Provide loose stone retaining wall where indicated on drawings on west side of parking area.

7. This contractor shall be responsible for all excavation work for the building and for all excavation for mechanical, electrical and related work within and without the building, except as noted otherwise. Excavation shall also include excavation work shown on drawings and specified under this section.

8. Excavations and graded areas shall be kept drained at all times. Contractor shall provide and operate all pumps or other equipment necessary to keep excavations free from water. Water removal shall be accomplished in a manner that does not damage adjacent property or any item of temporary or permanent site improvement or any other structure.

9. Rough grading, fill and backfill:

   a. Do all cutting, filling, backfilling and grading necessary to establish smooth subgrade parallel to finished grades shown on drawings and at proper depths below finished grade to permit proper installation of floor slab on porous fill, topsoil, and such other materials as may be indicated on drawings or called for in these specifications.
   b. Remove all debris and deleterious materials from excavations before backfilling. Do not use frozen materials for backfill.
   c. Deposit fill and backfill in layers not exceeding six (6) inches under buildings and other surfacing, compacting each layer. Where

rolling is impossible, hand tamping shall be employed. All fills over 2′ in depth shall be jetted with water, (weather permitting), in accordance with standard practice, in addition to being compacted by rolling or tamping.

d. Fill outside the building from the top of scraped subsoil to underside of the bank run gravel sub-base fill shall be earth, compacted as described above.

e. Bank run gravel for use as fill within the building and on driveway-parking areas shall be approved by the architect. Provide compacted gravel from the top of existing asphalt paving to underside of slab within the building perimeter and 6″ compacted gravel in the driveway-parking areas.

f. The Contractor shall be responsible for any settlement of fill materials and shall make good any damage caused thereby.

10. Provide 4″ Orangeburg pipe from mechanical room to concrete slab at rear.

11. Concrete curbs and walks:

a. Concrete to conform to Section 3.

b. Expansion joints in curbs to be ½″ premolded non-extruding filler. Use Flexcell by Celotex.

c. Protect concrete after pouring for 6 days with kraft paper.

d. Provide construction joints every 6 to 15 feet.

e. Walks to be reinforced with 6 × 6 #10 wire mesh, and poured on 5″ bank run gravel base.

f. Provide dummy joints in walks, ½″ deep.

g. Seal all expansion joints with bituminous rubber compound.

12. Bituminous Concrete Paving:

a. Paving shall consist of 1½″ of surface course of asphaltic concrete placed over 6″ of compacted bank run gravel placed on a prepared subgrade.

b. Asphaltic concrete shall consist of one course conforming to section 4.06 Dense Graded Bituminous Concrete of the State Highway Department Specifications.

c. Completed subgrade shall be parallel to the finished surface and shall be crowned or pitched to an even gradient. Do all necessary excavation and filling. Soft and yielding material, and other portions of the subgrade which will not compact readily when rolled or tamped, shall be removed, and all loose rock or boulders found in the earth shall be removed or broken off to a depth of not less than one foot below the finished surface of subgrade. Holes or depressions made by the removal of materials, as described, shall be filled with suitable non-plastic materials, and the whole surface compacted uniformly by rolling the entire area with an approved power roller weighting not less than ten tons. Any portion not accessible to a roller shall be thoroughly compacted by an approved pneumatic tamper until a smooth surface is obtained. Any creepage of the grade while being rolled shall indicate insufficient compaction. All fill is to consist of porous non-plastic material, throughly rolled and tamped.

d. Precautions shall be taken as necessary to protect the subgrade from damage. Construct and maintain the crown or pitch or shoulders necessary and maintain the crown or pitch on such a condition that it will drain readily and correctly.

e. Provide wood edging above all perimeters of asphalt paving.

f. Provide traffic lines and tire blocks, 6′ long pinned to surface as shown.

13. Connect roof drain line from point 5′ from outside building to drain line as shown.

14. Provide headwalls, manholes, RCP pipe as shown on draw⋅ .gs, all in accordance with drawings.

15. Provide 6″ of topsoil in areas shown on drawings seeding same on completion of job, and maintaining same until acceptance of job. Grass seed to consist of the following; used at the rate of 5# per 1000 square feet:

Proportion by Weight	Minimum Purity	Minimum Germination
60% Creeping Red Fescue	98%	85%
25% Kentucky Bluegrass	90%	75%
15% Domestic Ryegrass	95%	90%

Commentary. Because this is a business building in a restrictive zone (adjacent to residential) and because the site is on filled ground, the sitework and excavation called for are much more extensive than that usually required. The contractor should understand, however, that he cannot ever depend on the "usual" or the "normal" conditions governing any work he is to do. He can encounter filled land or sink holes or ledge rock or even very large boulders almost anywhere. He should cover himself by asking for a test pit or borings as in this case and by clauses in his estimate (see Chap. 3). (The borings in this case were recommended by the architect-engineer and paid for by the owner.)

The more important items in the specification follow.

Paragraph 2. This general provision calls on the contractor to provide excavation, backfill, rough and finish grading, additional fill, drainage lines, retaining wall, manholes, curbs, sidewalks, paving, and seeding. This general recital of the work required should immediately alert the contractor. He must study the site plan very carefully to find the full extent of his obligations, noting words like "additional fill," "drainage lines," "retaining walls," etc.

Paragraph 3. The contractor is held responsible for the staking of all lines including the setting of grade stakes. This means that the contractor must perform his own survey work or employ a surveyor. In this connection, the contractor is urged to learn the proper use of a transit so that he can lay out corners of a structure from fixed points, determine whether a structure is plumb, and "shoot" levels, among other things.

Paragraph 5. The contractor is held responsible for the disposal of the septic tank. It may have to be removed. This tank has been abandoned.

Paragraph 6. The "loose stone retaining wall" should be carefully estimated *after* the contractor has determined exactly what the architect requires.

Paragraph 8. This section calls for keeping the excavation drained at all times. If the water table is high this may call for constant pumping, which is very expensive. It may even call for well points. It should be carefully investigated.

Paragraph 9. This entire section must be carefully evaluated. Note the requirements for removal of debris and deleterious materials and refilling with bank run gravel tamped in place. The cubic yardage of the removal and backfill must be carefully determined. (There is an alternative for this.)

Paragraph 11. The contractor is responsible for all concrete curbs and walls.

Paragraph 12. The contractor is responsible for all black topping.

Paragraph 14. The headwall, etc., in this case is necessary because a small stream flows through the property. With new wetlands codes, the contractor will most likely have to obtain the exact requirements of the town authorities. Meeting such requirements can be very costly.

Paragraph 15. The contractor is responsible for topsoil and seeding.

2.5E. Concrete (Office Building)

SECTION 3—CONCRETE

1. The General and Special Conditions shall apply to this Section of the Specifications.

2. Included in this Section of the Specifications shall be all concrete work for the building. (All concrete work for the site work is in another section of this specifications). Included in this section shall be all reinforcing steel.

3. All concrete shall be in accordance with Standard specifications of the American Society for Testing Materials. All concrete shall be mixed and placed in accordance with the A.C.I. Standards to obtain 3000 psi strength in 28 days.

4. All sand used for mixing shall be clean, course, and free from loam or other foreign materials. Water shall be clean drinking water.

5. All reinforcing steel shall conform to A.S.T.M. specification A615, grade 60.

6. All wire fabric reinforcing shall conform to A.S.T.M. A-185.

7. Include all spacers, chairs, ties, and other devices for necessary spacing, placing and supporting reinforcement. Provide zinc coated, rustproof accessories in all exposed concrete work.

8. All exposed concrete work shall have added to it DAREX AEA air entraining agent by the Dewey and Almy Chemical Co., in accordance with manufacturer's instructions.

9. All exposed concrete floors shall receive Lapidolith floor hardener.

10. Vapor barrier under all slabs shall be Moistop.

11. Finish all interior concrete slabs with a steel troweled finish. Exterior slabs and steps shall be finished with an even wood or canvas surface.

12. Set all anchor bolts furnished by others as well as bearing plates using Embeco packing as detailed on drawings.

13. All concrete lintels shall be carefully precast with reinforcing as shown on the drawings using light weight 3000 psi concrete and with a color added as approved by the architect. Color shall be accurately measured to produce even color in all lintels. Color shall be by Frank Davis Company. Contractor to submit shop drawings of lintels and samples of concrete for color approval.

14. Fill steel stairs using metal reinforcement mesh.

Commentary. This is a standard concrete specification. The strengths of concrete should be a matter of certification from the ready-mix dealer to the contractor. Because this site is filled land, the plans call for extra large footings so that the weight may be distributed evenly according to the bearing capacity of the soil.

2.5F. Masonry (Office Building)

SECTION 4—MASONRY

1. The General and Special Conditions shall apply to this Section of the Specifications.

2. This Contractor shall provide all items, articles, materials, operations or methods listed, mentioned or scheduled on the drawings and/or herein, including labor, materials, equipment and incidentals necessary and required for the completion of masonry work.

3. Materials:

    a. All brick face work to be selected by Architect and shall conform to A.S.T.M. C216-60, Grade SW, type FBS. Allow $95.00 per thousand, delivered to site, unloaded and stacked. If brick selected by Architect costs more or less than allowance, the exact amount of the difference will be added to or deducted from the contract price.

b. Common brick for back-up work shall conform to A.S.T.M. C62-58, Grade NW.

c. Concrete masonry units shall conform to the following A.S.T.M. standards using Pumice or Celocrete lightweight aggregate as selected by the Architect.

1. Hollow load-bearing   C90-64T, Grade U-1
2. Solid load-bearing (under all concentrated load points)   C145-64T, Grade U-1

d. Mortar for exposed brickwork shall be either masonry cement or lime mortar as follows:

1. Masonry cement shall conform to A.S.T.M. C91-58, Type II, mixed C-144-52T.
2. Lime Mortar shall be type N, consisting of one part by volume Portland cement conforming to A.S.T.M. C-150, Type I, one part and six parts sand conforming to A.S.T.M. C-144-52T.
3. Water shall be clean and free from deleterious amounts of acids, alkalies or organic materials.
4. Mixing of masonry cement mortar or lime mortar shall be done in a mechanical mortar mixer with sufficient water added for desired consistency, and mixing time shall be not less than four minutes after all materials are placed in the mixer. Retempering of masonry cement will not be permitted.

e. All cavity masonry walls shall be reinforced with standard cavity (SC) Duro-O-Wall (drip crimp, galvanized cross wires) placed every second (16″) horizontal course. Provide corner assembly reinforcement at same second course. Reinforce interior masonry walls with standard Dur-O-Wall placed every third (24″) horizontal course. Provide corner and intersection assembly reinforcement. All of the above Dur-O-Wall Products, Inc., Block-Lok Standard or Walmesh. Provide galvanized ties to secure face brick to reinforce concrete walls or to wood stud walls.

f. Premoulded expansion joint filler, where required, shall be Flex-ell, manufactured by the Celotex Corp., or Kork-Pak, Code 1321, manufactured by Servicised Products Corp.

g. Below grade damp proofing shall be Thoroseal Foundation Coating, two coats, as recommended by Standard Drywall Products, Inc.

h. Dampproof all aluminum frames in contact with masonry with Hydrocide 128 Spray by Sonneborn Building Products, Inc.

4. This contractor shall construct a sample of brick wall not less than 3′-0″ square for the Architect's approval of brick and jointing.

5. Workmanship:

a. This contractor shall provide batts, headers, as indicated or required in laying up brick.

b. Brick shall be throughly wet before being laid, except in freezing weather.

c. No brickwork shall be installed when the temperature is below freezing. When temporary heat is provided for installing interior brick, temperature shall be maintained at 50°F for 36 hours.

d. Brickwork shall be covered at the end of each day's work or whenever work is stopped on account of inclement weather or other cause.

e. Push, lay and throughly group all brick at every course so that all joints are solidly filled throughout.

f. All brickwork shall be laid to a line with all surfaces plumb and true, horizontal joints level and vertical joints plumb.

g. Brickwork generally shall be modular, 3 courses equal to 8″ with joints approximately ⅜″ wide. All joints shall be tooled to form a concave joint. Brick shall be laid in running bond.

h. Joints at openings, and where indicated, shall be raked out to receive caulking.

i. Do all cutting and patching of brick as required for the installation of the work of other trades.

j. Build in whistles or wood grounds at door and window jambs.

k. Build in flashings furnished under another section.

l. Where necessary to acquire a uniform, flush surface brick shall be cut with a carborundum saw.

m. Fill top (2) courses of block solid where load bearing. Fill full height to a length of 12″ minimum under concentrated loads, such as beams and at exterior door jambs.

6. Cavity walls:

a. Cavity wall reinforcement shall be placed 15″ o.c. horizontally,

b. Flashing shall be built into cavity walls as specified under Moisture Protection, Section 7. Keep the cavity clean of all mortar droppings by placing a removable wood strip across the metal tie and removing and cleaning it every third course of block.

c. Weep holes shall be provided in lower joint between brick formed with ⅜″ diameter solid sponge rubber tubing, withdrawn when the mortar has set. Weep holes shall be spaced approximately two feet apart.

d. Provide 2″ of ⅜″ washed gravel in bottom of all cavities.

7. Upon completion all exposed brick and concrete masonry shall be washed down, cleaned and repointed where necessary. Cleaning compound shall be Sure-Klean No. 600 Detergent as manufactured by the Process Solvent Co., Inc. and applied in accordance with manufacturer's recommendations.

Commentary. This is a wall-bearing building (the exterior walls plus interior columns support the weight of the structure). The plans show a cavity wall that is faced with exterior-grade face brick backed by concrete block. An allowance per 1000 face brick is mentioned. If the cost runs over the allowance the contractor gets the difference.

The plans show the details in section of the various parts of the exterior walls and both the plans and specification detail the kind and frequency of the reinforcing and how it shall be applied. The specification is quite clear about the protection of the space between the exterior brick and the concrete block backing. Cavity walls are so named because there is a space between the exterior and interior portions. These two masonry units are carefully bound together by both vertical and horizontal reinforcement but the space between, which serves as thermal and moisture insulation, must be kept clear. If it is filled with mortar drips or other material it loses its entire purpose. That is why such walls are usually carefully inspected during construction. The contractor should keep this in mind.

This specification also calls for concrete-block foundation walls filled solidly with mortar. Concrete block walls are perfectly satisfactory for a small building and are according to code.

2.5G. Metal—Structural and Miscellaneous (Office Building)

SECTION 5—METAL—STRUCTURAL & MISCELLANEOUS

1. The General and Special Conditions shall apply to this Section of the Specifications.

2. Included in this Section shall be the fabrication and erection of all structural and miscellaneous steel work including joist hangers, bearing plates, anchor bolts, stairs, rail supports, etc.

3. Submit shop drawings of all structural and miscellaneous steel.

4. All steel shall be designed, fabricated, and erected in accordance with the latest specifications of the American Institute of Steel Construction.

5. All structural steel shall be type A-36.

6. All structural steel shall receive one coat of paint in the shop with a touch up coat in the field after erection.

7. All joints and connections noted on drawings, other than bolted connections, shall be welded.

8. Fabricate and install steel stairs as shown on the drawings, all to be built in accordance with the National Association of Architectural Metal Manufacturers.

Commentary. As mentioned previously, this is a wall-bearing building with floors consisting of wood joists supported by interior steel columns and steel girders.

This portion of the specification states that in addition to the structural steel as shown on the drawings, the contractor must also furnish miscellaneous iron work such as joist hangers, bearing plates, anchor bolts, stairs, rail supports, etc.

The contractor is to note the "etc." He should carefully examine the plans for ladders, hatch covers, steel cover plates, and ornamental iron rails.

The specification mentions that there are both bolted connections and welded connections. The contractor should be sure that his structural steel and miscellaneous iron contractor employs certified welders.

Because structural steel shapes are fabricated in a shop before being delivered they must fit exactly with each other and with the other parts of the structure. That is why shop drawings, which are checked by the architect/engineer for correctness of size and shape, are required and must be approved before the fabrication commences. Failure to do this is the contractor's responsibility and any corrections in the field (very expensive) are at his expense.

2.5H. Carpentry (Office Building)

SECTION 6—CARPENTRY

1. The General and Special Conditions shall apply to this Section of the Specifications.

2. This Contractor shall provide all items, articles, materials, operations or methods listed, mentioned or scheduled on the drawings and/or herein, including all labor, materials, equipment and incidentals necessary and required for the completion of carpentry and millwork. Provide all wood doors under Section 8.

3. Materials:

   a. Rough structural lumber, except otherwise specified, shall be Standard grade Douglas Fir, $E = 1,600,000$ psi and $f = 1500$ psi minimum. (Hemlock is not allowed).
   b. Rough carpentry shall be No. 2 white common pine or spruce.
   c. Interior woodwork and trim to be painted shall be choice grade Idaho White Pine or unselected birch.
   d. Studs 2 × 4's 16" o.c., doubled at openings, tripled at corners and as detailed.
   e. Plywood roofing shall be (1) layer of ½" Plyscord with exterior glue.
   f. Building paper shall be 15# asphalt saturated felt.
   g. All exterior nails shall be galvanized.
   h. Subflooring to be ⅝" Plyscord with exterior glue.
   i. Underlayment to be ½" Plyscord with exterior glue, plugged and touch sanded. (Use ⅝" thickness under alternate #1)
   j. Exterior sheathing behind brick panels to be ½" Georgia-Pacific Co. Firestop gypsum sheathing, asphalt impregnated.
   k. Provide 1 × 3 wood bridging 8' o.c.
   l. Oak to be clear red oak.

4. Framing, blocking, grounds and furring:

   a. All wood furring and blocking and subsills in exterior walls shall be treated with a 5% solution of pentachlorophenol, such as Penta by Monsanto Chemical Co.
   b. Provide wood blocking for interior work as indicated or required including wood door frames, wood partitions.
   c. Provide rough hardware, bolts, lags, anchors, ramsets, etc. for installing rough framing, blocking, furring.

5. This Contractor shall include labor to install finishing hardware and toilet accessories to be purchased out of an allowance carried by the General Contractor.

6. Dry-wall construction:

   a. Scope of work to include all gypsum board walls, fascias, soffits and ceilings on wood framing and on urethane insulated walls.
   b. All wallboard shall be gypsum board of thicknesses and type shown on drawings. Joint treatment shall be PERF-A-TAPE system including metal corner and trim accessories as detailed. All exterior angles shall receive metal corner reinforcement. *Casing beads shall be National Gypsum Co. #200.*
   c. Secure gypsum board to wood with nails as recommended by the Gypsum Coated Board Manufacturer. Gypsum board shall be laminated to urethane wall insulation with sheets placed vertically. Provide horizontal treated nailing strips at wall-ceiling and wall-floor intersections. Use nailing strips $\frac{1}{32}''$ thicker than insulation and $2''$ nominal wide. Use MC or Black Drywall Adhesive as recommended by the manufacturer. Use bracing as necessary to hold board to foam and allow $\frac{1}{4}''$ joint at floor.

7. Provide Formica window stools as shown, color selected by architect.

Commentary. Except for the exterior walls and the interior supporting columns and girders, this building is of wood construction, including the floors, the partitions, and the roof. The quality of the materials to be used is given as follows:

The structural lumber is to be 1500 psi Douglas fir. The rough carpentry lumber is to be No. 2 common pine or spruce. The interior wood work is to be choice-grade Idaho white pine or unselected birch. The partition studs are to be 2 × 4 in. on 16-in. centers doubled at openings and tripled at corners. Subflooring is to be ⅝-in. exterior grade plywood and underlayment* is to be ½-in. exterior plywood. Roof surface to be ½-in. exterior-grade plywood. All furring, blocking, and subsills in exterior walls to be treated with preservative. These are the highlights—there are many more items.

---

*The underlayment takes the place of a finish floor, which is not in the contract (NIC). The floor then consists of two layers of plywood—½ in. over ⅝ in.

The contractor should carefully study such a list to find the quality of material and the workmanship required. There are wide variations in the cost of various types of framing lumber and trim, for instance the additional cost for exterior grade plywood or certified 1500-psi strength Douglas fir.

The sixth section of the specification has to do with the interior dry-wall construction both for partitions and for the furring of the exterior masonry walls. The interior partitions are of gypsum wallboard nailed to wood studs, the wallboard to be of thicknesses and fire resistance shown on the plan. The exterior furring is to be laminated with adhesive to a urethane insulation board which has been supplied by another contractor. This contractor, however, supplies nailing strips at the ceiling and at the floor.

Here again, as was recommended for the private residence, the contractor would be well advised to obtain a price from a subcontractor who does nothing but dry wall. The exterior laminating is skilled work and can cause trouble to workers who are not used to it.

There is one little sentence at the very end of this section of the specification. It says "Provide Formica window stools as shown, color selected by architect." It is really necessary to read a specification carefully.

2.5I. Moisture Protection and Insulation (Office Building)

SECTION 7—MOISTURE PROTECTION & INSULATION

1. The General and Special Conditions shall apply to this Section of the Specifications.

2. Included in this work shall be all roofing, flashing, caulking and building insulation.

3. Roofing shall be 20 year bonded type by Barrett, series 720PC system as follows: Apply dry layer of 15# asphalt felt nailed to wood deck. Mop on 1.2″ Barrett Urethane roof insulation on to felt with Hot Crystal Steep Asphalt. Mop on Vapor Bar layer lapped 4″ on sides, 6″ on ends. Apply 2 layers of Barrett #33 coated roofing felt, lapped 19″ with Barrett Steep Crystal Asphalt, 23# per 100 square feet. Extend all plies up face of cant. Apply gravel surfacing in Barrett Specification Pitch.

4. Gravel stops to be Cheney prefinished type 5, 20 ounce Chinc in color selected by architect. Provide concealed splice plates. Set roof vents, fan, roof drains, supplied by others all in accordance with roofing company's bonded instruction. Deliver 20 year bond to owner on completion of job.

5. Flashing:

    a. Through-wall wall flashings shall be 3 oz. Copper Armed Sisal-kraft 371 Duokote. Start ½″ from outside wall and turn up at least 8″ on back up masonry and 1″ into joint. Lap joints 3″ and cement with asphaltic mastic.

b. Miscellaneous flashing shall be 16 oz. copper. Roof drains shall be flashed with 3 lb. lead pan.

6. Insulation:

a. Perimeter insulation; all perimeter walls to be 24″ wide, 1½″ thick styrofoam.

b. Masonry Walls: 1″ Dow Thurane insulation adhered to walls with Dow Mastic II in accordance with manufacturers instruction.

c. Wood stud walls, with brick veneer: Johns Mansville Ful-Thik with aluminum foil face.

d. Ceiling overhands; J. M. Company Super-Thik, foil faced.

e. Sould insulation; 3″ mineral blankets.

7. Caulking shall be Unicrylic, by Pecora Co., color selected by architect. (this caulking contractor shall do all caulking of control joints and between door frames and masonry, around air conditioner units and underside of subsills. The window contractor is to do all caulking around windows.) Use polyurethane backing in all joints.

Commentary. *Paragraph* 3. This calls for 2-in. polyurethane insulation laid in hot pitch and for a 20-year bonded roof.

Paragraph 4. The contractor must set and waterproof all roof fans, vents, etc.

Paragraph 5. Note copper flashing.

Paragraph 6. Heat insulation is called for in walls and ceilings. Sound insulation is to be 3-in. mineral blanket. Contractor must be sure to correctly estimate the quantities.

Paragraph 7. This contractor is called upon to caulk all joints except around the windows. The window caulking is to be done by the window subcontractor. It is to be hoped that there will be no conflict later on as to who is responsible for leakage.

2.5J. Doors, Windows, etc. (Office Building)

SECTION 8—DOORS, WINDOWS, GLASS, HOLLOW METAL WORK, CAULKING

1. The General and Special Conditions shall apply to this Section of the Specifications.

2. Windows and fixed glass, except at entrance and exitway lights, shall be as detailed, series #300 by Ruscoe Industries, Inc. complete with subframes, sills, etc. prefinished in standard colors. Submit shop drawings for approval as well as color samples. All steel shall be hot-dipped galvanized. Windows to have Fiberglas screens, and to be factory glazed with ½″ insulating glass DSB quality. Window installer

to do all caulking around windows using Unicrylic by Pecora Co. Colors selected by architect.

3. Hollow metal frames shall be by Atlantic Metal Products or Pioneer Fireproof Door Company. Frames shall be 14 gauge for exterior doors and 16 gauge for interior doors. Frames shall be combination type with integral turned over edge, integral stop with screw applied glazing beads. Provide special anchors for wood stud H.M. frames. Provide concealed reinforcement for all screws used for hardware. Provide for concealed closers at all exterior doors. Fill jambs solid with mortar. Provide holes for rubber silencers on all frames except exterior doors.

4. Hollow metal doors to be mineral filled, labeled type where indicated, with 16 gauge faces. Reinforce and drill as required for all hardware at factory. (Closers to be concealed type). Submit shop drawings.

5. Wood doors shall be Weldwood Co., Staved Lumber Core doors, vertically veneered, with plain sliced red oak veneer. Stile edges shall be ¾" red oak. All wood to be thoroughly dry.

6. Glazing:

a. Exterior entrance doors; to be shingled glazed with tempered ¼" P.P. Glass.
b. Side light of front entrance; to be single glazed with tempered ¼" P.P. glass.
c. Lights above exterior 'B' label doors to have ¼" Misco glass by Mississippi Glass Company.
d. Steel windows to be factory glazed as indicated above.
e. Glazing compound to be color as selected by architect.

Commentary. This section is a miscellany of requirements for several trades and kinds of material. The contractor will have to separate them into their several catagories.

Paragraph 2. This paragraph refers to the windows and applies to the subcontractor who will furnish, install, and caulk.

Paragraphs 3 and 4. These paragraphs call for a subcontractor to furnish hollow metal frames (bucks) and doors. The carpentry subcontractors usually install these.

Paragraph 5. Calls for wood doors. The carpenters install them.

Paragraph 5. Calls for miscellaneous glazing. The windows are factory-glazed.

This mixing of trades occurs frequently in the case of small buildings where the architect/engineer does not devote an entire page or section to a one- or two-paragraph specification. It is therefore up to the contractor to sort out the trades and to make sure he does not miss any. He should keep before him a standard estimating trade list so that he can insert each item that is mentioned in the specification into its proper trade classification. Chapter 3 will give such a list and guide the contractor so that he may insert each item into its correct category, thus avoiding both duplication and missed items.

2.5K. Finishes (Office Building)

SECTION 9—FINISHES

1. The General and Special Conditions shall apply to this Section of the Specifications.

2. Included in this section of the specifications shall be all finishes including taping and spackling of gypsum board; painting; vinyl asbestos tile work; acoustical tile ceiling system; and quarry tile work which is Alternate #1.

3. All gypsum board shall be carefully taped and spackled using the PERF-A-TAPE system, in a three coat method. Note that the casing bead and corner beads are to be spackled in with the walls.

4. Painting:

   a. Included shall be all exterior miscellaneous metal, air conditioner baffle panels, door frames, and soffits. On the interior include all walls and gypsum board ceilings, doors and door frames, miscellaneous metal, wood trim, etc.
   b. All colors to be selected by architect. Prepare samples as required.
   c. Do all necessary puttying of nail holes and touching up between coats. Wash metal carefully with mineral spirits before painting. Sand carefully before and between each coat.
   d. Finish tops and bottoms of all doors after fitting to frame.
   e. Remove all paint from glass, etc. on completion and protect other finishes during the work.
   f. Use Devoe and Reynolds Co. material, or approved equal.
   g. Miscellaneous metal and doors (exterior and interior): 1 coat #57 Krome-Kote, 2 coats Bar-Ox metal paint.
   h. Soffits (exterior): 1 coat exterior primer; two coats all weather house paints.
   i. Interior natural wood work (rails, doors, etc): one coat D&R Sanding Sealer #8052; two coats Rez Super Satin Wood Polyurethane.
   j. Interior painted woodwork: 1 coat D&R #8030 enamel undercoat; one coat D&R Velour Semi-gloss enamel.
   k. Gypsum board walls and ceilings: 1 coat D&R Vinyl Primer; one coat D&R Eggshell Enamel.
   l. Concrete block: 1 coat D&R Blox Fill and one coat D&R Satin Eggshell Enamel.

5. Vinyl asbestos tile and base:

   a. Supply and install 4" vinyl base where indicated, square edge type where carpet (by owner) is indicated and cove base elsewhere. Base to be by Kentile, color selected by architect.

b. Allow $.75 per square foot for vinyl tile material cost in base bid where indicated. Tile to be 9″ × 9″ × ⅛″.

c. Floor treads to be square edged type, plain colors as selected by architect, commercial grade by Johnsonite or approved equal.

6. Acoustic lay-in type ceiling:

a. Grid system: National Rolling Mills Company exposed grid system consisting of Main Tees at 4′-0″ o.c. with metal thickness of .016″, web 1½″, flange ¹⁵⁄₁₆″ and Cross Tees at 2′-0″ o.c. with metal thickness of .018″, web ⅞″, flange ¹⁵⁄₁₆″ and Wall Angles metal thickness of .020″, web ¹⁵⁄₁₆″, flange ¹⁵⁄₁₆″. All members shall have a factory baked white enamel finish. Hangers shall be #12 wire, located not over 4″-0″ o.c. Cut tees to rest on wall angles. Provide framing and supports for light fixtures.

b. Acoustic tile to be: 2 × 4 × ⅝″ lay-in type panels, Armstrong Fire Guard system. Tile to be Armstrong Minaboard, Georgian Design, item #763.

7. Quarry tile: (Alternate #1)

a. See finish schedule for location of this alternate in place of vinyl asbestor tile in base bid. Include stair treads and risers at exterior front entrance steps and slab at entrance.

b. Allow $.75 per square foot for 6″ × 6″ × ½″ quarry tile material.

c. Tile to be laid according to Tile Council of America's specifications #106-70 on wood floors and #103-70 over concrete slabs. On concrete slabs use Latex mortar setting bed, and L&M gray Epoxy Grout. On wood floors use L&M Surpoxy thin-set mortar and L&M gray Epoxy Grout all in *strict accordance with manufacturer's instructions.*

Commentary. This section is again a miscellany pertaining to several trades.

Paragraph 2. This mentions the trades that are involved

Paragraph 3. This calls for the taping of the gypsum-board walls. The contractor can give this work to the painting contractor, or he can sublet the entire dry-wall job, including erection and taping, to a single subcontractor.

Paragraph 4. This includes the painting of all exterior miscellaneous metal, door frames, soffits, and all interior walls, ceilings, doors, trim and miscellaneous metal. Because this is an office building, which gets harder wear than a private residence, the materials to be used are sturdier (and more expensive). For instance, all walls get a coat of a vinyl primer and a coat of alkyd-base eggshell enamel; woodwork gets a coat of sealer and two coats of satin finish containing polyurethane; and metals get one coat of rust inhibitor and two coats of special metal paint. The contractor is also called upon to remove all paint from glass (this clause is just stuck in at the end).

Paragraph 5. This calls for 4-in. vinyl base of color selected to be furnished and installed where shown on the plan. It also states the allowance per square foot of vinyl tile (9 × 9 × ⅛ in.) that the contractor will get for the installation of such tile when called for. As stated before in such cases, if the owner or architect chooses a tile that costs more than the allowance, the contractor is entitled to an extra.

Paragraph 6. This calls for a hung acoustical ceiling with an exposed grid system. It gives the sizes and finishes of the tee-bar supports, the method of their hanging, and the size and finish of the acoustic lay-in panels. This is all identified by manufacturer's name and catalog names and numbers. There are acoustic-ceiling contractors in towns of any size who are completely familiar with this type of work. The contractor himself need only be sure that he has placed the straps for hanging this ceiling in the correct location by the use of inserts in concrete floors or by nailing the straps to joists in the case of wood construction. (Architects' plans should show locations.) A caution: hung ceilings also support flush recessed lighting fixtures—provisions should be made for this.

2.5L. Specialties (Office Building)

SECTION 10—SPECIALTIES

1. The General and Special Conditions shall apply to this Section of the Specifications.

2. Toilet partitions and urinal screens shall be by Flush-Metal Partition Company, floor braced type, without headrails. Doors and panels to be 1″ thick, made of galvanized 20 gauge material over honeycomb filler, reinforced with galvanized 18 gauge channels. Pilasters to be same construction, 1¼″ thick, 18 gauge metal, 16 gauge reinforcement. Metal shall be bonderized and primed before receiving two coats standard color selected by architect. Hardware to be forged 302 stainless steel. Floor shoes to be 14 gauge 302 stainless steel. Provide coat hooks and paper holders.

3. Floor mats and sinkage to be Parco Company with Hi-Rib corrugated rubber mat, color to be selected by architect.

Commentary. This section specifies the type, the manufacture, and the method of hanging toilet-compartment partitions. Toilet partitions are furnished and installed by special contractors. The contractor himself must furnish the necessary wall, floor, or ceiling supports. Information regarding such supports is obtained from the manufacturer's catalog which the company will be glad to send on request. If there is any problem it will also send a representative.

2.5M. Plumbing (Office Building)

SECTION 15—PLUMBING

1. The General and Special Conditions shall apply to this Section of the Specifications.

2. This Contractor shall supply a complete system of water supply and sewage disposal from the connection on the street water line and to the waste line 5′ from the building. The septic system and excavation and backfill and electrical work shall be done by others.

3. Materials:

    a. Comply with all codes with regard to materials and labor.
    b. Copper pipe underground shall be Type 'K' tubing.
    c. Copper above grade shall by Type 'L' tubing.
    d. Exposed traps, stops, supplies, etc. shall be chrome plate on brass.
    e. Outside hose bibs shall be Wade W-8605 non freeze type.

4. Supply and install Josam roof drains to be flashed and set by roofing contractor. Roof drains to be Josam #413. Provide clean outs at all bends. Run drain to point 5′ from building.

5. Provide 30 gallon electric hot water heater, glass lined tank, quick recovery type, by A. O. Smith Company or approved equal.

6. Sewer line to run five feet beyond building to be connected to septic system by others.

7. Connect onto existing ¾″ copper water line as shown on drawings.

8. Provide all tests before closing up of walls and ceilings.

9. Fixtures: (all fixtures to be American Standard, white in color, acid resisting type, free of cracks and chips, with stops at every fixture).

    a. Lavatories: 20″ × 18″ Lucerne vitreous china, cast in soap dish, wall hanger. #351.023 with single lever #2181.014 faucet.
    b. Water closets: Elongated Cadet, #2109.056 with wall supply, and open front white seat with cover by Church.
    c. Urinals: Washbrook #F-6500, vitreous china, washout type, ¾″ top spud, wall hangers, and Coyne-Delaney #451 flushboy valve.
    d. Slop sink: Lake 24″ × 20″, #7602.022 with faucet #4141.263, drain plug #4362.034, and P-trap #4432.019.
    e. Drinking fountains: Manitou #8340.135.

Commentary. This building contains two women's and two men's toilets, two drinking fountains and two slop sinks, roof drains, and hose connections. The plumbing contractor is also to furnish and install a 30 gal electric hot-water heater with a glass-lined tank. The quality of materials is specified, such as extra-heavy bell spigot, cast iron for wastes, type-K copper water lines below grade, and type-L above grade. All fixtures, roof drains, and other fittings are specified by name, size, and catalog number. Every town in the country requires plumbing to be done by a properly licensed plumbing contractor.

2.5N. Electrical and Heating (Office Building)

SECTION 16—ELECTRICAL & HEATING

1. The General and Special Conditions shall apply to this Section of the Specifications.

2. Scope: It is the intent of this section of the work to cover a complete electrical and heating system as outlined herein, and on the drawings, as well as a temporary electric service for use during construction. The system shall be complete with emergency lighting system.

3. All work and equipment shall conform to all local, state, and federal codes and utility company requirements.

4. The following work shall be done by others:

   a. Excavation and backfill.

5. Furnish complete 600 AMP, three phase, four wire, 120/208 volt service underground in (2) 4″ conduits from transformer pole to main switch including risers and ground bushings and secondary service conductors. All metering etc. shall be in accordance with utility company requirements. There will be a single meter used in this building located where directed.

6. Supply complete distribution system as shown in the drawings providing eight, 12 circut flush panel boards as shown. Stub up from panel boards to ceiling space from each panel with (4) ¾″ conduit for future connectors. Run empty conduits to second floor and to outside concrete pad location for future connection of air conditioning unit. Provide all conduit for wiring of this unit. All conduit to be ¾″ minimum.

7. Provide and install complete with bulbs, all light fixtures as shown. Outdoor fixtures as shown to run to 7 day time clock similar and equal to "Tork" #1962.

8. All switches, receptacles, and cover plates to be specification grades; coverplates to be brushed stainless steel.

9. Provide and install a complete 32 volt emergency lighting system as made by Dual-Lite Company. Console shall be sufficient to carry emergency system as required by the State of Conn. Fire Marshall.

10. Provide an underground conduit 2″ diameter from pole to mechanical room terminating on the board as shown for telephone wiring.

11. Provide and install a roof fan with 24″ prefab roof curb with cant strip and *no* back draft dampers. Fan to be Exitair Model CX-1232, rated 650 cfm against ³⁄₁₆″ SP with ⅛ HP, 850 RPM direct drive motor.

12. Provide ductwork for toilet room ventilation. Accoustically line horizontal member of toilet room duct. Registers shall be U.S.

Register Co. #608 stamped steel face with fusible link and key operated opposed blade dampers. Provide capped off ductwork in ceilings as shown for future air conditioning unit. Duct work shall be fabricated and installed in conformance with the latest minimum recommendations of the ASHRAE Guide and all requirements of governing authorities. Insulate and vaporproof supply ductwork in ceilings with vinyl clad wrap around insulation.

13.   Provide for installation by General Contractor of one 1'4" × 1'4" exterior wall grille with bird screen, manual damper, 14 gauge min. extruded annodized aluminum bronze color grille where shown in drawings.

14.   Provide all heating and cooling devices as shown in the drawings. Wall units to be complete with exterior baffle kit, wall sleeve, and shall be connected by receptable to power source. Each unit to have automatic night set back with manual override feature. Baseboard radiation and heating/cooling units to have individual integral thermostats and built in disconnects. Provide plain baffle to be painted by others.

15.   Alternate.
Indicate additional cost of supplying and installing the following air conditioning unit equipment:

a. Condensing unit—York CM60 pre-charged with starting accessory, low ambient accessory, quick-connect adaptors for field piping and concrete support piers to below frost line footings.
b. Evaporator unit CEB62 pre-charged with heating/cooling thermostat suspension package and 12 KW 2 stage electric heating coils.
c. Furnish and install the above units and all required refrigerant and condensate piping with anti-sweat insulation and control devices including wiring. Connect duct work indicated in base bid into unit located suspended in second floor mechanical room. (Connectors from terminal ends of ducts would be done by others).

16.   Heating and Airconditioning to be balanced on completion of work.

Commentary. This is an all-electric building and therefore the heating and cooling is under the same contractor as the light and power. There is no central system and the heating and cooling is done by individual window units. The specification gives the size and capacity of the service lines which here are run underground from a pole transformer. There is a schedule of the interior distribution system on the drawings, which also show locations of panel boxes, base outlets, lighting fixtures, window units and all other devices which use electricity.

The contractor furnishes and installs all the devices, fixtures, window units, etc. as shown and as specified by size, capacity, manufacturer's name, and catalog number. The installation of telephone lines is also included.

Because of code requirements the specification also calls for a 32-volt emergency lighting system and one other item—because there is no heating contractor, the light and power contractor is called on to furnish and install ventilating ductwork and roof fans.

2.50. General

The foregoing samples of specifications have not attempted to give more than the important portions of the work to be done by the various trades. The contractor will find that each specification is slightly different, depending on the owner's requirements and the architect/engineer's preference. That is why it is so important that the contractor read and understand every word. It may seem a chore, but specifications represent dollars.

3
ESTIMATING
AND BIDDING

3.1. STARTING THE ESTIMATE

The contractor should not start to estimate and bid on a job until he thoroughly understands the intent of the plans and specifications. He should know exactly what he is supposed to do and what is expected of him by the owner and the architect no matter how small the job is. The foregoing chapter has emphasized the points of information he should look for.

The first step in estimating is to read carefully through the plans and specifications to determine which trades are involved. The contractor should make a list of these:

Excavation and sitework
    Finish grading
    Planting
    Seeding
Foundations
    Concrete
    Masonry
Carpentry and millwork
Brickwork
Roofing and sheet metal
Waterproofing
Glass and glazing
Ceramic tile
Painting and finishing
Plumbing
Heating

Electrical
Finish hardware
Miscellaneous iron
Bathroom accessories (including medicine cabinets)
Finish cleaning

This list covers the basic subdivisions of a construction job, but there are many loose ends which must be assigned to a trade. These items must be in the estimate and therefore the contractor has to decide who is to do them. Chapter 2 calls attention to many of them, such as:

Rubbish removal
Cleaning windows (if called for)
Cutting and patching
Miscellaneous metal such as lintels, lally columns
Structural metal (columns, girders, channels)
Insulation (both for sound and weather)
Weatherstripping
Temporary weather protection
Temporary water
Temporary sanitary facilities
Temporary heat and electricity
Dry-wall partitions (who does?)
Special floor, wall, or ceiling finishes
Special scaffolding
Special site work (backfill and grading)*

The items of work listed above are usually in the specification or plan from which the contractor prepares the estimate. Most of them have been shown as part of a trade subdivision but some are not. The contractor must not assume that the various subcontractors will include them in their bid, especially if the items mention work not normally done by the subcontractor.

Some of the items are not in any trade divisions but are in the General and Special Conditions. The contractor cannot expect any of his subcontractors to do any of the work mentioned unless he calls their specific attention to these items and puts it in writing, for example: cleaning and rubbish removal; temporary heat, light, water, or sanitary facilities; underground wiring; etc. Therefore it is up to the contractor to assign to himself the items he can do best and cheapest and to place into each trade subdivision those items which require the special skills or equipment which he does not have.

*This is work over and above the normal backfill against foundations.

After each subcontractor has been assigned (in writing) both his normal work and those bits and pieces that have been taken out of the General and Special Conditions, then the contractor is ready to start estimating the cost of his own share of the work.

3.2. THE BUILDER'S OWN WORK

The estimate in this case is on a one-story ranch house with three bedrooms, a living room–dining room, two baths and a powder room, a kitchen-laundry room, a two-car garage, and a mudroom or pantry.

3.2A. Checklist for the Builder's Own Work

In Sec. 3.1 a checklist of subcontractor's work was described and it was suggested that the contractor himself perform some of the work which would be easier and cheaper for him to do than to assign it to subcontractors. To estimate his own work properly he must make a list of all the work necessary to complete the structure, ready for occupancy. The list follows:

- *The Survey.* The structure should be placed on the site in its proper location, with setback and other zoning regulations observed. The architect or owner is presumed to have located the building on the site in its proper place. If the addition or the building is nonconforming, the owner should have obtained proper official authorization. It is wise for the contractor to check this before he proceeds. The owner should provide an approved survey.

- *Site Work.* One of the very first things a contractor must do when he is asked to bid a job is to carefully investigate the site. He should look for outcroppings of ledge rock, any slopes that grade down to the building site, wet land (in this case a test pit is indicated), large trees, heavy underbrush, and other natural features that may impede his work. (The subject of topography of the land is treated exhaustively in Chap. 18.) Having seen and noted these things, he must allow for them in his bid and in the bids he receives for excavation, foundations, and sitework.

- *Excavation and Foundation.* Can this work be sublet as a single subcontract to include all footings, concrete block walls, and block piers (if any) for central girders? It must also include comeback time for the excavator to redistribute topsoil and backfill and to remove excavated material. If this subcontractor has masons on his payroll, this contract can also include the fireplace chimney and furnace flue. Does the contractor want to do any of the work himself? Such as exterior steps, the concrete garage floor, stuccoing of exposed foundation wall, an outdoor terrace or porch floor.

- *Carpentry and Millwork.* The contractor should plan to build the entire structural frame and enclosure including sills, girders, interior and exterior wall framing, joists, sheathing, roof framing, underfloor and finish floor; all interior and exterior millwork including stairs; shelving; all trim, doors, windows, mantel, siding, insulation, roof shingles, kitchen cabinets, door hanging, and the locks for interior and exterior. He should decide who is to do the wallboard and taping. Can he get a subcontractor to install and tape or can he do it more cheaply himself? How about weatherstripping of doors and windows? How about storm windows and screens?

- *Brickwork* for fireplace and chimney is mentioned in *Excavation and Foundation.* If the contractor does not get the foundation masonry contractor to perform this work, should he place a bricklayer on his payroll or hire a small subcontractor? Who purchases the brick, the flue lining, the hardware—ash trapdoor and damper? Perhaps the specification calls for a built-in cast-iron heating unit with registers. Who supplies it?

- *Roofing and Sheet Metal.* If the contractor plans to lay the shingles, he will require a subcontractor to furnish and install flashings, leaders, and gutters. Or perhaps he can purchase ready-made leaders and gutters and purchase copper, etc., for flashings to be installed by him. This calls for experience and skill. Flashing leaks are very hard to locate. The contractor will know the capabilities of himself and his men.

- *Waterproofing.* This is mostly for foundation walls. If the specification calls for a trowel coat of mastic, it can be applied by the contractor. If hot pitch is called for, the contractor will have to figure on renting some heating equipment for the pitch. There is also the furnishing and laying of drain tile plus the necessary ditching. This can be done by the excavator or the contractor.

- *Other Trades.* The contractor is advised to sublet the following trades: glass and glazing, ceramic tile, resilient floor tile, painting, electrical, and heating and plumbing. These are all specialty trades and some require special licenses. The subcontractors who do this work can obtain special prices and technical advice that the contractor cannot get. Finish hardware and bathroom accessories should be allowance items that depend on the choice of the owner or architect.

- *General (and) Supplementary Conditions and Miscellaneous Items.* The contractor will find it easier to perform many of the items listed under these headings, except for the ones that require a special trade. If he does not wish to do them then they must be placed specifically in a subcontractor's contract. Such items would include temporary light, temporary water, special sitework, driveways, grading, and extra backfill (see list in Sec. 3.1). The contractor could assume responsibility for such items as rubbish removal, cleaning windows, cutting and patching after all trades, miscellaneous metal such as lintels and lally columns, and structural metal such as beams, channels, and girders, temporary weather protection, and special scaffolding. However he must be sure to include these items in his own estimate.

3.2B. The Quantity Take-Off

The first item to estimate is the lumber list. Lumber is sold by the thousand board feet, and a board foot is a piece of wood that is $12 \times 12 \times 1$ in. thick. Millwork is sold by the linear foot. (The figures in the following example illustrate how board feet are measured.) Now the contractor studies the specifications and plans again. Usually the structural lumber to be used consists of 2×6- or 2×8-in. sills, 2×8 or 2×10 headers, 2×4 studs, 2×4 soles and plates, 2×6 rafters, 2×8 or 2×10 joists, girders which may be 2×8 or 2×10 doubled or tripled, window heads which may be doubled 2×6 or 2×8, corner bracing, collar beams, subflooring, sheathing, and siding.

The specification or plan, for instance, may call for studs 16 in. on center, doubled at window and door openings and tripled at corners. It will give the size and spacing of all the structural lumber. If it does not, the contractor should ask the architect. If there is no architect, there is always the local code. Any contractor who follows the local code cannot be faulted, although most architects specify above code, which is, after all, minimal.

3.2B1. THE LUMBER COUNT

This is done to determine the number of pieces of lumber of the various sizes and lengths that are required. The lumber count is to be made as though there were no openings—interior or exterior.

CALCULATION OF BOARD FEET

All structural lumber is sold by the thousand board feet (MBF). In ordering such lumber, the contractor should give the size and length of the lumber and the number of pieces of each he requires. He must then reduce it to board feet.

A board foot can best be described by a piece of lumber that is 1 in. thick, 12 in. wide and 12 in. long. The cross section is 1 × 12 in. or 12 sq in. Multiplied by 12 in., this gives 144 cu in., or 1 board foot.

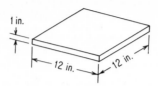

A simple formula for determining board feet is as follows: Thickness in inches, or 1, times width in inches, or 12, times length in feet, or 1, divided by 12; that is, 1 × 12 × 1 = 12 ÷ 12 = 1.

In a 2 × 4 the cross section is 2 × 4 in. or 8 sq in. Because the cross section is smaller than 12, it takes more than 12 in. to make a board foot. Since

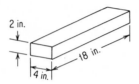

eight goes into twelve 1½ times, it takes 1½ ft or 18 in. to make a board foot.

Using the formula above: Thickness in inches, or 2, times width in inches, or 4, times length in feet, or 1½ (or 3/2), divided by 12; that is 2 × 4 × 3/2 = 12 ÷ 12 = 1.

Or to use another simple formula: Thickness in inches, or 2, times width in feet, ⁴⁄₁₂ or ⅓, times length in feet; for example, 2 × ⅓ × 3/2 = 6/6 = 1.

Take a 2 × 4, 8 ft long.
Formula 1. Thickness in inches 2, times width in inches 4, times length in feet 8, divided by 12; 2 × 4 × 8 = 64, 64 ÷ 12 = 5⁴⁄₁₂ or 5⅓ board feet.

Formula 2. Thickness in inches 2, times width in feet ⅓, times length in feet, 8; 2 × ⅓ × 8 = 16/3 or 5⅓ board feet.

There is still a third formula: Thickness in inches 2, times width in inches 4, times length in inches 96, divided by 144 (cubic inches in a board foot): 2 × 2 × 96 = 768, 768 ÷ 144 = 5⁴⁸⁄₁₄₄ or 5⅓ board feet.

One more example is a 2 × 8: In a 2 × 8 the cross section is 16 sq in. Because the cross section is larger than 12 it takes less than a foot of length

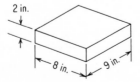

to make a board foot. 12 sq in. is ¾ of 16 sq in., so that ¾ of a linear foot is a board foot.

To prove this by formula:

Formula 1. $(T'' \times W'' \times L' \div 12)$ $2'' \times 8'' \times \frac{3}{4}' \div 12 = 1$

Formula 2. $(T'' \times W' \times L')$ $2'' \times \frac{2}{3}' \times \frac{3}{4}' = \frac{12}{12} = 1$

Formula 3. $(T'' \times W'' \times L'')$ $2'' \times 8'' \times 9'' = 144 \div 144 = 1$

Note: For the thickness of a piece of lumber in a board foot calculation, use multiples of 1. Thus any piece of lumber between 1 and 2 in. thick is counted as 2 and so on.

TABLE FOR CONVERTING TO BOARD FEET

2 × 4	Multiply linear feet by 1.5			
2 × 6	"	"	"	" 1
2 × 8	"	"	"	" 0.75
2 × 10	"	"	"	" 0.60
2 × 12	"	"	"	" 0.50

The house is 30 ft wide by 56 ft long including the garage, which is 18 × 30 ft. This is a typical ranch house.

The perimeter is 30 × 2 = 60 plus 56 × 2 = 112 or 172 feet.

3.2B1a. The Number of 2 × 4s, 8 ft Long, That Are Required*

Studs are 16 in. on center or every 1⅓ ft. Multiply 172 ft × ⅔	115
Add three pieces for each corner	12
Add two pieces for each opening interior and exterior incl.	
closets (approx). 16 openings × 2	32
There is one sole plate and two top plates. 172 × 3 = 516 ÷ 8	65
There is bridging at center of the studs. 172 ÷ 14	
(14-ft lengths cut into 14-in. pieces evenly)	12
There are 16 openings, 3 ft wide or 48 ft (approx)	
Use double studs at door heads and at window sills	
48 × 2 = 96 ÷ 12	8
There are 140 ft of interior partition	
Studs are 16 in. on center 140 × ⅔	93
The partitions have one sole and two plates	
140 ft × 3 = 420 ÷ 8 ft (each piece)	53
Total 2x4/8'–0" long	370
Total 2x4/12'–0" long	8
Total 2x4/14'–0" long	12

*If the contractor will sketch out his framing plan he may find that he can mix in some 12-ft lengths which cut into four 3-ft lengths without waste or some 14-ft and 16-ft lengths for long stretches of sole plates and top plates. The coat is almost the same and there can be a saving in lumber and labor.

3.2B1b. The Number of Floor and Ceiling Joists and Girders

The house is 30 ft wide and the floor joists will be supported on girders resting on lally columns or cement block piers (if there is no basement) at the half-way mark or 15 ft. The ceiling joists will be supported by the double plate over the central bearing partition or at 15 ft. This means that all floor and ceiling joists can be 16 ft long and can be dropped in place with no cutting and no waste. (This is an example of what a modular house should be.) For a clear span of 14 ft, 3 in., the code calls for 2 × 10s on 16-in. centers. The house is 56 ft long but the last 18 ft is a garage. There are therefore 38 ft of house. Dividing 38 ft by 16 in., or multiplying by ⅔, gives 25 joists on each side or fifty 2 × 10 floor joists, 16 ft long. The ceiling joists may be 2 × 8 on 24-in. centers (code). Because of the 24-in. centers, there are only 34 ceiling joists. The girders should be three 2 × 10s, 14 ft long, to span 36 ft or a total of nine 2 × 10s, 14 ft long (three spans of 12 ft, 8 in. each).

3.2B1c. Roof Framing

The house is 30 ft wide. The roof pitches 4 in. in 12. To span 15 ft, an 18 ft length of 2 × 6 is needed. Because of its length and the possible deflection it will have to be trussed. The greater the pitch the less need for trussing. A roof with a pitch more than 6 in. in 12 in. can be framed with 2 × 8s on 16-in. centers with 2 × 8 collar beams at one-third the distance from ridge to attic floor. The architect should say how it is to be trussed. If there is no architect, the builder can use the truss shown in the appendix (the monoplanar). This is built of 2 × 4s with steel connector plates.

These trusses can be on 24-in. centers. There is some headroom for storage space in the attic. Some lumber yards will sell such trusses ready to assemble. The other truss also distributes the roof load at three points of the supporting structure, but does not use steel plate connectors and uses 2 × 6 rafters instead of 2 × 4. The best way to decide between them is to lay out half the truss to scale ¼ in = 1 ft and scale off the lengths of 2× 6s or 2 × 4s. Then reduce them to board feet and figure which uses less lumber and labor. The truss made at the lumberyard ready for assembly will probably be cheaper.

3.2B1d. Other Members.

There are other structural members such as sills, bands or headers, diagonal bracing, wall sheathing and roof sheathing, underfloor, finish floor, siding, lumber for grounds and for forms. Sills in this case should be 2 × 8s. Dividing the perimeter of 172 ft by 16 gives eleven 2 × 8 pieces, 16 ft long.

Headers in this house are 2 × 10 because the floor joists are 2 × 10. Again divide 172 by 16 to obtain eleven 2 × 10 pieces, 16 ft long.

Lintels over exterior windows of ordinary size (up to 3 ft, 8 in.) are doubled 2 × 6s. Lintels over garage opening can be two 2 × 12s.

Sheathing should be figured as though there were no exterior openings. It is usually ½-in. exterior-grade plywood (plyscore). It comes in sheets that are 2 × 4, 4 × 4, or 4 × 8 ft. The contractor should spend some time to figure how he can work out his sheets with minimum waste. After all, ½-in. plywood costs about 40 cents per square foot, and the cost is going up.

The underfloor should be figured in the same way as sheathing. It is usually ½-in. plyscore. Use ¾-in. underfloor in kitchens and baths.

Finish floor is usually 25/32 × 2¼ red oak T&G strip flooring. Measure the square footage of the house and add 30 percent for waste. The house is 38 by 30 ft, or 1140 sq ft. Subtract 320 sq ft for kitchen and baths. Then 820 sq ft + 30% (or 240 sq ft) is 1060 sq ft.

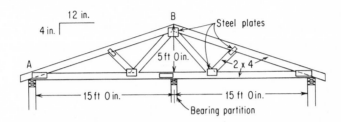

HOW TO CALCULATE SQUARE FEET OF SHEATHING AND UNDERFLOOR

Roof area: The roof slope is 4 in. in 12 in. The span is 15 ft, and the rise at the center is 5 ft. The length of roof between A and B is the square root of sum of squares; 15 squared (225) plus 5 squared (25) is 250. The square root* of 250 is 15.81, or 16 ft. Add 1 ft overhang to make 17 ft.

17 × 56 × 2 = 1904 sq ft, which divided by 32 (or 4 × 8)
   equals 60.   60

Exterior perimeter: 172 ft divided by 4-ft width = 43.   43

Underfloor: 38 ft long by 30 ft wide.
1140 sq ft divided by 32.   36
Number of 4 × 8-ft sheets.   139

Siding comes in a variety of woods. The most common is 1 × 8-ft red cedar bevel siding. More and more vertical siding is now used. Red cedar rough sawn 1 × 6, 1 × 8, or 1 × 10 ft board and batten or shiplap are examples. Add approximately 20 percent for waste and purchase by the linear foot.

3.2B1e. Calculations of Board Feet

(See diagrams in "Calculation of Board Feet," p. 72)

- 2 × 4s. There are 370 pieces 8 ft long, or 2960 lin ft. There are 12 pieces 14 ft-0 in. long, or 168 lin ft.

*See Appendix for table of square roots.

- 2 × 10-in. floor joists. There are 50 pieces 16 ft long, or 800 lin ft.

- 2 × 6s or other sizes for roof rafters. If the contractor uses trusses, he can obtain a price per truss; otherwise he can figure board feet.

- 2 × 8-in. ceiling joists. There are 34 pieces 16 ft long, or 544 lin ft.

The above figures are just a sample of how the contractor works up a lumber list. Other materials such as sheathing, underflooring, etc., are listed by square feet. Rough construction lumber may be listed by so many 1 × 2-in. furring strips 12 ft long (for instance) or sheets of rough plywood or T&G roofers for forms, etc. Such lumber is usually called utility grade lumber.

In all cases, 10 percent should be added for wastage (except where it has already been added). The exact amount of the board feet of lumber involved must be estimated first, and would be correct if every piece of lumber were used in the right place and if there were no waste, but anyone who has been around a construction job knows this is not so! Therefore the contractor must add for wastage and spoilage. A good overall figure is to use 10 percent over the actual board measure for each size of lumber. If the contractor can use modular lengths of lumber just as they come, and if he and his workers are careful, a great deal of this wastage can be eliminated, effecting a real saving, especially at today's lumber prices.

3.2B1f. The Materials List

The contractor is now ready to make up his lumber and materials list (see example shown in Fig. 3-1), which he is advised to submit to two or three local material dealers for bids. He must specify the kind and grade of lumber. Structural lumber is usually No. 2 or better Douglas fir, although No. 2 or better Southern yellow pine is coming into use. This is more difficult to cut and the longer lengths are likely to twist as they dry. The plywood usually has to be approved by local or state code.

There are other materials in addition to construction lumber that the contractor has to purchase from a material dealer and it is a good idea to obtain a bid for all material at the same time. The contractor is likely to get a better overall price than if he obtained his material piecemeal. For instance there are nails, screws, anchor bolts, metal straps, metal railings, steel bridging (if used instead of wood), buckets, small tools, trap doors, leaders, interior trim such as ¼-in. round, moldings, chair rail, bookshelf millwork including shelf brackets, door and window trim, and doors and windows.

There is also wallboard. The majority of construction now uses wallboard for all the interior partitioning. It comes in different thicknesses and has standard fire ratings which are accepted by building code and fire underwriters. The average private house uses ½-in.-thick gypsum board for walls and

Materials List Sheet 1 of 3

Contractor _Thomas Smith_ Date _Oct. 12, 197_

Property _32 Wilson Ave., Jonesboro_

Material	Location	Size	Length	Number of pieces	Lineal ft (l.f.) or sq ft	Board feet	Price per MBF (sq ft) or lineal ft	Total cost
#2 and	Studs	2x4	8'-0	370	2960 l.f.	1973		
better	Studs	2x4	14'-0	12	172 l.f.	120		
	Studs	2x4	12'-0	8	96 l.f.	64		
Douglas Fir	Sills	2x8	16'-0	11	176 l.f.	270		
"	Floor Joists	2x10	16'-0	50	800 l.f.	1340		
"	Ceiling Jsts.	2x8	16'-0	34	544 l.f.	727		
"	Headers	2x10	16'-0	11	176 l.f.	300		
"	Girders	2x10	14'-0	9	126 l.f.	210		
"	Lintels	2x6	12'-0	14	168 l.f.	170		
"	Roof Framing	see section of roof framing in this chapter						
Plyscore	Sheathing	4x8	Sheets	139	4448 sq. ft			
Ext. Grade	and Underfl.	½" thick						
"	Bath & Kitchen	4x8	¾" thick	10	320 sq. ft.			
Red Oak	Finish floor	25/32 x 2¼ T&G	No length less than 6'-0					
	"				1000 sq. ft.			
White pine, red cedar or as called for	Siding	Various widths and styles vertical or horizontal. Sold by lin. ft.						
Utility	Forms	1x8	12'-0	40 T&G	480 l.f.			
Grade-Const.	Furring	1x2	12'-0	50	600 l.f.			
Lumber	Bridging	"						
Shingles	Roof	235#-Asphalt			1900 sq. ft.			

Figure 3-1 Sample of materials list.

either ½-in. or double ⅜-in. gypsum board for ceilings. Between house and attached garage it uses ⅝-in.-thick fire code board. The wallboard comes in sheets 4 × 8, 4 × 9, or 4 × 10 ft. If it is not to be taped and painted, it can be purchased with textured finish and with various edges.

The material list when completed should be handed to at least two material dealers for bid. The contractor should make it clear to the material dealer that:

• There will be partial shipments to the job, to be ordered as required. (There should be a discount if contractor picks up material.)

							Price per	
Material	Location	Size	Length	Number of pieces	Lineal ft(l.f.) or sq ft	Board feet	MBF (sq ft) or lineal ft	Total cost
Wall Board	Walls	4x8x½		106	3400 sq. ft.*			
Wall Board	Ceilings	4x8x⅜ DOUBLE LAYER		72	2280 sq ft.			
Wall Board	Garage	4x8x⅝ FIRE CODE		15	450 sq. ft.			
Idaho Pine	Shelving for Closets and Bookcases	1x10	8'-0	24	192 l.f.			
By manufacture and catalogue #	Windows Doors Stairs†	Obtain number, size, etc., from plans and spec. and obtain approval of Owner or Architect. Are ordered ready made.						
	Trim	Contractor to check catalogue for standard trim sizes and shapes for windows, doors, molding etc. Obtain owner's or architect's approval.						
	Mantel Trapdoor and Stairs to Attic Kitchen counters and Cabinets	Order by style with prior approval — Order by catalogue number — Order with Architect's or owner's approval. Ready made or custom.						

Materials List — Sheet 2 of 3

Contractor *Thomas Smith* Date *Oct. 12, 197_*
Property *32 Wilson Ave, Jonesboro*

* 140 ft int. partition 2 sides. 136 ft perimeter 1 side. 280 + 136 = 416 lin ft 8'-0 high. To obtain number of 4x8 sheets divide 416 by 4 = 104 call 106 sheets.

Figure 3-1 *(continued).*

†Contractor requires (1) headroom, (2) floor-to-floor height, (3) height of riser, (4) width of tread, and (5) length of run. See table in text. The architect should provide this information.

- The prices quoted on the bid sheet are to be itemized for each kind of material.

- The contractor may purchase additional material for the job at the same price. (In this case he may have to truck it himself.) This additional material is to allow for wastage which was not in the original order. The only exception is the flooring, and here,

Material	Location	Size	Length	Number of pieces	Lineal ft (l.f.) or sq ft	Board feet	Price per MBF (sq ft) or lineal ft	Total cost

Materials List — Sheet 3 of 3

Contractor *Thomas Smith*   Date *Oct. 12, 197—*
Property *32 Wilson Ave, Jonesboro*

Finish Hardware. Order by style and catalogue number.
  pair 3½" x 3½" butts. Paint grade.
  pair 4" x 4" butts. Paint grade
  latch sets. #   polished brass.
  lock sets #   polished brass
Builder's Hardware
Anchor Bolts ½" x 8"   30
Pounds of nails of various sizes
Gross of screws of various sizes
Buckets, ladders, etc., etc.

Glass wool Insulation — Ceiling — 5½" x 24" vapor barrier — Rolls (107 sq ft)
Walls — 3½" x 15" vapor barrier — Rolls (705 sq ft)

Figure 3-1 *(continued).*

because of a possible grain or color variation, it would be well to add 30 percent to the original order. *Note:* The contractor must not forget to add 10 percent for wastage in his bid.

3.2C. The Builder's Labor Cost

It is very difficult to pinpoint the cost of labor, because there are so many variables. To start with, even if union labor is employed, there are different scales of pay in the various union jurisdictions and there are different benefits such as pension plans, insurance costs, unemployment taxes, etc.

Also craftspeople do not all work at the same rate and a construction job differs from an assembly line in which a worker has just so much time to install a certain piece of equipment. On a large job or a development employing many workers, the contractor can average out the time it takes a worker to install so many studs or joists or so many square feet of shingles, but on a small job employing one or two workers it is difficult to do this. The contractor must figure from his own experience how many days of labor it requires to rough-frame a house, to shingle it, to install finished millwork including doors, windows, stairs, finish floors, etc. The very first job may be an educated guess based on his own experience, but if he keeps accurate cost records on his jobs (see Chap. 8), he will soon build up a body of information that will be very important to him in future bidding and will also take the guesswork out of construction bidding. It should be emphasized that guesswork instead of solid record keeping is a major cause of serious loss or failure in the small construction business. Of course it takes time, but what worthwhile endeavor does not?

3.3 THE FINAL CHECKLIST OF SUBCONTRACTORS

Secion 3.2A, Checklist for the Builder's Own Work, analyzed the various trade subcontracts to help the contractor to decide which work he wishes to perform when it is not clearly defined as the subcontractor's work. A study of the sample specifications in Chap. 2 will help the contractor to avoid loose ends. (The author is now actively engaged in construction work. At least once a week there is a dispute between the architect/engineer, the general contractor, and the subcontractors as to who is responsible for a certain piece of work.) Of course, a single-family home or other small construction is not nearly as complicated as a hospital or large office building, but the principle still holds. The contractor must make sure that none of the work falls in between subcontractors. Items such as medicine cabinets, mirrors on doors, fireplace dampers, special wiring for hi-fi, underground pipe for electric or telephone service, drainage, waterproofing and many other miscellaneous items can easily be overlooked.

Each item in a plan and specification must be assigned to a subcontractor in writing, or the contractor must plan to do it himself and include it in his bid.

3.4. ASSEMBLING THE BID

3.4A. The Contractor's Work

The contractor has now prepared his lumber and material listing and has obtained at least two bids. He should ask the material dealers if they can suggest any savings either in material cost or in the use of a new material that saves labor cost. He should also ask about the availability of the materials.

The next step after obtaining the material bids is to add the labor cost (see Section 3.2C). The labor costs should be added for the structural and other carpentry work and also for all the miscellaneous work that the contractor has decided to do himself.

In completing the estimate for his own work, the contractor should be aware of the amount he must add to his labor cost for Social Security benefits, unemployment funds, workmen's compensation insurance, pension funds, hospitalization, and federal, state, or city income tax (which he simply collects and sends on to the proper authorities). All of these can be reduced to a percentage figure in his estimate, although he will have to separate them later in his payroll. (*Note:* This is only for his own work.)

At this time the contractor must decide about the overhead and profit on his own work. If he performs some of the work himself, then of course he has included his own pay in the labor cost. But in any case he must be paid for his time in making up the material lists, the bid sheet, expediting, supervision, etc. He can calculate how many hours this will take him and charge for it at a suitable hourly rate. This hourly rate can be made large enough to include a profit. For instance if his normal hourly rate is $10.00 per hour, then he can charge $12.00 an hour for the time he has spent and will spend in supervising, expediting, assembling bids, etc.

3.4B. Subcontractors' Work

Section 3.1 contains a list of the usual trade subcontracts that combine to make a finished structure ready for occupancy. When the subcontractors' bids come in (and some will not come in without a great deal of telephoning and coaxing), the contractor should go over them very carefully to be sure that they include all the extra items the contractor asked for. The bids should be in writing. People have short memories where their own money is concerned. All the trades should be entered on a bid sheet (see sample in Fig. 3-2).

After the bids from the subcontractor have been added to his own, the contractor must add overhead and profit to this amount. From the list in Chap. 1, he has determined his overhead or his cost of doing business. He must now apportion part of his overhead cost to this job. At the beginning of his business year he can only guess what portion of the year's buiness this job will be. He must also include the salaries for supervisory help, the cost of permits, sales taxes, license fees, insurance other than workmen's compensation, and all expenses that he can directly attribute to the job.

With regard to the profit he must remember that he has already added some profit to the estimate of his own work. He must also remember that each subcontractor has added a profit in his bid. The contractor has also charged for his time in supervising, etc. In putting a final figure on his estimate he must be guided by the apparent circumstances of his client. (If the bid is too high the client may drop the whole project.) He must also take

Bid Sheet

Estimate for _____   Date _____

Location _____

Owner _____   Architect _____

Cubage _____ Unit price _____ per cu ft

Floor area _____ Unit price _____ per sq ft

Garage area _____ Unit price _____ per sq ft

Basement area _____ Unit price _____ per sq ft

Trade	Contractor	Price
1. Excavation and sitework (finish grading, planting, seeding)		
2. Foundations (concrete and masonry)		
3. Carpentry and millwork		
4. Brickwork		
5. Roofing and sheet metal		
6. Waterproofing		
7. Glass and glazing		
8. Ceramic tile		
9. Painting and finishing		
10. Plumbing		
11. Heating		
12. Electrical		
13. Finish hardware		
14. Miscellaneous iron		
15. Bathroom accessories		
16. Finish cleaning		
17. Miscellaneous		
18. Overhead		
19. Profit		
20. Total bid		

Figure 3-2   Sample of a bid sheet. *

into account his own flow of work and ask himself how much he wants this job. Then there is the competition. In other words, determining profit in a competitive bid is a very delicate matter. The time and circumstances must be the determining factors.

3.5. ALTERNATES AND ALLOWANCES

Very often the architect or the owner asks a contractor to quote prices for alternates or for omission or addition of some piece of work. For instance,

*Note: Contractor to check list on page 68.

"Quote add or deduct cost for: Spruce prefinished plank floor in random 6 in. and 8 in. widths or for Rough sawn vertical shiplap Red Cedar siding in random 1 × 6, 1 × 8 and 1 × 10 widths or for Omission of painting for ceilings, walls, and doors or for Waterproofing basement floor with Ironite or etc."

The contractor must not forget that these add or deduct alternates are added to or subtracted from his bid price. The author has seen many jobs decided by the alternates. When an alternate is asked for, especially an add alternate, it means that the owner really wants it but is not sure he can afford it. Sometimes the cost price without profit may get the contractor the job.

Allowances are another matter. They do not affect the bid price because if the actual cost of the material is lower than the allowance the owner gets the difference, and of course the converse is true. Allowances are given for items like hardware, lighting fixtures, and special finishes where the owner's personal taste will dictate the quality of the material and the cost. The contractor is paid only for what he actually spends.

3.6. THE BID

Although a sample bid sheet is shown in Fig. 3-2, there is no particular set form for submitting a bid on a small construction project whether it be an alteration, a private residence, a small store and office building, etc. There are, however, very definite items that the contractor must include in his bid so that he can not only give the architect and owner a complete and clear understanding of how much the job will cost, but also protect himself against unwarranted later claims.

- The bid should be on the contractor's letterhead.

- It should give the date of the bid.

- It should say how much time the owner has to consider it.

- It should completely identify the property, by the owner, the architect, the address and by block and lot number.

- It should then identify the drawings and specifications, i.e., plans Nos. 1 through 4 inclusive, dated January 1, 197—, specifications sheets Nos. 1 through 15 dated January 1, 197—, addenda Nos. 1 and 2 dated January 1, 197—, General and Special Conditions dated January 1, 197—.

- It must detail any other instructions that have been given to the contractor either by word of mouth or in writing.

- It should then give the amount of the bid, i.e., "The contractor will furnish all labor, material, equipment, tools, licenses, supervision and temporary facilities as called for in the above enumerated Plans and Specifications for the sum of $_____

___. This sum does not include Alternates and Allowances and certain other exceptions as listed below. Building Permit by Owner."

Alternates

1×6 and 1×8 spruce plank floors in living room and bedrooms Nos. 1, 2, and 3 instead of red oak as specified.

Add $_____

Installation of Henrick Co. heating unit, catalogue No. 521, in chimney above fireplace, complete with finish registers.

Add $_____

Omit all painting of interior ceilings and walls throughout.

deduct $_____

Allowances

Lighting fixtures, dining room, kitchen, bath.　　$_____
Finish hardware as per hardware schedule.　　　$_____

- The bid must also include several other items: "The contractor proposes to complete the structure ready for occupancy in four calendar months from the start of the excavation unless there are delays beyond his control such as caused by strikes, unforeseen shortages of material, fire, or acts of God. This bid does not include other than earth excavation for the foundations down to firm bearing at levels shown by the plans. Rock excavation and special footings other than as shown will be charged for at time and material cost plus 10 percent." Additionally: "The contractor also calls attention to the site. The present bridge over the stream at the front of the building site seems insufficient to carry the heavy equipment and trucking necessary for the construction. The contractor can assume no responsibility for its repair other than to cover its surface with 2×12-in. rough planking." And: "The contractor suggests that some saving can be made in the cost of construction by the use of less expensive materials than those specified and by the omission of certain pieces of work."

3.7. PUBLIC BIDDING

The contractor is warned that bidding on public work is quite different than that for private work. The prescribed forms are set and cannot be changed. The time and place of the bidding cannot be changed. (A bid that is 10 minutes late can be thrown out.) The contractor must bid on the plans and specifications and alternates, etc., exactly as they are shown. Except for small work for a small town or village, the contractor must be bonded. (See Chap. 10, Insurance and Bonding.) In public bidding, unlike private work, there is no selected list of bidders. Anyone who can meet certain set requirements can bid, and usually he can come from anywhere in the state. In federal work, he can come from anywhere in the 50 states. And in conclusion, the quality of the material and workmanship as set forth by the plans and specifications is rigidly enforced.

Nevertheless a number of large contractors have made a great deal of money in the performance of public work. The small contractor is advised not to try it until he has accumulated some experience and is sure of his estimating.

Note: Bid forms as prepared by the A.I.A. are available.

4

CONSTRUCTION CONTRACTS

4.1. THE FUNCTION OF A CONTRACT

The function of any contract is to spell out in as simple language as possible the terms and conditions of an agreement between two or more parties. The construction contract in its simplest form should do exactly this. The contractor is advised to study "The Standard Form of Agreement Between Owner and Contractor" as published by the AIA.* This standard form contains the essentials of any contract. First there is the date, which is followed by the names of the parties to the agreement, i.e., the owner and the contractor. This is followed by a description of the work, the name of the architect (if any), the contract sum, the dates of commencement and completion, the manner of payments, and finally a listing of the contract drawings, specifications, general conditions, addenda, special instructions, etc. The contractor will note that what this all says is "Who is going to do what for whom for how much and how long it will take."

In Sec. 3.6, a sample form of a bid was shown. This form contains the date, the parties to the contract, the work involved, the amount of the contract and the time of start and finish. The only item missing is the matter of how payment is to be made. If this is added and the owner signs at the bottom of the bid "accepted, John Jones, Sept. 15, 197—" it could become a perfectly valid contract. And that is why the contractor must be sure that this bid contains everything he wants to say about the job and everything he is committing himself to do.

*AIA Document A107, obtainable from the Documents Director, The American Institute of Architects, 1735 New York Ave., N.W., Washington, D.C. 20006.

4.2. THE TYPES OF CONTRACTS

4.2A. The Lump Sum or Stipulated Sum

The contract as described within this section is a lump sum contract. It obligates the contractor to perform certain work for a certain fixed sum of money. Such a contract places certain responsibilities on the owner (and architect) as well as on the contractor. For instance, the owner must have a valid survey of the land, and a site plan should show the outlines of the house with the distances shown from boundary lines. If the job is an addition to an existing structure, the lines of the existing and new structures should be shown. If the plans are approved by the local authority, then the contractor can safely assume that they meet with the local zoning code. In some instances, however, when there is only a sketch plan, the contractor himself must be sure that it meets code requirements. In any case there must be an original survey showing the present house on the site.

Another responsibility of the owner is the matter of payment. This should be clearly spelled out in the contract.

This type of lump sum contract is almost exclusively used in public work because it exactly defines the owner's liability.

4.2A1. POSSIBLE CHANGES IN A LUMP-SUM CONTRACT

There are several ways by which a contractor can obtain more money than the contract calls for. The first is when the owner or architect specifically asks for an item of work that is *clearly* outside of the contract obligation. In this connection it may be stated here that the word "clearly" is very often the subject of argument. When he is asked to do an item of work that he does not think is covered by his contract, the contractor can partially protect himself by stating immediately after studying the plans and specifications that this is not in his contract. If he succeeds he will then obtain a change order (see Chap. 8).

Another way to obtain more money is by the proper use of qualifying clauses in the bid. For instance if he encounters ledge rock, large boulders, soft wet ground, or heavy ground water he should be paid extra for rock excavation, stepped footings, spread footings, pumping, etc., *but only if he has stated so in his bid.*

A third way is by use of the "escalator clause." If there are several union contracts coming up for renewal, the contractor can cover himself by stating in his bid that he is to be paid an extra amount to equal his extra out-of-pocket payroll and benefit costs.

The contractor is advised not to do too much "qualifying." Owners and architects do not like it, and, after all, the contracting business is a risk business—if the contractor tries to protect himself too much, he just won't get the job.

4.2B. The Cost-plus-Fixed-Fee Contract

This kind of a contract is difficult to obtain and is difficult to administer. It can only occur when an owner does not know exactly what he wants (mostly in an alteration or addition) and when he is willing to pay the contractor for all of the out-of-pocket costs incurred by the work and for all his supervisory time on the job in addition to a fee or profit, which can be an agreed percentage of the cost of the work. (This fee should include a part of the contractor's office overhead.) The problem with this type of contract is that when there is no set plan, the cost tends to wildly overrun any budget, and the owner, in spite of his expressed willingness to pay, is shocked by the final cost. The owner, of course, has the right to inspect the contractor's books and other cost records.

Before entering into such a contract, the contractor must tell the owner what his obligations are. Some of these are: the cost of labor including benefits; the cost of supervisory help stationed on the job or of the contractor's own time at a stated rate; cost of material, supplies, and equipment built into the job; rental charges for equipment used in the construction including rental charge for small tools; a proportion of the transportation charge of the contractor and his employees; cost of temporary services such as water, sanitation, and electricity; cost of insurance and bonding premiums that are attributable to the job; sales and use taxes; permit fees and license fees; royalties; cost of telephone calls and telegrams; payments made by the contractor to subcontractors.

The contractor who enters into such a contract must make every effort to keep the cost down. It is wise not to tell the workers that it is a cost plus job. Such a job, when and if it comes, takes all the risk out of the business. The contractor is paid all his costs and he is paid for his own time on the job. In addition he is paid a portion of his office overhead and a profit (the fee). This is too good a thing to abuse and it must not be abused.

4.2C. Other Types of Contracts

There are several other forms of construction contracts but they are used only for very large work or when time is of the essence and the owner cannot wait for the plans to be completed. It is well, however, for the smaller contractor to know about them.

4.2C1. THE GUARANTEED-MAXIMUM-PLUS-FIXED-FEE CONTRACT

In this type of contract, the contractor guarantees a maximum price for all of the work as set forth in the plans, specifications, etc. In addition he states what his fixed fee is to be. On such construction jobs the contractor's field labor, including payroll, purchasing, supervision, and engineering, is paid for by the owner. Equipment, transportation, subcontractors' costs, materials, insurance, permits, and licenses are paid for by the owner. In addition, the contractor gets a share of any savings he makes under his guaranteed maximum. Up to this point it is somewhat like a cost-plus contract. The difference is two-fold. First, the contractor must bid competitively (frequently in a severely restricted list). The one with the lowest combined guaranteed maximum plus fixed fee gets the job. Second, if the contractor runs over his guaranteed maximum it is *his* money.

4.2C2. THE NEGOTIATED CONTRACT

This type of contract is just what its name implies. An owner who knows and trusts a contractor may ask him to "look over an architect's shoulder" while the plans are being developed, or he may ask for the contractor's advice and guidance in coming to a conclusion as to what kind of a house or alteration or addition he can get for the money he wishes to spend. There is a negotiated price based on a very definite understanding (in writing) of what the owner is to get. This is somewhat like a guaranteed-maximum contract except that in this case there is no competition involved.

4.2C3. THE SCOPE CONTRACT

This contract is a mixture of the maximum-guaranteed and negotiated contracts. It can occur at any time when an owner cannot wait for full plans to be completed before construction starts. It can happen when someone owns a piece of land and is approached by a prospective tenant who has only a limited time to move, or where an owner wishes to beat the deadline on a new zoning ordinance, building code change, or a mortgage commitment. In such a case an architect/engineer must produce a set of scope drawings and specifications which outline in some detail the size, shape, and structural characteristics of a building and the type and capacity of the lighting, heating, ventilation, air conditioning, and elevatoring. These are not, however, the final drawings and specifications.

This is an extremely difficult kind of a contract to fulfill without endless discussion and argument. Only a highly experienced contractor is advised to offer a bid on this kind of a contract.

4.2D. Subcontractors' Contracts

The basic provisions of this type of contract* should contain the same terms and conditions as the contract between the owner and the contractor. These items should be in the contract between the prime contractor and the subcontractor.

---

*AIA Document A401, also obtainable from the Documents Director, The American Institute of Architects.

The subcontractor is bound by the same plans, specifications, general conditions, addenda, and plan modifications that bind the prime contractor.

The prime contractor must put in writing any work that he wishes the subcontractor to do over and above the performance characteristics and work as called for by the plans and specifications for that trade, which are of course the subcontractor's primary obligation.

The amount of money to be paid is stipulated. It must be understood that the subcontractor is paid only after the prime contractor is paid.

There are some general provisions which include the amount of insurance the subcontractor is to carry and which hold the general contractor harmless in case of an accident caused by him; define the character of the help he is to employ; and spell out the obligations to furnish shop drawings where these are necessary in a complicated job and to obtain the necessary permits and approvals from the public authority having jurisdiction.

The prime contractor, of course, has the obligation to pay the subcontractor within a few days after he is paid, to coordinate the work so that the subcontractor is not unduly delayed, to provide on-site storage space, to allow the subcontractor to use any on-site equipment (at a charge), and to generally provide a working environment that will allow the subcontractor to perform his work most efficiently.

A contract imposes obligations on all the parties to it.

5

PROGRESS SCHEDULING AND PURCHASING

5.1. ORGANIZING THE JOB

5.1A. Site Planning

The contractor will have visited the property and roughly located the position of the structure he is to build before submitting his bid. Now he has to place the structure exactly. On p. 387, a diagram shows how a structure on a small surveyed plot is laid out. This method can be used even if the side lines are not at right angles to the front and rear lines as long as they are parallel to each other. This can be determined from the survey.

If the plot is irregularly shaped, however, and there are extreme changes in levels, it is best to employ a surveyor (preferably the one who made the original survey), unless the contractor owns a transit, knows how to use it, and can make the proper calculations from his readings. The cost of this survey should be included in the original estimate.

Once the structure is located, the next step is to locate the areas to be used for the various parts of the construction, for instance: the locations of the piles of stored topsoil from the excavation and of the stored earth to be used for backfill against the foundation walls; of the ditches for water, sewer, electricity, and telephone (if the last two are to be concealed); of drainage ditches from the foundation walls; of the oil storage tank; of the septic tank and drain field (if any); of the driveway; of a drive for bulldozers, shovel, and concrete trucks, and finally and most important the location of the access to material storage by truck and from the structure. The proper layout of the material storage area and ready access for concrete or mason supply trucks can be a great saving in construction cost. There should be enough room to sort the material and the materials dealer must not be allowed to drop lumber or any other material haphazardly. The material dealer should also be instructed to load his truck so that the structural lumber to be used first is on top. For instance the load should have rafters on the bottom, then ceiling joists, floor joists, studs, sills, and finally rough lumber for forms, batter boards, etc., which should be on top of the load because they will be needed first. Material such as sheathing, underfloor, and shingles should come later when required. Millwork, finish floor, and wallboard should not come until the house is reasonably weathertight. Wallboard must be carefully protected. (See Fig. 5-1 for a suggested site layout.)

Above all, let the contractor beware of blocking himself from complete access to his own site. The author knows of a case where the contractor so blocked himself that he had to drive across a neighbor's lawn to deliver material to his own building site. He was arrested for trespass and sued for damage.

5.2. PREPARING A PROGRESS CHART

5.2A. What a Progress Chart Does

After the site layout, the next step in progress scheduling is the preparation of a simple bar chart. This chart will act as a constant reminder to the

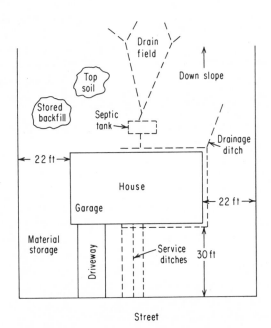

Figure 5-1 Suggested layout of site. If foundation is poured concrete, allow access on four sides for concrete trucks. If foundation is concrete block, allow for trucks to dump blocks near walls.

contractor and will tell him when various subcontractors and materials are due on the job. In its simplest form, a bar chart lists every trade and sets a date when each trade is to start work and when it should be complete. The chart can also break down each trade into its important components and can list the time when important materials are due. The contractor who carefully prepares such a chart has a track to run on and will find it will help a great deal in bringing in a job on time. This always pleases an owner and cuts down on the builder's overhead. The preparation of a good progress chart is an exercise in organization.

5.2B. How to Prepare a Progress Chart

Following is an example of how to prepare a progress chart (see Fig. 5-2): The job is to start on January 2 and the owner must move in before the end of May. This gives the contractor 5 months for the actual construction. After he is awarded a contract, the contractor should have at least an additional 2 weeks to arrange his own schedule, award subcontracts, purchase materials, obtain a building permit, and lay out the corners of the structure. This is the time when the site should be cleared and made ready for the excavation. Any trees that are in the way should also come out at this time.

5.2B1. EXCAVATION

The excavation contractor has been notified that he is to have his equipment on the site ready for work on January 2. When he was awarded the contract, he could complete the excavation including the cuts for the footings in 3 weeks, even allowing for weather.

Start the bar chart and draw a line for excavation for 3 weeks.

5.2B2. FOUNDATIONS

The foundations consist of poured concrete footings for the basement walls, the chimney, central supporting columns, and any other heavy equipment or structure that must have a permanent base. The walls can be of concrete block or poured concrete. The contractor will probably prefer to do the footings himself and should be prepared with form lumber and reinforcing rods very shortly after the excavation contractor has started. As the excavator proceeds on his cuts for footings, the contractor follows closely behind with forms and reinforcing. Start the footing line a week before the excavation is completed and continue for a week after excavation is completed. If the foundation wall is of poured concrete, the builder can start his forms a week after the start of the footings. If the wall is of concrete block, it will undoubtedly be done by a mason contractor. The builder must be sure that the block, cement, sand, etc., are delivered on time (at least 2 days before the work is to start). The mason contractor has said he will need three weeks. Start the

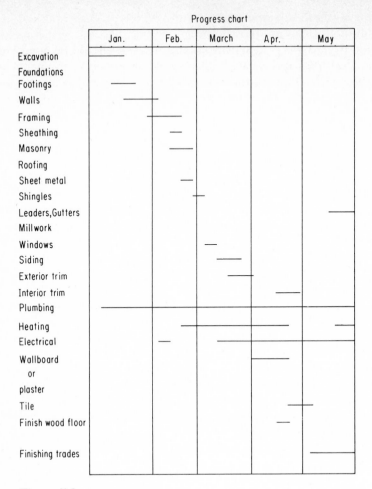

Figure 5-2

foundation wall line a week after the footings have started and run it for 3 weeks.

5.2B3. FRAMING

This can be broken down into sills, supporting girders, floor joists, under-floor, stud exterior walls with soles and plates attached, stud-bearing partitions, ceiling joists, rafters, framing for doors and windows, etc. The contractor must have his material delivered not more than a week after the foundation walls are started. He will require 3 weeks for framing. Start the framing line 2 weeks before the foundation walls are completed and continue for 3 weeks.

5.2B4. EXTERIOR

The walls and roof should be sheathed as soon as possible. Sheathing should be delivered at least a week before framing is completed. Sheathing will take 1 week. Start the sheathing line 1 week before the framing is completed, and complete it at the same time as the framing.

5.2B5. MASONRY

This work includes building chimneys for fireplaces and furnace, front steps, porch or terrace retaining walls, and any other miscellaneous brickwork. If the building is of brick veneer over a wooden structural frame, the veneer starts immediately after the sheathing. If the masonry is confined to chimney, etc., start the masonry line at the same time as the sheathing line and run for 2 weeks.

5.2B6. ROOFING AND SHEET METAL

This is separated into roof shingles, gutters, and leaders and flashing. As soon as the roof is sheathed the builder should immediately cover it with water-proof felt paper (weight 15 to 30 lb) to keep the weather out. If the contractor expects to do the shingling himself, he should have the material delivered at least a week before it is to be used. At the same time he should order the roofing contractor (if there is one) to start on the flashing. Start the flashing line when the sheathing is complete and run for 1 week. Then start the shingles immediately after and run for 2 week. Leaders and gutters should not be placed until after the exterior is completed.

5.2B7. WINDOW FRAMES AND SASH

At this time the house is sheathed, the roof is shingled, and the underfloor is in place. Now is the time to install the window frames and sash (which usually come glazed). The contractor should order his sash and frames to be delivered as soon as the roof is tight. The material should be prime-coated before it is installed. If the weather is bad, the material can be stored inside. Start the window line at the end of shingling and run for 1 week.

5.2B8. PLUMBING

The plumbing contractor should be on the job almost immediately after the excavation has started. He can run his sewer line and his water line for temporary water in the ditches that have been dug for him. The depth of the ditch is determined by the weather pattern of the area. It can be as much as 4 ft-0 in. deep and must always be deep enough so that the lines cannot be accidentally broken. The plumber can then work on the waste and vent lines in the basement or crawlway as soon as the foundation walls are near completion. Water supply lines follow as the framing and underflooring proceed, and all the concealed lines must be in place before the wallboard is started. Fixtures are installed last.

Start the plumbing line 1 week after excavation and continue to the completion of the job.

5.2B9. HEATING

The heating installation, whether it is hot water or hot air, does not start until the building is enclosed. Provisions must be made to get the heating plant into place before passage is blocked. Radiators or registers are placed last after wallboard. Start the heating line when sheathing is complete and continue for 9 weeks.

5.2B10. EXTERIOR SIDING AND TRIM

The siding can be started at any time after the windows are in place. Start the siding line after windows are completed and run for 2 weeks, then in the middle of the siding line start the trim line and run for 2 weeks.

5.2B11. ELECTRICAL

The electrical contractor should be on the job as soon as the foundations are completed. He obtains the necessary permits for temporary power and light and arranges with the local power company to provide wiring and metering. The contractor does not start on interior wiring until the structure is weather-tight and has to come back several times until completion.

Start the electrical line at the end of the foundation line and run for 1 week. Then start again at the completion of exterior windows and run to completion.

5.2B12. WALLBOARD, PLASTERING

Wallboard must not start until the house is weathertight and until all concealed plumbing and heating lines or hot air ducts are in place and the electrical circuit wiring is completed.

Start the wallboard line 3 weeks after the electrical line starts and continue for 3 weeks. This includes taping ready for painting.

5.2B13. TILING

Tile work in bathrooms comes after wallboard and any plastering. Start the tile line at the end of wallboard and continue for 2 weeks.

5.2B14. FINISH WOOD FLOORS

Finish wood flooring is almost the last item that is installed. It is installed at the time when the finishing trim is started and when there is no longer any heavy traffic in the house.

Start the finish-wood floor line 1 week before wallboard and plaster are complete and run for 1 week completing just after wallboard is taped.

5.2B15. INTERIOR TRIM

Start interior trim, doors, and hardware to follow directly behind finish flooring and run for 2 weeks.

5.2B16. THE FINISHING TRADES

These include floor scraping and finishing, painting, wallpapering, lighting fixtures, resilient tile floors, medicine cabinets. Start the finish trade line when the interior trim line is almost completed and run to completion of the building ready for occupancy. This is also the time when the leaders and gutters are installed.

5.3. PURCHASING OWN MATERIAL

Chapter 3, Estimating and Bidding, explained in detail how the contractor goes about obtaining bids for his own material and from subcontractors. The contractor now has been awarded the job and probably the main reason that he has the job is because he was the low bidder. In normal circumstances he does not know how low his bid was and therefore must proceed carefully with his own purchasing. There are several factors that should be considered.

5.3A. The Price

The contractor has received bids on his own materials list and now has the opportunity to compare prices. It will be remembered that the materials list asked for separate prices for the various categories of material. The contractor should see the material dealer who has submitted the lowest total price. He should negotiate for those particular materials where a competitor has come in with a lower price. There is no reason why the material dealer should know that he has the lowest gross price; negotiating for a better price is an important part of a contractor's business.

5.3B. Availability of Materials

During the purchasing negotiations the contractor should keep in mind the availability of the materials when he requires them. He has his progress chart which tells him when such items as roof shingles, doors, windows, flooring, siding, special trim, finishing, hardware, etc., will be required, and it should be part of his contract with the materials dealer to be sure that they are available.

5.3C. Stockpiling

Stockpiling for a small job is not always advisable. There are problems of protection from the weather, pilferage, vandalism, payment, and insurance. But sometimes when certain materials are in short supply because of strikes, demand exceeding supply, or weather or other acts of God, it becomes necessary for the contractor to assure himself of having the material when he needs it by purchasing it in advance and storing it. Advance purchasing and storage of material is a very common practice in large construction and there is no reason why it cannot be done on smaller jobs.

The contractor should go to the owner or the financing institution and explain the situation. He should arrange for its storage on site or in the material dealer's own warehouse. He must have it insured whereever it is and must produce invoices to show he owns the material. Under such circumstances any financing institution or owner will advance the required amount.

5.3D. Substitution of Material.

There may be instances where the material that is specified is simply not available within the time frame of the job. Such material may be special windows or doors or hardware. In many instances the contractor will not know this until he tries to place a firm order with a guaranteed date of delivery. In such cases the contractor has to get together with the owner or architect or both and offer substitutions. An owner without an architect will depend on a contractor's advice. The contractor is advised to offer substitutions of *equal quality* and with very little or no premium price.

5.4. PURCHASING SUBCONTRACTS

It is hoped that the contractor has obtained more than just one subcontractor's bid so that he can compare prices and have some leeway to negotiate a satisfactory price. In the letting of such subcontracts, there are several very important factors that must be considered and written into the contract or letter of acceptance or whatever document is used.

5.4A. Assurance that Subcontractor Has Included All the Work

In previous chapters on plans and specifications and bidding procedures, it was emphasized that the contractor should make certain that every item of work is covered by either himself or by a subcontractor. Now, before he lets any subcontract, is the time to check the list of items which he has asked each subcontractor to include. For instance, has the excavator included the trucking in and spreading of bank run gravel for the base of the driveway? Or have the plumbing and electrical contractors included the providing of temporary water and electricity? Or (if it is in a cold-weather area and wintertime) has the heating contractor made provisions for connecting radiators or hot air ducts so that temporary heat may be provided for taping of wallboard, tiling, finish flooring and painting?

There should be a clear understanding that such items are included. The contractor is advised to put it in writing.

5.4B. Compliance with Progress Schedule

The completion of a job on time is most important. The contractor has a progress chart which shows when each trade is to start and complete its work. The wise thing to do is to give each subcontractor a copy of this chart and have him agree to it or to make suggestions for changes which will not affect the completion date. When this has been done, either the original or the revised progress chart becomes a part of the contract.

5.4C. Availability of Subcontractor's Material

While the builder checks over the progress schedule with the subcontractor, there is one more important point to be determined. The owner or the architect may specify or request a certain color of ceramic tile or bathroom fixture or a special wallcovering or even a special type of heating plant. The author has known of 12- or 14-week delivery dates or even more on special items such as ceramic tile, lighting fixtures, wallpapers, etc. The subcontractor should be asked to report on any item which he finds requires a long lead time, and the contractor can then either ask for a change in the specification or warn the client, in writing, that the special items will not be available in time to complete the job on schedule.

5.5. ORGANIZING LABOR TO MEET SCHEDULE

In looking over his progress schedule, the contractor will note that there are certain times when several workers are necessary and other times when one worker alone can work more efficiently. For instance, during the period when the structure is being framed and sheathed, the contractor should have several workers on the job to get the framing up and to get the structure covered with sheathing and the underflooring in as soon as possible. Although wall and roof sheathing do not make a structure weathertight, they do provide a shelter of sorts so that internal framing can proceed. The underflooring is really part of the structural framing because all interior and exterior studs rest on it. Of course it also provides a safe working area within the structure.

At other times during construction one worker on flooring and one on interior trim can be sufficient. The problem is to deploy the men when and where they are needed. There are always men available on a day-by-day basis, but they must be notified in advance.

The contractor should keep planning ahead on a 2-week basis so that he has room to change if necessary.

6

THE CONSTRUCTION PROCESS

The actual construction of any structure is a complicated process. There are of course certain basic procedures which any contractor should know. They concern the order in which a structure is built and the items of construction which must be installed first so that subsequent items may follow in an orderly manner. Tearing out and rebuilding is expensive and is not reimbursable.

6.1. BEFORE THE START OF CONSTRUCTION

There are certain things the contractor must do before actual construction commences:

- Obtain a building permit.
- Cover the job with insurance (as mentioned in Chap. 10).
- Have the plumbing subcontractor obtain a permit to connect to the public water supply (or have a well dug).
- Have the plumber obtain a permit to connect to the sewer or obtain approval for a septic tank and drain field.
- Have the electrical contractor arrange for a power connection.
- Arrange for a pay telephone.
- Arrange for a portable sanitary accommodation.
- Lay out the site and stake it.
- Remove any brush and trees which will interfere with the construction.

6.2. EXCAVATION AND FOUNDATIONS

Figure 5-1 shows a sample site plan which can be used as an example for a site layout. The contractor is advised to draw such a sketch for his own site. The site plan is used as soon as excavation starts. It tells the excavator where to dump the topsoil for storage and where to dump enough of the excavated material for backfill against the foundation. It also shows the location of the utility ditches, the future driveway and the areas which must be kept clear for storage.

As the excavation nears bottom the contractor should not forget that the local building official must be called to inspect the soil or other underlying material on which footings are to be poured. Every building code has such a provision and the building official has the right to condemn the footings if he has not made this inspection.

The concrete footings and the foundation walls, which may be of concrete or concrete block, must be readily accessible to the material trucks. Concrete walls must be poured into forms and it is much cheaper to do this directly from a mixer truck than to wheelbarrow it. Concrete block is heavy and should be palleted as close to where it is being used as possible. The contractor should lay out the holes through the foundation walls for water and sewer lines, electrical and telephone lines if underground, and oil or gas lines. Even in a block foundation it is much cheaper to leave a hole than it is to chop one out later, and this is very expensive for concrete. The top course of block should be filled solidly, and holding-down bolts must not be forgotten.

6.3. THE STRUCTURE

The structural portion of a private residence depends on the location in the country. This book has concentrated on wood structural framing, but there are localities in which brick or stone may be used for bearing walls and there are also brick or stone veneer exteriors which, however, use wood as the actual structural frame. Small business buildings may use wall-bearing brick exteriors with lumber or light steel floor and roof joists. However, the wood structural frame is most frequently used for small buildings and especially private residences.

Erecting the frame and covering it against weather is probably the most important part of the construction of a private residence. This work should be done as expeditiously as possible so that other work can follow without being hampered by inclement weather, which can ruin a progress schedule. The contractor must therefore organize his men and material for this task. Lumber should be delivered several days before the foundation wall is completed and should be so delivered and stacked that little sorting is necessary. Extra workers must be alerted. It is safe to start laying sills three or four days after a block foundation is completed and, if high-early-strength concrete is used for the foundation walls, four days is enough to wait for it to set.

However, the contractor must not allow the concrete forms to be removed for several weeks.

As soon as the floor joists are in place, the subfloor follows. In the meantime, another team can be assembling sections of the exterior stud frame and of the interior bearing walls so that sections can be erected immediately after the subfloor is laid. The ceiling joists follow immediately after the first floor is framed. If there is a second floor, the same process continues. The rafters follow the top-floor ceiling joists, then sheathing can start. However, before sheathing starts, the contractor should check the frame for squareness and should check the walls for squareness with the floors which *are presumed to be level*. The sheathing fastens the frame in a fixed position and it is extremely costly to have to change any direction after the sheathing is nailed.

For a brick-veneer or stone-veneer exterior wall, the framing procedure is the same and the veneer can be applied at any reasonable time during the construction. But in the structure which has exterior masonry bearing walls it is the speed with which the masonry is erected that determines when the building can be enclosed. The contractor can help himself by framing each floor and the roof as soon as the bearing-wall mortar has set, and he can frame the first floor before the mason starts because he has the foundation walls as support.

The contractor may expect at least one visit from the local building authority during the framing. If the contractor is complying with the code (or better) such inspections are just routine.

6.3A. Fire Retarding

According to building codes, single-family or two-family houses* and small business buildings† require very little fire-retarding provisions. For instance, the only requirement for a one- or two-family house is that the exterior walls be firestopped between floors (that there be no open space in the wall between floors) and that there be one stairway not less than 3 ft in clear width. For the small business building the contractor need only enclose the stairway with fire-retardant material. (See Chap. 14, Building Codes.)

6.4. SUPERVISION OF MECHANICAL AND ELECTRICAL WORK

The contractor must closely follow plumbing, heating, and electrical work so that it will mesh first with the structural work and then with the finishing work. He should be especially vigilant to see that all concealed lines are

---

*Single- and two-family houses having total height of 2½ stories and not more than 35 ft, and a total floor area of not more than 4000 sq ft.

†Business buildings having total height of 2 stories and 30 ft, and total floor area of no more than 6000 sq ft.

installed in their proper location. Since patching work is usually part of the contractor's work, he should make sure that no structural member is seriously weakened. For instance, the author has seen many cases where a plumber or heating man has cut more than halfway through a supporting stud or a floor or ceiling joist. Even in a large reinforced concrete structure, a mechanical tradesman has been known to core-drill a concrete floor slab right next to a supporting column.

It will be noted from the progress chart that plumbing continues throughout the course of the job but it is not continuous. For instance the bathtubs should be delivered soon after the underfloor is installed but before the interior framing is complete. But then there is a wait until the framing is complete before the plumbing contractor starts installation of water lines, wastes, and stacks. Again there is an interval until the wallboard is completed and the bathroom tiling or wall finish is applied. At this time the plumbing contractor installs the fixtures. Some fixtures such as the kitchen sink and the bathroom basins may not go in until just before completion, when the cabinets and counters that receive them are in place.

This all means that the contractor must be vigilant to give the subcontractor sufficient notice before each portion of his work so that he will fit smoothly into the schedule and will not delay any work that must follow him.

The heating subcontractor must conceal his piping or ductwork in the walls and floors and he must therefore complete all the work before the wallboard can be started. He then waits until after the finish flooring and wallboarding to install radiators or outlets for the grilles. Baseboard or recessed radiators should have heavy reflecting foil behind them.

If the construction is a cold-weather job, one of the most important things for the contractor to remember is that he must have heat in the building as soon as possible. Until the building is heated (to at least 55°F) no wallboard taping, no tiling, no finish flooring, no interior finish trim can be installed.

The heating contractor must be made aware of this when the contract is signed. The heating plant should be on the job before the piping is complete. With its original crating and a heavy tarpaulin to protect it, it should be put in place. The fuel-oil tank, gas connection, or electric connection should be ready while the piping is being installed. The radiators or ducts or wall heaters should be delivered as soon as the house is tight. The finish floor and wallboard must go in before the radiators, but the radiators should follow immediately, and it is possible to do just enough flooring and wallboarding so that radiators or other outlets can be installed and heat can be supplied while the rest of this work is being done.

If there is an absolute emergency whereby the construction must stop dead because there is no heat, the contractor can avail himself of emergency temporary heat. Almost every building department allows propane-fired space heaters for temporary heating. These are available on a rental basis almost everywhere in cold-weather country. Two or three of them will do the job. They must of course be watched if they go all night and this means a watchman for a week or so until the permanent heating system is ready. The contractor should check with his local building inspector and with his insurance carrier. Since it is the owner or financial institution that usually carries the fire insurance he must check with either of them also. Something in writing is preferable.

The supervision of the electrical work closely follows the pattern set by the mechanical work. Here again the electrician is on the job right at the start to furnish temporary power. He does not come back again until the structure is securely weathertight. At this time he installs all his BX or conduit in the walls, floors, and ceilings, where it will be eventually concealed and then runs his circuit wiring to the panel box. In the meantime he should also have the power company install the permanent electrical feeders and the electric meter (which should, if possible, be located where a meter reader can read it without entering the premises).

Finally, after the wallboarding and finishing are completed, the electrical subcontractor installs the switch and base plates and the lighting fixtures.

Again, as for the mechanical work, the contractor should give the electrical subcontractor sufficient notice before each stage of his work.

6.5. EXTERIOR FINISH AND TRIM

When the exterior openings are all closed and weathertight, it is time to start the exterior siding, which is followed by the exterior trim. At the present time, with the saving of energy being of major importance, the contractor is advised to cover the sheathing with felt paper as additional protection against weather. If the specifications do not call for this, it can be a suggestion (to be paid for). As mentioned in previous chapters, exterior siding now comes in many varieties of wood and finish. It should be on the job even before the sheathing is completed.

Trim follows the siding. The contractor must make sure that every window head is flashed properly. Exterior trim should be stored indoors and back-painted before it is applied.

6.6. INTERIOR SURFACES

The finish floor goes in as soon as the building is weathertight. This means flashing, shingles, windows, doors, siding are all completed so that there is no chance of moisture. In cold weather the house should be kept warm. Installing a kiln-dried, tightly joined finish wood floor in a building with wet plaster or in damp cold can be disastrous. If the wood swells it can cause severe damage. The floor should go in just before the wallboard. It should be covered with heavy building paper immediately after installation. The contractor should watch that this is not scuffed aside by muddy feet or hobnailed boots.

Nearly all interior walls and ceilings are of wallboard. Wallboard is extremely perishable and has to be very carefully protected against moisture. It is also quite brittle. It should be palleted if possible but in any case must be kept off the ground. If possible, it should not be delivered until just before it is to be installed.

The contractor should be sure that all the concealed plumbing, heating, and electrical work is completed and tested. Plumbing and electrical work also has to be inspected and approved by the local authority before it is covered. Any called-for pipe covering must be applied. The stack or stacks which pierce the roof must be flashed and watertight. The exterior walls should be insulated. It is not until then that the wallboard can be applied. While carpenters are perfectly capable of applying wallboard, taping and spackling the joints is another matter. It takes three operations, and an expert can do it better and faster.

6.7. INTERIOR TRIM AND HARDWARE

Interior trim and finishing hardware consist of window stools and aprons, baseboard, chair rail (if any), door and window trim, doors, kitchen cabinets and counters, and lock sets and latch sets. They should be installed just before the painting. Door knobs, window latches, cylinders, and kitchen-cabinet hardware should not be installed until the painting is completed.

Interior trim should be back-painted before it is applied.

6.8. STAIRS

Stairways should be built by professional stair builders. The contractor is advised not to do it with his own workers if it can be avoided. Cutting the stringers exactly to receive the treads and risers, proper installation of the reinforcing blocks and wedges to prevent creaking, fitting the balusters are all precision jobs which should be done in a plant having the proper machinery and jigs.

Great care, however, must be taken in ordering a stair. There is a relation-ship between floor to floor height, the floor area that is available, the number of risers and the width of treads and the height of risers. The accompanying table gives some examples of these relationships.

Floor-to-Floor Height	Total Run	Number of Risers	Riser	Tread	Height of Handrail
8'-0	10'-3"	13	7⅜"	10¼"	2'-9"
8'-6	11'-4½"	14	7¼"	10½"	2'-9"
9'-0	12'-3"	15	7¼"	10½"	2'-9"

When stairs are ordered, the stair builder must know the clear width (which is 3 ft-0 in. as usually called for by the code) and the total run, which is the distance between the first and last risers. This information is usually on the plans but in some cases it may not be, and the contractor should be familiar with the procedure. The stair builder should also be told the number of risers required.

6.9. MASONRY

The foundation wall has been discussed in Sec. 6.2. The other masonry items in a wood structure are the chimney, the fireplace, the front or rear entrance platform and steps, a terrace or outdoor patio and other miscellaneous items. The most important of these are the chimney and fireplace. If these are located on an outside wall the contractor must frame around them and he must remember that there will be exposure to weather until the brickwork is completed. This is also true of chimneys and fireplaces anywhere in the house. Building codes are very specific about the size of the flue lining, the thickness of the brickwork, and how the wood framing is to be built around a chimney.

Building a good fireplace is an art. There is a very definite relationship between the height and width of the fireplace opening, its depth and the size of the flue. For instance:

Width	Height	Depth	Flue Size
3'–0"	2'–6"	1'–6"	12" x 12"
3'–4"	2'–6"	1'–6"	12" x 16"
3'–6"	2'–6"	1'–8"	12" x 16"
4'–0"	2'–8"	1'–8"	16" x 16"

If the building is of brick veneer over a wooden structural frame, the foundation has to be built to accommodate the brick veneer as well as the sill which supports the joists. The brick veneer must rest solidly on the foundation wall or on masonry built over the foundation wall, and the brickwork must be reinforced by corrugated wall ties fastened to the studs (if possible) rather than to the sheathing. Most building codes call for a wall tie for every 4 sq ft of wall area. (See sketch, p. XXX.) When there is a brick (or stone) veneer wall, openings are rough-framed until the masonry work is completed. This can cause a delay in closing-in the building because masonry takes longer to complete than siding and it must stop completely in very cold weather unless the mortar is heated and protected and quick-setting mortar is used. If there is the possibility of a long delay, the contractor must close all openings with heavy plastic and cover the roof with heavy felt. (Shingles should not be started until all flashing around masonry is completed.)

Solid masonry walls which are to be bearing walls (they support the upper floors as well as the roof) are usually of the cavity type, that is, there is a space between the exterior brickwork and the interior backing whether this is brick or concrete block. The cavity is an air space which is usually 1½ to 2 in. wide. The two walls are connected by wall ties. Building codes are very specific (see Chap. 14) about how such walls are to be built. Section 6.3 explains how the solid masonry wall can be worked into the progress schedule.

6.10. ROOFING, FLASHING, DRAINAGE

According to the progress schedule, the roofing should be started immediately after the sheathing is completed. First, all construction which pierces the roof must be flashed. This requires skilled workmanship and the contractor is advised not to do it himself unless he has someone on his payroll who is so skilled.

The shingling is not done until the flashing is completed because it is the shingles over the flashing that keep the roof watertight. The entire process of the flashing and finished roofing should be carefully supervised by the contractor because leaks through flashing or a roof are extremely difficult to pinpoint. It is not necessary for the contractor to watch every shingle being installed, but he should see to it that the installers know what they are doing and are following the plans and specifications.

After the gutters and leaders are completed, the contractor should give some thought to the drainage. Some specifications call for dry wells to disperse water coming down through the leaders but others are either silent or call for splash blocks. Dry wells or splash blocks are satisfactory if the land slopes away from the house, but if the house sits in a hollow, the drained water may find its way into the basement. In such cases it is well for the contractor to warn the owner or architect of this possibility and to suggest tiled drainage lines to run water away from the house. These must, of course, be paid for as an extra.

6.11. TILING, PAINTING, FINAL FINISHING

Each item under this heading is very important. The failure to complete any one of them on schedule can substantially prevent the owner from occupying the building on time and can cause the contractor substantial sums of money for comeback time, and will certainly create ill will. It is well, therefore, for the contractor not to lose sight of these numerous small but important items:

- *Tiling* was mentioned in connection with the completion of the plumbing. Plumbing fixtures in bathrooms cannot be installed until the tiling is completed. In the author's experience, tiling subcontractors in small work consist usually of a journeyman and helper and they must be constantly exhorted to get to a job on time and to stay there until the work is completed. This is true sometimes even in large multistoried construction with larger subcontractors. The main problem seems to be in material delivery. With the small contractor, a problem is also the lack of proper scheduling. The contractor should therefore have the tile ordered as soon as he is awarded the job. If there is any question about color, size, or shape, it should be settled right then. If the tiling contractor places the order, the builder should get a copy of the order with all the details, so that he can follow up with the tiling contractor or the tile manufacturer for a delivery date (which should be at least 3 weeks before the tile is required). This item both as to the labor and the material requires constant vigilance.

- *Floor finishing* is another small item which must be done on time. In a pinch an owner can put his furniture in a house before some finishing items are completed but he cannot do this until the floors are sanded and finished. This work can be done soon after the completion of the wallboard and just before the interior trim is completed. As in tiling, floor sanding and finishing are usually done by a small independent contractor who must be followed up carefully to see that he is on the job when it is ready for him.

- *Lighting fixtures.* In the modern home there is very little overhead lighting except for the kitchen, dining room, and baths. Nevertheless these fixtures should be installed before completion and the contractor should make sure that the owner and/or architect choose them well before they are due to be installed. In an office building the lighting is fluorescent and most of these fixtures, if they are of stock size and design, can be obtained on short notice. But if there are special sizes or special lenses, delivery may take much longer. The contractor should allow plenty of lead time for possible out-of-stock items and should certainly check even the stock items. The architect or owner should choose them and the electrical subcontractor should order them not long after the job has started.

- *Painting and decorating.* If wallpaper is involved there may be a delay because of delivery of material and the shortage of paperhangers. Choices of material should be made well before it is to be used. In cold, wet weather, exterior painting cannot be done at all. Provision should be made for this in the contract.

- *Final grading, planting, driveway.* All of these must be done in favorable weather. If possible the contractor should rough-grade as soon as the foundation is completed and the backfilling is done. In the particular job that was described in Chap. 5, completion is shown in May, but if a late summer job is scheduled to end in cold weather, the contractor will have to come back for the final grading. He should make allowance for this in his estimate. The driveway must be dug out and be filled with at least 8 in. of bank run gravel as soon as heavy trucking is over, and possibly with a layer of 1½ in. crushed stone later so that the owner may be able to use it through wet (and muddy) weather and so that it may pack down before any top dressing is applied.

There are other small items such as weatherstripping, caulking, and medicine cabinets which should be arranged for in advance of their installation. The contractor should make note of these and keep a "follow up" note on them.

7

FIELD INSPECTION FOR QUALITY OF THE WORK

7.1. HOW THIS CAN BEST BE DONE

The successful builder must not only build as economically as he can and produce the job on time, but he must also produce a quality product. Among his other duties, therefore, he must constantly check for quality of construction. The inspection items that follow may seem like a great deal of extra work, but they are not really. After a job or two they will become automatic, and the trouble that can be prevented is worth the effort 10 times over. This inspection can be done as he is supervising the progress of the job if the contractor is aware of the importance of this aspect of the work. When he visits the job to see whether the plumber is on time with his work, he can also check the caulking of a cast-iron waste line or the soldering of a copper pipe. This kind of quality inspection can be done for every trade *and without any extra expenditure of time.* Although the local building inspector is directly responsible for compliance with the local building code, it is important for the contractor to be familiar with its basic provisions for all trades. This constant inspection may also prevent the condemnation of completed or almost completed work which could cause serious delays and extra expense.

7.2. THE INSPECTION PROCEDURE

7.2A. Excavation

As the excavation proceeds and trucks are loaded with the excavated material there are several things to note:

- The angle of the earth banks should be shallow enough so that they will not slide back into the hole or on the footings. The

113

angle depends on the kind of soil excavated. Slippery clay requires a shallower angle than firm gravel.

- Trucks receiving the excavated material should not come too close to the edge of the banks.

- If there is any sign of a steady flow of water, or if water keeps seeping into the excavation, it may mean that the bottom of the excavation is below the water table. If there has been no preliminary test pit dug, this may be the first indication. It is hoped that the contractor has covered himself in his contract. In any case the bottom must be dry before concrete can be poured.

- Footings must be dug to good, undisturbed bottom. *There must be no backfill.*

- Backfilling against the completed basement wall is part of the excavation contract. The builder must see that heavy bulldozers do not get too close to the basement walls. A heavy weight too close to the wall can cause a collapse.

- As mentioned in a previous chapter, the water lines or sewer lines should be installed far enough below grade so that they will not be crushed by bulldozers or trucks. These ditches should be filled in and tamped down immediately after official inspection. In cold areas they must be installed below the frost line.

7.2B. Concrete Footings and Foundation Walls

- The footing excavation should have reasonably sharply defined banks or else it must be formed. The concrete subcontractor may choose to use more concrete rather than erect forms, and this is satisfactory if he maintains the proper depth of footing and does not "slop" over more than an inch or two on either side.

- On a cold-weather job, the contractor must make sure that the earth is not frozen when concrete is poured. It is advisable not to pour concrete footings at temperatures below 40°F. If the ground is frozen and is thawed just before concrete is poured, it may not regain its full bearing strength until the moisture has been driven from it. If the earth is not frozen but there is a threat of cold weather, the contractor should see to it that high-early-strength concrete is used and is thoroughly protected by salt hay and tarpaulins until it sets.

- Reinforcing rods must be located at least 2 in. above the bottom of the footing. The contractor should make it clear that such rods are to be watched when concrete is being poured so that they do not become misplaced.

- If the foundation wall is of reinforced concrete it must be doweled to the footing and the dowels must be tied to the footing reinforcement. The plans will show this and the specification will mention it. If the wall is not reinforced, then it need only be keyed to the footing. The key can be made by pressing a 2 × 4 into the concrete and then removing it just before the concrete sets.

- The specification will call for a certain strength of concrete. The ready-mix people should supply a certificate, or if the concrete is mixed on the job, Chap. 2 has given the proportions for the most common strengths.

- If the foundation is of concrete block the contractor should see to it that the blocks are laid up with full bed and cross joints. If they are to be waterproofed, a rich mortar mix should be plastered on the outside and smoothed to take a membrane or other waterproofing. The top course of blocks should be solidly filled with mortar *after* the holding-down bolts are in place.

- The top of the foundation wall should be checked to be sure it is level and that it forms a smooth bearing for the sill.

7.2C. The Structure

- In a wood structure it is the sills that form the base on which the entire structure rests. Therefore the sills must be firmly secured and absolutely level. The contractor can use wood shims to level the sills but must be sure to use a thinned-out mortar mix or a rich cement-sand mix for a permanent level. It is advisable to carefully paint the sills with a wood preservative before they are installed. If termite shields are to be used, the contractor should have them on hand before the sills are laid.

- The contractor should be constantly aware of the strength of the structure and should see to it that sufficient nails of the right size and kind are used. (See nailing schedule on page 393.) The structural timber itself should be examined to see that it is straight, square-edged, and free of knots and other imperfections. The supporting girders must be level with the top of the sill, but here the contractor must be sure that the girder timbers are thoroughly dry. If they are not sufficiently dry and should shrink or warp after they are installed, they can cause a great deal of trouble, because while one end of the floor joists rests on a sill over a masonry wall which does not shrink, the other end rests on a girder which will be from 8 to 12 in. wide and can shrink. This can produce uneven floors, cracked walls, and other problems. There is one way of making sure that the structural lumber is of good quality. Specifications for lumber are not always clear, so that various organizations such as the Southern Pine Association, the Western Pine Association, and others have banded together to protect their reputations. They brand the end of each piece of lumber to distinguish it as structurally sound. Certain large lumber companies also have their distinguishing trademarks branded on the end grain. There is a simple test which can be made in the field before the timber is used. A 2-in. piece is cut from the end of one or two timbers. The piece is then cut along the grain (longitudinally) with one or two saw cuts, depending on its thickness, to within ½ in. of the bottom. The pieces are left in a warm dry place for 24 hours. If the prongs of wood that are left bend inward or outward to any degree, the wood should be rejected.

- Girders and joists must bear solidly on their supports. On the sill end, the joist bears solidly on the sill and is nailed to the header. (See illustrations in Appendixes to Part 2.) On the girder end the joist should go beyond the girder but must at least rest solidly on the girder for its entire width.

- Bridging between joists and studs should not be nailed solidly into place until the structural frame is complete and the underfloor and sheathing are in place. Bridging braces the structure and therefore is not done until the joists and studs have had a chance to adjust to the weight upon them. Bridging between studs somewhere at their midpoint, with pieces of 2 × 4, is strongly recommended whether or not called for.

- The contractor should be aware of the methods for nailing the sheathing. Since studs are 16 in. on center and stock sheathing is 48 in. wide, each piece of sheathing should be nailed to the first and fourth stud of each 48 in. span and, of course, to the two intervening studs.

- Rafters or roof trusses must bear solidly on the exterior walls. Rafters should be carefully notched to fit over the double cap plates and must be thoroughly toe-nailed. The contractor should also see to it that rafters are braced or trussed with collar beams not farther than one-third down from the top.

- The contractor should constantly check to see that horizontal structural members are level in two directions as well as diagonally, and that vertical members are at perfect right angles. This can be done by the use of squares, levels, plumb bobs or by a transit. The structural frame must be perfectly level and exactly vertical before the sheathing is nailed. Cut-in corner bracing is important for this purpose and for additional structural strength.

- The structures must finally be checked after the rough plumbing, heating, and electrical work are done and before this work is covered with wallboard. The contractor should examine the entire structure, the joists, studs, bottom and top plates, and bracing to see that no holes have been cut for pipe, electrical conduit, or hot air ducts that will affect the structural strength. Any such breaks can be repaired by the use of strap iron well nailed or by the use of an additional stud.

7.2D. Safety and Fire Protection

The safety of the workers is one of the important responsibilities of the contractor. Observing safety precautions can save broken limbs or worse. A safe job also promotes better workmanship, better production, a lower insurance rate. When the contractor inspects the job, safe working conditions should be a primary concern. Some of the things to look for:

An excessive accumulation of rubbish
Boards with protruding nails
Ladders with defective side rails or rungs
Scaffold plank with cracks or splits
Scaffolding that is insecure
Badly chafed rope
Insecure hoisting pulleys
Top-heavy material piles
Haphazard storage of materials which may block passage for workers or trucks
Icy conditions where workers or equipment may slip
Excessive mud where equipment may become mired

Fire protection should also be a serious concern of the contractor. A fire causes serious delays, and even with adequate insurance nobody can come out ahead. It becomes even more serious in the case where a contractor is performing an alteration or addition to an inhabited house. Some dangers which should be guarded against:

- An excessive accumulation of flammable rubbish

- Carelessly thrown cigarettes or other burning tobacco

- A space heater left burning with no one to watch it

- Smoldering wood or rubbish where a plumber's torch has been used or a welder has been working

- Frayed electrical wire—the main switch should be turned off unless there is a permanent heating system in place and in use

The contractor is advised to make one thorough inspection after all workers are gone or to have a reliable worker do it. The contractor's attention is again called to fire-stopping and other fire safety regulations of the local code.

7.2E. Brick Masonry

Brick walls, whether brick veneer or solid masonry, must bear solidly on the foundation wall. The contractor must check to see that the veneer wall is securely attached to the structural frame with a metal wall tie at least every 4 sq ft of wall. He should also note that all brickwork is to be laid with full bed and cross joints.

Most brick-masonry bearing walls are of the cavity type, i.e., there is a space usually 2 in. wide between the front and the backup or rear wythes. The contractor should be sure that the cavity is not filled up with mortar droppings and that there are weep holes (small plastic tubes) set into the front wythe at the bottom of every floor just above the fire-stopping. The front and rear wythes must also be tied together at every fifth course by continuous wall ties made of galvanized steel. The best way to keep the cavity clear is by the use of a strip of wood 2 in. wide laid over the wall ties and which can be lifted out by strings or wire when the next level of wall ties is reached. The thickness of the walls is set by code and relates to the height and the unsupported width.

Chimneys are to be inspected for the size of the flue lining and fireplaces are to be inspected for the correct width, height, and depth according to the plan and for the thickness of the brick walls.

Cold-weather masonry construction requires that special precautions be taken. The contractor should not allow any brickwork to be performed below 40°F unless the following work is done:

- The sand for the mortar mix must be kept dry and should be on a raised metal platform so that it can be heated.

- The mixing water should be heated so that it is over 70 but not over 160°F.

- The mortar boxes should be raised above the ground so that the mortar can be kept warm by a fire underneath.

- The top of the wall should be protected at all times when brick is not being laid.

- The entire wall should be covered with tarpaulins when work is finished for the day.

These are all simple and inexpensive things to do. On a small job, the extra precautions that must be taken in extreme weather, such as all-night heating by salamanders, are not worthwhile, and it is better and safer to wait until the temperature goes up.

7.2F. Waterproofing

Waterproofing a basement is an expensive item of construction. There are several ways of doing it and the method depends on the amount of water that is present.

Membrane waterproofing consists of one or more layers of heavy tarred felt laid in hot asphalt. It is applied to the outside of a basement wall and lapped over the footing. If the basement wall is of concrete block, it must be allowed to become thoroughly dry so that any shrinkage cracks in the mortar may be patched, and it must be free of sharp projections before the membrane is applied. A concrete foundation wall must also be thoroughly dry. The hot tar in membrane waterproofing becomes brittle when it dries, and the contractor should see to it that the tar is not cracked during backfilling, which should be done carefully.

For integral waterproofing, a manufactured additive is mixed in concrete. There are a number of such additives and the directions for mixing the material into the concrete and the recommended proportions of the concrete must be carefully followed. It is best for the contractor to have this done by a reliable "ready-mix" material dealer and then make sure that the concrete is poured evenly into the forms and is well rodded.

For surface waterproofing, a waterproofing compound is mixed with a rich cement mortar and applied to the inside of a basement wall and floor. The contractor must see to it that the walls or floor are sufficiently rough to form a bond with the waterproofing. It is best to have this done by professional waterproofers.

7.2G. Roofing and Sheet Metal

Section 6.10 states that the contractor must carefully inspect roofing and flashing because leaks are very difficult to find, and there is nothing more annoying to a client than a roof leak.

Flashing can be of various materials. There are heavy "copper-plated" paper, aluminum, sheet copper, and many others. The architect should specify the material to be used. The important thing is for the flashing to overlap enough so that water cannot be driven up under it even in the heaviest storms. The diagrams on p. 389 show an example of flashing. In every case the contractor should see to it that the sheet-metal contractor uses sufficient flashing material. The contractor should also make sure that the flashing material is not pierced by even a pinhole.

Thermal insulation board for residential roofs is now available. This is applied over the felt paper which covers the roof sheathing and is laid under the shingles. The board must be kept absolutely dry and should not be laid when there is any threat of wet weather. (If this board is not specified the builder may suggest it as an extra.)

The finished shingle roof is laid over the insulation boards (if they are specified) and over the flashing. It must be laid closely to any vertical surface whether it be dormer, chimney, higher abutting wing, or protruding pipe. Shingles should not be laid in wet weather and heavy tarpaulins should be readily available in case of sudden storms. Shingles or any roofing laid over a wet surface can cause endless trouble.

In instances where there is a flat roof, the roofing contractor must use built-up roofing which consists of several layers of tarred felt, with each layer in a mop coat of hot pitch. The walkover surface of such a roof can be gravel laid in a bed of hot pitch. Such roofs are usually laid according to specifications written by the manufacturer of the roofing and the contractor should make sure that these specifications are followed. If there is a railing around the roof the posts should have pitch boxes around them to prevent leakage where the post supports pierce the roof.

7.2H. Plumbing and Heating

In small private residences the plumbing and heating work is very often performed by the same subcontractor. The plumbing work must be done by a licensed plumber and according to a strict code.

Inspection of plumbing should concentrate on tight joints in copper lines and in the screw pipe, cast-iron pipe, or plastic pipe of the waste and vent lines. Copper lines should not have sharp bends that can restrict flow. The local code should call for a water test of the wastes and vents and a pressure test of the water lines. The local inspector and the contractor should attend these tests.

Basins and water closets should be shaken to see that they are firmly attached. They should also be examined for chips and cracks. If bathtubs are of light metal they should be packed underneath to eliminate the unpleasant drumming noise that is caused by a shower. There is a device now on the market that eliminates water hammer when water is shut off suddenly.

If the heating is by hot water, the only testing that need be done is a pressure test to see that the joints are tight. If the heating is by hot air, a sheet-metal subcontractor is usually required. There should be a specification or plan which notes the size of each sheet-metal duct and locations of the supply and return air registers. The contractor can make a spot check of duct sizes and look for tight joints. Sharp bends in duct work without turning vanes inside the elbow will cause whistling. Generally on any job of more than three or four bedrooms there is a representative of the architect or heating engineer to make such inspections. This is especially true if air conditioning is called for. In such cases the contractor need only check for structural integrity.

7.2I. Electrical

The electrical work must be performed by a licensed electrical subcontractor and in accordance with a strict code which is national in scope. Inspection is usually made by the local building inspector who is presumed to be familiar with the code.

The only inspection work that the contractor can do here is to make sure that all boxes for wall outlets, switches, ceiling outlets, and accessory outlets are in the correct places and wired before the wallboarding starts.

7.2J. Wallboarding

Wallboard must be carefully covered against weather. It should be placed and nailed in accordance with the manufacturer's instructions. The contractor should see to it that fire-rated wallboard is placed where it is called for. Holes for outlet boxes and other openings should be carefully cut to fit.

The taping of the wallboard requires several inspections. Taping is performed in three operations, each one of which is sanded down before the next coat of spackle is applied. The final coat of spackle must be feathered and made so smooth that there is no discernable edge if a hand is run over it.

7.2K. Windows and Doors

Wood windows, whether double hung, casement, sliding, or awning, usually come to a job ready-glazed and ready for setting into the framed openings that have been left for them. There are U.S. standards for wood windows that are used by the American Wood Window Institute. There is nothing more annoying than windows that stick or bind or do not close tightly. The contractor should see to it that the windows are made by a recognized manufacturer (if one is not specified) and that they are weatherstripped and open and close properly. The frames should be carefully braced so that they are not pushed out of plumb or out of square when the siding or brick veneer is applied. A frame even slightly out of square can cause binding of movable sash.

Doors must be hung properly and square with the trim to prevent binding.

It is advisable to choose larger butts if the door is heavier than usual or if there is any doubt. The contractor should also check for the swing of the door as per plan and for the proper insertion of the latch set or lock set to see that it meets the striking plate squarely and without binding or rubbing.

Windows and doors should be delivered only in dry weather and be kept completely dry until they are installed. The contractor should be sure that the windows are carefully prime-coated before or immediately after they arrive on the job.

7.2L. Millwork and Flooring

Millwork and wood flooring should not be delivered to the job until there is a warm dry place to store them, and they must be kept warm and dry after they are installed. They should not even be delivered on a wet day. Millwork should be prime-coated as soon as it comes on the job. Wood flooring must be perfectly kiln dried. There are several large manufacturers of flooring as well as trade associations which label wood flooring. The contractor should ascertain the name of the manufacturer from his materials dealer. He would also be wise to note where the materials dealer stores finished doors, windows, millwork, and flooring.

7.2M. Tiling and Painting

Tilework is now mostly done by pasting the tile to a heavy mastic that is spread directly over the wallboard. The contractor need only note that there are no cracked or chipped tiles and that the temperature is kept over 50 for 24 hours after the tile is set. If the tile is laid in a mortar bed it must be kept warm for at least 72 hours. If the floors are tile they are laid in a thin mortar bed (thinset) and this too must be kept warm.

Painting must not be started until the walls, either exterior or interior, are perfectly dry. For interior painting the contractor must see to it that all hardware, cover plates, and other material that can be stained by paint are removed and stored in a safe place. It is best not to do any interior painting in cold, damp weather until there has been heat in the house and the wallboard has had a chance to become thoroughly dry. Any knots in woodwork should be shellacked before any finish coats are applied. Nail holes in wallboard must be spackled and carefully sanded. Exterior painting should not be attempted unless the temperature is over 50°F and likely to stay there. Exterior woodwork should have at least a week of over 50°F fair weather before painting. Painting over moist wood causes bubbles and discoloration.

There are other inspections that can be made but the foregoing are the most important. They can all be done while the contractor is checking the progress, personnel, and delivery of material, and will be well worth the time and effort it took to ensure the safety of the workers and the quality of the work.

COST CONTROL

8.1. THE IMPORTANCE OF PROPER COST CONTROL

The construction contractor should never forget that he is operating a business and that all the rules for the successful operation of business must be followed. The most important difference between a construction business and other businesses is that construction is more complicated than most.

In the performance of a construction contract the contractor has to assemble dozens of many different kinds of materials that are manufactured in widely scattered places. He has to see to it that all of these materials are available when they are required. Unlike other owners of businesses, he cannot build up much of an inventory because each job is different, and in fact it is not advisable to do so because inventories tie up operating funds.

The building contractor also cannot build up an "inventory of workers." Unlike the operator of a store, a small factory, or any kind of an office, the contractor is faced with many different kinds of craftsmen—carpenters, plumbers, roofers, laborers, electricians, etc., each of whom performs only his part of the work and then has to wait for another craftsman to do *his* part of the work before coming back. If this sounds complicated, it is. The building contractor must depend on all of these craftsmen to appear when they are needed and to complete their portion of the work on time.

In the construction of a private residence or small business building, for instance, there are times when three or four carpenters may be necessary and there are other times when only one carpenter is required. The contracter must constantly look ahead to be able to "juggle" his workers at the least payroll cost and still have them on the job when they are needed.

The foregoing is meant to show how important it is to maintain tight cost control on a construction job. The entire success of the business depends on it. The contractor must stay within his estimate, cover his overhead cost, and make a profit, and he can only do this through cost control.

8.2. THE ELEMENTS OF COST CONTROL

Cost control starts at the very beginning of a construction job with the layout of the site. This is discussed in Chap. 5 from the standpoint of job progress and is equally important for cost control. The contractor does not need to be told twice that convenient and adequate material storage areas that enable the craftsmen to get at the material quickly without time-consuming sorting will save labor cost. This holds true also for a solidly based driveway for heavy trucks or equipment to get close to the building site. The proper location and protection of ditches for the plumber or electrician will help them to avoid delays.

Cost control has to take into account many different aspects of construction, such as progress control and scheduling; material control with respect to original cost, delivery, and ultimate use; labor cost control; equipment costs and rentals; use of utilities during construction; control of a subcontractor's requests for any additional funds over his contract; and control of overhead.

The best way to combine all of these important components into easily understood figures is through the use of simple forms. These can be used for each separate project and will show at a glance how the job cost compares with the original estimate. These forms, samples of which will be shown in this chapter and Chap. 9, must of course be kept up to date. Some of them can be filled in on a weekly or even monthly basis, but others must be kept on a daily basis if they are to be utilized to their full extent.

8.3. PROGRESS CONTROL AND SCHEDULING

A major ingredient of a cost-control program is to get the job completed on time with no necessity for comebacks to complete or repair poorly done or incomplete items. This cuts overhead, labor costs, utility costs, and equipment rental, and enables the contractor to obtain his progress and final payments on time. This in turn can save him interest on loans and provide working capital. Therefore Chaps. 5 and 6 should be read very carefully with particular attention to ways of making and keeping the progress chart on a current basis.

In this connection, Chap. 7, which is about quality control, can save the contractor comeback time for defective or incomplete work.

8.4. MATERIAL CONTROL

The cost control of material can be separated into a number of different parts. Throughout this book, the "general contractor" or "contractor" is assumed to be the carpentry contractor (although he can be anyone with a knowledge of general construction). While the contractor's responsibility covers all the trades, his prime responsibility is for the carpentry and structural work and for the materials used in this work.

8.4A. Delivery of Material

8.4A1. THE TIMING OF DELIVERIES

The delivery of the correct material on time and the placement of the material at the designated place is the first step. The contractor or his foreman or someone he can trust should be on the job when lumber is delivered so that it is not dumped in a disorderly manner and in the wrong place. This also refers to other materials, some of which are fragile or susceptible to damage by wet weather, such as wallboard, millwork, etc. The material dealer must understand that any such material that is exposed to bad weather when it is delivered will be rejected.

The structural lumber should be delivered in several loads, depending on the size of the house. The contractor should insist on this for several reasons. First, he can control the use of the lumber much better if it is delivered in smaller quantities. Second, large piles of fresh lumber are an invitation to pilferage. As an example of how materials should be delivered, the first delivery might consist of sills, girders, floor joists, nails, and anchor bolts. The second delivery might be the underfloor for the first floor, plates, and studs. The third delivery might be ceiling joists (or second floor joists), underfloor for the second story or rafters, bracing, and lintels.

The above sample is just a partial listing of the material to be delivered. The timing of the deliveries depends on the progress of the job, i.e., the size of the crew, the weather, etc. The contractor cannot tie up the trucks of the material dealer, however, and must therefore take a chance on the delivery dates in advance.

8.4A2. QUANTITY CHECK

The contractor must receive a detailed material slip (delivery ticket) with every delivery of material. This form should say how much of each kind of lumber, builder's hardware, window frames, sash, etc., is being delivered. For instance: 2×8 16/16, 12/14, 10/12; or 12/2 ft-8 in. $\times$ 4 ft-6 in. frames and double-hung sash; or 50/4 ft-0 in. $\times$ 8 ft-0 in./$\frac{1}{2}$ in. wallboard; or 1 keg nails, 16d. There should be an immediate count of the material to be sure that the material slip is correct. If the contractor is on another job he should get back to make this count on the day it is delivered, or the next day at the latest, or have a trusted assistant do it. It must not be forgotten that three of four sticks of $2 \times 8/16$ ft can represent \$30 or \$40 and it does not take too many of these sums to make the difference between profit and loss.

If there is any shortage in count, the material dealer should be immediately notified. Any reputable material dealer is as anxious as his customers to stop carelessness or pilferage. If the count is correct the contractor should transfer the items on the material slip to a permanent record (delivery slips are easily lost and they do constitute important records).

8.4A3. QUALITY CHECK

The delivered material should then be checked for quality and for conformance with the original order and the specifications. Lumber has branded marks on the end grain. These marks must be identified as the product of a lumber association or a well-known lumber mill. If the specification or the order calls for a certain kind and grade of wood, these must be identified by the branded marks or by the material dealer. It is even better if the contractor himself can tell by the grain, the absence or presence of knots, the straightness, and the general appearance whether the lumber meets his requirements. All other material should carry the manufacturer's name in a readily available spot.

8.4A4. COST

The contractor's permanent record of material delivered to the job will serve him well when he is billed by the material dealer. First, he can check quantities. Second, he can check prices against the estimate which he originally received from the material dealer when he was making up his estimate of cost. It is at this point that it becomes most useful to have had the estimate priced by separate items as was suggested in Chap. 3.

8.4A5. USE OF MATERIAL ON JOB

Materials delivered in several steps will enable the contractor to keep close account of their use. This serves two important purposes. The first, is, of course, to prevent pilferage and misuse of materials, and the second is to enable the contractor to closely follow labor progress. Figure 8-1 shows a suggested form for doing this. The first three columns indicate the day and hour of delivery and the quantity delivered. The fourth column shows the day and hour when the material was counted. By the time of the count, some of the material has been used and this quantity is placed in the "In place" column. Column 6 shows the quantity of material "Left on site," and this quantity plus the quantity of the material shown in the "In place" column should equal the total quantity delivered. If it falls short, then some of the material has been wasted or taken from the job.

The contractor should note carefully the advantage of keeping this type of record. It tells him how much of the various kinds of material have been used in how many hours by his crew and it will start to build a record of labor costs which he can use to great advantage in estimating future labor costs. And it does not take much time.

There is one other job record that should be kept if the contractor has more than one job going at the same time. This is a record of material transferred. It can happen that one job runs out of 2 × 4s or plyscore or wallboard too late for a delivery on a working day. (Of course this should not happen—but it

Material Delivered and Used							
Project J. Wilson Residence					Job #11R		
Date received	How delivered	Material (by delivery ticket)	Date counted	In place	Left on site	Difference	
1/5/7— 8 A.M.	Jones Lumber Co. Truck	Ticket #4285A	1/6/7— 12 noon				
		2x10 9/14		9/14	0	—	
		2x8 11/16		10/16	0	1	
		2x10 61/16		40/16	20	1	
		2x4 10/12		10/12	0	—	
		2x4 100/8		—	100/8	—	
		1 Keg 16 d			3/4 K	—	
		1 Keg 10 d			3/4 K	—	
		Plyscore 60 - $\frac{1}{2}$" (4x8)		10	50	—	
1/5/7— 10 A.M.	Acme Steel Truck	3 - 4" Lally 8'	1/6/7— noon	3	0	—	

Figure 8-1

sometimes does.) The contractor can then transfer material from one job to another, but he must keep a record of it and deduct it from one job and charge it to the other. (See chart in Fig. 8-2, which shows material transferred on 1/10 and 1/15.)

There is one more important matter that should be discussed under the heading "Use of Material on Job," and that is the *misuse* of material on the job. Construction jobs large or small are notorious for the amount of waste material that is left to be thrown away or burned. On smaller jobs the sites are

Material Transfer				
Project J. Wilson Residence			Job #11R	
Date	Material	Quantity	Price	Transferred to
1/10/7—	2x4	16/8	$38.00	O.T. Smith residence
1/15/7—	2x6	8/16	$47.50	O.T. Smith residence

Figure 8-2

usually covered with various cut-off lengths of all sizes of structural lumber, plyscore, wallboard, flooring, siding, etc. This is normal, but much waste can be avoided. If the studs are to be 7 ft-2 in. long, then a 10-in. piece must be cut off every 8-ft length. But if there is to be bridging between studs for which 14-in. pieces of 2 × 4 are required, a 14-ft length of 2 × 4 should be used, which divides into 11 pieces with almost no waste. If 2 × 6 lintels 4-ft long are called for, then 12- or 16-ft lengths should be used. The larger sizes of lumber such as 2 × 8, 2 × 10, or 2 × 12 need not be cut at all if they were ordered in the correct modular lengths. A worker who is seen cutting a short piece from the end of a modular length of lumber should be reprimanded (unless he has a very good reason for it). Even if the worker is not seen wasting lumber, the experienced contractor can tell about the wastage by noting the discarded ends. This subject is worth the effort of an occasional 5-minute job meeting.

8.4A6. INVENTORY

As has been stated before, the construction business (unlike most businesses) does not require any construction materials to be kept in stock. Construction projects can be widely scattered and most of the structural materials, such as lumber of all kinds and sizes and builder's hardware of various kinds, are stocked in a material dealer's yard ready for delivery. Other items of construction such as finish hardware, tile, roofing, lighting fixtures, etc. vary so widely from job to job that it would be impractical and a useless tie-up of capital funds to keep any stock even as a protection against a price rise or a coming shortage. The only inventory that is at all practical is the surplus from a completed job that is made up of standard-sized structural lumber, reinforcing rods, wire mesh, rolls of plastic, nails, screws, and other builder's hardware.

To store and keep such an inventory safe, the contractor must have some kind of a small storage yard where he can also keep his inventory of equipment. A typical materials inventory sheet is shown in Fig. 8-3, indicating the flow of material to and from the yard.

Stockpiling of material is only done under certain conditions, which are discussed in Chap. 5.

8.4A7. PILFERAGE AND MALICIOUS MISCHIEF

The problem of pilferage or the robbery of stored materials or equipment, whether on the job site or in the contractor's storage yard, can be serious in certain localities. There are areas in the country where almost anything can be left out without fear of its being molested or stolen, and there are areas where nothing is safe. Insurance is available to cover the contractor and the owner against these hazards, and this will be discussed in Chap. 10, Insur-

Materials Inventory				
Project *J. B. McArthur*			Yard *1421 Stone St.*	
Material	Quantity	Date of storage	Date of removal	Now in stock
2 x 6	5/16 2/18	2/18/197_		5/16 2/18
Plyscore 4 x 8 ½ 2 x 8 ½	5 pcs. 4 pcs.	2/24/197_ //		5 pcs. 4 pcs.
2 x 10	8/16	3/1/197_		8/16
Plyscore 4 x 8½	5 pcs.	2/24/197_	3/1/197_ 5 pcs.	None

Figure 8-3

ance and Bonding. However, there are many areas where insurance is not really necessary and where only simple precautions need be taken with a consequent saving in insurance premiums.

One of these precautions is to have material delivered as it is used. This was discussed previously in this chapter. Another precaution is to place smaller items under lock and key until they are used. The contractor is strongly advised to lock or barricade the building under construction as soon as all the openings are closed. The casual amateur thief will usually hesitate to break and enter, whereas he would have little hesitation in picking up loose items.

8.5. LABOR COST CONTROL

8.5A. Availability of Workforce

It would seem obvious that one of the important items in maintaining good cost control over labor is the presence of a sufficient number of workers when they are needed and over whom the contractor can exert some control. As a rule construction workers do not stay in one place. To earn a livelihood they must follow the work, which can be widely scattered. In order to get workers on the job when he requires them, the contractor can keep an inventory of names and addresses of individuals and some notes as to their capabilities and skills.

8.5B. Productivity

Once a sufficient crew of reasonably capable workers is available, the contractor must then look to their productivity. In present times construction labor, whether union or nonunion, is highly paid and extremely independent. Except perhaps in isolated communities the average laborer will balk at constant supervision or any feeling that he is being "pushed."

The contractor can determine the capability and the productivity of a worker only by observation and by the use of a form such as that shown in Fig. 8-1. From such a carefully maintained form, the contractor can tell how much structural framing is being accomplished in a day or how many sheets of plyscore or square feet of siding are being erected. This also applies to doors, windows, roofing, flooring, and trim. Among a team or crew, it is reasonably simple to observe who are the workers and who are the laggers. As soon as there is a reduction in the crew (or any excuse for a reduction) the laggers should be the first to go.

8.5C. How to Increase Productivity

The productivity of individuals can be increased to a large extent in several ways. First, there should always be a sufficient supply of material on the job to act as a "pusher" to those workers who may see it as an incentive to get it up into place. Second, the delivery of such items as window frames just as the roof is tight or flooring and trim just as the house is weathertight assures crew members of continuous work and prevents loafing until these items arrive. This of course goes for all trades and all materials, such as piping, tile, electrical equipment, and plumbing fixtures. All of these items of construction which fit into a schedule must be delivered on time so the other trades depending on their completion may also fit into the schedule. A third way of increasing productivity is through the use of a good working foreman (or "pusher" as he is sometimes called). This person, or the contractor himself, should always be a step ahead of the crew. For instance, while the sills and girders are being installed, the foreman should be cutting studs to the right length, or as the studs are being installed, he should be notching the rafters. He should determine how the sheets of underfloor or wall or roof sheathing are to be laid before the crew gets to this work.

8.5D. Use of Daily Progress Report

Another important tool in labor cost control is the daily progress report (Fig. 8-4). If this is kept on a daily basis it will give the contractor an overview of not only what his own crew is doing but also what the other trades are doing and how the work in place fits in with his progress schedule. For instance, he must note if bathtubs are in place so that he may complete his framing, or make sure that electric BX is in place so that he can start the wallboarding, or check if vents are through the roof so that flashing and roofing can start. Delay caused by such unfinished items interrupts the rhythm of the work.

8.5E. Comparison with the Estimated Cost

The contractor is now ready with the help of the daily progress report and the form given in Fig. 8-1 to compare the actual labor cost with his estimated cost. As an example:

1. The contractor has estimated that the framing of the house including underfloor interior stud partitions and rafters will take 80 man-hours.

2. The daily progress report states that sills, girders, and floor joists are complete, that underfloor is 60 percent complete and that two exterior stud walls are in place.

3. On a given day, Fig. 8-1 may show that 25 percent of the 2 × 4s and all the material for floor joists and girders has been used. It may also show that 20 sheets, or 15 percent, of the plyscore have been used.

4. For a single-story house he can safely assume that the framing is approximately 20 percent complete and can compare the worker-hours actually spent with his estimate.

5. The same process can be gone through for exterior sheathing, shingling, siding, etc.

As the job proceeds, if the contractor finds his labor costs are exceeding his estimate, he must supervise the job more closely to determine and correct what is wrong. If the cost is running considerably below, then he should look for shoddy workmanship (the use of fewer nails, studs out of square, something left out, etc.).

8.6. OVERHEAD CONTROL

Chapter 1 shows a list of the overhead charges that are likely to be incurred by a typical small builder. As stated in that chapter, the builder new to the business can only estimate the cost, but as he proceeds with various contracts (whether alterations or new work), he can start to check actual expenditures against his estimated total cost.

In estimating for each separate job the contractor has added a percentage of his total estimated overhead to the bid. Such percentages should be calculated on the assumption that the total of all the sums included in the various successful bids will equal the total of the overhead cost (not including his own compensation).

As a job progresses and as the budget year progresses, the contractor, if he has kept accurate records, can calculate what part of his total budgeted overhead cost has been spent and what part of it is chargeable to this job. This gives him a chance to review future bids; for instance, if he is anxious to be awarded a certain job and if his overhead is running below the budget, he can cut the overhead charge in his bid. If his overhead is running over the budget he has a choice of economizing on such things as salaries, renting of equipment, accounting, and legal fees or of increasing the overhead charges in future bids (if in his judgment this will not lose him a contract).

				Daily Progress Report	
Weather _____				Temperature _____	
Project _____				Job _____	Date _____
Supt. _____					
	J*	L*	F*	Work Completed or in Progress	
Excavation					
Foundations					
Masonry, Brick					
Carpentry (rough)					
Structural steel					
Insulation, sound, and heat					
Windows					
Plumbing					
Heating					
Electric					
Roofing and sheet metal					
Lath and plaster					
Wallboard					
Tile					
Carpentry (finish)					
Floors, Wood					
Floors, Resilient					
Waterproofing					
Painting					
Accessories					
				(over)	

*J—journeymen; L—laborers; F—foremen. How many and hours worked.

Figure 8-4

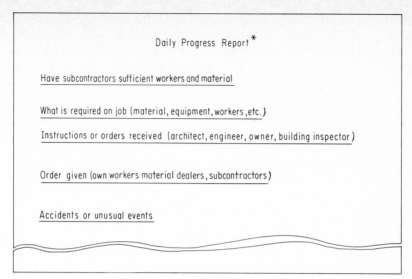

Daily Progress Report*

Have subcontractors sufficient workers and material

What is required on job (material, equipment, workers, etc.)

Instructions or orders received (architect, engineer, owner, building inspector)

Order given (own workers material dealers, subcontractors)

Accidents or unusual events

*Back of form.

Figure 8-4 continued

8.6A. Equipment, Owned and Rented

Except for heavy equipment such as power shovels, cranes, bulldozers, ditchers, etc., which are the property of the excavator, power equipment and power tools used on a job are either owned or rented by the contractor. He usually also owns at least one truck and a number of smaller tools such as picks, shovels, wheelbarrows, scaffold brackets, ladders, buckets, possibly a small mortar or concrete mixer, and other miscellaneous equipment.

In addition to his owned equipment he may on occasion rent equipment such as an extra truck or a small bulldozer for final grading, or salamanders for winter heating, or even heavy tarpaulins for extra weather protection. It is very often cheaper to rent such equipment than to own it and it does not tie up capital funds.

To keep account of his own and rented equipment, the contractor must keep an equipment inventory and a running equipment rental account so that he will at all times know where his own equipment is located and when his rented equipment has come on the job. Rental rates for some equipment are high, and rented equipment should not be kept on the job one day more than is necessary. (See Fig. 9-2.)

8.7. CHANGE ORDERS

8.7A. What They Are

Change orders come as a result of changes in the scope of the work during the course of construction. These changes can be additions or deductions.

The deduct change orders come when the architect, the engineer, or the client requests that the contractor omit an item of work which he has included in his estimate and which he is prepared to perform. It could be the omission of the finish wood floor because the client has elected to carpet all the floors. In such an instance, the contractor must prepare a proposal to the owner or the architect to state the allowances he will make in the contract price for this omission. This is not as simple as it sounds. First, the contractor has to refer to his original estimate to ascertain how much he allowed for the finish flooring (labor and material). Second, he must deduct at least 20 percent from this cost as the allowance because he anticipated the covering of some of his overhead as well as a profit on this item. Third, he should make sure that the material dealers will allow him to deduct from their bill the entire cost of the flooring. Fourth, he should call attention to the fact that the ½-in. plywood underfloor—which is called for and which is assumed to be in place—must be covered with at least another half inch of finish-grade plywood, and the cost for labor and material for this must be deducted from the allowance. If his figure is accepted, he and the owner can then sign a change order which reflects the new contract price (change-order form Fig. 8-5).

8.7B. How to Handle a Change Order

The contractor is strongly advised to look very carefully at every request for a change in construction from either the architect or the owner, especially when something is already in place and has to be torn out and rebuilt or replaced by something else. We must not forget that the prices he quotes, whether plus or minus, will usually be met with resistance and sometimes outright hard feelings. The client thinks he should get a larger deduct allowance and in many cases feels that the price quoted for a plus change is much too high. The contractor is unfortunately caught in the middle.

But whether caught in the middle or not, the contractor should not lose money on changes. On minus changes, he should at the least preserve his originally estimated profit and overhead, and on plus changes he should add sufficient profit and overhead to the new item of work. It must not be forgotten that change orders of any kind interrupt the rhythm of the work. Many change orders involve one or more subcontractors from whom firm prices must be obtained before any price is quoted.

One other important fact about change orders is that they must be promptly estimated and promptly accepted or rejected. Whether it is a change that benefits a job or a deduction of an item of work, in its very nature any proposed change in construction interrupts the work. The contractor may have to work around some item that has to be changed, and this is expensive. The contractor must make it clear that his proposal must be accepted within a certain time limit (that is, if he has submitted the proposal in good time).

Change Order

Change Order No. _____ Date _____

Project _____ Contractor _____

You are hereby authorized to proceed with the following changes described below
based on the following drawings and specifications or other communications.

_____

_____

_____

Description of change	Add	Deduct	Cost

Subtotal $_____ $_____

Net add (or deduct) $ _____

Total all preceeding change orders $ _____

Total all change orders (to date) $ _____

Original contract price $ _____

New contract price $ _____

Figure 8-5

8.7C. Beneficial Change Orders and Others

Although, as inferred previously, all change orders are something of a
nuisance, some kinds meet with less resistance. The change in construction
that is beneficial to the owner such as better-constructed and better-looking
kitchen cabinets, or a plank floor instead of oak, or the enlargement of a
family room, etc., will usually meet with less resistance than the demolishing
and rebuilding of a partition because the owner is unhappy with the size of
the room (although originally he approved the plan). The contractor can be
guided, therefore, by the kind of change that is requested. If it enhances the
looks of the structure, interior or exterior, or if it adds a desired fireplace or
sturdier wall, or if it is just added insulation for weather or sound that will
make living more comfortable, the contractor may assume that his price will

meet with minimal resistance and can act accordingly. If, on the other hand, it has been caused by a mistake in judgment of the architect or owner and will be of no particular added benefit, any price he gives will be too high. In such cases the contractor should tread carefully, although he must never lose his overhead and profit.

8.8. CONTROL OF SUBCONTRACTORS' COSTS

In previous chapters, the contractor has been warned to read the plans and specifications carefully and to make sure that every item is covered either in his own work or in the work of a subcontractor. It is the items that "fall in between" that can cause serious losses. But there is another "nonspecific" matter which is embodied in any plans, specifications, and general conditions. This is the *intent* of the plans and specifications. For example, the author once encountered a seemingly ridiculous situation which took weeks to settle. It involved a unit price which had been quoted for electrical wall outlets. Several hundred additional outlets were ordered before it was discovered that the electrical contractor's price did not include the wiring of the outlets. This kind of situation can happen and does. A fireplace damper may not be shown, the plumbing specification may say that hot and cold water lines are to be extended to a future bathroom but is silent about the waste and vent. These items come under the *intent* of the plans and specifications. If a fireplace is built it must have a damper in it to prevent the escape of warm air in the winter. If water lines are extended to a future bath, what good are they if there is not a waste and vent?

These kinds of items are the ones that are often claimed by subcontractors as extras. Reimbursement for such extras is almost impossible to collect by the contractor. Such claims must be resisted. When a subcontract is awarded there must be a meeting of the minds. The subcontractor must be given to understand that he is expected to provide a complete job and that any extras for obvious omissions, without which a job would not be complete, will not be allowed.

8.9. FORWARD PROJECTION OF COST

All of the items in this chapter will have to be set up in a simple bookkeeping system in which the various pieces of cost control as shown in the several charts and tables can be assembled as a whole, so that the contractor can come up with a profit-and-loss statement for each job. If the contractor is keeping accurate records of his cost, he can not only see at a glance what his current financial situation is, but he can also forecast the future with some degree of accuracy.

Figure 8-6 shows how the final cost of a job may be forecast. The items that are in the estimate form are used and the original estimated figures are entered. By the time such a sheet is prepared, the contractor has sublet most

		Changes				
Item	Original estimate	Add	Deduct	Revised estimate	Projected final cost	Under or over
Excavation						
Foundations						
Masonry						
Structural						
Lumber						
Labor						
Payroll extras						
Hardware						
Equipment						
Roofing						
Sheet metal						
Plumbing						
Heating						
Finish carpentry						
Floors						
Trim (interior and exterior)						
Wallboard						
Electrical						
Other trades						

Forecast of Final Cost — Project _____ Job _____

Figure 8-6

of the trades and his own work is past its initial stage. He can therefore make an educated guess as to what the final cost of each part of the work will cost. Since this is done by trades and of course includes his own work, the contractor has a chance to forecast his final profit (or loss) and be guided in any estimating he may be engaged in for future work. It also gives him a chance to make future commitments, arrange for further loans, cut down or increase his work force, and preserve his assets.

The control of the cost of a job and the keeping of accurate and *current* records of such costs is one of the most important things a contractor can do. Without such records he cannot succeed.

9

RECORD KEEPING FOR A CONSTRUCTION BUSINESS

9.1. WHY IT IS NECESSARY

It has been mentioned several times in this book, and it is generally agreed, that the quickest way to lose a business is through the failure of the owner to keep adequate records on a current basis. The previous chapter, on cost control, has described how the construction contractor can maintain adequate control over each piece of his business. But the forms (which must be kept on a current basis) that are necessary to do this must be gathered together into a whole so that the contractor can see how each aspect of his business has contributed to his profit, which after all is what business is all about.

As a matter of fact, the contractor is forced to keep some sort of books to satisfy the various governmental authorities who very often may want to examine his records. A glance at the Federal Tax Guide reveals some highlights that are worth repeating:

"You must keep records to determine your tax liability . . . your records must be permanent, accurate, complete and must clearly establish income, deductions, credits, employee information, etc."

"You must elect an accounting method . . . for income and expenses of the business."

"If you have one or more employees you may be required to withhold Federal Income Tax from their wages. You may also be subject to the Federal Insurance Contribution Act (FICA) [which is Social Security] and the Federal Unemployment Tax Act (FUTA) [unemployment insurance]."

These three quotes should be sufficient to show why a contractor must keep books. But there are other reasons such as sales tax records, state and local income or real estate taxes, and so on. From this it would seem that a contractor goes into business in order to fill out tax forms and pay taxes, but this is not so. The reason for going into the business is to make a profit, and a well-run contracting business can be richly rewarding.

9.2. THE FUNCTION OF THE BOOKKEEPER

This chapter does not presume to discuss general bookkeeping or accounting practice. However, it will show the contractor what records he must keep so that a person with a basic knowledge of bookkeeping can keep his books in order on a current basis and so that an accountant can go over these records and books at periodic intervals. The simple bookkeeping can be performed by the contractor himself or a member of his family until the business becomes large enough to warrant the employment of outside help. Such current bookkeeping should be in sufficient detail so that the contractor can almost at a glance tell what state his business is in.

9.2A. Labor Cost

As soon as a contractor employs outside labor, he is faced with a series of forms required by the federal, state, and municipal governments. These forms are for tax purposes, unemployment benefits, Social Security, and possibly union benefits. There are weekly payroll sheets to be prepared. The contractor himself has to keep a daily time book showing the hours worked by each employee and the hourly rate. Many of these forms are available in standard printed material that can be purchased at stationery shops specializing in this material. The Social Security people will be helpful in advising the contractor on how he should keep his payroll records.

The payroll records must be kept on a current basis in a bound book which is subject to inspection. It is from this book that the accountant calculates insurance premiums, payments to Social Security, to unemployment, and to any other agency which has to do with the welfare of the worker.

9.2B. Distribution of Labor Costs

Figure 8-1 is an example of how a contractor can keep account of the productivity of his workers. There is one other record that the contractor should have. This is the one that shows how his labor cost is distributed among the various activities such as framing, roofing, trim, siding, flooring, etc. The contractor can keep such a running record by notations in his time book and eventually transfer them to a permanent record which will be of invaluable help to him in estimating future jobs. Figure 9-1 shows what such a record might look like. This is for pure labor cost. Insurance, payroll taxes and all other attributable costs can be kept separately and added as a cost per hour of labor.

9.2C. Distribution of Material Costs

The contractor who wishes to keep an accurate record of his costs must also distribute his material costs. In Chap. 3, on estimating, there is an illustration

Distribution of Labor Costs				
Project *J. Wilson Residence*			Date *June, 197—*	
Kind of work	Total time	Hourly rate	Total cost	Cost per unit
Framing 1st floor Setting lallys, girders, sills, plates, joists, underfloor, studs, ceiling, joists. *Framing roof Rafters, plyscore, felt paper. Ready for flashing and shingles*	*60 hrs J** *40 hrs A**	*$10.00* *$6.00*	*$ 600.00* *240.00* *$840.00*	*2 M Board Feet 1000 sq ft plyscore $640. for framing $320./MBF $200. for underfloor $.20/sq ft*

*J—journeyman; A—apprentice.

Figure 9-1

of a lumber list which the contractor uses to obtain bids on the required material. This list is broken into various sizes of lumber, kinds of trim, flooring, windows, doors, etc. If the contractor asks the material dealer to bid this list by the separate items, he will have a ready-made list of his material costs. He can then adjust this for current costs when bidding a new job and for keeping account of his present costs as compared with his estimate.

9.2D. Other Records

Other records that must be kept are the material receipts and the entries referring to them, material transfer records to show when material is transferred from one job to another, equipment cost records, subcontractor payment records, equipment costs, overhead costs, cash receipts, interest payments and others.

9.3. WHAT THE ACCOUNTANT REQUIRES

Following is a general outline of what an accountant requires in order to prepare a balance sheet, a statement of net worth which is required by all lenders, and a profit-and-loss statement for IRS and others.

Equipment Inventory

Project _J. B. McArthur_   Date _March, 197_

Tool or equipment	Total number	Date purchased or date rented	Number and where located	Date counted
Wheelbarrow Gen. Purpose 4½ c.f.*	6	Oct. 8, 197_ XY Lumber Co.	Yard - 4 J. Wilson 1 O.T. Smith-1	3/17/197_
Skilsaw 7¼" J.Z. #215	3	Jan. 4, 197_ O'Brien Tool Co.	O.T. Smith-1 J. Wilson-1 Yard -1	3/17/197_
Tarpaulins 10 X 12	6	Jan. 10, 197_ XY Lumber Co.	Yard-2 J. Wilson-4	3/17/197_

*Simplified abbreviation for "cubic feet."

Figure 9-2

- A payroll record which conforms with all laws having jurisdiction. The record should include time sheets and hourly wages paid.

- The inventory ledger, which records all supplies and materials on hand and shows the inflow and outgo of material.

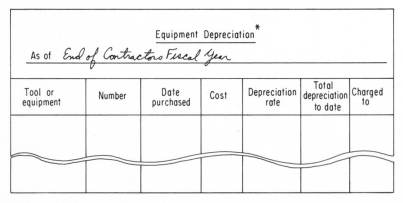

Equipment Depreciation*

As of _End of Contractors Fiscal Year_

Tool or equipment	Number	Date purchased	Cost	Depreciation rate	Total depreciation to date	Charged to

*This should be filled out by an accountant from the contractor's records.

Figure 9-3

- The subcontractor's ledger, which shows all contracts made for the particular job, their cost, what has been billed, and what has been paid.

- An equipment ledger which shows all equipment on hand, when purchased, and how much it cost (Fig. 9-2). Periodic inventories must be made to keep this record current. This record is also used for depreciation (Fig. 9-3) and insurance purposes.

- The contract ledger, which records the various contracts entered into and their present status, including amounts paid out and amounts received on each contract.

- The general ledger, which combines all the above and acts as a control on them. It is from this ledger that the accountant prepares the balance sheet and all the other records which show the "state of health" of the business.

10

INSURANCE AND BONDING

10.1 INSURANCE AND THE CONSTRUCTION BUSINESS

By its very nature the construction contracting business is subject to many risks. Because a construction job consists of the assemblage of many materials from many places, it is subject to delays. Because such assemblage takes place in the open and often in high or restricted places, it is subject to accidents. Because it is mostly an outdoor activity, it is influenced by weather. Because the usual construction job employs many different trades and subcontractors who may default before their work is completed, the contractor is subject to financial loss.

Construction insurance, while it cannot protect against every risk, can protect the contractor against the more common ones and the premium paid for such insurance is small compared with the contractor's liability if he were forced to pay for losses from a fire or a major accident to an employee or a member of the public. It should also be mentioned here that carrying proper insurance is not always at the contractor's discretion. Many kinds of insurance and their face amounts are a matter of contractual obligation and at least one kind (workmen's compensation) is enforced by the law.

The following list shows the type of insurance which should be carried by a building contractor and some insurance coverage which is discretionary and dependent upon the kind of job and its location:

- Workmen's compensation and employer's liability insurance
- Builder's risk fire insurance with extended coverage, such as for vandalism, malicious mischief, pilferage, and others
- Fire insurance on contractor's own property
- Contractor's comprehensive general liability insurance

145

- Comprehensive general liability insurance
    Public liability
    Property damage
    Automobile owned and nonowned liability
    Automobile owned and nonowned property damage
    Contractual liability
    Owner's protective liability

- Disability insurance

- Discretionary
    Contractor's equipment insurance
    Group hospitalization insurance
    Business interruption insurance
    Completed operations insurance

10.2. WORKMEN'S COMPENSATION INSURANCE

Every state has a workmen's compensation law whose purpose is to protect the worker against financial loss caused by an on-the-job accident. The law is administered by the courts, by a state fund, or by a state commission. The contractor should know that, because construction is a high-risk business, his compensation insurance premiums will be one of his largest insurance expenses. There are a few states in which the contractor can choose his own method of coverage. However, the contractor who does not cover himself through insurance is taking a very dangerous risk. One serious accident could put him out of business.

One of the basic provisions of the workmen's compensation laws is that the employee is covered even if he is guilty of contributory negligence. Even if a worker does not wear his hard hat or safety goggles, or if he wears thin-soled shoes and steps on a nail, the employer is still liable. As a matter of fact, some states have become so liberal that even if a worker trips and falls on his way to his car he can still collect compensation (compensation laws have also been amended to cover workers against work-connected disease).

The premiums for this coverage vary in the different states, as do the amounts awarded for various kinds of injuries. In some states there is a state compensation fund and every employer must join this fund and pay its premiums as set by the commission that administers the fund. In other states the contractor may purchase the insurance through his own insurance broker in a company of his choice. In all cases the policy limits and rates are set by the law. The contractor is obligated to thoroughly investigate the compensation laws of the state in which he does business. This can be done through a reliable broker *who has experience* in construction insurance.

10.2A. Job Safety

Chapter 7, on field inspection, gives a check list of possibly unsafe conditions on a construction job. These things are under the contractor's control. What he cannot protect himself against are careless workers and careless working habits. *But he can try.*

On large construction jobs no one may enter a building under construction without wearing a hard hat. There are safety posters everywhere. There may even be a part-time or full-time safety man. The smaller contractor can ask his workers to wear goggles when operating a power saw, to wear hard hats and heavy-soled shoes, and not to throw boards with protruding nails just anywhere (the man who throws such a board may be the one to step on it). The contractor can talk to his crew when he distributes the pay checks, he can post safety posters, he can see to it that open stair wells are railed, and so on. If his accident rate is reduced, so is his premium cost. In the past few years a new force for job safety has been introduced. The Occupational Safety and Health Administration (OSHA) is a Federal body created by the Congress. Its inspectors visit construction jobs to check on the Administration's published safety regulations (which can be obtained from the Department of Labor in Washington, D.C.). These inspectors have the power to levy heavy fines or even shut down a job if they find the contractor and his crew in violation of safety regulations and guilty of noncooperation. The contractor is warned that he *must* file accident reports immediately or suffer severe penalties.

10.2B. Workmen's Compensation Rating Systems

Premium rates for compensation are set by compensation rating bureaus of the various states and are reviewed annually. It is a fact that the larger companies obtain better premium rates because: (1) they pay larger amounts and therefore the insurer is better able to absorb the cost of an occasional bad accident, (2) the large contractor enforces safety standards, and (3) the large contractor keeps better payroll and other records so that the carrier itself does not have to audit his books.

It will be recalled that the smaller contractor has been urged to keep good records and enforce safety rules for himself and his workers.

The rate set by the rating bureau for the various trades and kinds of work are based on the overall experience of claims and payments for these trades. These published rates are known as the "Manual Rates." They vary widely from the highest rates for a structural steel worker to a low rate for an office worker. Some trades themselves are subdivided by risk. For instance a painter who paints outside windows from a scaffold carries a much higher rate than one who paints interior walls or ceilings, and a carpenter who shingles a roof carries a higher rate than one who is hanging interior doors or working on trim. *These may be the same person.* The contractor must therefore be very sure that he notes exactly when a single craftsman goes from one job to another in *either direction.* If an audit shows that he is claiming lower rates for high-risk jobs his claims are liable to cancellation.

Premium rates are set by multiplying the worker's weekly pay by the rate set for his classification. As the rate can vary by 7 times from one job to another for the same worker, the contractor is well advised to keep good records of shifts in the work.

One other important factor in setting the individual contractor's rate is his experience rating. It is very obvious that the contractor with a poor accident rating will have to pay more for his insurance than the safe-working contractor. As a matter of fact, if a safety record is too bad the contractor may be refused insurance coverage or can be forced to pay such high rates as to effectively put him out of business.

All contractors pay their compensation insurance premium in advance based on their estimated payroll and the set rate for this kind of work. This deposit premium is audited at the year's end and the contractor must make up the difference, if any.

10.3. BUILDER'S RISK FIRE INSURANCE AND EXTENDED COVERAGE

Builder's risk fire insurance, unless otherwise stated in the contract, is always carried by the owner. The contractor must check to see that he and his subcontractors are named in the policy as their interests appear. The usual form of Builder's Risk policy covers not only the structure in place but also materials and equipment stored on the site. For example:

> This policy covers the (described) building or structure while in course of construction, including additions, attachments, and all permanent fixtures belonging to and constituting a part of said building. . . . This policy also covers temporary structures, materials, equipment and supplies of all kinds incident to the construction of said building or structure . . . only while on the premises or within 100 feet thereof.

Builder's risk insurance automatically cancels when the premises are occupied in whole or in part and the contractor should not allow such occupancy unless there is an endorsement by the insurance carrier specifically allowing such occupancy.

The contractor who engages in alteration work or in an addition to an existing structure is particularly cautioned to see to it that the owner covers this work as an addition to his existing fire insurance policy with a suitable endorsement that covers the contractor, his subcontractors, and all material and equipment stored on the site.

10.3A. Extended Coverage

The usual coverage for fire and lightning does not cover all the risks that can be encountered during the course of a construction job. Therefore a policy can be endorsed to cover certain extra selected risks (at an additional premium). There are, for instance, windstorm, hail, explosion, riot, civil commotion, aircraft, vehicles, smoke. There can also be "named perils" such as vandalism and malicious mischief, flood, and earthquake. There is also an "all risks" policy written which covers almost everything except war, radioactivity, and nuclear fission. But such policies are expensive. The contractor and the owner should agree on what constitutes a reasonable risk and forget the others.

10.3B. Business Interruption Insurance

This can be considered as an extension of the builder's risk coverage. It covers the contractor against loss of earnings caused by a delay in the construction because of fire or other insured peril.

10.3C. The Available Form

One form that can be used on small jobs is called the *straight form*. This policy can be taken for any specified amount and for any specified period of time during the construction period. If the contractor does not make sure that the policy is kept up to date by endorsements for added time or increased value as the construction progresses, he may find that in the event of a loss he is underinsured or not insured at all. This means that the owner or the contractor must make good the loss out of his own pocket. Another form is the *reporting form* of insurance which requires that the contractor advise the insurance carrier of the increased value of the job on a monthly basis. The premium is paid in installments as the value increases. The contractor must report increased values and do it on time in order to be sure that his interest is fully covered.

The third form is the *completed value form*. This type of policy is written at the beginning of the job before the completion of the foundations (which are always excluded in fire insurance coverages except in earthquake areas). It is written for the full amount of the completed value and the premium is payable in a lump sum in advance. This form of insurance saves the contractor and the owner the trouble of reporting the progress of the job and for jobs of short duration is probably the most economical. The premium rate is 55 percent of the rate that would be charged in the reporting form of insurance. This, of course, is because the entire value of the job is covered from the beginning. It is suggested that in earthquake areas the builder make sure that his foundation is covered for its cost through extended coverage.

10.4. CONTRACTOR'S (EMPLOYER'S) LIABILITY INSURANCE

This insurance is written in conjunction with workmen's compensation insurance. It covers the contractor against claims by workers who are not covered by workmen's compensation, which can occur in states where it is not obligatory for the contractor to insure in any particular way. It also protects the contractor against claims by dissatisfied workers that are over and above the awards granted by compensation.

10.5. DISABILITY INSURANCE

Many states now have laws that force an employer to pay disability benefits to employees who are disabled or injured off the job. In some states the contractor is obliged to pay this insurance premium to the state by means of payroll taxes but others allow the employer to carry such insurance in a private company. In construction where there is no steady labor force, the best way to carry this insurance is by means of payroll taxes (if the law allows). In any case the contractor must be sure he is not paying premiums for people who are not working for him.

10.6. PUBLIC LIABILITY AND PROPERTY DAMAGE INSURANCE

This type of insurance comes under a comprehensive general liability policy. The contractor has not only to protect his own employees against loss caused by on-the-job injury (workmen's compensation) but he must also carry insurance to protect himself against the claims for property damage or bodily injury that may be made by the general public. He should not only cover himself against such claims caused by his own actions, but he should also cover himself by contingent liability (see Sec. 10.7) against claims caused by the actions of his subcontractors.

Most construction contracts call for the contractor to carry such insurance and the limits of the coverage are usually defined. Even if they are not, the contractor is well advised to carry a policy with high limits. Jury awards for injury are notoriously high and it is poor economy to skimp on this coverage.

The premiums that are paid for this type of insurance vary with the contractor's experience. As is true for compensation rates, a contractor with a good safety record enjoys a lower rate than the regulation rate. The contractor is advised to carry both his workmen's compensation and his public liability insurance with the same company. Insurance carriers will give more consideration to an employer who carries more than one line of insurance with them.

10.7. CONTINGENT LIABILITY INSURANCE

Contingent liability insurance comes under a comprehensive general liability policy and protects the contractor against bodily-injury or property-damage claims caused by the actions of his subcontractors. Any person who claims injury to person or property caused by an act of the subcontractor can sue both the subcontractor and the prime or general contractor. A worker who is injured on the job may refuse a compensation award and sue both the subcontractor and the general contractor. The premium for this type of insurance is low *if* the general contractor makes sure that all his subcontractors carry public liability and property damage insurance.

10.8. CONTRACTUAL LIABILITY

Many construction contracts contain a clause which states that the contractor must protect the owner (and possibly other parties at interest) against any claims arising from either the contractor or the subcontractor's actions. This clause is commonly known as a "hold harmless" clause and must be written into the contractor's policy. The contractor is warned against including any "hold harmless" clause other than the so-called "limited" one which holds the owner harmless against only the actions of the contractor and his subcontractors. He should avoid any broad forms which say more than this.

10.9. SUBCONTRACTOR'S INSURANCE

In order to protect himself and the owner to whom he is solely responsible, the general contractor should make sure that his subcontractors carry the following insurance:

Workmen's compensation
Employer's liability
Public liability and property damage
Motor vehicle insurance and any other required by law

As a matter of fact, many state laws hold that if the subcontractor does not carry workmen's compensation, then the general contractor assumes full legal liability for any accidents that may occur.

10.10. MOTOR VEHICLE LIABILITY AND OTHER INSURANCE

This insurance comes under the comprehensive general liability policy and covers the contractor against claims arising from injuries to persons or damage to property caused by the contractor's motor vehicles that are used in his work. The policy should cover vehicles, whether owned, nonowned, or hired, which are used during the course of construction. The policy should also cover the contractor's owned vehicles for fire and theft. Collision insurance can also be carried but it is advisable for the contractor if he wishes to avoid very high premiums to include a deductible amount which reduces the net recovery from the insurance company. "Nonowned" vehicles as mentioned above means the vehicles of his employees when they are engaged in the employer's business.* "Hired" vehicles sometimes carry their own liability and property damage insurance. If they do, the contractor can obtain a reduction in his own premium provided certificates evidencing coverage are obtained and filed with the contractor's carrier.

One other important matter is the amount of coverage. As has been stated before, juries sometimes award astounding amounts. Although most contracts state the amounts of personal liability and property damage to be carried, the contractor is advised, if he can afford it, to carry an "umbrella" policy which carries limits over and above his regular policy.

10.11. CONTRACTOR'S OWN INSURANCE

Up to now this chapter has confined itself mainly to the insurance that the contractor must carry to protect the owner and himself against the hazards that are created by the actual construction. This section is about the insurance that the contractor should carry to protect himself as a prudent business man. Some of the coverages that are considered essential are:

- Fire and extended coverage on his own premises.

- Workmen's compensation and contractor's or employer's liability on his employees who are not engaged in actual construction.

- Motor vehicle liability and property damage on vehicles not used in his business. (If the contractor drives his personal automobile to inspect a job, it is considered business.)

- Contractor's equipment floater. This is carried only if the contractor owns heavy, valuable equipment such as cranes or bulldozers which travel from job to job. This policy can cover almost any peril for which the contractor is willing to pay.

- Business interruption insurance covers the contractor against loss of business because of fire or other peril.

10.12. CONSTRUCTION CONTRACT BONDS

10.12A. The Purpose of Bonding

The average small contractor who stays with private work such as residences, small office buildings, or multiple dwellings will seldom run into a requirement that he must be bonded. The contract or surety bond does not provide

---

*If an employee uses his own car to drive to a hardware store for any material to be used on the job and has an accident, it will be covered by the "nonowned" vehicle clause.

any protection for the contractor. What it does is assure the owner that the contractor will carry out the work and deliver it free and clear of liens and encumbrances to the owner, or on the contractor's failure to do so, the bonding company will make good the contract. Before a bonding company will guarantee any such thing it must be sure that the contractor is completely reliable.

10.12B. The Requirements for a Bond

Bonding is always required for public work, and the contractor may sometimes wish to bid on such work. If he does he should know what is required of him before he can obtain such a bond. Following are some of the requirements of the surety company:

1. The surety company will want to know about the professional ability, experience, and reputation of the principal or principals of the firm.

2. It will investigate the volume of work that the contractor has on his books (including the work for which he requires a bond) to determine whether he can handle it all or will get into difficulty.

3. It will want to know about the jobs the contractor has completed that compare in size to this one.

4. It will investigate the adequacy of working capital and the availability of credit. It will want to see a financial statement that is prepared by a certified public accountant. The contractor who deals with a single financial institution which considers his credit a good risk should have no difficulty with this condition.

5. It will want to know how much lower his bid was than the next highest. A swing of over 5 percent is considered dangerous and surety companies will hesitate before granting a bond to such a low bidder.

6. It will want to know how the contractor is to be paid so that an evaluation can be made as to whether he is strong enough to carry the job financially between payments.

10.12C. The Various Kinds of Bonds

10.12C1. THE BID BOND

The bid bond is probably the first type of surety bond that a contractor will encounter. Under this bond the surety company guarantees to the owner that the contractor will honor his bid to construct the building in accordance with this bid if he is awarded the contract within a certain fixed time. If the contractor defaults the surety company is obligated to pay to the owner the difference between the low bid under the bond and the next highest bid which the owner has been able to obtain (in good faith).

10.12C2. THE PERFORMANCE BOND

This bond guarantees that the contractor will perform all the work necessary to complete the building within the terms of his contract. In this case if the contractor defaults during the job the surety company will pay to the owner the difference between the value of the work already completed and the value of the completed job up to an amount equal to the face value of the bond. Many bonding companies will work with a defaulting contractor if they find that he has defaulted through no direct fault of his own. The contractor should always remember that he is liable for any loss to the bonding company.

10.12C3. LABOR AND MATERIAL BOND

This bond is always required when a performance bond is called for. It guarantees payment for labor and material furnished to either the general contractor or his subcontractors. Suppliers of material are specially happy when there is such a bond. This bond also is a partial guarantee against liens.

11

FINANCING A SMALL CONSTRUCTION BUSINESS

11.1. INITIAL FINANCING

If the contractor signs the proper contracts with responsible owners, he will have very little difficulty in financing his operation. This applies to the small contractor who confines himself to additions or alterations and to small projects such as private residences, stores, office buildings, and small multi-family units that are built under contract with an owner. It is the very first financing that is troublesome.

To start with, the contractor should make a budget showing projections of expense and of cash flow (Fig. 11-1). He is now an independent contractor and is no longer on anyone's payroll. All the money he now earns, less his expenses, is his own. But he must have some capital to start with and he should first make a list of his own resources. These resources consist of current assets or liquid assets which are readily convertible to cash, such as savings and checking accounts, stocks and bonds, insurance policies with cash values, and fixed assets such as land, a house, machinery, a truck, etc. Until he obtains his first job the contractor will have to live on his own current assets. From these assets he will have to pay for the following:

His own salary for living expenses
Office rent or taxes and interest on his house (if used as an office)
Electricity and fuel oil
Telephone
Printing and office supplies
Car expenses

This cash outlay will continue until the contractor obtains his first job. Whether it be an addition or alteration or a new house, he knows that he will

155

Assets (liquid)
Cash in bank (savings)
Cash in bank (checking)
Stocks and bonds
Cash values of insurance policies
One-quarter share Uncle Joe's house
(can sell any time)

Assets (fixed)
Automobile
Truck
Tools and equipment

Expenses (business)
Advertising (newspapers, flyers)
Telephone
Extra use of car
Stationery

Furniture
(These figures should represent how
much total money the builder must
spend over a 6-month period.)

Expenses (personal)
Household expenses
Mortgage payments
Taxes
Electricity
Fuel oil
Telephone
Insurance
Car expense (gas and oil)
Miscellaneous expense (clothing,
laundry, etc.)
Medical expense (possible)

Note: The budget should represent very frugal living and a contractor must be able to get by for up to 10 months on this budget if no unexpected bills have to be met.

Figure 11-1   Thomas Jones—balance sheet and budget.

be paid—but when? If the alteration is small, he can bill upon completion or on a larger one he can bill monthly. This means that there will be a lapse of from 2 to 6 weeks after he gets a contract and before he obtains any income. He must be prepared to pay for his living expenses and other fixed charges but in addition lay out money for:

Insurance (public liability and motor vehicle)
Insurance (workmen's compensation if he employs any help)
Advertising for new work
Payroll
Materials, supplies, and equipment

He can obtain credit from a local dealer for 30 days if he can show a contract. He may not have to lay out cash for some of his insurance, but the payroll is payable weekly. Up to this point the contractor may have difficulty in borrowing money from any lending institution and may have to depend on his own resources or on personal loans from friends and relatives.

As a conclusion to this section the contractor is urged to make sure that he has sufficient cash either on hand or readily available, to carry him for at least 6 months and then to add 20 percent to this for unforeseen expenses.

11.2. FINANCING DURING CONSTRUCTION

As soon as the contractor starts working for owners who will pay him at fixed intervals during his work, his ability to obtain credit and loans increases greatly. Certainly on major alterations he should have the method and intervals of payment written into his contract, and if he is building a new house the lending institution will have a fixed method of payments during construction upon which he can depend.

11.2A. The Payment Schedule

All lending institutions have schedules of payments during construction and the contractor can have such a schedule written into his contract. A typical payout schedule is:

1. At the completion of the excavation and foundations and the start of framing

2. At the completion of the framing and the start of rough plumbing and heating

3. When the structure is enclosed and all the mechanical and electrical roughing is complete

4. When lathing and plastering and wallboard are completed and finish carpentry and cabinet work are under way

5. At full completion when a certificate of occupancy is issued

Any of these stages can be combined to make a four-payment plan. The mortgagee will always send someone to inspect the construction before the payment is made. Very often it will also require the approval of the architect (if there is one). The smart contractor will anticipate these payout times by notifying the mortgagee and/or the architect several days before he has reached the point of payment and will make an appointment for that day so that he can be there personally to answer any questions. In this way he can obtain his money several days earlier. This makes for good relations with the mortgagee, and it is good business to obtain cash as early as possible.

11.2B. Working Capital between Payments

One of the most frequent causes of failure in any business, and especially in the construction business, is a shortage of working capital. The amount a contractor requires depends upon the kind of work he is doing. At the beginning of an alteration job or an addition to an existing structure the contractor should prepare, for his own use, a statement of his cash requirements during the job. For example, suppose he obtains a contract to alter a private home in a business zone so that it will comply with the building code for small office buildings. The plans and specifications require him to enclose an open stairway, to provide direct access from the stair to the outside, to shift radiators, to provide an additional toilet, to change the locations of some partitions and to provide new fluorescent ceiling lighting and electrical outlets.

The contractor knows he will require lumber, wallboard, builder's hardware, and other material. He will also have to employ at least two subcontractors—a plumber and an electrician—and a carpenter on his own payroll to help him at least part time. The contract is for $4500 and the contractor estimates that it will be completed in a month or less, at which time he will bill for the job, and he hopes he will be paid not more than two weeks later. In this case he can obtain 30 days credit from the material dealer and can arrange to pay his subcontractors when he is paid. The only extra cash he requires is to pay the part-time carpenter and possibly his insurance coverage. He should certainly be able to manage this without having to borrow money.

While he is performing the alteration, the contractor bids on another job. It is the addition of two rooms and a bath to an existing house plus an alternate price for a major alteration of the kitchen. His bid of $20,000 is accepted. He can wait until he completes the first job before he starts this one—but he should not. The contractor who is willing to complete one job before starting another must also be willing to settle for a day's pay instead of for the profit that can come from a well-managed small construction business. In order to earn such a profit, the contractor should be working on more than one job at any one time. Even in the case of a fairly large job ($50,000+), he should not hesitate to start another job some weeks before the first project is completed. In this way he can keep his good workers and subcontractors.

Instead of waiting, he should start ordering lumber and other material and should complete negotiations with his subcontractors for this new job. He estimates this job will take 10 weeks. He can arrange a four-payment schedule as follows:

- When the excavation and foundation is complete and the framing is well started (first floor joists, exterior studs)—25 percent or $5000

- When the framing is complete, the heating and plumbing roughing is complete, and the structure is enclosed and weathertight—25 percent or $5000

- When the electrical roughing is complete, the wallboard is complete, the flooring is complete, and the finish trim is well underway—25 percent or $5000

- At completion and on the issuance of a certificate of occupancy—25 percent or $5000

This schedule is designed to bring in a periodic supply of money that should enable the contractor to partially keep pace with his obligations to pay his workers, subcontractors, and material dealer. Also, during the progress of this job, the contractor has collected his $4500 from the alteration, and after paying for his material and his subcontractors he should have about $1500, which includes 4 weeks pay plus profit (if he estimated correctly and came within the estimate). The contractor should now make up a schedule showing his cash payments for payroll, his commitments for lumber, material, subcontractors, insurance, etc., and when he expects to be paid.

11.2B1. SCHEDULING CASH FLOW

The cash flow chart (Fig. 11-2) shows the following:

- *Column 2, Cash outlay.* This is out-of-pocket expense which has to be met weekly. It includes the contractor's drawing account of $200 plus any payroll which must be paid in cash when due. It will be noted that the contractor in this example has employed a craftsman to help him complete the Keyes alteration before he gets involved in the Addis addition. The payroll expense then keeps on going through the first 7 weeks of the Addis job.

- *Column 3, Committed.* This column shows the amounts of the lumber and other materials that the contractor has ordered for his own use plus the amount of the subcontracts he has sublet. This is a list of all his obligations.

- *Column 4, Date due.* This column shows the dates when lumber bills, subcontractor bills, and all other obligations are due.

- *Column 5, Paid.* When the various bills are paid (and in order to build a good credit record the bills should be paid when due), the amount of these bills is added to Column 2, Cash outlay, and the total is entered in *Column 6., Total cash paid.*

- *Column 7, Cash received.* The contractor should enter in this column the amounts of money he expects to receive for his work and when he expects to receive it. The contractor is warned to allow a week or so of leeway between the time when he thinks he should be paid and when he is paid.

						Total		Total	
Week No.	Date ①	Cash outlay ②	Committed ③	Date due ④	Paid ⑤	cash paid ⑥	Cash received ⑦	cash received ⑧	Cash balance ⑨
0	Keyes 1/2					Col. 2+5			Col. 8 / Col. 6
1	1/9	200.	$2700. (K) Lumber, Bus. etc.			200.	0		−200
2	1/16	200.				400.	0		−400
3	Addie 1/23	200. PR 200 (K)	$250 Insurance		$250	1050.	0		−1050
4	1/30	200. PR 250(AD)	3800. (AD) Lumber, Excav.			1500.	0		−1500
5	2/6	200. PR 200 (AD)	4500. (AD) Plumbing Elect.	$2700. (K)	$2700. (K)	4600.	4500. (K)	4500.	−100.
6	2/13	200 PR.300(AD)				5100.	4500.	4500.	−600.
7	2/20	200 PR.300(AD)	2500. (AD) Lumber, Tiling Board			5600.	5000. #1 ADD	9500.	+3900.
8	2/27	200. PR 450(AD)		$3800 (AD)	3800. (AD)	10,050.	0	9500.	−550.
9	3/5	200. PR 200(AD)		$4500(AD)	4500. (AD)	14,950.	0	9500.	−5450
10	3/12	200. PR 200(AD)				15,350.	5000. #2 ADD	14,500.	−850.
11	3/19	200.		$2500 (AD)	2500. (AD)	18,500.	0	14,500.	−3550.
12	3/26	200.				18,250.	5000. #3 ADD	19,500.	+1250.

Figure 11-2

- *Column 9, Cash balance.* This column shows the difference between what the contractor has paid out (Column 6), and the amount he has received (Column 8).

It can be seen from this sample chart that payments do not always come in time to pay payrolls and bills when they are due. This is the time when the contractor must make up the temporary shortage in cash from his own capital and it is also a good time for the contractor to think about borrowing money in order to keep his cash flow secure and in order to build up his credit standing. It will be noted that on the seventh week in Fig. 11-2 there is a cash balance of $3900, but this becomes a minus $5450 by the ninth week. It is true it will be for only a short time, but it provides the perfect opportunity for the contractor to approach his local bank for a short-term loan.

The contractor has completed one job successfully, is working on a second job under contract and has bid on a third job which he hopes to get. He has made a profit on his first job and his inflow of cash for the second job is assured. If the lending institution is the one with which he has been doing business, the contractor should have very little trouble in borrowing up to $5000 for 60 days. He knows he can repay it on time. If in the meantime he is awarded another contract he has every possibility of renewing the period of the loan. This type of financing is an excellent way of building a credit rating. This is one of the more important things the contractor must do if he wishes to build a successful contracting business.

There are other financial advantages of borrowing besides the building up of a credit rating. Even in these days of high bank interest, borrowed funds can earn a higher rate of interest when used in the contractor's business. There is also a tax advantage because the interest paid on borrowed money is tax deductible. A third reason is that the borrowed funds can be used to pay material bills within 10 days and thereby gain a 2 percent discount or they can be used to build an inventory of equipment that may be advantageous in gaining future work. Borrowed funds also give the contractor more flexibility than using his own capital. He can pay off a loan when he does not require the money rather than have his own money tied up over a period of time when it could be earning interest from outside investment.

11.3. HOW AND WHEN TO BORROW WORKING CAPITAL

11.3A. The Basic Information That All Lenders Require

In order to borrow money, the contractor must be able to furnish complete information about himself and his business. Such information would include a financial statement or a balance sheet (usually prepared by an accountant), a profit-and-loss statement, and the contractor's record in paying his bills. Even if this is the first time the contractor has asked for a loan, he will certainly have a credit rating on installment payments, mortgage payments, credit card payments, personal loan payments, etc. The lender will also want to know about the work in progress, the work that has been completed, and the prospects for future work. The lender may also want to see a projected financial statement for the period to be covered by the loan.

11.3B. The Kinds of Loans That Are Available

11.3B1. THE COLLATERAL LOAN

It is possible that the lender, especially in the case of a small new business, may require collateral. This means that the loan is secured not by the business in hand and the contractor's past record of meeting his obligations, but by the cash value of an insurance policy, stocks and bonds, improved real estate (his home), and savings accounts. The contractor should resist such a loan. Illness or death or any unforeseen catastrophe can cause the loss of a home or the loss of long-time savings. Since it is a secured loan, the basic information in Sec. 11.3A is not required. It is better to ride through a short period of financial stringency than to take such a loan.

11.3B2. THE PERSONAL OR CHARACTER LOAN

This is an unsecured loan which is based on the lender's appraisal of the contractor's ability to pay it back when called for. In this case the lender will want all the information he can get about the contractor as noted in Sec. 11.3A. Such loans to a small business will usually run from 30 to 90 days before they come due. Banks which are acquainted with the contractor through having had his accounts or perhaps through paid-off automobile loans or home-improvement loans will always give a sympathetic hearing to a request for a short-term loan for the purpose of providing a cash flow for a going business. It is well for the prospective borrower to confine his accounts and his personal borrowings to a single bank in order to build a credit and character record. The contractor must also remember that he is personally responsible for the repayment of such a loan.

11.3B3. THE REVOLVING CREDIT LOAN

This type of loan is also known as a "line-of-credit loan". It is rarely used by the small custom builder. It is granted to contractors who have a good record of profitable building over a period of at least 3 or more years. In this case the bank agrees to lend the contractor up to, say, $50,000 for a period of one year. He can then borrow and repay the amount of cash he requires at any time during the year, but can never have more than $50,000 outstanding at any one time. At the end of the period he must either get an extension or repay the entire outstanding balance of the loan.

11.3B4. THE INSTALLMENT LOAN

This is somewhat the same as an installment loan on a car. This loan is discounted in advance, i.e., the lender takes all of his interest for the entire term of the loan out of the face value of the loan before the contractor (borrower) gets the money. The contractor then pays it back in monthly installments. Very often, if the contractor has been faithful in his payments, when the loan is paid down he may be able to get it refinanced for an additional term and at a more favorable interest rate. This is almost the same as a line-of-credit loan.

11.3B5. THE ACCOUNTS-RECEIVABLE LOAN

This is not the type of loan a small contractor would ordinarily take. Here is an example of how it works, however. If the contractor has a sum of money owed to him by a credit-worthy client who for one reason or another is delaying the payment, and if the contractor has to meet payrolls or material bills that are due now, he can borrow money from a bank by pledging the accounts receivable. For instance, if he is owed $5000 he can usually borrow about $4000 from a bank to pay his bills and repay the bank when he receives the money from his client.

11.4. THE SOURCES OF FUNDS

There are a great many sources of funds for the contractor who has started a small construction business and can show a record of contracts which have been performed on time and with a profit.

11.4A. The Small Business Administration

This is a federal agency which was formed to help small businesses that cannot otherwise obtain financing from regular lending institutions. It is more suited for the use of a speculative builder who requires larger amounts of money than the custom builder. It will be discussed in the second portion of this book under speculative building.

11.4B. The Local Bank or Building and Loan

These represent the most reliable sources of funds. The kind of loans they will make has been discussed in Sec. 11.3.

11.4C. The Equity Loan

This is a loan usually made by friends or relatives who will invest in your business to obtain a share of the profits. The terms and conditions of such loans are subject to negotiation. The contractor is warned to be very careful about taking this kind of loan unless he is willing to have a "partner" who may give him a lot of advice!

11.4D. Miscellaneous

There are also equipment loans which can be obtained from a bank or from the company selling the equipment. Such loans from the manufacturer or agent are usually sold to finance companies whose interest rates are much higher than those charged by banks.

There are also venture capital loans which will be discussed in Part 2 of this book.

12

THE LEGAL ASPECTS
OF CONSTRUCTION

12.1. WHAT IS INVOLVED

The contractor who is conducting a small construction business does not have to be a legal expert. But he certainly should be familiar with the laws, regulations, ordinances, etc., that relate to the construction business, and he should be familiar with their intent. Some laws, while not related to the building business as such, are related to business in general. Some of these latter are the laws regarding income tax, Social Security tax, sales tax, workmen's compensation laws, the law of contracts, labor laws, and laws regarding the organization of a business. Then there are other legal requirements and ordinances that refer directly to construction. These include such items as permits, licensing, highway use requirements, and building and zoning codes.*

While this chapter will provide a sufficient outline of the various laws, etc., with which the contractor should be familiar, it in no way intends to replace the services of an attorney who specializes in this field.

12.2. THE BUSINESS ORGANIZATION

This book is addressed to the building contractor who is in business for himself. From the legal standpoint he is solely responsible for the obligations of the business. Any profit or loss is his alone. This type of business organization is known as a sole proprietorship. The only money in the business is from the owner's own capital or the money he may be able to borrow from banks or other lenders, or his own friends and relatives. Any obligations he incurs while doing business must be paid for out of the profits of the business or from assets, even including any real property he may own.

*Building and zoning codes will be discussed in Chaps. 13 and 14.

He can draw as much money as he wants from the business, but if, as a result of this, he cannot pay his bills, then his creditors have the legal right to attach anything he owns.

If the contractor desires, he can do business under a firm name. Joseph Smith can call his company the Apex Construction Company. Depending on where he is located, the law may require that he file a certificate showing that he is the person that owns the company. This certificate, which gives the name of the company and Joseph Smith's name and address, may have to be filed with the office of the county clerk or other official and it becomes a public record. He may also have to file a copy with his bank and to post a notice in his office so that everyone doing business with him will know that Joseph Smith is the sole owner of the Apex Construction Company and therefore legally liable for its obligations.

There are, of course, many other forms of ownership such as partnerships or incorporated businesses, but the laws regarding these vary widely and the contractor is advised that the only way to protect his personal interest in such ownerships is to employ an attorney.

12.3. THE TAX LAWS

12.3A. Internal Revenue Service

The federal income tax is one that is familiar to everyone in the country. But there are certain regulations that apply to a sole proprietorship with which the contractor as a businessman should be familiar even though he will (if his business prospers) have to employ a bookkeeper and an accountant to keep his records and prepare his tax returns. As the sole owner of the business he pays income tax based on his entire income whether it be income from investments, income from outside activities, or income from his business, all of which are added together. Chapter 9 describes the records that are necessary in order for him to determine his business profits. In addition to his own tax liability, the contractor must withhold income tax from his employees. The amount of such withholding depends on the allowance claimed by each employee on a W-4 form, which must also note the employee's Social Security number. The money that is withheld must be paid over to the designated IRS depository on a quarterly basis.

12.3B. Social Security

In addition to withholding income tax from his employees' pay, the contractor must also withhold money for Social Security, as required by the Federal Insurance Contributions Act (FICA). The contractor must not only withhold the proper amount from his employees' pay but must also match these contributions with his own money. These withheld and employer-contributed funds must be reported and deposited quarterly in a designated federal depository. In addition, the self-employed contractor must pay FICA tax on the income from his business. This is known as the "self-employment tax." This of course, at a later time, makes him eligible for Social Security benefits.

12.3C. Federal Unemployment Tax

Any contractor whose payroll exceeds $1500 in any one calendar quarter or who has had someone on his payroll for at least part of a day for any 20 calendar weeks is subject to the Federal Unemployment Tax Act (FUTA). The FUTA tax is not deductible from employees' wages, but is a percentage of the total payroll.

12.3D. State or Municipal Income Taxes

Many states and even municipalities now levy some form of income tax. Although the tax structure has many variants, many of such taxes are levied on the total combined income of the businessman-contractor. State and municipal taxes are deductible from the federal income tax as business expenses.

12.3E. Sales Taxes and Personal Property Taxes

Most states now levy sales taxes on all the material the contractor has to purchase. Many states also levy personal property taxes on the contractor's equipment, larger power tools and his motor vehicles. The sales taxes on the material and the personal property taxes on the equipment which is used by the contractor in his business may both be deductible on his federal tax as a business expense.

It is hoped that the contractor is aware of the taxes he is called upon to pay when he estimates a job. These are all overhead expense.

12.4. GENERAL BUSINESS LAWS

12.4A. Insurance

Insurance has been discussed in Chap. 10. A great deal of insurance coverage is voluntary, but there are some forms of insurance that are mandated by law. An example of this is workmen's compensation insurance and some forms of liability insurance.

12.4B. Labor Laws

If the contractor plans to employ outside help, he should be familiar with the labor laws. Most states have their own labor laws. These refer to safe working conditions, to maximum permitted hours of work, and to the employment of minors and women. There are variations in these laws, and the contractor should become familiar with the laws of the state in which he works. There is always the possibility of a labor department inspector dropping in.

The federal labor laws to a great extent confine themselves generally to national labor problems. The National Labor Relations Act and the Taft-Hartley Act may be quoted as examples. These have to do with union representation and other matters which are not of great concern to the small contractor. Then there is the Fair Labor Standard Act which covers the legal minimum wages that can be paid, a definition of which categories of workers are covered under the act (which under new amendments consist of practically everybody who works), a definition of what constitutes a work week and when overtime must be paid, child labor provisions, and what records must be kept. There are also Fair Employment Practices laws and regulations. These bar discrimination in hiring practice based on race, creed, color, or national origin. This law is especially effective in any work involving any governmental body.

Last but far from least is the recently enacted Ocupational Safety and Health Act (OSHA). This law, which is exactly what its name implies, is administered by the United States Department of Labor, and its provisions for workers' safety are strictly enforced. This act overrides state laws referring to its subject matter.

12.4C. The Law of Contracts

12.4C1. A DEFINITION

A contract has been defined as an agreement enforceable by law. In order to be so enforceable, the contract must consist of an *offer and an acceptance.* It is not enough for the contractor to assume that he has been awarded a job because of what the owner has said, nor is he legally guaranteed the job even if the owner puts it in writing but he (the contractor) has not formally accepted it. The contractor may order materials and prepare to perform the work based on the owner's say so, but if the contractor has not signified his acceptance the owner can still change his mind.

12.4C2. HOW DISSENSION CAN BE AVOIDED

It is best and safest to have all agreements in writing. The contractor should make his bid in writing (this is an *offer*), but he should not start any work until the owner has *accepted* the offer in writing. This avoids one of the most frequent causes of dissension between the owner and the contractor. To repeat—if the contractor states clearly what work he intends to do and for how much (see Chap. 3), and if the owner accepts this offer in writing, there is very little likelihood that there will be any arguments.

12.4C3. CHANGE ORDERS

Another cause for argument is the change order, which occurs especially often in residential construction. The owner or the architect may not like the size of a room or the kitchen layout and may ask the contractor to make a change. If the contractor proceeds on the basis of such a verbal order he does so at his own risk. There has been no offer and no acceptance. The contractor should make an estimate of his cost, should put it in writing on his letterhead, and should have the owner sign it.

12.4C4. DELAYS IN THE WORK

Delay in the performance of the work can become a legal matter. After the work has started, if the owner for some reason decides to halt the job for a period of time, the contractor has every right to establish a claim for losses caused by the delay. These losses must be documented. On the other hand, an owner can also sue a contractor for unwarranted delays if he (the owner) can establish loss. Very often the delay is not caused by the contractor himself but by one of his subcontractors or material dealers. This becomes a "tricky" legal problem which often leads to endless law suits. This liability for delay very rarely arises in small jobs. In larger work the contractor is advised to have a clause inserted in his contract which holds him harmless against any claims for delay caused by circumstances beyond his control.

12.4C5. PAYMENTS

The contractor must be sure that his contract calls for interim payments as the work progresses. If it does not, he may find that he is not entitled to any payment until the work is completed. Where there is an institutional mortgage there will be a plan of payment as various portions of the work are completed. The contractor must be sure that this payment plan is included in his contract. In the case of large alterations or other work for which the owner is to pay directly, there should be a clause in the contract that calls for monthly payments for the work in place.

Failure to make these provisions can cause serious loss through high interest rates on loans to bridge the cash flow gap until the contractor can obtain his payment.

12.4C6. ERRORS IN BIDDING

It is possible that a contractor who is distracted or makes a mistake in arithmetic when he is making up his bid may submit a bid which is lower than he intended. If he discovers the error before the owner has accepted it he can withdraw the bid without penalty. If the owner accepts it before the error is discovered, it becomes another matter. In most cases the contractor can convince the owner that he has made an honest mistake. If he cannot do this and the owner insists that the work be done at the price quoted, the contract becomes a case for arbitration or for a law suit. Courts have held that if the contractor can prove that he has made an honest mistake and that no damage has been caused to the owner, the contractor need not perform. The best way to avoid all this is for the contractor to go over his bid very carefully immediately after he has submitted it, when the "pressure is off."

12.4C7. BREACH OF CONTRACT

The breaking of a contract by a contractor is extremely difficult. Difficulties in obtaining material or labor or financing are not sufficient grounds. The contractor must show that it was impossible to perform the work because of a catastrophe beyond his control.

If an owner breaches a contract by stopping the work completely or by nonpayment of money as called for by the contract, the contractor can not only collect for all of the work he has performed and for much of the material delivered but also for his lost overhead and profit.

If the contractor breaches the contract, the owner is entitled to collect sufficient money to complete the work as called for in the contract at the best price he can obtain from another contractor. The owner is also entitled to collect all the money he has paid the original contractor over and above the value of the work in place.

12.4C8. THE CONTRACTOR'S LIABILITY FOR POOR DESIGN

Chapter 2 of this book contains a sketch that a builder might make for a client who wants to add a room to his house. The owner does not wish to employ an architect for such a small job and he confines himself to telling the contractor what he wants, leaving it pretty much to the contractor to design it as well as build it. This happens many times in alteration work and can even happen in the case of a small house.

The contractor should know that when he does this he is assuming responsibility not only for the construction but for the design. In the great majority of such deals no difficulty is encountered. But should there be any defects in the construction caused by faulty design, then the contractor has to make it good at his own expense.

12.4C9. CONTRACTOR'S RESPONSIBILITY FOR CHANGES IN BUILDING CODE

This situation rarely arises in small construction jobs but it does happen that a town will adopt changes in its building code during the course of construction. This may occur because of pressure from state or federal authorities.

Specifications always state that all work must conform to all codes and to all the rules and regulations of all governmental and other authorities having jurisdiction. Who then is responsible for the possible extra cost involved in conforming to the new rules? Unfortunately it is the contractor. When he signs a contract obligating himself to conform to all codes, rules, etc., it means just that, and he must comply at no expense to the owner.

12.5. ARBITRATION

12.5A. Why Arbitration?

The preceding section defined the various difficulties which can be encountered in the course of a construction contract. The contractor was warned about these difficulties and was given some cautionary advice on how to avoid them. The difficulties mentioned, however, were the ones most frequently encountered. There are many more, but to go into these would require this to become a law book. In settling these claims and counterclaims several methods can be used, the most evident one being direct negotiation between the contractor and the owner. If the architect or engineer is brought in to settle the dispute, he can settle matters relating to quality or quantity of materials, standards of workmanship and the interpretation of the plans and specifications. However, he cannot settle questions of law involving such matters as the interpretation of the contract, breach of contract, errors in bidding, and others which require legal interpretation.

There are then only two ways to settle disputes which involve legal as well as construction matters. One is to go to law and the courts. With crowded calendars in the courts and the possibility of protracted legal maneuvering, this method is time-consuming and expensive. The other way of settling disputes is through arbitration. This is recommended as a relatively quick and inexpensive way of settling construction quarrels.

12.5B. The Arbitration Process

All contracts for large construction projects contain clauses which state that in case of dispute between owner and contractor, the dispute will be submitted to arbitration. A typical clause in a large contract will state, "Any dispute, claim or question arising between the Owner and the General Contractor under the Contract shall be submited to arbitration under the Construction Industry Rules of the American Arbitration Association."* This clause is applicable to any contract, no matter what its size. But the clause need not even be written into the contract. All that is required is that both parties to the dispute agree to submit their case to arbitration. This must be done in

*The American Arbitration Association has offices in 22 major cities.

writing and the contractor should note that the decision of the arbitrators is binding on both parties and will be upheld by the courts.

The way to start the process is to apply to the nearest office of the American Arbitration Association. The Association will submit a list of names. The contractor can choose one and the owner can choose one. Usually the two then choose a third arbitrator. The time and place of the hearing is set and the owner and contractor may bring their respective evidence to the hearing. They also can be represented by counsel. There are some fees involved but they are relatively small.

The contractor will find that the arbitrators are either architects, engineers, contractors or others of high standing in their community who are familiar with all aspects of construction.

12.6. LIEN LAWS

The word "lien" means a charge on real or personal property for the satisfaction of a debt. It was originally applied to the right of a creditor to retain property of a debtor as security for a debt owed him by the debtor on this property.

The particular portion of the lien laws which concerns the contractor is the mechanics lien law. This was created to protect the rights of the worker for compensation due him for having added to the value of real estate by performing work or supplying material or both. The lien laws in general now cover general contractors, subcontractors and material suppliers. Some states have amended the law further to include architects, engineers, surveyors, and landscape architects. Each state has its own lien laws and the contractor should employ counsel who is familiar with the law to make sure that his rights are protected.

12.6A. Some General Provisions

The mechanics lien actually gives workers, contractors, etc., a claim on the real property on which they have done work or for which they have supplied material. In some states this lien, if properly filed, has precedence over the mortgage. In other states it is inferior only to the mortgage. All liens filed against a property have equal rights except the lien for wages, which takes precedence over all other liens.

12.6A1. FILING A LIEN

State laws provide that a person claiming the lien must file his claim in a designated public office (usually with the town clerk) and personally on the owner or his agent within a certain time (usually 60 to 90 days) after the last of the claimant's work has been completed. The lien must state in detail what work or material the worker or contractor has performed or delivered and what amount he is claiming for it. The contractor must be sure that the work he has done on the property has been done with the consent of the owner of the property or his accredited agent. If he cannot prove this the contractor's lien rights may be jeopardized.

After filing a lien the contractor must start legal action within a designated time (usually 1 year) to foreclose the lien. This is the same as a mortgage and means that if the owner cannot satisfy the lien, the property must be sold.

12.6A2. WAIVER OF LIENS

Most construction contracts require the contractor to furnish the owner with a complete release of liens. This means that, if the general contractor signs such a release, he has given up all his rights to file such a lien. The contractor is therefore warned that he must not sign such a release unless he has received prior releases of liens from all of his subcontractors and suppliers of material. Sometimes it is difficult for the contractor to obtain such releases in writing. In that case, if the contractor has asked them in writing to sign such a waiver before they have accepted a subcontract or purchase order, they are held by law to have agreed to the release.

By signing a release of lien, the contractor has not given up his rights to be paid for his work. If the owner defaults on his payments the contractor can always sue him for breach of contract and collect his money through the courts.

12.6A3. STATE LAWS

As previously mentioned, each state has its own variations of the mechanics lien law. That is why it is necessary to have an attorney in order to file a lien in accordance with the state requirements. Some state laws favor the contractor more than others. In some states the contractor's interest is protected to the point where, if he performs work on any structure on a piece of land, his lien will hold against the owner's interest in all the land on which the structure is located. Most laws also state that the owner may withhold money from the general contractor if the owner is notified by subcontractors or material men that they have not been paid. The owner has the right to pay them directly.

12.7. LOCAL LAWS

A contractor who intends to perform work in any village, town or city must become familiar with the rules of the building department having jurisdiction. Many smaller towns do not have a local building official and are supervised by a county building department. There are, however, certain legal requirements that are common to all communities. They all require that:

- The contractor or the owner file for a building permit, for which a fee is charged

- The building contracting trades comply with state licensing laws

- The contractor or his subcontractor obtain a street-opening permit for the purpose of connecting to sewer, water, or electric lines

- The construction comply with the building and zoning codes having jurisdiction

- The contractor obtain a final certificate of occupancy before the owner can occupy the new construction

There may be other requirements but the foregoing are the important ones. Of course, one of the most important requirements is that the contractor be thoroughly familiar with the local building and zoning codes and that he acquire this familiarity before he commences any construction. The use of nonacceptable material or the violation of a side- or front-yard requirement can cause the contractor expensive trouble. In extreme cases he could even be forced to tear down what he has built. Chapters 13 and 14 will discuss building and zoning codes.

13

ANALYSIS OF ZONING CODES

13.1. THEIR GENERAL PURPOSE

In the normal course of his work, the small contractor does not have to be overly concerned with zoning regulations. It is assumed that he is building on contract from plans or is making alterations to existing structures. If there is no architect, he should make sure that the owner has ascertained that the new house or addition complies with local zoning. It is when the contractor starts building on his own in speculative ventures that he must become thoroughly familiar with zoning. The regulations will tell him what he can build and where he can build it.

Zoning regulations are designed to protect the general welfare and character of a community and, incidentally, the builder's own investment. Following are excerpts from the preamble of a zoning code:

- To guide future growth and development . . .

- To provide adequate light, air and privacy and to prevent overcrowding of the land and undue concentration of population . . .

- To protect and conserve the value of land and buildings appropriate to the various zones . . .

- To limit development to an amount commensurate with the availability and capacity of public facilities and services . . .

- To conserve and protect all of the natural resources including land, soil, ponds and lakes, wetlands, . . .

These purposes were excellent in their original concept but there are communities that have used them for restrictive purposes. The builder or developer or any group that feels that it has been unduly discriminated

175

against can bring a court action. Many code restrictions have been overturned by the courts.

13.2. TYPICAL REQUIREMENTS

13.2A. Zone Classification or Districts

Every zoning ordinance starts by defining the districts into which the community is divided and provides a zoning map which outlines the boundaries of these districts. The first step, then, in examining the requirements of the ordinance is to determine the district in which the site is located.

Some localities may have as many as eight single-family residential districts, each with its own requirements. Multiple-dwelling areas are included in the residential zones and are defined by the allowable density of population. Some regulations permit the merging of certain types of business zones into the higher-density residential zones. They may set aside small areas in residential districts for retail business or small office structures.

Business zones are also divided into various use areas. And so are industrial zones.

13.2B. Residential Zoning Requirements

The requirements for minimum land area and the amount of such area that can be covered by buildings vary widely between cities and smaller towns. Because land values in cities are much higher than those in small communities, the cities allow smaller lots and a much higher density of population.

For instance the minimum land area and maximum coverage in three different communities are as follows for a single-family residential area—highest zone:

- Large city: Land area 6250 sq ft   Maximum coverage 50%
- Medium city: Land area 7500 sq ft   Maximum coverage 50%
- Small town: Land area from 2 to 4 acres Maximum coverage 20%

All small towns do not have the extreme limitations shown in the last example but many have 1-acre zoning. Following are paraphrases of actual zoning codes.

13.2B1. RESIDENTIAL—MEDIUM ZONE*

Large city. 2500 sq ft of land per dwelling unit is the minimum land area allowed in this zone. The floor area ratio is 0.7, which means that a structure

---

*"Medium zone" is not called by this name in any code, but all codes classify areas by allowable land areas and density, and a "medium area" is one that is somewhere between the most restrictive and the least restrictive.

built on this lot can have a gross floor area of only seven-tenths of the land area. A single-family house on 2500 sq ft of land can therefore contain 2500 × 0.7 or 1750 sq ft gross.

Medium-sized city. A medium-zoned district requires a minimum land area of 3500 sq ft per dwelling unit and a minimum lot area of 6000 sq ft. There is no floor area ratio, but the regulation allows no more than 30 percent land coverage. Therefore the builder can erect a single-family house of a total gross area of 6000 × 30% or 1800 sq ft. If he wants to build a two-family house, he must have 3500 sq ft of land per dwelling unit, or 7000 sq ft of land.

Small town. In this particular town a medium district requires a minimum lot area of 10,000 sq ft per dwelling unit and a maximum land coverage of 25 percent.

13.2B2. MULTIPLE DWELLINGS

There are some smaller communities which do not allow any multiple dwellings at all. Many others will not allow multiple dwellings in their highest-grade residential zones. Even large cities have severe requirements on how much land a builder must use per family unit. The reason, of course, is to restrict the density of population and preserve some open land.

Large city. Some large cities do not allow any multiple dwellings in the two highest residential zones. In a residential zone which does allow such dwellings, the minimum land area required could be as much as 2500 sq ft per residential unit. Figure 13-1 shows a lot that measures 100 ft front by 250 ft in depth. According to the code, the builder can construct 10 family units (25,000 sq ft divided by 2500 sq ft per family unit equals 10). According to the front-side and rear-yard requirements, shown on the illustration, the builder can cover 17,600 sq ft of area, and if he builds a two-story structure he can build a total gross area of 17,600 × 2 or 35,200 sq ft. *But* on a 25,000 sq ft plot, he can only house 10 family units. Obviously 35,200 sq ft is too much building for 10 families. He is forced therefore to provide more open space.

Medium-sized city. Some medium-sized cities do not allow any multiple dwellings in any of their higher residential zones. In a residential zone that does allow multiple dwellings, there is a requirement for 3500 sq ft per family residential unit, 2500 sq ft for an efficiency unit (one bedroom) and 1750 sq ft for an elderly-housing unit (one bedroom). Maximum allowable land coverage is 30 percent.

If the 25,000 sq ft plot in Fig. 13-1 is used, then the builder can build 10 *efficiency* units (2500 sq ft per unit) and he can cover 30 percent of 25,000 sq ft or 7500 sq ft. The remaining land (25,000 minus 7500 sq ft) can be used for parking and planting.

Small town. When a small town allows multiple dwellings at all, the zoning code is very strict in its requirements for open space, lot coverage, height, and bulk. In this particular town, there is a minimum lot requirement of 11,250 sq ft with a minimum frontage of 100 ft and a density requirement

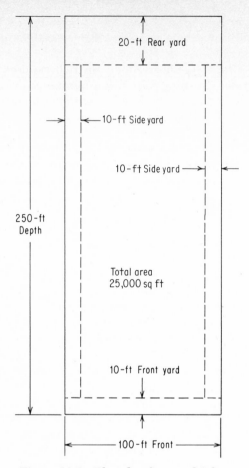

Figure 13-1   Plot plan for a multiple dwelling in a large city. There are 80 ft in width and 220 ft in depth available for building—or 17,600 sq ft. But there can be only 10 apartments on a plot that has a total area of 25,000 sq ft.

of only one family unit for every 3750 sq ft of lot area. Each family unit must consist of at least 750 sq ft.

In addition to the above there must be a recreational area of at least 200 sq ft per family unit and one car space per family unit. In this case, if the builder wishes to house 10 families, he must acquire 10 × 3750 or 37,500 sq ft of land. The minimum frontage required is 100 ft, but this would produce a long narrow lot which might be difficult to work with. Figure 13-2 shows a plot of 150-ft frontage by 250-ft depth. When the minimum side, front, and rear yards are taken out of the land area, there is still ample land to move around in, with plenty of room for the recreational requirement of 200 sq ft per family and even for covered garages, which can be a source of additional income.

A builder who does not wish to go into anything this large can build a lesser number of units in a smaller plot.

13.2B3. OTHER USES PERMITTED IN RESIDENTIAL ZONES

The term "single-family residential area" is to some extent a misnomer. All such areas allow other uses which are compatible with residential use but

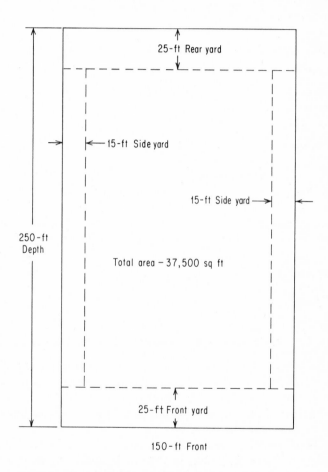

Figure 13-2   Plot plan for a multiple dwelling in a small town. A 10-unit building can be built anywhere in this envelope of 120 × 200 = 24,000 sq ft. The entire structure cannot cover more than 30 percent of 37,500 sq ft (11,250 sq ft).

which may not be compatible with the builder's future use of the land. When the builder is purchasing land he must therefore be aware of such possible use of the land, and this is especially true when there is a good deal of underdeveloped land around his proposed purchase. Such permitted uses in the *highest* residential zone could be:

> Public schools
> Public parks and playgrounds
> Private schools
> Professional offices housed in residences
> Churches and parish houses
> Clubs
> Golf courses
> Reservoirs and dams
> Public utility substations that serve the area
> Pumping stations
> Fire houses
> Post offices

Some communities allow these uses as "of right," others allow them only under special permit. The larger the community, the more the uses that are allowed.

It is to be noted that the above uses are allowed in the highest residential zones. As the required minimum lot areas go down and the allowable density increases, more uses are allowed, especially in the medium and large cities. Such uses may include local shopping, two-story store and office buildings, and two-story professional buildings. The builder must be careful about the possible future uses of the surrounding land.

13.2C. Business Zone—Requirements

Zoning regulations for business very rarely mention required land areas. Instead of a positive land area, business zoning limits certain zones to certain types of business use and then limits the area of the space that can be occupied by these businesses. Communities allow certain businesses in the lower grade of residential zones.

Local retail district. Some communities allow such a district to be used for convenience shopping with no establishment to be over 6500 sq ft. Such retail zones are usually restricted to main thoroughfares.

Restricted retail district. Other communities will allow a facility to cater to the needs of a larger population with single establishments limited to 12,500 sq ft.

These districts also have limited floor area ratios so that no one can build a high-rise anywhere in a local retail district.

Even small-town zoning will allow limited business uses in the lower grades of residential areas. Such business use, however, is confined to convenience shopping, professional offices, and even these uses are sharply limited by the allowable size of the single business enterprise.

13.2D. Other Requirements

In addition to the provisions for minimum land areas and maximum coverage of the land, either by a percentage or by a limited floor area ratio, codes give lists of permitted uses in each district. They also give the minimum allowance for side yards, front yards, and rear yards in these districts. All codes stipulate the allowable minimum of parking by size of building and its use and now many codes are concerning themselves with land fill, wetlands, and other environmental concepts.

13.3. ZONING CODES IN VARIOUS SITUATIONS

It would be impossible in a book of this size to list all the variations in zoning codes, and for the purposes of the smaller contractor it is not necessary. The best way to illustrate how a code works is by some examples.

13.3A. An Addition to a Private Residence in a Small Town

The contractor is called in to add two rooms and a bath to an existing private residence. There is no architect, but the owner has drawn a dimensioned sketch to show what he wants and has told the contractor what materials he wants to have and what existing windows, doors, hardware he wants to match. The contractor feels he has enough information to estimate the cost. There are several important matters, however, that may now be left in the hands of the contractor in cooperation with the owner. Plans must be filed (including a building plan and a plot plan), and a permit must be obtained to confirm that in the opinion of the local building official the plans comply with the building code and the zoning code.

The contractor should not, however, file a plan "cold" without knowing what these codes require, and if he intends to run a successful business he should not have to throw himself entirely into the hands of a building official. Chapter 14 of this book will explain the general provisions of a building code. The zoning regulations are meant to be easy to understand, and it is a simple matter once the contractor has gotten the hang of it to follow through, especially for smaller structures. The examples following are taken from specific zoning codes.

First, the contractor locates the property on a zoning map. It is in a zone which requires a minimum land area of 14,520 sq ft. The minimum frontage on a street must be 80 ft and the minimum depth 100 ft.

Second, the contractor finds that in this zone a building can cover only 20 percent of the land area. This means that the total area of the structure, including the new addition, cannot cover more than 2904 sq ft.

Third, the contractor finds that the minimum front yard must be 30 ft, that the minimum side yards must have a total of 25 ft with neither one to be less than 10 ft, and that the minimum rear yard must be 25 ft.

A sketch (Fig. 13-3) illustrates the situation. The existing house is 26 ft

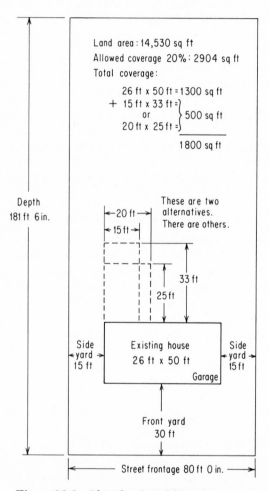

Figure 13-3 Plot plan for addition to a private residence (zoned ⅓ acre). The addition can be of either shape shown, or any shape that meets code requirements.

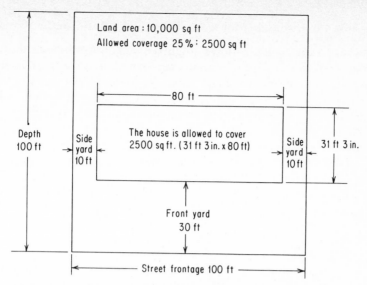

Figure 13-4 Plot plan showing possible envelope for a private residence in a small town (zoned "A" Residential). The diagram illustrates the maximum amount of house that could be built on this plot in this zone. A two-story house with each floor 1250 sq ft would be much more advisable.

wide by 50 ft long including a garage, or a total area of 1300 sq ft. The plot is 80 ft wide by 181.5 ft deep or 14,530 sq ft (⅓ acre). The side yards are 15 ft on each side, or a total of 30 ft, and the house is set back 30 ft from the front lot line. The house as it now exists complies with the zoning regulation.

To accommodate two bedrooms, closets, and a bath, the new addition must have an area approximating 500 sq ft and can be 25 × 20 ft or 15 × 33 ft. It will have to ell out in back of the house, since either side yard can be encroached upon for only 5 ft. The total building coverage will then be 1300 + 500 or 1800 sq ft, well within the allowable maximum of 2904 sq ft, and the side, front, and rear yards will all remain legal.

13.3B. Area Requirements for a Private Residence in a Small Town

The plot is in an "A residence zone." The minimum land area allowable in this town is 10,000 sq ft and the minimum dimensions cannot be less than a 100-ft frontage and a 100-ft depth. Side yards must be at least 10 ft each, front yard 30 ft, and rear yard 25 ft. Maximum allowed land coverage is 25 percent. The contractor can build a house that is 31 ft-3 in. wide by 80 ft long. See Fig. 13-4. Whether he should build such a large house on such a small lot is another matter.

13.3C. Area Requirements for a Small Business Building in a Small City

The land is in a zone which allows neighborhood convenience shopping and small office buildings. The regulation permits all retail activities and office occupancies such as professional, insurance, branch offices of any kind, etc. The ratio of building area to lot area is 2.0 with no restrictions on height. There are no side or front yard requirements and there is a 10-ft rear yard requirement.

Before he can estimate the size of the building he can build, the contractor must first take into account the very strict regulations that every zoning code has for off-street parking facilities. In this instance the code requires that one parking space be provided for every 600 sq ft of *net* office area and one space for every 200 sq ft of *total* retail sales or serving area. This is a fairly typical requirement throughout the country.

The contractor and his architect now have to go through a series of arithmetic calculations to ascertain how many square feet of office and store area he can build and still satisfy the parking requirement. It must be remembered that according to the code (with no parking requirements) he could build 2.0 times the land area or 20,000 sq ft. Obviously he cannot do this and still satisfy the parking requirements.

Figure 13-5 is a fairly accurate diagram of what he can build. The lot is 100

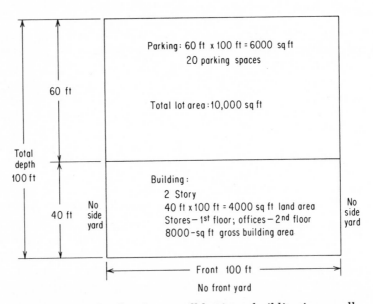

Figure 13-5   Plot plan for a small business building in a small city (zoned Business "A"). *Note:* If there is no back entrance to parking, a driveway will have to be provided. This will require a different building conformation.

ft in front by 100 ft deep. If he builds on the entire 100-ft front, which is the most valuable part of the property, how deep into the lot can he go? A depth of 50 ft would be very desirable but it does not work out. If a depth of 40 feet is used it still represents a viable office or retail store depth. The building will then be 100 ft wide by 40 ft deep or 4000 sq ft on each of two stories.

The second floor can be devoted to office space which requires one parking space for every 600 sq ft of *net* office space.* If stairs and toilets and other utility spaces are omitted, the *net* space may be 3000 sq ft, or five spaces. The first floor can be all retail or part retail and part office (real estate, insurance, etc.). If it is all retail, then one parking space is required for every 200 sq ft of *total* retail area. If space is taken out of this for toilets, hallway, and a minimum of "back-room activities," a total figure of 3000 sq ft can again be used, and this divided by 200 gives 15 spaces. Thus a total of 20 parking spaces or 6000 sq ft is required, and presents a practical solution.

Of course the building need not be of the shape that is shown or used for the purpose as set forth, but this illustration does show what a builder can accomplish even with strict parking regulations.

13.4. NONCONFORMING BUILDINGS, STRUCTURES, AND USES

Unlike building codes, which date back to historical times, zoning codes are of comparatively recent origin. Many codes are not much older than 50 years, and of course there are many thousands of structures in this country that are much older than this and which to a great extent do not conform to present zoning regulations. All zoning regulations have taken cognizance of this, and rightfully so because no public body should deprive a person of the use of his property except for very special reasons—and zoning is not one of these. Zoning regulations for nonconforming land or buildings have therefore been adopted with this in mind.

13.4A. Discontinuance of a Nonconforming Use

While not directly ordering the discontinuance of a nonconforming use or stating a definite time limit, many codes state that "buildings and structures which substantially and adversely affect the orderly development and taxable value of other property in the district will not be permitted to continue indefinitely," or words to this effect. Such a use might be, for instance, a bulk storage yard, junkyard, or auto wrecker in a residential or "A" business zone. Most codes state that no nonconforming use can be continued if the property is not used for a period of one year.

---

*This is only for the parking space calculation. It does *not* mean that the tenant does not have to pay rent for more space than this.

13.4B. Exempted Buildings, Structures, and Uses

All codes recognize that a nonconforming building has a legal right to be there and do not attempt to change its character or its use for as long as the building exists. These legal uses may be nonconforming in:

- Floor area ratio

- Yards—front, rear, or side

- Lot area per dwelling unit

- Maximum gross floor area

- Off-street parking and loading spaces

- Light retail or industrial activity which does not cause serious noise or other pollution

13.4C. Repairs, Alterations, Additions

In this instance, the regulation becomes stricter without actually prohibiting the continued use of a nonconforming building. Ordinary repairs and alterations may be made in a nonconforming building to keep it in sound condition. Some codes allow alterations that cost less than 50 percent of the assessed valuation of the building, but there are other codes which allow the cost for alteration to exceed 50 percent if the alteration is called for by law, and this can include OSHA regulations as well as building department requirements.

All codes, however, forbid the addition of more space to a nonconforming structure unless the structure is so altered or added to that it becomes conforming as to use, area, and bulk. This may not be as strict as it sounds. A building may be nonconforming only in use but may conform to the code in land area covered, yard widths, floor area ratio, etc. In this instance an addition can be made up to the top limit of the present code if the use is changed to a conforming use. An instance would be the changing of a warehouse or loft building to an office building or to a multifamily building.

The intelligent use of a code can lead to many opportunities for the advantageous purchase of property. It must also be remembered that codes are not static. As neighborhood and community use of land and buildings changes, so can the code.

14

BUILDING CODES

14.1. THE PURPOSE OF CODES

Building codes of some kind have been in existence for well over 100 years. The purpose of the codes is to protect the householder against poor planning and workmanship and the use of inferior or dangerous material. In this country the larger cities have had written codes and have enforced these building codes for many years, and these in turn have been the foundation for the state and national building codes now in existence. A building code has the force of law.

14.2. THE CONTRACTOR'S USE OF BUILDING CODES

Instead of being annoyed by the building code, a reputable contractor should make use of it. If he becomes acquainted with the code under which he is working, he will find that:

- By establishing minimum standards for design and material, it protects him against shoddy construction.

- By establishing such standards it can act as a guide to him in his selection of material. A respected contractor will not confine himself to minimum standards.

- It can prevent serious miscalculation in the use of structural members which may not be satisfactory for the work they will have to do.

- By its very existence, it inspires confidence in the owner.

Most people do not know very much about construction, and an occasional visit from a building official will assure them that they are being taken care of. This is good for the contractor. It is true that codes are not changed as rapidly as some people think they should be, and some people call them regressive. Many of these people state that codes are very slow in the approval of new materials and methods of construction. This may be true, but in the author's opinion some of these new materials require prolonged testing and many of them have not proved to be as good as their producers say they are. For instance, elevator push buttons which are heat sensitive have proven dangerous; certain plastics and compounds used for insulation emit noxious fumes when they are heated (as by a fire); sprayed-on fire-resistant material for steel has been found dangerous to health, and so forth.

14.3. THE FUNDAMENTAL PROVISIONS OF CODES

All codes contain certain fundamental provisions. Various codes elaborate on these provisions for local conditions, for instance, depth of foundations in different climates or extra strength of framing for snow loading or earthquake. The contractor should become familiar first with the meaning and purpose of the general provisions before he goes into the detail required by the locality in which he is building. Following is a listing of the general provisions of a typical building code.* Each of these will be explained so that the contractor may become aware of what the code is trying to accomplish. The contractor is to remember that this chapter presents the contents of many codes, and that the order in which the contents are presented here does not necessarily follow the order of any single code.

14.3A. Administration and Enforcement

Definitions and classifications
Building limitations
Use and occupancy requirements

Having defined the kind of buildings and occupancies to which the various requirements of the code apply, it now goes on to specifics.

14.3B. Structural Requirements

Footings and foundations
Structural requirements for lumber, masonry, steel, etc.
Chimneys and flues

---

*The author has used three large-city codes, one small-city code, one town code, one state code, and one national code.

14.3C. To Make the Structure Livable

Heating equipment

Plumbing and drainage

Air conditioning and mechanical ventilation

Electric wiring

14.3D. Health and Safety

Means of egress

Fire protection

Light and ventilation

Protection of workers and the public

Some codes have requirements for plastic construction and prefabricated construction. Several have now added provisions for the handicapped. Many of the code requirements that are mentioned here apply mostly to private residences or alterations to them, but they also apply to multifamily buildings, small office buildings, warehouses, etc., which the contractor will want to bid on as his business grows.

14.4. ADMINISTRATION AND ENFORCEMENT

The code is interpreted and enforced by a building department or by a building official. Following are some specific requirements under such a section.

No part of any existing building can be altered, or added to or repaired unless the new portion complies with the code.

If alterations or repairs whose cost is more than 50 percent of the value of the building are made to a building and all of this work is done within a 12-month period, then the entire building must comply with the existing code.

If more than 50 percent of the value of a building is damaged by fire, then the entire building, when repaired, must comply with the existing code.

The building official is specifically charged with the duty of inspecting the construction at periodic intervals. In the event of a violation of the code which he is unable to have corrected by the contractor, the building official is charged with the duty of reporting the violation to the city, town, or county attorney for legal action.

Permits are required for all repairs costing over $100, and the contractor is forbidden from making any structural, plumbing, or electrical changes without a permit no matter what the cost.*

*This may seem a rather petty provision. But what if a contractor unknowingly closes a legal exit, or overloads an existing electric circuit that may cause a fire, or cuts a supporting joist or stud?

Permits for all new construction, alterations, additions, repairs, etc., are issued by the local building department. The contractor must provide a statement of the proposed cost of the work. The cost of the permit is based on the cost of the work.

He must also provide two sets of plans and specifications for inspection and approval by the building official.

Except in the case of a small private residence, most codes require that plans be prepared by a licensed engineer or architect.

The contractor is obliged to file any change from the original plans and specifications with the department.

Before any new construction, alteration, etc., can be occupied, the building official must make a final inspection and issue a certificate of occupancy.

14.4A. Definitions and Classification

This portion of a code does two things. First it defines all the terms used in the code so that there will be no mistake about their meaning. For example:

14.4A1. DEFINITIONS

Apartment. One or more rooms comprising a dwelling unit for an individual, a family, or a household.

Building, height of. The vertical distance of the highest point of the roof above the mean grade of the ground or street curbs adjoining the building.

Fire resistance. The property of a material which restricts the spread of flames.

Fire resistance rating. The time in hours or fractions of an hour that materials will resist fire exposure.

Load, dead. The weight of all permanent construction including walls, floors, roofs, partitions, stairways, and fixed service equipment.

Load, live. The weight superimposed by the use and occupancy of the building, not including wind load, earthquake load, or dead load.

There are almost 200 definitions of this kind in most codes. The contractor should find the definitions that apply to his work before he goes any further in his study of the code.

14.4A2. SIZE AND OCCUPANCY

The second part of this portion of the code classifies buildings by size and type of construction and by use and occupancy. The reason for this is that many requirements of the code refer only to structures of a certain area or height or type of construction, and these in turn are subject to limitation by the use and occupancy of the building. For instance, a wood frame residence that houses no more than two families cannot be more than 2½ stories or 32 ft in height, whereas a wood frame building that houses more than three families cannot be more than two stories or 25 ft in height.

The simplest way for a contractor to determine which portions of the code apply to his work is to cross-reference it by occupancy, by type of construction, and by height and area.

14.4A2a. Occupancy and Fire Rating

Each of the following is given a group rating:

Public buildings
Assembly buildings
Institutional buildings
Residential buildings, small
Residential buildings, large
Business buildings and others

For instance in one code, residential buildings, small, is C1, residential buildings, large, is C2, and business buildings is D.

In addition there are definitions of each type of occupancy so that the exact occupancy can be pinpointed. Each type of occupancy is then broken down by the use to which it will be put. For instance, an assembly hall may be 50 × 50 ft or larger or smaller; a residential building may have 10 apartments or 50 apartments. Each C2 occupancy (in this case residential buildings, large) is then separated by the type of construction (fireproof masonry, frame, etc.), which depends on the size of the building and its exact use.

The builder must then combine the type of occupancy with its specific use in order to determine how large a building he can build and what its fire rating must be.

14.5. STRUCTURAL REQUIREMENTS

Having defined the kind and size of structure that can be built for various uses and occupancies, the code now goes on to the requirements for structural strength and stability.

14.5A. Footings and Foundations

The code will state that all footings for foundation walls, piers, and other permanent supports of buildings must go down below the frost line of the locality and shall be of such size as to properly distribute the load within the allowable bearing value of the soil. No footings are allowed on frozen soil. Many codes contain a table of the allowable bearing values of the various bottoms. If they do not, the contractor must ask the building official.

Foundation walls must be built to resist the action of frost and must be of at least the same thickness as the walls that they support. In some areas, foundations must be designed not only to take the ordinary live and dead loads of a building but also to resist lateral loads such as those from an earthquake. Fortunately, the structures that are most mentioned in this book, such as one- or two-family dwellings, minor accessory buildings, or buildings not over 35 ft in height, are exempt from these structural requirements. Other larger building foundations in such areas must be designed by an expert in this field.

14.5B. Framing

14.5B1. WOOD FRAMING

The code usually states that the structure shall be of sufficient strength and rigidity to withstand the forces that it will be called upon to bear. This is a general statement which has to be interpreted by the architect or builder into specific sizes and lengths of lumber. Many codes have tables showing the limits for the use of various sizes of lumber for different spans and loading. If these limiting sizes are not shown, and if the contractor has any doubts and there is no architect, he should speak to the building official. The sizes and lengths of joists, studs, rafters, girders, and plates in small construction are standard everywhere, and a contractor should be familiar with them. Following are a few examples of the requirements of a code for strength and rigidity of a structure:

- All joists shall bear at least one-quarter of their depth but not less than 2 in. except when supported on a ribbon board and nailed securely.

- Ceiling joists must be nailed securely to sloping rafters, or metal ties must be used.

- Corners of buildings must consist of at least three 2 × 4s and the corners must be braced diagonally.

- Framing around openings shall be of sufficient size to transfer all loads equally to surrounding members.

- Framing over openings (windows and doors) must be of sufficient size to transfer all superimposed load to the nearest vertical members.

- Roof rafters must either be vertically supported at the ridge or be tied with not less than 1 × 6-in. collar beams at not less than

5-ft intervals, and each rafter must be securely fastened to the wall plate or wall stud. There are also tables for wind and earthquake loading in codes where such information is required.

14.5B2. MASONRY

The provisions of a code for masonry construction mentioned here are for small structures only. Some of the general stipulations are:

- Masonry bearing walls in residential buildings with a total height of 35 ft (including subgrade) must be 8 in. thick.

- In residential buildings which exceed 35 ft in height, the second and third stories may be 8 in. thick but the first floor and subgrade must be 12 in. thick.

- In cavity walls, neither the facing nor backing can be less than 4 in. thick. The entire wall cannot be less than 10 in thick, and the wall cannot be over 25 ft high. The thickness of a cavity wall for heights up to 40 ft cannot be less than 14 in.

- There must be a header course or a heavy galvanized tie at least at every sixth course and not less than one tie for every 1½ sq ft.

- Masonry walls must be supported at right angles at intervals not less than 14 times the wall thickness for cavity walls (vertically or horizontally).

- Masonry veneer walls over wood frame construction must be securely attached to the wood frame with corrosion-resistant anchors at vertical intervals of not more than 16 in. and horizontal intervals of not more than 20 in. Fourteen-pound waterproofing felt must be attached to the frame before the veneer is applied, and necessary flashing must be provided to keep moisture from seeping in between the masonry veneer and the wood frame.

14.5C. Chimneys and Flues

Codes are particularly strict about the construction of chimneys and flues and about how a structure must be framed around them. The reason is obvious. Poorly constructed chimneys or flues are a common cause of fire and may even leak noxious gases.

Codes do not allow more than one heating apparatus on a single flue. A furnace and a fireplace require two separate flues.

Chimneys must extend at least 3 ft above the adjacent roof and not less than 2 ft above any roof within 10 ft.

No combustible material such as header and trimmer beams which frame the chimney opening can be closer than 2 in. to any chimney and no trimming around the fireplace opening can be closer than 6 in.

14.6. REQUIREMENTS TO MAKE THE STRUCTURE LIVABLE

Codes not only have requirements for structural integrity but also for the amenities of life and for the health and safety of the occupants. All of these requirements refer to the kinds of materials that may be used and how they should be installed to provide comfortable and safe living.

14.6A. Heating Equipment

Codes never mention the capacity of any heating system because this function depends upon the use of the building and the requirements of the owner. There are laws in effect to protect the occupants of rented dwelling units but these laws simply state that interior temperatures must be maintained at a certain level during the heating season (this varies according to the various climates). Codes confine themselves to the safety of the heating systems and to the prevention of fire from illegal or poorly installed systems.

Oil burners must be approved by the public authority having jurisdiction and must be installed under special permit from the building official. Oil tanks must be approved by public authority and inspected by the building official.

All oil burners must have approved safety devices such as high and low water limits, stack temperature limits, and a device for shutting off the flow of oil. There must also be a switch, located at a safe point, which can shut down the entire system.

14.6B. Plumbing and Drainage

Here again the code does not attempt to dictate the type of fixture to be used but confines itself to the general welfare and safety of the occupants. It is well known that poor plumbing and drainage have been responsible for outbreaks of typhoid, dysentery, and other dangerous illnesses. Some general provisions follow:

- All premises intended for human habitation shall be provided with an adequate supply of pure and wholesome potable water which must not be connected to any unsafe water supply or subject to backflow or back siphonage.

- All plumbing fixtures installed in buildings intended for human habitation that abut on a street or easement containing a public sewer must be connected to the sewer. If there is no public sewer, then a suitable disposal system must be provided and this is subject to approval by the local authority having jurisdiction. The contractor should consult the local health authority before bidding on a disposal system.

- Each dwelling unit shall have at least one water closet, one tub or shower, one lavatory, and one kitchen sink. Fixtures must be of nonabsorbent material and must have water-seal traps.

- Every plumbing system must have a venting system that vents to the outer air and sanitary cleanouts where necessary. If necessary, the sanitary lines should have backwater traps and provisions against siphonage in which the pressure could be great enough to force a trap seal.

- All plumbing contractors must be licensed.

- Permits must be obtained whenever additional fixtures are added or the system is altered in any way.

14.6C. Air Conditioning and Mechanical Ventilation

Air conditioning and mechanical ventilation systems are treated from a safety and good workmanship standpoint, except that in closed areas the code will call for a certain volume of air to be delivered in accordance with the size of the area and its use. There are no requirements for absolute temperature differentials.

The small contractor will not normally encounter air conditioning requirements. Residences or business buildings with requirements for air conditioning are designed by architects and engineers and the contractor's contact with it would be through an air conditioning subcontractor who specializes in this work. Normally also, the system, including the duct work, the required air damper, fire dampers, smoke detectors, etc., is inspected by the architect or engineer and a certificate of compliance is issued by the building authority.

The contractor's duty is to see to it that the proper inspections are made and that the proper approvals are issued.

14.6D. Electrical Wiring

The electrical code is a countrywide code whose provisions are strictly enforced by local authority. There is a National Electrical Code and a Fire Underwriters' Code. All electrical contractors must be licensed and even in small private residences their work is inspected before it is covered over. Faulty or undersized wiring is a serious cause of fires. The code concerns itself with the use of the proper material and with competent workmanship.

The contractor should be sure that the electrician he uses for any job is properly licensed and that he has obtained a certificate of approval before his work is covered over by other construction.

14.7. REQUIREMENTS FOR HEALTH AND SAFETY

14.7A. Means of Egress

This portion of a code concerns itself with the design, construction, and arrangement of exit facilities so as to ensure a safe means of egress from a building. Because safe exit from a building can be a matter of life and death, the code becomes very specific about how such exit facilities must be built. Some important examples follow.

In every one- or two-family dwelling there shall be at least one exit stairway from upper stories not less than 3 ft in clear width between enclosing walls or enclosing wall and banister. A handrail may project into this clear width but not more than 3½ in.

Such a stairway cannot have a height of rise of more than 12 ft between landings. In one- or two-family dwellings, the risers cannot be over 8¼ in. high and the tread not less than 9 in. wide, plus nosing.

In multifamily dwellings of wall-bearing masonry construction, approved exitways must be located so that the maximum travel distance from the entrance of each apartment to an enclosed interior stairway is no more than 50 ft.

In multifamily dwellings every apartment must have access to at least one additional exit separated from and independent of the primary interior stairway.

Basement recreation rooms in multiple dwellings must have direct access to a street exit by means of a fire-retardant stair.

There are many other requirements for exit widths, for widths of stairways in accordance with the occupancy in commercial buildings, and for the fire-retardant quality of stairway walls. All of these are for the purpose of making it as simple and safe as possible for the occupants to leave any imperiled building.

14.7B. Fire Protection

The code requirements for fire protection and fire extinguishing equipment are comparatively simple for small residential and commercial buildings. They confine themselves to stopping the spreading of fire between dwelling units and between floors.

Fire walls are required between building units when they exceed a certain allowable fire area.

Basement ceilings in all buildings, except one- and two-family residences, must be of ¾-hour rating.

Firestopping is required to close all concealed draft openings and to form effective fire barriers against the spread of fire in all subdivisions of any one story and between all stories of a building.

The open spaces around pipes or ducts that penetrate floors or between the backs and sides of chimneys and fireplaces and combustible framing must be firestopped with noncombustible material.

So far as fire extinguishing equipment is concerned, such equipment as sprinklers, standpipes, fire dampers, CO_2 systems, etc., are only for large structures, must be designed by engineers, and need not concern this contractor.

14.7C. Light and Ventilation

A large portion of this section of the code applies to older multifamily buildings. It does, however, require that no alteration can be made that reduces the size of a room or its window space to less than the amount required for new buildings. It also states that new rooms cannot be added unless they conform to the requirements for new buildings.

If a basement does not have more than one-half its height above grade, it cannot be used for habitable rooms. It can, however, be used for recreation, etc. Some codes give standards for the required natural light and the required volume of air for habitable rooms. The entire thrust of the code is toward healthful living accommodations.

14.7D. Protection of Workers and the Public

The building construction business has one of the worst safety records of any industry, and because of this there are usually at least two agencies that make and enforce safety rules and inspect the construction to see that these rules are complied with. The local building inspector is the primary agent, but many states have labor departments which have rules about sanitary facilities, scaffolding, etc., and in the past few years there has been the Occupational Safety and Health Administration (OSHA) which was created by the Congress and is now becoming pervasive. Some typical requirements are as follows.

- A first-aid kit must be available at every building site, and every site must have provisions for prompt transportation to a doctor or a hospital.

- An adequate supply of potable water shall be provided and any container used for this purpose must be clearly marked and not used for any other purpose. Common drinking cups or dippers are prohibited.

- Every building site shall be provided with a temporary toilet, and if the site is on a sewer line this toilet must be connected to the sewer.

- Employees working in areas where there is danger of head injuries from falling or flying objects must be provided with head protection (hard hats).

- Employees working on machinery that may present a potential eye hazard must wear protective goggles.

- Safety belts shall be provided for all employees engaged in hazardous work in unprotected situations.

- Flammable and combustible liquids shall be stored only in approved metal containers. Such liquids in excess of 15 gal must be stored in an approved storage cabinet.

- When heaters are used in confined spaces, sufficient ventilation must be provided to sustain proper combustion. Heaters must rest on suitable noncombustible and heat-insulation materials.

- Walkways, runways, and sidewalks shall be kept clear of excavated material or other obstructions.

- No person shall be permitted under loads handled by power shovels, derricks, or hoists but shall be required to stand away from any vehicle being loaded.

- Trees, boulders, and other surface encumbrances that are located close to the excavation must be removed or made safe.

- Excavated or other material shall not be stored closer than 4 ft from the edge of the excavation.

- Trenches more than 4 ft deep must be shored and earth banks more than 4 ft deep must be either shored or sloped to an angle of repose (the angle at which the slope will be stable).

- There must be provision for the use of inhalators against rock dust and other dangerous materials.

- Material that is stored in tiers must be stacked in such a way as to prevent sliding or collapse.

- All scrap lumber, waste material, and rubbish shall be removed from the work area as the work progresses.

- There are published standards for the strength and construction of ladders, scaffolds, etc.

- There must be provisions for the protection of the public, although these requirements will not normally affect the smaller contractor. For example, there must be provision for protection of sidewalk crossings by vehicles, for sidewalk sheds, for providing fences around dangerous sites, for protection of the public against contaminated air, etc.

The contractor who has noted these sample code requirements will know which ones apply to his particular job. He is cautioned to comply with those requirements. Safety inspections at the most unlikely sites are becoming more common and more rigorous as the result of a national effort to cut down on construction accidents. The contractor is advised to allow for safety costs in his original estimate.

15

THE ALTERATION CONTRACTOR

15.1. THE SPECIAL CHARACTER OF ALTERATION WORK

Up to now this book has confined itself to the principles of construction work in general. These principles, which cover estimating, progress and cost accounting, codes, legal problems, etc., hold true for alteration work as well as for new construction. The difference is that in alteration work the contractor is dealing with a completed structure and often with the client who occupies this structure. Except in large additions or alterations, there is rarely an architect, and at best the plans and specifications are sketches. The contractor is therefore to a great extent "on his own" and should take proper precautions to avoid losing time or money.

15.2. ESTIMATING AN ALTERATION OR ADDITION

Before a contractor can start to estimate on work involving an existing structure he must know how the structure is built, what lies concealed behind the walls, how he will gain access to the structural frame, the location of the piping and the electrical wiring that he must connect to, and their condition. There is nothing more disconcerting to a contractor than to find the soil or water line to which he must connect crumbling in his hand or breaking off at a fitting, or to find rotted sills or other deteriorated structural members.

A thorough investigation of the existing structure is therefore very important. An inspection of the basement will tell a great deal. The experienced contractor can tell the condition of the structure from the exposed piping, the heating plant, or any exposed framing. If the proposed work includes electrical, plumbing, and heating work, he should certainly have subcontractors examine the structure so that there will not be any future claims for charges for unforeseen extra work (which are very difficult to collect from the owner).

If the contractor finds any signs of advanced deterioration in an existing structure, it is strongly recommended that he tell the owner about it and show him the condition.

Very often the owner will ask the contractor to match certain paneling. It is possible that some of these items are unobtainable. While a mill will tool up for a large run of anything, it will not do so for small orders. The owner should be told in advance about items that cannot be matched except under special order or perhaps not at all. The contractor should make a list of substitutes available for these unobtainable items and should have illustrations or substitute colors of paneling, etc., to show.

The estimate is then put together, listing all the subcontractors' prices which should include not only the cost of new work but also the cost of tearing out and connecting to the existing work. The subcontractors' bids should clearly indicate that this is included. The contractors' own costs should of course also include these items (see sample estimating form, Fig. 15-1).

15.2A. Effect of Changed Building Code

The contractor must remember that the provisions of building codes are constantly being amended and sometimes changed entirely to reflect the changes in building technology and materials. Materials or techniques that were allowed when the house was built may no longer be valid. For instance, all present-day codes have increased their requirements for light, ventilation, fire safety, means of egress, and safety of workers. Many codes state that if a certain percentage of the value of a structure is spent for an alteration, then the entire structure must conform to the new code. The contractor is especially cautioned about restoration work after a fire.

The same provisions of the code regarding the value of the restoration holds for a fire restoration as it does for any other alteration. There may be hidden damage that is not quickly discernible. The contractor must be particularly careful about his bid on the electrical work. Fire damage restoration gets special attention from building officials and from insurance claim adjusters and inspectors.

15.2B. Effect of Changed Zoning Codes

Zoning regulations are of comparatively recent origin, and there are many structures everywhere that were built before there was any zoning at all. This is especially true in smaller communities. Many of these structures are now "nonconforming," which means that they can stay where they are and how they are *until the owner decides to alter them.* It is at this point that the zoning regulation comes into effect. Chapter 14 tells what can and what cannot be done. There are of course many structures which, although they were built before zoning codes were in effect, happen to conform.

Before starting to estimate on any alterations or additions to an existing structure, the contractor is advised to investigate the zoning regulations to ascertain whether the proposed work is in compliance.

15.3. ORGANIZING THE WORK

15.3A. The Occupied Residential Building

15.3A1. PROTECTING THE STRUCTURES AND THE OCCUPANTS

Before any work can be started, the contractor must plan to protect the existing structure and the plantings and trees against weather and against damage from workers and equipment. The contractor must be sure to have enough weatherproof tarpaulins, sheets of heavy plastic, sheets of plywood, tarred felt, and any other protective material for protection of the structure against weather. All openings must be closed every night and over weekends and of course at all times during inclement weather. Any valuable shrubbery may have to be boxed in and trees close to the new construction may have to have some plank protection. All of this costs money and the contractor should have it clearly understood with the owner that while his contract does include protection of the structure itself during the alterations, all other protection will be done only at the request of the owner.

The protection of the occupants against noise, dirt, and weather can be accomplished by the use of plywood or wallboard partitions, plastic sheets, and tarpaulins. While such temporary partitions cannot be noiseproof, they can be made weatherproof and dustproof, and this is very important if the contractor wishes to retain the good will of his clients.

His public relations with his clients is also very important to the contractor. If the occupants are told what is going on and about how long it will take, and are kept informed about the progress of the work, it will make the contractor's job much easier. Good communication in this case is very simple.

If the work is to be done on an existing residence with the owner occupying the house, the contractor cannot approach it as if it were a new construction job where he has an empty plot to work on. There are undoubtedly an existing driveway, a lawn, shrubbery, and trees. The existing structure restricts the areas into which the contractor can bring heavy equipment or dump material. Means of access to the garage or the front door must be maintained. Rubbish must be removed—and not through the front door! The contractor must not dump materials on the front lawn. All of this sounds complicated but it need not be if some advance planning is done.

15.3A2. SITE PLANNING

The situation is easily handled if the alteration work does not involve large quantites of material or extensive demolition, but if the work is extensive, the

Estimating Form for Alteration Work

Description of work	Labor	Material	Total
PROTECTION. Tarpaulins plastics, plywood, etc., for protection against weather and dust	30 hours @ $10. = $300.	Use of tarps. Plastic rolls. Plywood 6'·¾" $100.	$400.00
DEMOLITION. Exterior–Tear out W. gable end. Save windows and leave studs in place. Interior– Remove all non bearing partitions in 2W. bedrooms	30 hrs. Exterior 15 hrs. Interior 45 hrs. @ 10. = $450.		$450.00
RUBBISH REMOVAL & CLEANING	10 hrs. to start 30 hrs. During job 40 hrs. @ $10. 400	Use of truck, Brooms shovels, scrapers, etc. $100.	$500.00
EXCAVATION & FOOTINGS FOUNDATIONS (incl keying to existing foundation)	J.C. Francini Bid of 2/10/7–		$1,250.00
NEW EXTERIOR FRAMING. (incl. shopping and other connection to existing work)	56 hrs. @ $10. = $560.	Bid on lumber list XYZ Lumber Co. 2/12/7– $650.	$1,210.00
NEW INTERIOR FRAMING.			
MILLWORK & TRIM, etc.*			
SALVAGE	For cleaning trim, doors, and windows for reuse. Cleaning special bathroom tile for use in new powder room 45 hrs. @ $10. = 450.		$450.00

*See Chap. 3 for millwork and trim estimating form.

Figure 15-1

contractor should make up a plot diagram just as he would for a new building. If there is no other way, he will have to use the existing driveway as his means of access. He will have to make it clear to the owner that a power shovel and heavy trucks will have to cross a lawn. He may have to dig a new ditch for sewer, water, or electrical lines.

A place will have to be set aside for the delivery and storage of new material. This can consist of anything from concrete blocks for the foundation, brick for a new chimney, wallboard and paneling, to the finish hardware. Much of this material must be kept under cover. Material must be delivered in sequence so that mason material and millwork (for instance) do not come together.

Rubbish removal is another problem. There is nothing more unsightly than broken wood, hunks of wallboard, and the other miscellaneous junk that results from a demolition job. The best way to handle this material is to remove it daily. It is a fire hazard, it is dusty, and it can cause accidents and injury to workers. Its continued presence also makes the occupants very unhappy.

15.4. SALVAGE

In demolishing existing work, the contractor very often has the choice of reusing some of the material. Such material can be brick, marble, wood trim, or siding. With the present cost of field labor, however, it is usually cheaper to purchase new material than to pay for cleaning and salvaging the old. Of course, if there is wood trim of a certain pattern, or marble or brick that is no longer on the market and cannot be matched, it should be salvaged. The contractor should be aware of which material to salvage so that he can make allowance for the cost of removing it carefully and cleaning it up for reuse. Even if the material that is being torn out is not to be reused on the present job it may be of such character or value that it can be used on another job or sold to a used material dealer. This is especially true in the remodeling or alteration of an older house.

15.5. SAFETY

The contractor must at all times remember that he is working in an occupied structure. He should bear in mind that people are eating and sleeping in the building. There must be no carelessness regarding workers' smoking or leaving sparks after a cutting torch or a plumber's torch is used. It is one thing to burn a building and another to burn people. The plumbing, heating, and electrical work have to be made safe at all times. There must be no possibility of a short circuit or contamination of the water supply. Material should be stored so that there is no tripping hazard or any danger of stepping on protruding nails. Openings in floors must be kept covered.

Working in any occupied structure means that people other than the contractor's employees are involved. Accidents can be terribly expensive.

15.6. JOB PROGRESS

One of the most important things to bear in mind when performing work in occupied premises is to pay close attention to a proper progress schedule. No matter how badly the owner wants to improve his quarters, by adding a garage, terrace, or bedroom, changing partitions, or modernizing a kitchen, he does not want workers under foot. He tolerates them but he is not happy until they have completed their work and left.

It is therefore wise for the contractor to make up a progress schedule and to *keep to it*. There should be no waiting for days for a tiling contractor or a carpenter to appear to complete a bathroom or to hang doors or complete a floor. The sequence should be the same as for a new building so that the foundations start as soon as excavation is complete, framing starts when foundations are complete, and so on.

Many contractors who graduate from alteration work to building new houses continue to perform alteration work for many reasons. It enables them to keep in contact with many people, some of whom may build new houses in the future. It also provides them with a place to employ their workers when new construction is slow or when they are between operations. The contractor is warned, however, that he must not remove his workers from an alteration job when it is partially completed and hope that the occupants of the structure will not mind—they will! Leaving an alteration job partially completed for any length of time can lead to all kinds of unpleasantness—lawsuits, three-day notices, refusal to pay bills, and certainly a poor reputation.

There is one other matter for the contractor to keep in mind. Very often when working on the electrical, plumbing, or heating systems, the contractor must shut down these systems for a time until necessary connections are made. The occupants of the building should be warned well in advance of any such shutdown so that they can make proper preparations.

15.7. ALTERATIONS IN BUSINESS BUILDINGS

Alteration work in a business building is much simpler than that in a residence. The building is normally occupied only during business hours so that work which necessitates a great deal of noise and dirt can be done out of normal business hours. This of course involves overtime for the workers. However, tearing out partitions, erecting ceilings, and installing lighting fixtures can be done so much more quickly when there are no occupants underfoot. The contractor can make some allowance in his estimate on the cost of the overtime, especially if it is a competitive job.

Generally the subcontractors who work on commercial structures are more businesslike and are more likely to keep to a tight schedule. As in a residential building, it is an excellent idea for the contractor to keep the office occupants advised of what is going on and how long it will take, and they will be much less likely to complain. And finally, let the contractor remove his rubbish as quickly as it accumulates.

Summary of State Licensing and Qualification Requirements

ALABAMA

PREQUALIFICATION *required* in order to bid on highway work.

CONTRACTOR'S LICENSE, *having the effect of Prequalification, required* before undertaking any projects, public or private, costing $20,000 or more.

PREQUALIFICATION

Prospective bidders on highway work must prequalify with State Highway Department, Montgomery, Alabama. They must furnish sworn statements, on forms prescribed, giving detailed information with regard to financial resources, equipment, past record, experience of both the firm and personnel of organization, credit lines established with material and equipment houses, and any other information Department may deem necessary. Financial statements must be prepared either by CPA or independent licensed public accountants approved by the Highway Department. (CPA or accountant not needed for certificates under $50,000.) Foreign corporations must obtain a certificate of authority to do business in Alabama from Secretary of State, Montgomery 4, Alabama (fee $1.50). This is needed for Highway Department qualification. It is not necessary for bidding only on Federal participating contracts.

Within 30 days after submission, if applicant is found to possess required qualifications, certificate of qualification will be issued, valid for not more than one year. Certificate will set forth amount of work applicant may be allowed to have under contract at any one time, and may specify types of work upon which applicant will be permitted to bid.

Once prequalification has been accomplished, the Highway Department can accept bids and make awards on work up to $20,000 without a license being issued.

LICENSING

Contractors on both public and private work must obtain licenses before undertaking projects costing $20,000 or more.

Licensing supervised by:

State Licensing Board for General
    Contractors
Room 604
State Administrative Building
Montgomery, Alabama 36104.

Work performed for Federal governmnent on government-owned land exempt. Also, exempt, construction of one-family residence or one-family private dwelling.

Application for license, on form prescribed by the Board, must be filed not less than 30 days prior to any regular or special meeting of Board and must be accompanied by a certified check for $50. Renewal fee is $35 per year, after qualification.

If application is satisfactory to the Board, applicant may be required to take examination to determine his qualifications. Examination may be oral or written or both and may cover, in addition to financial responsibility and past record, the qualifications of the applicant in reading plans and specifications, estimating costs, construction, ethics and other matters.

License, when and if issued, will stipulate type or types of work applicant is found qualified to perform, also setting out a letter symbol indicating the maximum limits on which he is permitted to bid or perform in a single contract.

STATE AND COUNTY PRIVILEGE LICENSE: In addition to the above license requirements, a State and County license must be obtained from the Probate Judge of the county in which the contractor maintains his principal office, or in which the contract is to be performed. Payment in one county of the State shall be sufficient. Cost, based on gross amount of contracts, ranges from $15.50 to $375.50

ALASKA

PREQUALIFICATION *not required.*
CONTRACTOR'S REGISTRATION *required.*

PREQUALIFICATION

Prequalification was discontinued in 1967. (Department of Highways.)

LICENSING

A construction contractors registration law was enacted in 1966. On October 16, 1967 we were informed that construction contractors are now required to be registered. Fee for registration is $100.00 for general contractors and $50.00 for specialty contractors. Proof of bonding to the State and proof of liability and property damage insurance must also be submitted. A business license (fee $25.00) still must be obtained from the Department of Revenue. (Central Licensing Section, Department of Commerce.)

ARIZONA

PREQUALIFICATION *required* in order to bid on highway work.
LICENSE *required* in order to bid on any work. (See below.)

PREQUALIFICATION

Under regulations of the State Highway Commission, contractors desiring to bid on State highway work must prequalify.

Applicants must submit a statement of experience and financial condition on forms supplied by the Arizona Highway Commission. The forms must be fully completed, and the Financial Statement made by a certified or licensed public accountant. Prequalification must be filed not later than 15 days prior to the date set for opening bids.

This information is good for fifteen months after its date, but right is reserved by the State to request additional information on current assets and liabilities. The contractor also may be required to show the amount contracted subsequent to the date of his Financial Statement, and to furnish a list of available equipment.

Prequalification is complete when this information has been approved by the Commission and the contractor holds a valid license. On Federal-aid projects license from the Arizona Registrar of Contractors is not required for submission of bids or consideration of award, but will be required to complete the award of contract.

Communications regarding prequalification should be addressed to:

State Highway Engineer
Attention: Division of Contracts and
  Specifications
Arizona Highway Department
206 S. 17th Ave.
Phoenix, Arizona 85007

LICENSING

Title 32, Chapter 10, Arizona Revised Statutes, requires all contractors to be licensed before doing work or submitting bids on work in the State. Fees range from $50 to $100. Bids are permissible on Federal Aid Highway Construction without first securing an Arizona Contractors license. However, an Arizona license must be secured for such work prior to executing any contract or performing any work.

To obtain a license under this Act the applicant must remit the required fee and submit, upon such forms as the Registrar of Contractors shall prescribe, a duly verified application including (1) a complete statement of the general nature of his contracting business, giving the names of principals or officers of the organization (2) if a foreign corporation, a statement showing that the corporation is qualified to do business in the state (3) the certification of two reputable citizens of the county in which the applicant resides, that he is of good reputation, recommending that license be granted, and containing the statement that the applicant desires the issuance of a license under the terms of the Act and (4) a contractor's license bond in an amount ranging from $500 to $2,000 depending upon type of license, or in lieu of bond a cash deposit may be made with State.

An applicant must be of good reputation and must show, by written examination, experience in the kind of work he proposes to contract and a general knowledge of the building, safety, health and lien laws of the State and of the rudimentary administrative principles of the contracting business and of the rules and regulations promulgated by the Registrar of Contractors pursuant to this Act.

A foreign corporation, before applying for a license, must have maintained both an office and a residence for one or more of its principals in the State for at least 90 days prior to date of application, except that office and residency requirements may both be waived to correspond with any such requirements imposed by applicant's home State upon Arizona residents seeking similar licenses in such State.

The Examinee will be the individual applicant, member of a co-partnership, corporate officer or responsible managing employee of the applicant and must have had four years experience in the classification for which the applicant applies for license. This experience must have been as a journeyman, foreman, supervising employee or contractor and must have been within the ten years immediately preceding the date of filing the application. The applicant proves his experience by securing certified experience certificates.

The application must be complete in every detail before filing. When a satisfactory completed application has been filed the applicant will be notified of the time and place of the written examination. After the applicant has passed the examination, his name and address and the name of those associated with him are publicly posted for 20 days prior to issuance of the license. The license will either be issued or refused within 60 days from the date of filing application.

All contractors must have licenses issued in names under which they do business. Licensees are required by law to notify the Registrar within 30 days of a change of address. Applicant must secure privilege sales tax license.

All licenses expire June 30th of each year but are renewable on or before July 30th of the same year. Unless renewed by that date licenses will be suspended. Reinstatement for the balance of the fiscal year would involve payment of a double renewal fee.

ARKANSAS

PREQUALIFICATION *required* in order to bid on highway work.
LICENSE *required* in order to bid on all projects of $20,000 or more, public or private.

PREQUALIFICATION

State Highway Department, Highway Building, Little Rock, Arkansas, prequalifies contractors for all highway work.

Each prospective bidder will be required to file a Prequalification Questionnaire consisting of a Financial Statement, Experience Record and Equipment Schedule on a form furnished by the State Highway Commission.

A questionnaire, reflecting the status of the prospective bidder as of the terminal date of his fiscal year, will become the criterion for issuing proposals and awarding work during the following year. In any case a bidder's period of qualification will be for one year beginning with the effective date of his statement plus a two-month grace period. Prospective bidders may file a current questionnaire at any time but no proposal will be released to a bidder unless a rating has been extended based on a questionnaire filed with the Commission at least seven days before the date set for receipt of bids *Questionnaire must be transmitted through the U.S. Mail.*

Contractors will be rated in accordance with the maximum amount of work that it is deemed they can satisfactorily prosecute through any given period, generally, such amount not to exceed twenty times the net quick assets reflected in the current financial statement. The maximum amount of work considered will include the unfinished value of going contracts. In the event a contractor submits a low bid on more than one project, and the aggregate amount is greater than the amount the contractor may be allowed to undertake the Commission will exercise its discretion in the particular project or projects to award.

In addition to the annual questionnaire required, the contractor will file an affidavit at each period proposal forms are issued citing active contracts in force and the unfinished value of such work. Proposal forms will not be issued until such affidavit is on file and the amount of work the contractor may be allowed to undertake so determined.

Proposal forms will be issued only upon the written request of the contractor, to the contractor in person or to a member of the contractor's organization.

Proposals must be accompanied by either a certified or cashier's check drawn on a solvent bank or trust company or a bidder's bond executed by an approved surety company. The proposal guarantee shall be made payable to the Arkansas State Highway Commission and in the amount shown in the proposal form. A lesser amount will not be accepted. Individual checks or bidder's bond must be furnished with each proposal submitted. Bid bonds must be signed by a resident agent domiciled in Arkansas.

Checks drawn on banks or trust companies not located in the State of Arkansas shall not exceed twenty-five (25%) per cent of the combined capital and surplus of the banking institution on which drawn, and a statment to this effect, signed by either the president or cashier or such banking institution, must accompany the check.

LICENSING

Contractors including sub-contractors on both State and private work must obtain license *before bids are submitted*, if individual projects amount to $20,000 or more.

Licensing supervised by:
Contractors Licensing Board
Room 350, Gazette Bldg.
Little Rock, Arkansas 72201

Application for license, on forms prescribed by the Board, must be accompanied by a certified check for $50 and be submitted at least 30 days prior to any regular or special meeting of the Board. License expires on June 30th of each year. Renewal is by application, with renewal fee, maximum $50 to be determined by the Board. (Presently $15.)

In determination by the Board of the applicant's qualifications, the following are considered: "(a) experience, (b) ability, (c) character, (d) the manner of performance of equipment, previous contracts, (e) financial condition, (f)

ability and willingness to conserve the public health and safety, (g) any other fact tending to show and (h) default in complying with the provisions of this Act, or any other law of the State."

Recipients of certificates of license must record same with the Secretary of State with the date of recording to be shown thereon. Until such recording holders of license certificates shall not exercise any of the rights or privileges conferred thereby. Failure to record within 60 days of date of issuance shall invalidate the certificate of license. Fee, $1.00.

License NOT required where contractor bids on or performs contracts for Federal Government, on Government land. Sub-contractors, however, must be licensed. License NOT required for BIDDING on Federal Aid Highway Projects with the Arkansas State Highway Department but the bidder receiving an award of contract must be licensed before a contract may be executed. License NOT required for builders of single family residences.

Out-of-state licensed contractor is required to post a corporate surety bond or a cash bond with the county tax collector of each county in which the contractor is performing a contract to guarantee the payment of personal property taxes which may become due from said contractor.

CALIFORNIA

PREQUALIFICATION *required* in order to bid on State work in excess of $50,000.

LICENSES *required* of general and sub-contractors bidding on projects of $100 or more public or private, with exceptions noted below.

PREQUALIFICATION

All contractors bidding on State work costing over $50,000 must prequalify with the Department of Public Works, the Department of Water Resources, or the Department of General Services, in accordance with provisions of Article 4 or Chapter 3, Part 5 of Division 3, Title 2 of the Government Code.

The standard form, "Contractor's Statement of Experience and Financial Condition," may be obtained from the:
Disbursing Officer
Department of Public Works
1120 N Street
Sacramento, California 95805

LICENSING

Contractors on both State and private work must obtain license, with exceptions noted, *before* bids are submitted.

Chapter 9 of Division III of the Business and Professions Code requires all contractors, including both general and sub-contractors to be licensed.

"The Board may adopt rules and regulations necessary to effect the classification of contractors in a manner consistent with established usage and procedure as found in the construction business and may limit the scope of the operations of a licensed contractor to those in which he is classified and qualified to engage.

"Under rules and regulations adopted by the Board and approved by the director, the registrar may investigate, classify and qualify applicants for contractors' licenses by written examination."

Application for license is made on forms prescribed by the Board. Application fee for original license is $50; also an initial license fee of $60 if license is to run more than a year and $30 if less than a year. A financial statement prepared by an independent certified public accountant or an independent public accountant showing applicant's net worth as exceeding $1,000 is required. Applicant must also filed or post $1,000 bond or cash deposit as a condition to the issuance of a license. Licenses expire on June 30 of each odd-numbered year. Fee is not proratable.

License is NOT required for any construction, alteration, improvement or repair carried on within the limits and boundaries of any site or reservation, the title of which rests in the Federal Government, nor to bid on or receive contract award on any state project involving Federal funds. However, before initial payment for work done on such contracts can be obtained there must be certification by State License Board that license has been issued.

Licensing supervised by:
Registrar of Contractors (Appointed by
Contractors State License Board)
1020 N Street, Room 579
Sacramento, California

COLORADO

PREQUALIFICATION *required* in order to bid on highway work.
CONTRACTOR'S LICENSE *not* required.

PREQUALIFICATION

Before submitting bids on highway work contractors must prequalify with Division of Highways at least 10 days before letting.

Application for prequalification is made by filing the standard form, "Experience, Equipment and Financial Statement," with the Chief Engineer, Division of Highways, 4201 E. Arkansas Ave., Denver, Colorado 80222.

The certificate of a certified public accountant will be required in all cases where the contractor desires to qualify for work in excess of $50,000. Bonds required on all public works contracts over $1,000. See CH. 86-7-4 through 86-7-7, CRS 1963. Also see STANDARD SPECIFICATIONS, Division of Highways $5 per copy.

LICENSING

There is no State law requiring contractors on either State or private work to be licensed.

CONNECTICUT

PREQUALIFICATION *required* in order to bid on highway work.
CONTRACTOR'S LICENSE *not* required.

PREQUALIFICATION

Contractor's Statement Form No. CON. 16 is required by Department ruling of all parties desiring to qualify for State Highway work; information required includes statement of type of organization and names of officers or principals, financial statement, description of equipment and performance record of the organization and experience outline of its key personnel. The statement of any organization having assets of over $50,000 must be prepared by a Registered Public Accountant. This form ordinarily is submitted on a yearly basis; new submissions must be received not less than ten days before a request for bid sheets.

Additionally, a current sworn Affidavit, on the Department's form, showing value of all work to be completed as well as pending bids must be on file with the Department before a contractor's request for bid sheets can be considered.

Each request for project bid sheets is considered individually on the basis of the Contractor's Statement, his Affidavit, and the Department's actual experience with the contractor; his qualifications then are determined for that particular project. Bid sheets are not transferable.

Forms may be obtained from State Highway Department, Wethersfield, the mailing address is P.O. Drawer A, Wethersfield, Conn. 06109.

LICENSING

There is no State law requiring contractors on either public or private work to be licensed.

DELAWARE

PREQUALIFICATION *required* on highway work.
LICENSE *required* of all contractors doing business in the State.

PREQUALIFICATION

To be qualified each bidder must submit at least every two years, on the standard forms of the Department, sworn statements as to his experience, organization, construction equipment and financial resources. These statements may be submitted in March, April or May of each year and qualification, if granted, will be vaild to May 31, of the second succeeding calendar year.

Written request may be made to the Director at any time for further qualification because of changed conditions or estimated cost of a project. The Department also reserves the right to request new qualification statements from any bidder at any time.

Bidders may qualify at other times during the year provided such statements are properly executed and submitted. Prequalification approval shall be made by the Director within 10 days of the submission, and bidders may submit bids immediately. Bidders must be prequalifed in order to receive unconditional bidding documents.

Before awarding the contract, a bidder may be required to show that he has the ability, experience, necessary equipment, experienced personnel and financial resources to successfully carry out the work required by the contract.

The above is being carried in all projects by Special Provision until the Department's new Standard Specification is issued, probably July 1, 1970.

LICENSING

Licensing of contractors is for revenue only. No examination for license is required.

Any individual, partnership, firm or corporation, or other association of persons resident of the State of Delaware, acting as a unit desiring to engage in, prosecute, follow or carry on the business of contracting as herein defined shall obtain a license from the State Tax Department and pay a license fee.

Any individual, partnership, firm or corporation or other association of persons not residents of the State of Delaware, acting as a unit desiring to engage in, prosecute, follow or carry on the business of contracting as herein defined shall obtain an original license from the State Tax Department for each contract or contracts on hand before engaging in business and shall pay a license fee for the execution of such contracts.

Every architect and/or mechanical engineer and/or general contractor engaging in the practice of such profession shall furnish within ten (10) days after any contract or contracts in the preparations or plans for which they were engaged are entered into with a contractor or sub-contractor not a resident of this State, a statement of the total value of such contract or contracts together with the names and addresses of the contracting parties. Failure to furnish each such statement shall subject each architect and/or mechanical engineer and/or general contractor to a penalty of twenty-five dollars ($25) which shall be collected and paid in the same manner as provided for the collection of delinquent licenses as provided in this Article.

Every architect and/or mechanical engineer and/or general contractor, engaging in the practice of such profession, before the payment of any award or amount payable to any contractor or sub-contractor not a resident of this State, shall ascertain from said nonresident contractor or sub-contractor and/or the State Tax Department, whether he has obtained a license and satisfied his liability to the State under this Section, and if said license has not been obtained and the license liability paid by said non-resident contractor or subcontractor, the architect and/or mechanical engineer and/or general contractor shall deduct from the award or amount payable to said non-resident contractor or sub-contractor, the amount of said license liability and shall pay same to the State Tax Department within ten days after final payment and settlement with the non-resident contractor or sub-contractor. Failure to ascertain the payment of license liability of any contractor or sub-contractor not a resident of this State, by any architect and/or mechanical engineer and/or general contractor, in accordance with this section, shall render the architect and/or mechanical engineer and/or general contractor personally liable for the license liability of the non-resident contractor or sub-contractor.

Licensing is under the supervision of:

State Tax Department

Wilmington, Delaware

License is NOT required where contractor performs contracts for Federal Government, on Government land.

Non-resident contractors and subcontractors not regularly engaged in business in Delaware must within 30 days after construction is commenced file for a permit.

DISTRICT OF COLUMBIA

PREQUALIFICATION *not* required in order to bid.
CONTRACTOR'S LICENSE *not* required.

PREQUALIFICATION

It is not necessary to prequalify in order to bid. Low bidders on public work may be required to demonstrate capacity to handle work before contracts are awarded.

LICENSING

Contractors, as such, need not be licensed. But any corporation or unincorporated business must obtain an annual license before engaging in a trade or business in the District; fee, $10.

FLORIDA

PREQUALIFICATION *required* in order to bid on State Highway work.
CONTRACTOR'S OCCUPATIONAL LICENSE *required.*

PREQUALIFICATION

Prequalification for bidding on highway work is by application to Florida Department of Transportation, Tallahassee, Forida, on a standard form, "Application for Qualification."

Each contractor is given a specified classi-

fication and a maximum rating which is the total amount of uncompleted work he will be permitted to have under contract at any one time.

LICENSING

State and County Occupational License Tax determined by the maximum number of persons actually employed, or to be employed during the license year, in the county in which the work is performed, at rates ranging from $9 for 1 to 10 employees to $375 for 201 or more employees. Also, license must be obtained in each county in which the contractor establishes headquarters or a separate place of business. County tax is 50% of the State tax. Both licenses obtainable from Tax Collector of any county. Certain municipalities also are permitted to levy a tax in an amount set by ordinance and others by an amount equal to 50% of the State tax.

License IS required where contractor performs contracts for Federal Government, on Government land.

GEORGIA

PREQUALIFICATION *is* required.
CONTRACTOR'S LICENSE *not* required.

PREQUALIFICATION

The State Highway Department of Georgia adopted and promulgated Rules and Regulations pertaining to Prequalification of all Contractors desiring to bid on projects of said Department. The effective date for implementation of the Regulations was June 4, 1965. All contractors desiring to obtain proposals for bidding on State Highway Department Projects must comply with said Rules and Regulations prior to receiving proposals to bid. Forms for Prequalification may be obtained from the Prequalification Officer, State Highway Department of Georgia, 2 Capital Square, Atlanta, Georgia 30334.

LICENSING

There is no State law requiring contractors on either public or private work to be licensed.

HAWAII

PREQUALIFICATION *may be required* to bid on all public work.

LICENSE *required* to bid on all work except Federal-aid highways.

PREQUALIFICATION

State law requires that prospective bidders file written notice of intention to bid at least six days before the date of opening. Engineer in charge may then require submission of Standard Questionnaire and Financial Statement on forms to be provided. Complete and notarized answers must be made at least 48 hours prior to date set for opening of bids. If deemed satisfactory bids will be received. See Section 103-25, Hawaii Revised Statutes.

LICENSING

All prospective bidders on public or private work, with the exception of Federal-aid highways where federal regulations applicable, must be licensed. Application forms obtainable from Professional & Vocational Licensing Division.

Licenses issuable in three classes—(1) General Engineering, (2) General Building, (3) Specialty.

License fees—Classes (1) and (2) $200, Class (3) $100. Responsible managing employee for Classes (1) and (2) $200, Class (3) $100.

Licensing year ends June 30th, prior to which date renewal required. Renewal fees—Classes (1) and (2) $75, Class (3) $25. Responsible managing employees, all classes $25.

IDAHO

PREQUALIFICATION is effected through operation of Public Works Contractors License Act.

LICENSE *required* of contractors and subcontractors on public works contracts in excess of $1,000.

PREQUALIFICATION

Contractors desiring to bid on public work must prequalify by obtaining a license.

LICENSING

The Act provides that it shall be unlawful for any person to engage in the business or act in the capacity of a public works contractor within this State without first obtaining and having a license therefor . . . unless such person is particularly exempted as provided in this Act, or for any public works contractor to sub-contract in excess of eighty per cent of the work under any contract to be performed by him as such public works contractor according to the contract prices therein set forth, unless otherwise provided in the specifications of such contracts or to sublet any part of any contract for specialty construction, as defined in the Act, to a specialty contractor who, at or before the time of the original bid opening, was not licensed in accordance with this Act; provided, however, that no contractor shall be required to have a license under this Act in order to submit a bid or proposal for contracts for public works financed in whole or in part by federal aid funds, but at or prior to the award and execution of any such contract by the State of Idaho, or any other contracting authority mentioned in the Act, the successful bidder shall secure a license as provided in this Act.

In the above "person" means any individual, firm, co-partnership, corporation, association or other organization or combination thereof acting as a unit.

Application for license shall be of form prescribed by the Public Works Contractors State License Board, shall include complete statement with regard to applicant's contracting business experience, qualifications, description of work completed during preceding 3-year period, description of machinery and equipment owned, statement of financial condition, and other pertinent data including evidence of good character and reputation.

Applications shall be sworn to and filed at least 30 days in advance of consideration by Board, whose meetings shall be on a day not later than the fifteenth day of the month in each of the months of January, April, July and October and at such other times as Board may designate. Applications shall specify class of license desired. AAA, AA, A, B, or C, and be accompanied by appropriate fee.

CLASS AAA—covering contracts for public works with an estimated cost of more than $250,000. Fee, $125; renewal, $125.

CLASS AA—covering contracts for public works with estimated cost of not more than $250,000. Fee, $100; renewal, $100.

CLASS A—covering contracts for public works with estimated cost of not more than $100,000. Fee, $75; renewal, $75.

CLASS B—covering contracts of not more than $50,000. Fee, $50; renewal, $50.

CLASS C—covering contracts of not more than $25,000. Fee, $25; renewal, $25.

ILLINOIS

PREQUALIFICATION *required* in order to bid on highway work.

CONTRACTOR'S LICENSE *not* required. (See below.)

PREQUALIFICATION

State of Illinois, Department of Public Works and Buildings, Division of Highways, requires contractors desiring to bid on highway work to submit a "Contractor's Statement of experience and financial condition" from which the contractor is rated and prequalified.

LICENSING

There is no State law requiring contractors to be licensed. Foreign corporations must be licensed to do business in Illinois prior to the execution of a contract.

INDIANA

TAXES AND FEES

PREQUALIFICATION *required* in order to bid on Highway Commission road, bridge and maintenance work, and on all other public work, except state college and university work, costing $20,000 or more.

CONTRACTOR'S LICENSE *not* required.

PREQUALIFICATION

Prospective bidders on Highway Commission work, except for the purchase of material, equipment and supplies and for the construction of buildings, must prequalify with Indiana State Highway Commission, State Office Building, Indianapolis, Indiana. Information required, on forms to be provided, includes detailed financial statement and outline of experience and available equipment. Financial statement must be prepared by CPA and all material submitted sworn to. Contractors will be rated according to types and amounts of work they are deemed qualified to perform. Any subcontractor for work costing more than $5,000 must also be prequalifed.

On all other public work, except state college and university work, costing more than $5,000 and less than $20,000, same type of information must be presented to awarding authority, along with and as part of bid. On such work costing more than $20,000, prospective bidder must prequalify with Public Works Division, Department of Administration, State Office Building, Indianapolis, Indiana, presenting same type of information.

IOWA

PREQUALIFICATION *required* in order to bid on highway work.

CONTRACTOR'S LICENSE *not* required.

PREQUALIFICATION

By regulation of the State Highway Commission contractors desiring to bid on State highway work must prequalify. Application for prequalification must be submitted on a standard form entitled "Iowa State Highway Commission Contractors' Financial-Experience-Equipment Statement," available from Iowa State Highway Commission, Ames, Iowa.

LICENSING

There is no State law requiring contractors on either public or private work to be licensed.

KANSAS

PREQUALIFICATION *required* in order to bid on highway work.

CONTRACTOR'S LICENSE *not required*, but certain contractors may be required to register and furnish bond to assure payment of taxes.

PREQUALIFICATION

Prequalification on highway work is by the State Highway Commission, Topeka, Kansas.

Prospective bidder must submit to the Commission, once a year, and at such other times as Commission may designate, but in any event at least seven days prior to date set for opening of bids, "a complete statement of his financial condition, equipment, experience and organization, on forms provided for that purpose." The contractor's financial statement must show his net worth and must be certified to by a certified public accountant holding an unrevoked certified public accountant's certificate in Kansas or in any State which has a reciprocity agreement with the State of Kansas. The certification by a certified public accountant may be waived where the contractor's net worth is less than $5,000 or where contractor does not desire a qualification of over $15,000.

Contractors are classified according to the type of work they are qualified to undertake and rated on the amount of work in dollars allowable in any one or more classifications of work which the bidder may have under contract at any one time.

LICENSING

There is no law requiring contractors bidding on or performing work in the State to be licensed.

However, Chapter 462 of the Session Laws of 1963 requires every non-resident contractor required to register any contract, as defined, before entering into the performance of such contract to file a bond of not less than $5,000 conditioned that all taxes (including contributions due under the Employment Security Law) accruing to the State or subdivisions thereof will be paid when due; to cover all contracts to be performed in current calendar year. (Director of Revenue.)

KENTUCKY

PREQUALIFICATION *required* of prime and subcontractors in order to bid on highway work.
LICENSING, as such, *not required*, but effected through prequalification.

PREQUALIFICATION

Highway Department Order No. 73757, revised October 1966, issued pursuant to KRS 176-140, sets up following procedures for prospective bidders on highway work. Contractors must apply for Certificate of Eligibility, on form to be provided. Application must be accompanied by (1) financial statement, certified to by independent CPA, authorized to do business in Kentucky or in home State showing condition at end of fiscal year, if applicant desires to limit eligibility to $100,000, financial statement certified by company official is acceptable, (2) evidence of experience and competency of personnel and adequacy of equipment, (3) certified copy of Articles of

Incorporation or Partnership Agreement, (4) if a corporation, copy of the articles of the incorporation and a certificate from the Kentucky Secretary of State are required.

If applicant meets Department's standards Certificate will be issued within 30 days from filing date, except that, if applicant states in writing that he intends to bid on U.S. Bureau of Public Roads projects, issuance may be made within 15 days.

Certificate establishes type or types and maximum amount of work contractor is qualified to have under contract at any one time.

Certificates must be renewed annually and are extended upon written application for period not to exceed 120 days during which time the applicant must file within 90 days a new statement of experience and financial condition which, if approved, will be followed by issuance of Certificate. Certificates are issued for the fiscal year of the applicant. Applications are processed by Divison of Contract Procurement, Department of Highways, Frankfort, Ky.

LICENSING

There is no State law requiring contractors on either public or private work to be licensed.

LOUISIANA

PREQUALIFICATION—see below.
CONTRACTOR'S LICENSE required to bid on most public and private work in excess of $30,000.

PREQUALIFICATION

Prior to submitting a bid, the bidder may be required to file an experience questionnaire and a confidential financial statement which shall be certified to by a certified public accountant. The statement will include a complete report of the bidder's financial resources and liabilities, equipment, past record, and personnel.

Bidders intending to consistently submit proposals shall prequalify at least once a year. However, prequalification may be changed during that period upon the submission of additional favorable reports or upon unsatisfactory performance. (Department of Highways.)

LICENSING

Act 113, 1964, requires contractors on both public and private work in amounts exceeding $30,000, with certain exceptions, to be licensed. Exceptions include private residential work, federal aid projects and projects for public utilities subject to regulation by State Public Utilities Commission. However, successful bidders on last two named shall, before start of work, secure license and pay fee. They must also comply with terms and provisions of Act and with Rules and Regulations of State Licensing Board created by Act.

Application for license shall be accompanied by statement outlining financial condition, experience and all pertinent facts bearing on applicant's responsibility. Board will rate successful applicants on basis of types of work upon which they may be permitted to bid. Board meets twelve times annually (monthly).

Foreign corporations are required to secure a certificate of authority to do business as a corporation in the State before a license can be issued. Secured through office of Secretary of State. Surety bond or cash deposit sufficient to pay all unemployment compensation taxes accruing to State must be filed with Administrator, Division of Employment Security, Department of Labor.

License fee, $100. License year ends December 31st. Renewal required on or before first Tuesday following January.

Licensing supervised by:

State Licensing Board for Contractors
2nd Floor, Capitol House Hotel
Baton Rouge, Louisiana 70821

Act 476, 1968, requires nonresident contractors, except foreign corporation authorized to do business in the state, to register with the collector of revenue each contract in excess of $1,000 and file a bond in a sum of not less than $1,000, conditioned upon the payment of all taxes, including contributions due under the employment security law, which may accrue to the state and to political subdivisions thereof on account of the execution and performance of such contract or contracts.

MAINE

PREQUALIFICATION *not* required in order to bid.
CONTRACTOR'S LICENSE *not* required.

PREQUALIFICATION

There is no law or regulation requiring prequalification for bidding on any work in the State. On State highway work, the State Highway Commission makes whatever investigation of contractors it deems necessary and may request statements of financial condition, equipment and experience before contracts are awarded. Such a statement must be filed with the bid of any contractor who has not been awarded a contract during the previous five-year period.

LICENSING

There is no State law requiring contractors on either public or private work to be licensed.

MARYLAND

PREQUALIFICATION *required* in order to bid on highway work, by both general and subcontractors.
LICENSE *required* all contractors obtaining work exceeding $5,000 per annum, public or private.

PREQUALIFICATION

Prospective bidders on highway work, both general and subcontractors, must prequalify with State Roads Commission, 300 W. Preston Street, Baltimore, Maryland 21203.

Statements must be on forms, to be supplied on request, submitted 15 days prior to any contract letting upon which it is desired to bid, or, in any event at least once during the period July 1-June 30. Information submitted must include application, sworn financial statement, outline of experience and equipment owned. Prior to award, bidder must submit a Plan and Equipment Questionnaire outlining a proposed plan for carrying on the work. Prime contractors must not sublet more than 50% of value of contract.

Above applicable for contractors desiring to bid on work for Maryland State Roads Commission only. Many contractors in Maryland perform work for other State agencies and are not covered by Maryland State Roads Commission prequalification.

Some counties in Maryland require that contractors bidding on highway work be prequalified with the Maryland State Roads Commission, and two of the larger counties have their own prequalification system. Contractors working within the City of Baltimore on City contracts must prequalify with Baltimore City.

LICENSING

No license is required to bid, but under Chapter 704, Section 184, Acts of 1916, any person or corporation accepting orders or contracts for doing work in a gross yearly volume exceeding $5,000, must be licensed. This applies to all work, public or private, performed within the State, with the exception of Federal work. The annual license fee is $15, plus $1 clerk fee.

MASSACHUSETTS

PREQUALIFICATION *required* in order to bid on any work to be awarded by the Massachusetts Department of Public Works aggregating fifty thousand dollars ($50,000) or more, excepting the construction, reconstruction, repair or alteration of buildings. Also required by Metropolitan District Commission.

CONTRACTOR'S LICENSE *not* required.

PREQUALIFICATION

Any contractor proposing to bid on work under the direction of the Massachusetts Department of Public Works aggregating fifty thousand dollars ($50,000) or more must furnish a notarized statement on forms provided by the Department setting forth his financial resources, adequacy of plant and equipment, organization and other pertinent facts. The financial data shall be prepared by a Certified Public Accountant based on an actual audit of the contractor's records within four (4) months of the filing date, provided no significant change in the structure of the firm, officers, ownership, status of equipment, name of corporation, or incorporation of an non-incorporated firm occurs between the date upon which the audit is based and the filing date.

In no case shall a request for prequalification be accepted after the twelfth day preceding the day set for opening of bids for work upon which a contractor intends to bid. A request for prequalification will not be considered until a properly and correctly completed questionnaire and financial statement, including all necessary data, has been submitted.

The "Regulations Governing Classification and Rating of Prospepective Bidders," Form R-110, and "Contractor's Prequalification Statement," Form C-93, may be obtained from the Massachusetts Department of Public Works, 100 Nashua Street, Boston, Massachusetts.

LICENSING

There is no State law requiring contractors on either public or private work to be licensed.

MICHIGAN

PREQUALIFICATION *required* in order to bid on highway work.

LICENSE *required* in order to bid on residential building. See below.

PREQUALIFICATION

Under Act No. 170, Public Acts of 1933, as amended, contractors proposing to bid on State highway construction are required at least 15 days prior to date set for opening of bids, to file with the State Highway Commission a "Confidential Experience Questionnaire and Financial Statement," using standard forms provided by the Department.

All bidders having a fiscal year ending on or after December 31, 1968, must complete and submit a Revised Form 1313, attaching thereto a copy of their certified audit report for the same fiscal year if they desire to become prequalified. Prequalification for work under $200,000.00 does not require certification of the financial statement, however, it is desirable. They should develop bidders' financial resources, equipment, facilities, experience and qualifications to satisfactorily carry out work to be performed. Information will be kept confidential.

Bidders who qualify will be rated to show the maximum amount of work allowable at any time. Following criteria will be used in determining the rating:

(a) Net liquid assets multiplied by 9.

(b) Net equipment value multiplied by 4.

Description of all major rating factors and their methods of application are set forth in "The Administrative Rules Governing the Prequalification of Bidders for Highway Construction Work," effective December 31, 1968. Joint bidding on a single contract may be engaged in by two or three contractors. See page 25 of said booklet.

A low bidder on two or more projects totalling more than his financial rating will be awaited such project or projects as will be to best advantage of Highway Department.

The financial statement as at the end of the fiscal year is required once each year for continuous prequalification.

LICENSING

Residential building contractors and maintenance and alteration contractors are required to obtain a license before bidding upon or contracting work of a residential or combination residential and commercial character. Application must be made in writing, on forms, prescribed by the Department of Licensing and Regulation. The applicant must undergo a written examination or submit satisfactory evidence of five years' experience in the type of work to be undertaken as a contractor. The Act prescribes various regulations, exemptions, and penalties.

Fee for a residential builder's license is $35; for a residential maintenance and alteration contractor, $30.

No license will be issued to a foreign corporation until such corporation has been duly authorized to do business in Michigan by the Department of Treasury. Foreign corporations must maintain place of business in Michigan.

MINNESOTA

PREQUALIFICATION *not* required.
CONTRACTOR'S LICENSE *not* required.

PREQUALIFICATION

No formal prequalification is required in order to submit bids on State highway work.

Each bidder shall furnish to the State upon request a statement showing the experience of the bidder and the amount of capital and equipment he has available for performance of the proposed work. (Department of Highways.)

LICENSING

There is no law requiring contractors bidding on or executing work within the State to be licensed. Bids submitted by foreign or non-resident corporations will not be considered unless these corporations have furnished evidence to the State that they have met all legal requirements for transacting business in Minnesota.

MISSISSIPPI

PREQUALIFICATION *required* on all public work costing in excess of $25,000.
LICENSE *required* before bidding on or performing public or private work costing over $10,000. (See below.)

PREQUALIFICATION

Contractors are required to prequalify before submitting a bid or being awarded jobs involving public funds of more than $25,000.

Application for Certificate of Responsibility must be made to State Board of Public Contractors on a form prescribed by the Board accompanied by a $100 deposit for special privilege tax. Board will classify the kind or kinds of public works or public projects that a public contractor is qualified and entitled to perform under the Certificate of Responsibility. The Board shall not require a financial statement but shall limit its inquiries to: Experience and ability, manner of performing work previously undertaken, equipment, personnel, work completed, work on hand, apparent ability to perform satisfactorily work under contract at the time of application, and written or oral examinations.

LICENSING

Before bidding on or performing public or private work, on jobs costing in excess of $10,-000 contractor must obtain a State-Wide Privilege License. Application must be on form prescribed by State Tax Commission. Cost of license, $75. (State Tax Commissioner.)

License IS required where contractor bids on or performs contracts for Federal Government on Government land.

On all contracts in excess of $25,000.00 involving public funds both the prime contractor and the subcontractor must obtain a license and a Certificate of Responsibility from the State Board of Public Contractors. Cost of license is $100. Application must be on form prescribed by State Board of Public Contractors.

MISSOURI

PREQUALIFICATION (as such) *not required* in order to bid on highway work.
CONTRACTOR'S LICENSE *not* required.

PREQUALIFICATION

Foreign corporations must furnish a certified copy of authority to perform the type of work involved in Missouri. All bidders must have on file a financial statement seven days before letting date. Those individuals doing business under a name other than their own must comply with registration requirements for fictitious names.

LICENSING

There is no State law requiring contractors on public or private work to be licensed.

MONTANA

PREQUALIFICATION *required* in order to bid on highway work.
LICENSE *required* of contractors bidding on public work costing over $1,000.

PREQUALIFICATION

Contractors desiring to bid on State highway work must qualify, before bids are accepted, with the State Highway Commission, Helena, Mont. Prequalification statements required annually. New bidders wishing to qualify for specific letting must submit qualifications not later than 7 days prior to opening of bids. A prospective bidder, submitting a statement for the first, or a former, prequalified bidder whose statement has expired, must submit data which is not more than 90 days old.

LICENSING

Contractors bidding on public works in excess of $1,000 required to obtain license.

In the language of the revised statute:

"There shall be three classes of licenses issued under the provisions of this Act; and such classes of licenses are hereby designated as Classes A, B, and C. Any applicant for a license under the provisions hereof, shall specifiy in his application the class of license applied for.

"The holder of a Class A license shall be entitled to engage in the public contracting business within the State of Montana without any limitation as to the value of a single public contract project, subject however, to such prequalification requirements as may be imposed and at the time of making the application for such license the applicant shall pay to the registrar a fee in the sum of Two Hundred Dollars ($200).

"The holder of a Class B license shall be entitled to engage in the public contracting business within the State of Montana, but shall not be entitled to engage in the construction of any single public contract project of a value in excess of Fifty Thousand Dollars ($50,000); and shall pay unto the registrar as a license fee the sum of One Hundred Dollars ($100) for such Class B license at the time of making application therefor.

"The holder of a Class C license shall be entitled to engage in the public contracting business within the State of Montana, but shall not be entitled to engage in the construction of any single public contract project of a value in excess of Twenty-five Thousand Dollars ($25,-000) and shall pay unto the registrar as a license fee the sum of Ten Dollars ($10) at the time of making application therefor."

Each public contractor must pay to the state an additional license fee equal to 1% of the gross receipts from public contracts during the income year for which the license is issued. The additional license fees may be used as a credit on the contractor's corporation license tax, or on the contractor's income tax. Contractors may also request direct refund of the additional 1% license fee by filing copies of tax receipts reflecting Montana personal property taxes paid on equipment used in their contracting business.

Licenses are issued by:
State Board of Equalization
Mitchell Building
Helena, Montana 59601

Since application must be held 10 days by Board before issuance of license, submission should be made sufficiently in advance to permit receipt of license before opening of bid on any project which contractor wishes to bid. Renewal, 50% of the original fee. Must be renewed before March 1st of each year.

License is required where contractor bids on or performs contracts for Federal Government, on Government land. License is not required to submit a bid where Federal funds are involved from Bureau of Public Roads or Department of Agriculture, but must be obtained before actual construction is started.

NEBRASKA

PREQUALIFICATION *required* in order to bid on State highway work, except on maintenance or repair jobs costing below $2,500, and emergency work.
CONTRACTOR'S LICENSE *not* required on any work.

PREQUALIFICATION

Contractors desiring to bid on State highway work must prequalify with the Department of Roads. Excepted are maintenace and repair jobs costing less than $2,500, and emergency jobs.

Detailed statements, certified to by a CPA, or by a public accountant holding a currently valid permit from the Nebraska State Board of Public Accountancy, must be submitted on forms provided for the purpose, at least seven days before date of contract letting on which it is desired to bid. Statements must provide information relating to finances, equipment, organization and experience, and must be sworn to. Statements will hold good for 15 months but Department may call for additional or new information at any time.

Department will rate applicants on basis of information supplied. Ratings will designate types and amounts of work for which applicants have been qualified to bid. Ratings will be of two types. A "maximum qualification" rating will first be issued to qualified applicants. After receiving same, applicant may request proposal forms for any specific letting, and state, on forms provided by Department, amounts and types of work then under contract, in Nebraska and elsewhere, and amounts thereof still uncompleted. Department may then grant a "current qualification" rating showing amount of work for which applicant may be qualified to bid at the particular letting. He may, however, be awarded contracts exceeding the "current" rating by 25%.

Proposal forms will be labelled with bidder's name and will not be transferable. They will not be issued after 5:00 P.M. of day preceding day of letting. Two or more qualified bidders may bid jointly.

LICENSING

There is no State law requiring contractors on either public or private work to be licensed.

L. B. 1415, 1969, requires nonresident contractors to register with the Tax Commission each contract in excess of $2,500 and file a bond or other form of acceptable assurance conditioned upon the payment of all taxes, including contributions under the employment Security Law, which may accure to the state and to political subdivisions, on account of the execution and performance of such contract or contracts. (Tax Commissioner.)

NEVADA

PREQUALIFICATION *required* in order to bid on highway work.
LICENSE *required* of contractors in order to bid on both public and private work. Bid by unlicensed contractor is unlawful, unless exempted due to conflict with federal law or regulations pertaining to federal aid contracts.

PREQUALIFICATION

Pursuant to Nevada Revised Statutes 408.-870, the State Highway Engineer shall before furnishing any person proposing to bid on any duly advertised work with the plans and specifications for such work, require from such person a statement, under oath, in the form of answers to questions contained in a standard form of questionnaire and financial statement, which shall include a complete statement of the person's financial ability and experience in performing public work of a similar nature. Such statements shall be filed in ample time to permit the department to verify the information contained therein in advance of furnishing proposal forms, plans and specifictions to any such person proposing to bid on any such duly advertised public work, in accordance with the department's rules and regulations.

LICENSING

State of Nevada State Contractor's License Law requires all contractors, including subcontractors, doing business in the State to be licensed.

Application for license shall be on form prepared by State Contractor's Board, and shall be accompanied by fee prescribed by law. Form calls for exhaustive information as to applicant's past record, competence, character, finances (supported by CPA report) and other pertinent data. All bids and contracts must carry license number.

Licensing supervised by:
State Contractors Board
P. O. Box 7497
Reno, Nevada 89102.

The Board, in its discretion, is authorized to fix application and annual license fees to be paid by applicants and licensees under the terms of this Act; provided, however, that the application fee shall not exceed $100 and the annual license fee shall not exceed $100.

A bond or deposit in an amount determined by the board up to a maximum of $20,-000 is required. Expiration of renewal date, December 15th.

License is NOT required where contractor performs contracts for Federal Government, on Government land.

NEW HAMPSHIRE

PREQUALIFICATION *required* in order to bid on public work.
CONTRACTOR'S LICENSE *not* required.

PREQUALIFICATION

All contractors desiring to bid upon work under jurisdiction of Department of Public Works and Highways must prequalify by filing therewith, on forms provided for the purpose, information setting forth their qualifications. Such filing must be made once a year and, in any event not less than eight days prior to opening of bids on any work on which they desire to bid. Department may require a prospective bidder to bring his statement up to date as of the last day of the month preceding that in which bids are to be opened.

A copy of the "Regulations for Prequalifying Contractors" and associated forms may be obtained from:
State of New Hampshire
Department of Public Works and
Highways
John O. Morton Building
85 Loudon Road, P. O. Box 483
Concord, New Hampshire 03301

LICENSING

There is no State law requiring contractors on either public or private work to be licensed.

NEW JERSEY

PREQUALIFICATION *required* of all bidders on State work, either new construction or repair, where same is advertised. Also required by State Board of Education from all school building bidders.
CONTRACTOR'S LICENSE *not* required on any work, except certain specified electrical work.

PREQUALIFICATION

Persons proposing to bid on any State work must prequalify.

Those proposing to bid on State highway or other Transportation Department work must furnish a statement under oath in response to a questionnaire to be submitted by the Commissioner of Transportation. Such statement shall fully develop the financial ability, adequacy of plant and equipment, organization and prior experience, including complete record of work done in past three years and such other pertinent and material facts as may be desirable. New statements required every twelve months, or oftener, if deemed necessary by Commissioner.

Applicant should indicate class or classes of work for which qualification is sought. Commissioner will classify approved applicants with respect to construction or repair work in grading, paving, bridge construction, heavy highway construction and miscellaneous work, such as the painting of bridges and other structures; landscaping; test borings; demolition of buildings or other structures; the furnishing and applying of surfacing materials; dredging; guard rail and fencing; signs; electrical work; underground utilities; fabrication and erection of iron and steel; pile driving; pavement marking; blasting; and the like. He will also stipulate dollar volume of work upon which applicants may bid, according to an alphabetical classification grading from A, for jobs between $50,000 and $100,000 to R, jobs with a value of over $25,000,000. For jobs under $50,000 a special classification also will be accorded.

In addition to prequalification requirements above, prospective bidders with ratings up to and including $2,000,000 must submit new statements bearing date as of the end of the month preceding month during which bids will be accepted, except that bids submitted between the 1st and the 15th of any month may carry statements dated one month earlier than here stipulated.

Bidders with ratings above $2,000,000 may submit an affidavit that there has been no material change in the financial condition since the date of submission for classification if the proper affidavits are completed and accompanied by the status of contracts on hand as of the most recent practical date.

BIDDING: Included in the bid envelope, in addition to the proposal being offered, should be (1) Revised Contractors Financial and Equipment Statement Form DC-74(b) as of the time specified in the advertisement; (2) Certified Check for 10% of the amount bid (minimum $500, maximum $20,000); (3) Proposal Bond in a sum not less than 50% of the bid; (4) Non-collusion Affidavit, in duplicate; (5) Appointment of Local Agent, by nonresident contractors.

State Board of Education requires prequalification of all contractors doing public work.

The State Division of Purchase and Property requires the filing of a financial statement questionnaire and sets limits on the amount contractors can bid on construction of state buildings.

LICENSING

There is no State law requiring contractors on either public or private work to be licensed, except certain specified electrical work which must be performed by an electrical contractor approved and licensed by the N.J. Board of Examiners of Electrical Contractors.

NEW MEXICO

PREQUALIFICATION *required* in order to bid on highway work.
LICENSE *required* in order to bid on both public and private work, except Federal projects.

PREQUALIFICATION

Contractors will be required to file an experience questionnaire and certified financial statement which must be a complete report of their financial resources and liabilities, equipment, past record, personnel of organization, and experience. This evidence must be submitted on forms furnished by the Engineer and must be on file with the Engi-

neer not less than ten (10) days prior to date of opening bids. Contractors will be prequalified, on the basis of the data submitted, not less than once each year.

The Commission will determine the qualifications of prospective bidders, based on the data submitted and will establish the type of work, the number of projects, and the total monetary value of the uncompleted work that the bidder will be permitted to have under contract at any time. The proposals of bidders exceeding the prequalification limit established by the Commission may be rejected.

LICENSING

Applications for Contractor's License must be made on forms furnished by the Construction Industries Commission. Failure to complete or to omit essential information will result in delay or cause rejection of the application.

The "Construction Industries Licensing Act of 1967" provides for the regulation, licensing and classification of "contractors".

Provides that each "trade board" may require a reasonable bond or surety in the penal sum of $500 with such board as obligee and conditioned for the payment of inspection fees provided in the Act.

Provides that an applicant for a license shall demonstrate financial responsibility as provided in this Act.

Provides that the Construction Industries Commission shall promulgate regulations setting forth standards for the determination of financial responsibility. The standards shall take into consideration, but not be limited to, such factors as credit ratings, net worth, total assets, net quick assets, business management experience, previous financial practices and experience, previous bankruptcies, and the size and scope of contracting or proposed contracting operations.

Provides that no applicant for a contractor's license or for the renewal thereof shall be issued a license until the commission determines that he is financially responsible to perform a specified aggregate dollar-amount of contracts at any one time.

Provides that any applicant for a contractor's license or the renewal thereof who is found not to be financially responsible shall be licensed by the commission only in the event such applicant furnishes to the commission proof of financial responsibility for the future. The proof of financial responsibility for the future shall be maintained for the period of one licensing year and for each succeeding licensing year, after a determination by the commission that the applicant is not financially responsible at the time application for renewal is made.

Provides that proof of financial responsibility for the future shall be: (1) a surety bond acceptable to the commission and underwritten by an authorized corporate surety; a net value to him at least double the amount; or (2) an agreement of cash collateral assignment, executed with a state or national bank or federally insured savings association authorized to do business in New Mexico, as trustee, in a form prescribed by the commission.

Provides that proof of financial responsibility for the future shall be furnished in amounts of $1,000, $2,500, or $5,000, thus authorizing the contractor to perform $25,000 or less, $100,000 or less, or over $100,000 gross annual business in New Mexico.

Communications regarding licenses and application forms should be addressed to:

Construction Industries Commission
P. O. Box 5155
Santa Fe, New Mexico 87501

NEW YORK

PREQUALIFICATION *not* required.
CONTRACTOR'S LICENSE *not* required.

PREQUALIFICATION

There is no law or regulation of any department letting contracts for public construction that requires contracts to prequalify in advance of bidding. However, Chapter 480 of the Laws of 1947 provides that non-resident contractors, partnerships, having one or more partners who is a non-resident, or corporate contractors not organized under the laws of New York State must prove that all taxes due the State of New York have been paid before receiving payments due under a contract for highway construction. A certificate from the State Tax Commission to the effect that all such taxes have been paid constitutes proof of such fact.

LICENSING

There is no State law requiring contractors on either public or private work to be licensed.

NORTH CAROLINA

PREQUALIFICATION *required* in order to bid on all other non-federal jobs costing $20,000 or more, through operation of State licensing laws.

LICENSE *required* of contractors bidding or undertaking projects of $20,000 or more, both public and private.

PREQUALIFICATION

State Highway project—Contractors bidding for the first time or who have not had a contract for one year must file prior to the time of receipt of bids an experience questionnaire and confidential financial statement which must be a complete report of the financial resources and liabilities, equipment, past record, personnel of organization, and experience. Contractors intending to consistently submit proposals on State Highway projects are to prequalify at least once a year. They shall comply with the act to regulate the practice of general contracting as contained in Article 1, General Contractors, Chapter 87, General Statutes of North Carolina.

There are two types of projects (1) those financed from State funds, and (2) those financed wholly or in part from Federal funds. Before a Contractor is permitted to bid on the first class of projects, it is necessary for him to be licensed by the North Carolina Licensing Board for Contractors, provided the bids submitted are $20,000 or more. This license is not a requirement when bidding on the second class of projects.

LICENSING

Licensing is supervised by:
North Carolina Licensing Board for
Contractors
508 Branch Banking & Trust Co. Building
Raleigh, North Carolina 27602

Contractors desiring to bid on or execute projects of $20,000 or more must make formal application and file with the Board at least thirty days prior to any regular or special meeting, a written application on such forms as may then be prescribed by the Board. The Board either issues or denies a license, basing its decision upon experience, organization, financial condition and performance record of the applicant, and successful completion of written examination.

Licenses are issued in three groups, as follows:

(1) Limited Group—permitting contractors to bid on individual projects up to $75,-000; Fee $40. Annual renewal, $20.

(2) Intermediate Group—permitting contractors to bid on individual projects up to $300,000; Fee, $60. Annual renewal, $40.

(3) Unlimited Group—permitting contractors to bid on projects of any size; Fee, $80. Annual renewal, $60.

All licenses expire on the 1st day of December. Renewal of license may be effected any time during the month of January, without re-examination, by payment of the renewal fee to the secretary of the Board.

Separate from the above, Section 122, Chapter 105-54, N.C. General Statutes, requires "Every person, firm or corporation who, for a fixed price, commission, fee, or wage, offers or bids to construct within the State of North Carolina any building, highway, street, sidewalk, bridge, culvert, sewer or water system, drainage or dredging system, electric or steam railway, reservoir or dam, hydraulic or power plant, transmission line, tower, dock, wharf, excavation, grading or other improvement or structure, or any part thereof, the cost of which exceeds the sum of ten thousand dollars ($10,000) shall apply for and obtain from the Commissioner of Revenue an annual Statewide license, and shall pay for such license a tax of one hundred dollars ($100) at the time of or prior to offering or submitting any bid on any of the above enumerated projects.

In addition to the above and before entering into such projects, a state-wide license must be procured.

Licensing year begins July 1st. Fee may be prorated where bidder places first bid between January 1st and June 30th.

NORTH DAKOTA

PREQUALIFICATION *required* in order to bid on highway work.
LICENSE *required* in order to bid on all work costing $500 or more.

PREQUALIFICATION

North Dakota State Highway Department requires that "Names of bidders must be on the Commissioner's qualifed list of Contractors, with a sufficient rating shown thereon to entitle them to bid upon the particular job in question before bid will be accepted. Each bidder shall furnish the Commissioner with satisfactory evidence of his competency to perform the work contemplated. A new prequalification statement must be filed each year by April 15, or 10 days prior to the first letting after that date in which the Contractor wishes to bid. This statement shall show the condition of his business as of the close of the Contractor's fiscal year. New statements shall be submitted by April 15 each year thereafter for as long a period as the bidder continues to offer proposals for work advertised for letting by the Commissioner unless specifically requested oftener. The prequalification statement consists of the builder's financial statement as attested to by a Certified Public Accountant, also information relating to his experience in performing construction work similar to the work on which he wishes to bid, and a list of machinery, plant and other equipment available for the proposed work. Experience questionnaire herein referred to shall be submitted on forms furnished by the Commissioner based on such statement, and the confirmation or verification of the fact set forth therein, together with such other material and pertinent data as the Commissioner may have to acquire relative to the competency of such a bidder. A rating will be assigned such bidder after receipt of the financial statement and questionnaire, which rating will set forth the maximum and type of work which will be awarded to him or which he will be permitted to have under contract and incomplete at any time."

No contractor shall be eligible to enter into a public contract with the state of North Dakota or any of its political or governmental subdivisions until the contractor has furnished to the public body a certificate from the State Tax Commissioner stating that the contractor has satisfied all of the requirements of the state income tax law, and use tax law.

LICENSING

Chapter 43-07 North Dakota Century Code as amended July 1, 1969, requires contractors to be licensed when contract cost exceeds $500.

A "contractor" is any person, as hereinbefore defined, engaged in the business of construction, repair, alteration, dismantling or demolition of bridges, highways, roads, streets, buildings, airports, dams, drainage or irrigation ditches, sewers, water or gas mains, water filters, tanks, towers, oil, gas or water pipelines, and every other type of structure, project, development or improvement coming within the definition of real or personal property, including the construction, alteration or repair of property to be held either for sale or rental and shall include subcontractor, public contractor, and non-resident contractor.

There are four classes of licenses issued. License (A) costs $250, covers contracts of any amount. License (B) costs $150, covers contracts up to and including $125,000. License (C) costs $100, covers contracts up to and including $60,000. License (D) costs $25, covers contracts up to and including $25,000. Bond required with application, Class A, $2,000, and others $1,000.

Registrant must hold application for license ten days. A contractor bidding on a "public contract" as defined in this law must have license ten days prior to date set forth for bids, to be a qualified bidder.

License may be renewed from year to year at 20% of original cost, if renewed between January 1st and April 1st. (Secretary of State.)

OHIO

PREQUALIFICATION *required* in order to bid on highway work.
CONTRACTOR'S LICENSE *not* required.

PREQUALIFICATION

Contractors desiring to bid on State highway work are required to file a financial statement and complete an equipment and experience questionnaire to be reviewed by the Administrator of Contractor Qualification.

For general work, statements must be submitted at least 10 days prior to date set for opening bids. For structures built to carry railroad traffic, whether permanent or temporary in nature, special prequalification necessary, with statements submitted at least 30 days before opening of bids.

Upon favorable action by the Administrator of Contractor Qualifications, a prequalification certificate indicating the amount and type of work the contractor is qualified to have under contract, is issued. Communications concerning prequalification should be addressed to the Administrator, Contractor Qualifications, Highway Administration Building, 25 S. Front, Columbus, Ohio 43215.

LICENSING

There is no State law requiring contractors on either public or private work to be licensed.

OKLAHOMA

PREQUALIFICATION *required* in order to bid on highway work.
CONTRACTOR'S LICENSE *not* required.

PREQUALIFICATION

Only prequalified contractors will be allowed to bid upon construction and maintenance work of the Highway Department.

A contractor, who desires to bid upon the construction or maintenance work of the Department, will submit to the Department, at least ten (10) days prior to the bidding date, a plan and experience questionnaire and a comprehensive confidential financial statement, showing all liabilities (current, deferred, and contingent), including equipment schedule, dated within the last sixty (60) days prior to receipt by the Department, on forms furnished by the Department for the purpose. The financial statement will be verified by a Certified Public Accountant with his certificate number shown. All blanks on the contractor's financial statement form will be filled in with either an amount or the word "none." The plan and experience questionnaire form will show, inter alia, contractor's past experience record, principal personnel and their experience, and at least six references as to the character and quality of work previously done.

Based upon a review by the Department, a contractor who has not performed any work for the Department may be prequalified for an amount which is not more than ten (10) times his net quick assets based upon reasonable grounds and experience and which shall not be subject to appeal.

The department will qualify, or refuse to qualify, any contractor for paving, grade and drain, bridge, or other Department construction work in accordance with such contractor's experience, equipment, and financial rating, provided, however, that the Department will determine the contractor's rating, or disqualification, and will notify him of its findings not later than four (4) days prior to the bid opening date in which the contractor desires to bid.

Any contractor not satisfied with a rejection of his application for qualification by the Department or with the rating given, may appeal therefrom to the Director by giving notice by registered mail addressed to the Director, of his objection within 24 hours from the date such contractor received notice of the Department's action.

If a contractor has previously done work for the Department, the maximum amount for which he may be prequalified will be not more than ten (10) times his net quick assets.

Every non-resident contractor, firm or entity including any corporation not domiciled in this State, will before it is permitted to transact business or continue business with the Department, appoint and maintain a service agent upon whom service of process may be made in any action to which said contractor, person, firm or entity may be a party. Appointment of such agent for service, properly executed and acknowledged will be filed with the Secretary of State, and will give the residence address or place of business of such agent. A certified copy of this filing will be furnished to the Department. Said service agent will not be an official, elective or appointive, of the United States, or any political subdivision thereof except as otherwise provided by law, or a bondsman, surety or materials supplier.

Every such foreign corporation, firm, association or legal entity will file a certified copy of its Articles of Incorporation, Partnership, or Association, with the Department.

No proposal for construction or maintenance work of the Department will be issued to any contractor after two o'clock in the afternoon of the day preceding opening of bids for any contract; and no individual proposal will be issued to any contractor in excess of the amount for which said contractor may be qualified. Should a contractor be low bidder on contracts totaling more than the amount for which he is qualified (less the amount of work on hand), the Commission reserves the right to reject any or all proposals, to waive technicalities, to readvertise for new proposals, or proceed to do the work otherwise, when the best interest of the state will be promoted thereby.

The prospective bidder should familiarize himself with the Oklahoma State Highway Commission Standard Specification, Edition of 1967.

For copy write to:
State Highway Commission
Jim Thorpe Building
Oklahoma City, Oklahoma 73105

LICENSING

There is no State law requiring contractors on either public or private work to be licensed.

OREGON

PREQUALIFICATION *required* in order to bid on public works projects in excess of $10,000.
CONTRACTOR'S LICENSE *not* required.

PREQUALIFICATION

Prospective bidders on all public works projects costing over $10,000 shall prequalify with awarding authority, not later than 10 days prior to date set for opening bids. Information required, on forms to be furnished, shall be sworn to and shall include financial statement, outline of experience, description of equipment available and other pertinent data that may be called for. Bidders once qualified before any public officer need not separately qualify for each contract later to be advertised, unless required to do so by said officer. Decisions as to prequalification submissions will be announced at least 8 days prior to time set for opening bids.

Prequalifying authorities include: State Highway Commission, Salem, Oregon; State Department of Finance and Administration, Salem, Oregon; State Board of Higher Education, Comptroller, University of Oregon Eugene, Oregon; and Oregon State Board of Control, Salem, Oregon.

LICENSING

There is no State law requiring contractors, as such, to be licensed on either public or private work.

PENNSYLVANIA

PREQUALIFICATION *required* of all contractors, whether bidders or subcontractors, in order to bid on highway work.
CONTRACTOR'S LICENSE *not* required.

PREQUALIFICATION

In determining qualifications of bidders the department shall consider the following factors; equipment, past record, experience, personnel of organization and financial condition. No bids considered from any bidder who is not qualified.

LICENSING

There is no State law requiring contractors on either public or private work to be licensed. Fictitious business styles and foreign corporations must be registered. (Secretary of the Commonwealth.)

PUERTO RICO

PREQUALIFICATION *not required* in order to bid.
CONTRACTOR'S LICENSE *not* required.

PREQUALIFICATION

Prospective bidders must accompany bids with a "statement of bidder's qualification" attesting to experience, equipment available, personnel and financial condition.

LICENSING

There is no Puerto Rico law requiring that contractors be licensed.

RHODE ISLAND

PREQUALIFICATION *not* required in order to bid.
CONTRACTOR'S LICENSE *not* required.

PREQUALIFICATION

A registered list of bidders, for highway and bridge work, is maintained and when there is work to be bid, contractors on the registered list are notified. The job is also listed in local newspapers. To be placed on the list, it is necessary only to make request to the State Department of Public Works Division of Roads and Bridges, Providence, R.I. Out-of-State contractors are requested to file authority for officers authorized to sign or, if a partnership, to give names and addresses of partners. A contractor is not required to file statement of finances and performance history until and unless he is a low bidder.

LICENSING

There is no State law requiring contractors on either public or private work to be licensed.

SOUTH CAROLINA

PREQUALIFICATION *required* in order to bid on highway work.
LICENSES of two types *required* of general contractors in order to bid on jobs of $30,000 or more.

If contractor has prequalified for highway work license will automatically issue, after 7 days following the date of application.

PREQUALIFICATION

Under "Rules and Regulations for Prequalifications," established in accordance with Section 33–223 of the 1962 Code entitled "State Highway Commission to Fix Eligibility of Bidders on State Highway Work," contractors desiring to bid on State highway work are required to submit a financial statement, an experience questionnaire and an equipment questionnaire to the South Carolina State Highway Commission, Columbia, South Carolina. The required forms may be obtained from the Commission.

LICENSING

Two types of licenses required for general contractors desiring to bid on or perform jobs costing $30,000 or over. Both licenses under Jurisdiction, Licensing Board for Contractors, P. O. Box 5737, 1300 Pickens St., Room 118, Columbia, S.C. 29205.

General Contractor's license obtainable by applying to Board, on form provided, at least 30 days in advance of regularly scheduled meeting and, upon being notified, submitting to examination. Approved applicants will appear on roster maintained by Board. Fee for this license $60, paid at time of application. Expiration date, December 31. Renewal required during month of January, same fee.

This license will be issued without examination, seven days after application, to those presenting bidder's or contractor's certificate issued by Highway Department. Same fees.

Bidder's license, issuable without examination those holding General Contractor's license upon payment of fee of $100. This license also expires in December and is renewable either the following January or prior to submitting the next bid. Renewal fee, $100.

All bids by licensed contractor must show license numbers, for both types of licenses held.

License is NOT required where contractor bids on or performs contracts for Federal Government, on Government land. Projects involving public or private funds augmented by Federal Aid are subject to license requirements.

SOUTH DAKOTA

PREQUALIFICATION *required* in order to bid on highway work.
CONTRACTOR'S LICENSE *not* required.

PREQUALIFICATION

All persons proposing to bid on State highway work must furnish a statement under oath on a form prescribed and provided by the Department of Highways. Statement shall fully develop the financial ability, adequacy of equipment, organization, prior experience and other pertinent and material facts. Information furnished shall be used to determine a contractor's classification and rating.

The financial statement shall be supported by a certificate as to the correctness thereof by a certified public accountant or a South Dakota licensed accountant.

Statements upon which a qualification is desired shall be received by the Department in Pierre not less than fourteen (14) days prior to the date of requesting proposals for a letting to provide sufficient time for the committee to properly analyze and consider the same.

Ratings are given for one or more of the following classifications:

Grading
Portland Cement—Concrete Paving
Bituminous Paving—Plant Mix Work
Bituminous Surfacing—Blotter Type
Gravel and Crushed Rock Surfacing Base Course
Bridges and Grade Separations
Guard Rail
Roadside Improvement

A rating on "maximum capacity," or largest amount that contractor may have under contract at any one time is also assigned.

Also assigned, for any particular letting will be a "current rating," bearing upon contractor's eligibility to be considered for that job.

Necessary forms for making application together with a copy of "Regulations Governing the Classification and Rating of Prospective Bidders" can be obtained from:
South Dakota State Highway Commission
Pierre, South Dakota.

LICENSING

There is no State law requiring contractors on either public or private work to be licensed.

TENNESSEE

PREQUALIFICATION *required* in order to bid on highway work.
LICENSE *required* of contractors undertaking work in excess of $10,000, public or private.

PREQUALIFICATION

The Department of Highways requires prequalification by contractors bidding on work under the supervision of that Department, regardless of the size of the project and irrespective of whether or not the contractor has been licensed by the State Board for Licensing General Contractors.

Prequalification questionnaires prepared by a Certified or Licensed Public Accountant, must be filed once a year and must reach office of State Construction Engineer at least seven days prior to date of contract letting in which contractor is interested. Forms may be obtained from:

Department of Highways
110 Highway Building
Nashville, Tennessee 37219

LICENSING

Tennessee Code, Section 62-601 et seq., requires general contractors to be licensed before undertaking any project costing more than $10,000.

Any person, firm or corporation desiring to be licensed under this Act must make application on the prescribed form thirty (30) days prior to any regular or special meeting of the Board for Licensing General contractors. Regular meetings of the Board are held in January, April, July and October of each year.

Written application accompanied by a remittance of $25 must be filed with the Board on such forms as the Board may prescribe. If the application is satisfactory to the Board, the applicant shall be entitled to an examination to determine his qualifications. If the results of the examination are satisfactory to the Board a certificate will be issued authorizing the applicant to operate as a general contractor in the State of Tennessee. Anyone failing to pass such examination may be reexamined at a regular meeting of the Board without additional fee.

Licenses expire on the last day of December following issuance or renewal. Renewal may be effected by payment of $15 to the Secretary of the Board.

Issuance of a certificate of license by the Board is evidence that the person, firm or corporation named therein is entitled to all the rights and privileges of a licensed general contractor, while the license remains unrevoked, provided that the contractor has paid his privilege tax (outlined below) and that the license is recorded in the office of the County Clerk in each County in which the contractor engages in business. Fee for recording of the certificate by the County Clerk of any county is $1.

Licensing is under the supervision of:
State Board of Licensing General
 Contractors
101 Cotton States Building
Nashville, Tennessee 37219

TEXAS

PREQUALIFICATION *required* in order to bid on highway work.
CONTRACTOR'S LICENSE *not* required.

PREQUALIFICATION

Contractors desiring to bid on State highway work must submit to the Texas Highway Department, Austin, Texas 78701, on forms provided for the purpose, a confidential questionnaire containing financial, equipment and experience data. The financial statement must contain complete information pertaining to the contractor's financial condition, including a balance sheet and statement of contractor's financial resources which must be certified to by an independent C.P.A., registered and in good standing in any state, or an independent Public Accountant registered under the Texas

Public Accountancy Act of 1945. Foreign corporations desiring prequalification must first obtain a Certificate of Authority to do business in the State of Texas from the Secretary of State's office.

LICENSING

There is no State law requiring contractors on either public or private work to be licensed.

House Bill 557, Texas Regular Session 1967 requires Non-Resident Construction Contractors, before commencing work or undertaking to perform any duties under a contract in Texas, to file with the Comptroller of Public Accounts a surety bond in the amount of 10% of the contract price payable to the state of Texas, conditioned upon compliance with the Tax Laws, the Unemployment Compensation Laws and the Workmen's Compensation Laws of Texas.

The law provides that if the Comptroller finds that the Non-Resident Contractor has property in Texas sufficient to comply with said laws or has a past record of compliance with these laws, the Comptroller may issue a certificate of exemption from the bonding requirement. The law also provides that a contractor whose principal place of business is in a state that does not require notice and bonding of non-resident contractors as provided by this law, said contractor is exempt.

UTAH

PREQUALIFICATION *required* to bid on projects under the jurisdiction of State Road Commission, and on State Building Board projects.
LICENSE *required* in order to bid on both public and private work.

PREQUALIFICATION

Under regulations of State Road Commission contractors desiring to bid on State projects must submit a Confidential Financial Statement, Equipment and Experience Questionnaire, on forms provided by the Department of Contractors, Salt Lake City, Utah. State Building Board requirements similar, with respect to projects.

Financial statements must be of a date not more than nine months prior to date of application for prequalification. Financial statements must be audited by independent

C.P.A., registered and in good standing in any State, or independent public accountant, licensed and in good standing in Utah. *If applicant desires qualification in excess of $100,000, accountant's audit must not contain nullifying qualifications.*

New statements required annually at least 30 days prior to expiration of current qualification.

Prior to being prequalified each applicant must have been licensed in compliance with Utah laws, and, if an out-of-State corporation, must have certificate from Secretary of State showing that corporation is duly qualified to transact business in Utah.

LICENSING

Applications for license must be on forms provided by Department and afford pertinent information regarding applicant's experience, financial responsibility and general competence.

Licenses to be issued will be of three types: (1) General Engineering (2) General Building (3) Specialty. Applicants should state type of license or licenses desired. A qualified applicant may be licensed in more than one classification.

58-23-2. Exceptions from Act.—This Act shall not apply to:

(1) An authorized representative or representatives of the United States Government, the State of Utah, or any county, incorporated city or town, irrigation district, reclamation district, or other municipal or political corporation or subdivision of this State.

(2) Any construction or operation incidental to the construction and repair of irrigation and drainage ditches of regularly constituted irrigation district and reclamation districts, or to quarries, sand and gravel excavations, well drilling, hauling and lumbering.

(3) Trustees of an express trust, or officers of a court, providing they are acting within the terms of their trust or office, respectively.

(4) Public utilities operating under the regulations of the public utilities commission on construction work incidental to their own business.

(5) Sole owners of property building structures thereon for their own use.

(6) Any person engaged in the sale or merchandising of personal property which by its design or manufacture may be attached, installed or otherwise affixed to real property who has contracted with a person, firm or corporation licensed under the provisions of this Act to install, affix or attach the same.

(7) Any contractor submitting a bid on a federal aid highway project; provided, that prior to undertaking any construction under that bid, the contractor shall be licensed under the terms of this act.

Licenses expire April 30 and applications for renewal must be made on or before that date. Fee, $60; renewal, $20. (Department of Contractors.)

Any contractor operating under an assumed name must register with the Secretary of State in order to have legal status in Utah courts.

VERMONT

PREQUALIFICATION *required* in order to bid on the highway and bridge work estimated at $50,000 or over. Statement also required of contractors desiring to bid on smaller jobs under jurisdiction of Highway Department, at time first bid of year is submitted.

PREQUALIFICATION

Contractors proposing to bid on State Highway projects must furnish a statement under oath on forms prescribed and provided by the Department of Highway at least once each year.

Prequalification year ends annually 3 months after close of contractor's fiscal year.

Proposals for contract work of $50,000 or over will not be issued to any contractor prior to establishing of prequalification status.

Request for prequalification, including properly executed statement on forms prescribed and furnished by the Department must be submitted on or before the eighth day before the opening of bids in order to receive proposals for a particular bid opening.

Contractors desiring to bid on contract work involving less than $50,000 are required to submit with their first bid of the year a properly executed financial statement and questionnaire, using forms prescribed and provided by the Department of Highways.

LICENSING

There is no State law requiring contractors on either public or private work to be licensed.

VIRGINIA

PREQUALIFICATION *required* with State Highway Commission in order to bid on State Highway work.

REGISTRATION and possession of registration certificate, issued by State Registration Board for Contractors, required to bid on or undertake all other works, costing $20,000 or more, whether private or public, and including highway work under jurisdiction of counties or local authorities.

PREQUALIFICATION

Contractors desiring to bid on State highway work in Virginia must prequalify. Application is by standard form, "Confidential Contractor's Financial Statement" (Form C-37) and "Application" (Form C-38) supplied by Commonwealth of Virginia, Department of Highways, Richmond, Virginia. Prospective bidders are rated and assigned a maximum bidding amount.

BIDDING: Procedure is to be in accordance with the requirements set forth in the 1966 edition of the Virginia Department of Highways' Road and Bridge Specifications which permits the bidder to (a) withdraw any proposal after it has been deposited with the Department provided the request for such withdrawal is received by the Department in writing one hour prior to the time and date set for receiving proposals. (b) A bidder who desires to bid on more than one project at a single letting and also protect himself against receiving the award of more projects than he is equipped to handle, may bid on any number of projects, securing the protection desired by making written statement signed by the bidder and attached to the proposal for each of the projects bid upon, on which this is to apply.

LICENSING

General contractors and sub-contractors bidding on or undertaking projects of $20,000 or more within the State, except highway work under the supervision of the State Highway Commission, must be licensed and registered.

Title 54, Chapter 7, Virginia Code, 1950, as amended, 1964, provides substantially as follows:

Any person, firm, association or corporation desiring to be registered as a general contractor or a subcontractor in this State shall make and file with the State Registration Board for Contractors 30 days prior to any regular or special meeting thereof a written application on such form as may then be prescribed for examination by the Board, which application shall be accompanied by thirty ($30) dollars.

Regular meetings are held in January, April, July and October and special meetings as determined by Board.

The Board may require the applicant to furnish evidence of his ability, character and financial responsibility, and if said application is satisfactory to the Board, then the applicant shall be entitled to an examination to determine his qualifications. If the result of the examination of any applicant shall be satisfactory to the Board, then the Board shall issue to the applicant a certificate to engate as a general contractor or a subcontractor in this State as provided in the certificate in any one or more of four classifications of work: (1) building, (2) highway, (3) public utilities, (4) specialty; and it shall be the responsibility of the Board, or the members of said Board, to ascertain from reliable sources whether or not the past performance record of the applicant is good, and whether or not he has the reputation of paying his labor and material bills, as well as carrying out other contracts that he may have entered into.

Before issuing certificate Board shall ascertain whether applicant has complied with laws respecting foreign corporations and/or any other laws of State affecting contractors or subcontractors as defined by statute. Any applicant failing to pass such examination may be re-examined at any regular meeting of the Board without additional fee. Certificate of registration shall expire on the last day of December following its issuance or renewal and shall become invalid on that date unless renewed, subject to the approval of the Board. Renewal may be effected anytime during the month of January by the payment of a fee of fifteen ($15) dollars to the secretary-treasurer of the Board.

Registration supervised by:
State Registration Board of Contractors
Ninth Street Office Building
Richmond, Virginia 23219

WASHINGTON

PREQUALIFICATION *required* in order to bid on highway work.

CERTIFICATE OF REGISTRATION required to bid or to do any work as a contractor. (See below.)

PREQUALIFICATION

Bid proposals upon any construction or improvement of any state highway shall be made upon contract proposal form supplied by the highway commission, and in no other manner. The highway commission shall, before furnishing any person, firm or corporation desiring to bid upon any work for which a call for bid proposals has been published, with a contract proposal form, require from such person, firm or corporation, answers to questions contained in a standard form of questionnaire and financial statement, including a complete statement of the financial ability and experience of such person, firm, or corporation in performing state highway, road or other public work. Such questionnaire shall be sworn to before a notary public or other person authorized to take acknowledgment of deeds and shall be submitted once a year and at such other times as the highway commission may require. Whenever the highway commission is not satisfied with the sufficiency of the answers contained in such questionnaire and financial statement or whenever the highway commission determines that such person, firm, or corporation does not meet all of the requirements hereinafter set forth it may refuse to furnish such person, firm or corporation with a contract proposal form and any bid proposal of such person, firm or corporation must be disregarded. In order to obtain a contract proposal form, a person, firm or corporation shall have all of the following requirements:

(1) Adequate financial resources, or the ability to secure such resources;

(2) The necessary experience, organization, and technical qualifications to perform the proposed contract;

(3) The ability to comply with the required performance schedule taking into consideration all of its existing business commitments;

(4) A satisfactory record of performance, integrity, judgment, and skills; and

(5) Be otherwise qualified and eligible to receive an award under applicable laws and regulations.

Applications for prequalification are filed with the Director of Highways of the State of Washington, Olympia, Washington.

LICENSING

Applicant for registration as a contractor shall submit an application under oath upon a form prescribed by the Division of Professional Licensing. Certificate of Registration is valid for one year and is to be renewed on or before August 1st of each year. Surety bond or negotiable security deposit required, general contractors, $2,000; specialty contractors, $1,000. Evidence of public liability and property damage insurance in certain limits is also required. Registration fee $15 per year for both general and specialty contractors. (Division of Professional Licensing P. O. Box 649, Olympia, Washington 98501.)

WEST VIRGINIA

PREQUALIFICATION *required* in order to bid on highway work.
CONTRACTOR'S LICENSE *not* required.

PREQUALIFICATION

Standard Specifications for Roads and Bridges Adopted 1968 pursuant to Acts of the Legislature 1937, revised July 1, 1941, provide that contractors desiring to bid on State Road Commission highway work must prequalify.

A Certificate of Qualification will be issued by the Commissioner, fixing the amount of uncompleted work a contractor may have under contract at any one time, and the type of work for which the contractor is qualified.

To obtain a Certificate of Qualification, the contractor must file, under oath, a "Contractor's Prequalification Statement," containing Financial Statements and Experience Records with detailed information as to available financial resources, equipment, property and other assets, together with an account of past experience, a record of work accomplished, personnel of organization and all other facts called for in the Prequalification Statement, and with such other information the Commissioner may desire for consideration in issuing said Certificate. Forms may be obtained from the State Road Commission of West Virginia, Construction Division, Contract Department, 1800 Washington Street, East, Charleston, West Virginia.

Application for Prequalification will be accepted by the Commissioner until 15 calendar days prior to the date set for receiving bids on projects on which the applicant may want to bid.

No contractor will be issued a Certificate of Qualification unless investigation and verification of the Financial Statement shows possession of net current assets, or working capital, sufficient for satisfactory fulfillment of all contracts that may be awarded, and payment of all obligations that may be thereby incurred. The Commissioner shall be the judge of the sufficiency of assets.

LICENSING

There is no State law requiring contractors on either public or private work to be licensed.

WISCONSIN

PREQUALIFICATION *may be required* on highway and other public work.
CONTRACTOR'S LICENSE *not* required.

PREQUALIFICATION

Prequalification optional with awarding authority. Where required prospective bidders must submit sworn, confidential statement containing information on finances, equipment and experience, not less than five days prior to time set for opening bids. Authority will rate applicants on the basis of information supplied. Once rated, applicants need not separately qualify on each contract let unless so required by awarding authority.

On State highway work, applications to Division of Highways, State Office Building, Madison, Wisconsin.

On other public work, to State Chief Engineer.

LICENSING

There is no State law requiring general contractors to be licensed.

WYOMING

PREQUALIFICATION *required* in order to bid on highway work.
CONTRACTOR'S LICENSE *not* required, except electrical contractors.

PREQUALIFICATION

The following are excerpts from the State Highway Departments Policy Statement of December 21, 1967:

"1. All persons, firms co-partnerships or corporations proposing to bid on any State road or bridge projects must first submit a statement under oath on a questionnaire furnished by the Wyoming Highway Department. Such statements shall fully develop the applicant's financial ability, the adequacy of his plant and equipment, organization and past experience, together with such other pertinent or material facts as may be desirable in the judgment of the Highway Superintendent. Pre-qualifications statements in excess of $400,000.00 must bear the unqualified certification of a certified public accountant. In an amount of $400,000.00 or less pre-qualification statements must be signed by a certified public accountant or a reputable public accountant. Reputable public accountants signing pre-qualification statements must not be a member or an employee of the organization or a relative of the owner or owners. Certification by a CPA must be current (current to be defined as within the contractor's fiscal year).

Pre-qualifications will be for a twelve-month period starting on January 1, April 1, July 1 or October 1. Contractors will not be allowed to bid if their pre-qualification period has expired."

"4. If the applicant is a foreign corporation, evidence shall be furnished of its authority to do business in Wyoming; however, such evidence shall not be required for the submission of bids but shall be required prior to an award of contract."

"6. Upon receipt of questionnaire statements the Highway Superintendent shall examine and verify the same and then either qualify the applicant and establish his capacity rating, together with character of work qualified for, or reject the applicant as unqualified. Final decision on every application must be taken by the Superintendent within ten (10) days after receipt of same and the applicant so notified by mail. Any applicant dissatisfied with the decision of the Highway Superintendent may appeal to the Highway Commission."

"7. All prospective bidders are requested to submit pre-qualification statements well in advance so that said statements can be acted upon at least four (4) days prior to the date of a letting. The bids of contractors who are not pre-qualified at least four (4) days prior to the time of opening bids may not be read or considered."

"11. The overall responsibility for prequalification of constractors rests with the State Highway Engineer. The financial capacity of the contractor will be determined by the Director, Accounting Division. The character of work for which the contractor is to be prequalified will be determined by the Senior Construction Engineer."

LICENSING

There is no State law requiring contractors on either public or private work to be licensed, except electrical contractors.

TWO
THE SPECULATIVE BUILDER

FOREWORD
THE APPROACH TO
SPECULATIVE BUILDING

The first part of this book was devoted to the art of construction. Its purpose was to set forth the aspects of construction with which a building contractor should be thoroughly familiar in order to carry on a successful business. A contractor should not consider entering the field of speculative building until he has mastered the fundamentals of estimating, purchasing, site planning, building and zoning codes, and cost and labor control.

Speculative building is just what its name implies. It is a venture requiring personal knowledge, effort, and risk capital in order to produce a structure for potential sale or rent at a profit. When he builds on speculation, the builder can no longer expect to receive monthly or progress payments, nor to be paid at the completion of an alteration. He may obtain progress payments from a lending institution on the mortgage which he has applied for, but this is borrowed money which he must pay back. Eventually he must use money of his own. This is called "risk capital."

Why then should the contractor build on speculation? The answer of course lies in the profit motive. Risk capital, if it is astutely managed, can bring a large return on the investment. If the contractor wishes to become a businessman and is not satisfied with a day's pay for a day's work, then his way to success may lie in speculative building. But it must be done carefully and with full knowledge of the risks involved.

So the contractor should start slowly. He should build a house or two and see how it goes while he is still engaged in contract building and in alteration work. The following section sets forth the fundamentals of speculative building so that errors and unnecessary risks may be avoided.

16

HOW TO DETERMINE
WHERE TO BUILD

16.1. THE REASON FOR THE STUDY

The determination of where to build is a very important part of the builder's business. Even if he proposes to start in speculative building with only a house or two, he must have confidence that the economic stability and the growth of the area will assure him of a quick sale at a profit. Therefore such economic stability and growth play a fundamental part in what and where the contractor should build. A declining area is not the proper place to start any speculative venture even if it is in his own or a nearby community. An example of this is the decline of an area when an entire industry which has been the main support of the area moves to another part of the country. A historic example occurred when the textile mills abandoned the Northeast. Southern speculative builders did very well in this shift. A dislocation in area growth may also come from other causes. For instance, a large corporation may decide to change the location of its headquarters. This move could motivate unrelated companies as well as satellites of the corporation to move along with it.

Such a move or series of moves can stimulate new construction in the new headquarters area, an increase in land costs, and an increased market for new housing of all types. New retail space, new small-office space, and possibly new institutional construction could all benefit the informed contractor.

16.2. HOW TO DEFINE THE AREA TO BE SURVEYED

Every area of the country has a large city or town as its center of influence. All such large centers of population and commercial activity also have satellite communities which are variously used. Some are dedicated to heavy industry or any industry whose noise or other pollution cannot be tolerated by householders. Others may be so called "bedroom towns" which are used almost exclusively for private housing. Some may be of mixed use, for example, by a combination of small office buildings, garden apartments, condominiums, and private homes.

The builder should study maps of the area which show roads, public transportation, and populations. He could choose an area for his activities which encompasses a part of the outskirts of the large center and several of the satellite cities (not the industrial ones) and try to stay within a 20-mi radius of his home or office. Depending on the roads, a less than 20-mi radius is preferable. After all, a radius of 20 mi encompasses an area of over 1200 sq mi. The area may jump county or state lines, and it may not be a perfect circle in order to take in the necessary good areas. Figure 16-1 illustrates this point. The particular map was chosen at random. The writer is not familiar with the area but it does show a city (Peoria) with a population of 126,000 and three smaller towns with populations of over 30,000 each. The statistical or metropolitan area in this case has a population of 342,000 (*World Almanac* and a standard road map). The area as marked for investigation is about 45 mi long by 15 mi wide.

The local builder who wishes to build on speculation can use this as an example of how to define an area for further investigation.

16.3. HOW TO MAKE AN AREA SURVEY

The contractor who wishes to know what is going on in his chosen area should begin by subscribing to the nearest large-city newspaper. Fifteen or twenty minutes spent daily in careful reading will tell him what industry is moving in or out of town, how retail sales are going, what is happening in the local college or university, how the city government is doing, what is going on at the state capitol, what real estate transactions have occurred, and so on. He should also examine the real estate section and advertisements, especially in the Sunday editions, to find out what is for sale, where it is located, and how much is asked for it. The contractor should also go through the

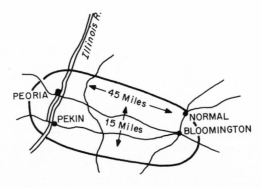

Figure 16-1

appropriate small-town newspapers. There will be listings of houses or land for sale, the local zoning boards' activities, who has moved in or out of town, and other matters of similar interest. There are also real estate periodicals and periodic surveys of area growth available to the contractor at his own bank.

All of this information gives the builder a general view of what is going on currently. However, there is always a pattern of underlying strength in every area which the builder must also take into account. This pattern does not change very rapidly, and it supplies the basic economic stability of an area. Following are some of the factors that contribute to such permanent stability.

16.3A. Institutional and Government Activities

A state capital and a county seat are examples of sources of underlying stability. A university and a large government installation * are others. These institutional or governmental activities provide work for many people, almost all of whom must live in nearby communities. These installations also attract many satellite uses. In times of economic pinch they may shrink, but the usual pattern is that of expansion, especially in governmental activity. Insurance and banking are also sources of economic stability. These can take the form of regional or national headquarters, or clerical or computer centers.

16.3B. Marketing and Retail Center

There are many cities in this country which have grown, and continue to grow, as area marketing centers for agricultural or manufactured products of various kinds. Examples of this are Chicago or Omaha, as meat packing and food processing centers. Pittsburgh is an example of an area of influence for basic industry. These cities and others like them have a diversity of manufacturing, institutional, and governmental activities as well. Such centers also become large retail centers.

At this point it is well to inject a word of caution. The speculative builder should be very careful about making any large commitments in a single-industry area unless he is certain that the single industry which is the economic mainstay of the area will stay prosperous. The aircraft, automobile, and heavy machine tool industries have brought prosperity and then depression and unemployment to a number of cities and surrounding areas. This in turn seriously affects the sale and price of new houses, rentals, etc.

Reports on all of these basic economic factors are available to the contractor. Any good public library either has or can obtain national market guides which list every city and town and give such information as the number of

*Examples of governmental installations which provide employment could be an IRS center, an arsenal, a naval installation, a large military camp, or any clerical center.

persons employed in the various industries and institutional activities, population growth, etc. Most states publish an economic guide which gives population growth, retail sales, industrial employment, etc., on a town-by-town basis. The *World Almanac* is always a good source. The U.S. Department of Commerce publishes economic surveys. These are usually available in libraries, as are real estate periodicals, zoning maps, and files of at least one big-city newspaper and one or more local ones. An hour a week spent in obtaining this valuable information will be well repaid. Librarians know what is available and will be helpful.

16.3C. Industry

The builder should determine the diversification of industry in the area. As mentioned before, it is not healthy for any area to depend on a single large industry. A state department of commerce or chamber of commerce should have statistics on this subject. A good mix would be a combination of various kinds of manufacturing, producing items such as metals, plastics, household wares, machine tools, aircraft products, automobile parts, electric appliances, electronic equipment, and processed food. Such a combination of industrial employment prevents the severe ups and downs of economic activity which can leave a builder with unsold houses or empty stores.

16.3D. Population Growth

Information about the rate of growth of the population and the various age brackets into which it is divided can be obtained from the state departments of commerce, the census bureau, and the state or local chamber of commerce. It is usually listed by town or county. The builder should look for an adequate percentage of the population to be of house-buying age. In this connection there are also published birth rates. This is an important factor in the demand for new houses.

16.3E. Transportation

Easy access to one or more major cities in the area by means of public transportation is important. Airports, railroads lines, and expressways enable the area manufacturers to ship their products to a large consumer market. The railroads and major highways also provide the means for numbers of people to work in a large or medium-size city and to live in the suburbs. Such satellite suburban centers are the "bedroom towns" which are usually prosperous and which provide opportunities for builders.

16.3F. The Bedroom Community

This is a commonly used expression for a (usually) small town which is used as a residence by the wage earner who works in a nearby city. Such a town has very little industry of its own but supplies facilities and amenities such as schools, a library, a cinema, retail shops, and small office buildings for the professionals who practice locally. Such towns tend to grow along with the large city, but they are also affected by the nearby larger towns. To an extent, the nearby larger towns have a life of their own and support light industry, shopping centers, branches of big-city department stores, and possibly even some governmental activities or a branch of a large university.

These bedroom towns are a prime target for the smaller speculative builder. Many of them have strict zoning regulations to discourage large-scale developers. But there is usually vacant land where small numbers of new houses can be built and there are also areas in such towns where small condominiums or small store and office buildings can be built.

16.4. TABULATING THE RESULTS OF THE AREA SURVEY

Table 16-1 is a sample of the way in which a builder can rate an area. (It does not refer to the area shown in the map in Fig. 16-1, but it is an actual area.) Each factor that goes into making an area economically stable and that helps the area at a rate that can be sustained from year to year (without severe ups and downs) can be assigned a weighted number, for a possible total of 100. The builder can use the information which he has obtained to rate each category in accordance with his best judgment. Any total rating under 50 is not a good risk.

The area rated in Table 16-1 is a county. Counties vary in size, and there are counties which are larger than entire states! There are also many counties that have very little population or industry. A tabulation of this kind is not very useful in such areas or in counties that are primarily resort areas, or are forested or mountainous, or contain range land and large farming areas. On the other hand, there are hundreds of counties that contain centers of population, industry, institutional activity, farmland, and so forth. These are the counties that can be studied advantageously. Also, if the builder's head-quarters is located at the edge or the corner of a county, he should certainly include the adjoining counties in his survey, even if they are in a different state.

The county surveyed in Table 16-1 has a conservative rating of 70 out of a possible 100. It is an economically stable area with every prospect for continued upward growth. It is an excellent area for speculative building of private residences, small office buildings, multifamily housing, and condo-miniums where zoning permits.

16.5. THE SPECIFIC COMMUNITY SURVEY

Having determined the potential and economic stability of the area, the contractor is now ready to select the site upon which he will build for the maximum profit in salability or rentability.

There are several ways of determining such locations. To start with, the

TABLE 16-1   EVALUATION OF JAMES COUNTY
Area 626 sq mi

		Maximum Points	**Rating**
1. Population growth	653,000 (1960) 792,000 (1970) + 21% 819,000 (1973) + 3.4%	10	8
2. Population age from 19–49	198,000 24%	5	3
3. Median family income $12,086		10	7

4. Institutional influence 22,300 students
  2 universities,
  1 community college
		5	3

5. Governmental activities—none		5	0
6. Marketing and retail centers 2 towns that are retail centers		5	3

7. Transportation
  1 main line, 2 spurs
  1 north-south expressway
  1 secondary airport—40 minutes to major airport
		5	4

8. Industry and employment in the county
  aircraft, machine tool—people employed
  91,000
  Total employment 260,000
		10	8

9. Bedroom communities—there are several around
City X and City Y
  Employment out-of-county over 30,000
  The majority of these people are well paid
		10	7

10. Agriculture Dairy farms and Truck farms		5	1

11. Banks
  170 including branches and building and loan
  associations
		5	5

12. Dwelling units   154,000 (1950)
  209,000 (1960)
  254,000 (1970)
  270,000 (1973)
  +21.8% from 1960
		10	9

13. Movement in or out of industry or office
  employment—movement is in from nearby large
  population center
		10	7

14. Contractor's judgment of overall economic stability		5	5

builder should decide how far from his home or office he is willing to travel. Large developers can, of course, build anywhere, because they can set up a local semiautonomous organization to take charge. The small builder, however, has no such choice. At least at the beginning he must be able to take personal charge of any project he builds if he wishes to be a success. He may also wish to work on the project. This limits his area of operation. About a 30-minute drive should be his limit. This can include a range of from 15 to 25 miles, depending on the traffic pattern of his location. This means he can look at an area of from 700 to 1900 sq mi, which should certainly give him enough scope. Of course if there is a location which presents an ongoing opportunity to build more than one project, he can travel much farther.

What locality within this area is showing the greatest growth? There is no substitute for an actual physical survey of the centers of population—the small and large towns. The builder should look for new construction of any kind. He should speak to the local building and zoning officials. Local newspapers, both daily and weekly, will report on building permits. He can ask someone in the local chamber of commerce what new business or industry has come or is coming. An educated look at the automobiles and the people at a shopping center should tell him something about the economic status of the community. He should enquire whether there is an influx of people who are moving from a city into the general area.

16.5A. How to Make a Table of Values for the Specific Community

Again, as for the large area survey, each item can be given a maximum value and the builder can use his best judgment to decide what value to assign to each.

He can make up a little table of values somewhat as follows:

	Maximum Points	Rating
1. The general look of the community	10	
2. How much new construction and what kind (industrial, housing, office)?	15	
3. How many banks?	10	
4. Is there an influx of new families?	15	
5. How do the shopping areas look?	10	
6. Any branches of large department stores? What class?	5	
7. Are there expensive shops and boutiques?	5	
8. How do the people look?	10	
9. What kinds of automobiles?	10	
10. The schools, the town hall, the library	10	

Any rating between 65 and 75 shows a community that is stable or on an upward trend. It should be a good place in which to build.

17

HOW TO DETERMINE WHAT TO BUILD

17.1. A MARKET SURVEY

A market survey in its simplest form is the determination of market needs, and the contractor who wishes to be a successful builder must ascertain these needs by performing several surveys. These need not be extensive, but they will require considerable time and effort in order to ensure a successful marketing venture.

Such surveys should include a study of the economic growth of the area, and the growth and stability of various specific communities as shown in Chap. 16. No matter how time-consuming this may be, the contractor should arrange his time so that he can continue his business during the surveys.

Having completed the initial surveys and site selection, the contractor can keep this data current by an occasional visit to the surrounding area, by reading the newspapers, and by speaking to and meeting with knowledgeable people in the area. This knowledge will be invaluable to him in determining the type, the location, and the extent of construction that has a good chance for quick sales and the turnover of his capital.

In determining what to build, the speculative builder must bear in mind at least two important factors. First he must decide what the community needs. Real estate brokers can help here. They are the ones who receive inquiries from prospective purchasers or prospective tenants. The local newspaper will have for-rent and for-sale listings. A personal survey of stores and offices in the community center can also help. Are there vacant stores? What do the small office buildings or condominiums look like? What is for rent or sale? The builder need not announce himself. He can be looking for a house or condominium to purchase, and as for the offices—a look at the tenant listings in an office building or in a two-story store and office building and a walk through the corridors will be rewarding. When the builder has completed this survey he must decide what kind of structure will best succeed.

17.1A. A Decision. What to Build.

Following is a list of questions he should answer:

Are there many vacant stores in town?
What is the condition of the store fronts in use?
Are there office vacancies?
How many private residences are being built? Of what size?
Are there any vacant houses or apartments?
Are there condominiums for sale?
Are there many private residences for sale by the owner?

If each of the foregoing questions is thoughtfully considered and given a value (and it must not be forgotten that the builder is on the scene and is therefore in the best position to know), it should be possible for him to arrive at a decision as to what kind of structure to build. Shall it be a small office building, a building with shops on the street floor and offices above, a small condominium (this can be extremely complicated), a private residence or two, a medical building?

17.1B. A Decision. What Price Range?

Probably the best way to ascertain the popular price range is through the careful study of the real estate section of the Sunday edition of a big-city newspaper. The following is a sample of typical advertisements taken from several central-city and small-town newspapers in widely scattered sections of the country. No cities or communities will be identified here, but in every instance the advertisements cover an area of well over a 25-mi radius and some refer to quite distant communities. The builder in studying his own area newspapers will of course be able to identify the localities of advertised properties.

17.1B1. SAMPLE ADVERTISEMENTS FROM SEVERAL CENTRAL CITY NEWSPAPERS

PRIVATE RESIDENCES
4 bedrooms, 2 1/2 baths, full basement, 2-car garage $69,900
2 bedrooms, 1 1/2 baths, split level 32,495
3 bedrooms, 2 baths, ranch 31,900
4 bedrooms, 2 baths, full basement 45,995

CONDOMINIUMS
2 and 3 bedrooms, 2 or 2 1/2 baths 39,750
2 bedrooms, 1 bath, living room, kitchen, ... 19,850
3 bedrooms, study, 2 1/2 baths, kitchen-dining space 85,000
Townhouse—2 bedrooms, 1 bath, living room, kitchen 22,299

These properties are located within a 30- or 40-minute drive from the central city. As can be seen from the wide range in price, they are located in communities with a wide variety in income. Not all central cities can present such a range. From such advertisements the builder can obtain a good idea of the price range and the type of property that seems to meet market requirements.

17.1B2. SAMPLE NEWS ITEMS FROM SEVERAL CENTRAL CITY NEWSPAPERS

The contractor should read the news items in the real estate section, such as:

- Vacancies drop in S.E. of city
- Foods division of X Corp. moving to Lakeside
- Bell Telephone building a $13 million complex
- Hilltop subdivision opens, sales going well
- Spring Park's new garden homes selling well
- Hillcrest homes grand opening
- A choice of homes (with floor plans and pictures)
- May figures noted, building is firm
- Court ratifies delay in zoning change at Eastlake
- Residents on the move. Sales of houses, condominiums
- Parkhill subdivision opens second phase. New models on display.

These news items can be analyzed. Telephone employees or Foods division employees may require housing, which in turn will bring shops and service business. Hilltop subdivision, if successful, may be pointing in the direction of city and suburban growth. The builder must carefully study his prospective market. No samples are given here of small-town advertisements or news items, but they do not differ from the ones shown except for price range.

17.1C. A Survey of Apartment and Commercial Rentals

If the builder has enough confidence in his ability to build and finance a strictly commercial venture such as a small apartment house or an office building with stores, he must ascertain the going level of rents for such units before he proceeds. In Sec. 18.6 there is a sample of an operating budget or profit-and-loss statement which indicates how much the builder should pay for the land for a commercial structure. By the same token this form should also be used by him to determine how much the building should cost.

The cost of the land and building will determine the amount of the mortgage and the builder's equity. These amounts plus an estimate of the ordinary operating expenses will have to be balanced against the expected rent roll.

A search through the Sunday real estate section of the nearest large city or town newspaper will give a good idea of the going rents for apartments and, to some extent, the going rents for offices and stores, although these latter rents are not often quoted in newspaper advertisements. One Midwestern and one Western newspaper show the following.

In Midwest:

- 2-bedroom apartments with carpeting, air conditioning, pool, and fully equipped kitchen—from $240 to $300 per month.

- 1-bedroom apartment, same facilities as above—$190 to $200 per month.

- Small office building—$4.10 per sq ft, all services.

In West (not Pacific Coast):

- 2-bedroom apartments, fully equipped—$175 to $240 per month.

- 1-bedroom apartment, same as above—$165 to $185 per month.

- Offices in new complex—$7.00 per sq ft.

Store rentals were not advertised, and would have to be researched through real estate brokers, landlords, and possibly the friendly banker. When the builder has determined his rent range, he can complete his calculation to balance the cost of land and building and all operating expenses against the expected rent roll.

17.1D. The Marketable Size and Style

17.1D1. DETERMINATION OF THE SIZE

When the builder has come to a decision on the general location in which he wishes to build and on the type and price of structure that he thinks will be most rentable or salable, he must decide on the size of the structure and its style. To a large extent, of course, the size of the structure depends on the amount of funds the builder has available. It may be, for instance, that he thinks he can readily sell a four-bedroom private residence for $85,000, but such a residence must be in a carefully selected area where zoning restrictions are tight and land prices are high. The builder must also be able to obtain a large mortgage and carry it until he has sold the house.

Or he may see the need for a small condominium (see Chap. 19) or an office building. The size of these ventures must be governed by the available funds. It is recommended that first ventures in speculative building be on a limited scale. The advertisements shown in Sec. 17.1B1 show that two- or three-bedroom houses are being built and sold in most places, and this kind of project can certainly serve to start with. If such starting ventures are successful and if, for instance, the marketing survey shows that larger houses are selling well, these can be the next venture, and so on. It would seem, therefore, that the size of the venture is determined by a combination of the financial aspect and the marketability

17.1D2. STYLE

Style in this context refers not only to the architecture but also to the interior arrangement. An attractive exterior is extremely important but it need not be stereotyped. Architectural styles vary in different parts of the country and if the prevailing style in an area is rough-sawn vertical spruce or cedar siding, the smaller builder may want to follow this fairly closely with only an occasional variation such as using a small quantity of cedar shakes or facing part of a wall with brick. If the prevailing style of exterior is brick, the builder may wish to face part of a wall with stone. Or, of course, he can completely follow the prevailing style and have his house look like every other house on the street with the possible exception of different windows or front doors.

The basic precaution in the builder's use of an architectural style is to avoid the "gimmicky." Split-level houses belong on sloping grounds; "picture windows" should be placed where there is some kind of view. Do not build an odd-shaped roof; stick to the style that has proven sales appeal, that people have been buying for years—the ranch house, the 1½ or 2-story Colonial, the flat-roofed adobe. This may sound ultraconservative, but it makes good sense for the small speculative builder.

There is also a variety of interior styles. In private residences there may be certain items that have a special appeal—a raised hearth or barbecue fireplace, for example, or an island kitchen counter, or a bit of paneling in the kitchen. A study of magazines that specialize in house styles will be rewarding. These magazines reflect present interior styles in addition to forecasting new ones. But again, let the builder be cautious about trying anything that is "way out" (and that could be expensive).

The architecture of small office buildings and condominiums also varies widely over the country. If there is a view, a small balcony may be a popular item in a condominium. On the other hand, the author has seen condominiums with balconies looking into dead-end corners or with a 1½-story living room with a ceiling that slopes up to clerestory windows that cannot be opened. Such windows can be cleaned on the outside only by getting out on a roof and, on the inside, by using a long ladder. This is "gimmicky" and will last only until the word gets around.

The exterior material of these buildings is an important factor in their salability or rentability. The small glass-and-aluminum office building boxes that have sprung up all over the country are giving way to a variety of styles. The use of brick or cast stone or even siding is coming back, and these structures certainly look more inviting. Intelligent spacing of columns and windows to make office layout easy is an excellent sales point.

There is also the very important matter of the use of energy. Smaller glass areas and materials with superior insulating qualities are becoming popular as part of a campaign to conserve energy. There are federal subsidies for some of these provisions (see Chap. 27).

17.2. HOW TO SUMMARIZE THE MARKETING INFORMATION

The preceding section has devoted itself to the whys and hows of gathering information about the market for new speculative construction. Now the prospective speculator should summarize this information so that he may make the most practical use of it. One way to do this is by means of a table like Table 17-1, covering:

- *Area in which to build.* From the summary in Sec. 16. (area survey), the builder has determined that James County (in which he lives) is an economically stable area with excellent prospects for continued growth and which therefore can absorb new construction of any kind.

- *Specific community survey.* From a tabulation like that in Sec. 16.5, the builder has determined that there are three towns within reasonable traveling distance from his office which show strong evidence of continuing their upward trend in population

TABLE 17-1   TABULATING THE MARKETING INFORMATION

Chap. 16, Sec. 4 Area in which to build	James County
Chap. 16, Sec. 5 Specific community in which to build	Town of Monmouth

Chap. 17, Sec. 1A
  What to build
	Three bedroom, two bath,
	  private residence

Chap. 17, Sec. 1B
  The price range—Central City newspaper and
    the Monmouth newspaper indicate
	$55,000

Chap. 17, Sec. 1D2
  Architectural style
	1½ stories, dormers, shin-
	  gled, colonial

and in economic growth. Towns A and B are bedroom communities that are attracting many residents who are "refugees" from Central City. The influx is so great that some of the town's facilities are being outgrown with a consequent heavy boost in taxes. Town C is a well-established university town which has been attracting new industry in the electronics and small machine tool fields for a number of years. It is also an established marketing center, and it is only 15 mi from the builder's office, whereas Towns A and B are 25 or more miles away in a heavy-traffic area. Town C (Monmouth) is the choice for a starting venture.

- *What to build.* Section 16.1A will help the builder decide. It will be a private residence—first, because there seems to be more need for private residences, and second, it does not take so much financial outlay.

- *The price range.* Section 17.1B gives a number of examples of newspaper advertisements. In his particular central city newspaper, the builder notes that three-bedroom, two-bath houses are being advertised at from $38,000 to $65,000. Town C's newspaper advertises houses starting at $42,000 because land in this more established town is more valuable. If the builder wishes to reach a middle bracket he should try for a $55,000 house. He should be able to appeal to Central City executives who will travel this extra distance and to the top echelon of the resident faculty as well as to the rising executives of the smaller companies that are growing in the immediate area around Town C (Monmouth).

- *Size and style.* The size of the project has to some extent been determined by the financial considerations involved. But the builder need not entirely preclude the small office building or condominium, especially when in the course of his explorations he comes across a piece of property in the right zone and at the right price that seems to be fitted for a particular business use. There is always money available for such a purpose from a local bank, or friends and relations, or the Small Business Administration. So long as he controls the property, the builder can always come back to it later when he is more financially sound. From the material summarized under *The price range*, the builder has now determined to build a three-bedroom, two-bath house with a two-car garage. What style of architecture and interior layout will have the most sales appeal in Town C? It is an established university town with an influx of new sophisticated businesses and some commuters from Central City. A two-story clapboard, a 1½-story shingled colonial, a one-story ranch house? It would seem that a 1½-story shingled colonial with dormer windows for the upstairs bedrooms would best meet the market.

The builder has now made up his mind. He will build in Monmouth, in James County. It will be a 1½-story, three-bedroom, two-bath colonial with a two-car garage. He will estimate it and build it to sell at a price of $55,000 with a minimum clear profit of 12 percent or $6000. for himself. This $6000 includes his builder's profit as well as his speculative risk profit.

17.3. AREAS OF EXTRAORDINARY GROWTH

Chapters 16 and 17 have gone into detail on how the small builder can start in the field of speculative building with minimum risk and with maximum return for his efforts. This advice is good for the normal everday business areas and communities.

However, there are areas in this country (and worldwide) where climate or general environment considerations have created a certain ambience. This has often resulted in mass migration regardless of economic factors. This migration consists to a large extent of retired or semiretired persons but there are also a surprising number of active wage earners looking for "the better life."

Speculative building has gone on in these areas without regard to normal economic considerations or anything else. The areas involved have taken belated steps to protect themselves against this unbridled construction, which threatens their ecology and overstrains their facilities. As a result of this and a cooling of the general economy, hundreds of speculative builders have been forced out of business.

The small builder is reminded that a careful survey of the future prospects of an area is important no matter what the current situation is.

18

THE PURCHASE
OF LAND

When the builder has defined his objective as to where and what to build and what the price should be for a quick sale, his next important task is to purchase suitable land. Although in the illustrative case below the builder has chosen to construct a private residence, this chapter will also explore the purchase of land for office buildings, combination offices and shops, and small condominiums. It is quite possible that during the course of his marketing survey the builder has seen several building sites that meet his requirements, but in a speculative venture it is well to examine all the alternates.

18.1. HOW TO FIND LAND (RESIDENTIAL)

The first part of this section will deal with the acquisition of land for single-family residences, usually the first venture for a speculative builder. In order to obtain available land at the most favorable price, the builder should examine every possible source.

18.1A. Local and City Newspapers

The local newspaper and the Sunday real estate section of a big-town newspaper are excellent sources. The large-town paper will advertise land for sale within a radius of many miles. Following is a current sampling from several newspapers all over the country:

- Lots 100 × 300, 100 × 240. Sewers, paved road. $13,500 to $15,500.
- 5-acre parcels $19,500. 3-acre parcels $15,500.
- 15 acres on a lake $33,000.

- Planned development of 268 lots. Single lots for sale.
- Golf course view ¼- to ⅓-acre lots $12,000 to $15,000.
- 2½ acres $14,750.
- 2 wooded home sites $8,250 each.
- Two 1-acre sites $11,950 each.

One or two local papers and one large-town newspaper will advertise dozens of buildings sites.

18.1B. Local Real Estate Brokers

Local real estate brokers not only list offerings of their own but have cross listings from out-of-town brokers. The builder who wishes to obtain these listings is advised to deal only with one of the principles of a reputable firm. Too often brokers employ part-time people whose only interest is in a fast sales commission. Such people are apt to send the builder off to see 20 properties in the hope that one may sell.

The builder should make very clear the kind of land he is looking for. In this particular case (Chap. 17), he wants a piece of land in a residential zone on a paved road with access to electric power and (if possible) sewers and water. With the last two services, of course, the price will be higher. He should also tell the broker the price bracket he is interested in. An experienced broker, who may have hopes of selling the finished house, will steer the builder toward the areas where sales have been good.

18.1C. Land Developers

There are many instances in every area of the country where a land developer will purchase a large tract of land and then subdivide it into building lots. Many developers will build on some of the lots as a speculative venture but in order to obtain ready cash they will also sell many of the lots to smaller builders.

The best way to preview such developments is through meetings of the local planning and zoning board. There is almost no place in this country where a land developer can go ahead without obtaining approval from local authority. Attendance at such meetings will enable the builder to evaluate the character of the development and to make up his mind whether he wishes to participate.

One important matter that the small builder must keep in mind when selling his own house is the competition he may meet from high-pressure advertising that may be started by the developer in order to sell his houses. Unless an understanding can be reached and *made part of the sales contract,* it may be best not to purchase land from a developer who will be in competition with the builder.

18.1D. Drive Around to Look for Vacant Land

Many owners of a single or a small number of building lots neither advertise nor list with brokers. They will, however, put up a "for sale" sign. Some very nice pieces of land can be found in this way. An occasional evening's drive through settled but somewhat outlying areas may turn up some pleasant surprises.

18.1E. Contacts

If a builder lets it be known that he is in the market for land through his service club, his insurance broker, his friends, etc., he may be able to obtain an occasional lead on a piece of property that has not even been put on the market.

18.1F. Obituaries, Probates

The builder should read the paper for obituaries and probates. There may be land for sale from the estate. He must obtain the name of the executor of the estate.

18.2. HOW TO LIMIT THE POSSIBLE CHOICES

In order to properly evaluate the land the builder should make up a table like Table 18-1 in which he enters information about every piece of land in which he is interested. This table should be kept on a current basis as the builder

TABLE 18-1   INFORMATION ABOUT POSSIBLE BUILDING SITES

Location	Distance in Time from Office *	Size of Land	Price	Remarks
Jonesboro, Kona Road near Rt. 6	25 min by Rts. 86 and 6	100 x 300 100 x 240	$15,500 $13,500	Zoning not known. On paved road, sewers.
Smithtown, ½ mi W. of Rt. 301	35 min by Rts. 86 and 301	268 lots; Size unknown telephone for info.	Call for info.	Check if developer is building any houses of his own. Zoning unknown.
Westlake, 1 mi from Turnpike	35 min by Rt. 86 and Turnpike	Not shown; two wooded homesites	$8250 each	Check for zoning, improvements, etc.

*The time is a guess based on builder's knowledge of area.

sees interesting advertisements or obtains information from brokers or other sources.

The table entries are just a sample of what may be 12 entries a week. The builder has picked these 12 possibles out of dozens of advertisements or other leads. Before he wastes time or gasoline to visit these sites, he should use the telephone to obtain a great deal more information about them. Essential questions are:

- The size of the land
- The zoning: use, minimum land area allowed
- The improvements in place—electricity, city water, sewers, paved road
- Whether the land developer plans to build any houses of his own
- The price (if not shown)

The answers to these questions may narrow down the possibles from a dozen to three. The builder should now be prepared to spend some time in closely examining these three and this should be done on a current basis by a quick visit to the site.

18.3. THE STEPS IN THE EVALUATION OF A BUILDING SITE

This section will confine itself to residential property. Multifamily dwellings and business sites fall under different rules which will be explained later in this chapter.

18.3A. Zoning

Chapter 14 explains zoning laws in detail and shows some illustrative examples of how zoning codes are applied. To some extent this section will be repetitious, but zoning is so important to the speculative builder that many of the provisions of the codes bear repeating. The builder who seriously intends to go into speculative building should purchase a zoning code and a zoning map from every community in which he intends to do business. Small communities charge a few dollars for these and even a major city code costs no more than $15 or $20. The maps are invaluable. The builder can locate the property he is interested in, in the proper zone, and he can examine the adjacent zoning to find how far his property is from less restrictive zones.

He can also find in the code whether the site is of the proper allowed area and how large a house he can build after allowing for side, front, and rear yards.

18.3B. Amenities and Adequacy of Transportation

It is very nice to build a house on a wooded lot out in the country but very few people will want to buy it. The builder should look for many things.

- How far is the nearest bus line? How far to town?
- How far is the nearest supermarket or shopping center?
- How far is the nearest school? Is there a school bus?

The builder should also look at any houses around his site. He should note their size, whether they are well kept, what kind of people live in them (Sunday is a good day to do this). His house should not be too much larger or smaller than the surrounding houses.

18.3C. Check for Adverse Uses

In Sec. 18.3A the use of a zoning map was advocated so that the builder could determine how far his site is from a less restrictive zone. This is extremely important. If the site is only a short distance from a business or industrial zone or a multifamily zone the wary buyer* may not be willing to take a chance on these zones encroaching in the near future especially if there is much vacant land around. Any nearby zone that allows trailer camps should be avoided. Unless extremely well run, these are neighborhood blights. The distance to main highways is also important.

One other thought here about location. There is an occasional situation, especially on the outskirts of large cities, where houses are built on a tract of land that is virtually an island. The tract is cut off on all sides by high-speed boulevards or by main highways. The housewife cannot go shopping, the children cannot go to school, and the husband cannot get his bus without crossing these thoroughfares (and there is not always a traffic light where it is convenient). This is not a major point and should not stand in the way of the purchase of an otherwise good building lot, but it is worth considering.

18.3D. Topography

Topography in this instance refers to the physical characteristics of the site itself. There are several things the builder should look for when examining the land—and there is no substitute for the personal examination of the land by the person who is investing money in it.

---

*With the current cost of houses, prospective purchasers are extremely well informed.

18.3D1. THE LAY OF THE LAND

The slope of the land can be important. If there are steep slopes at or near your boundaries there are several things to be wary of. If the slope is down to the lot, it could shed water which would make the land very wet and might preclude a basement or a split-level house. If the slope is sharply down, it may not appeal to prospective house purchasers. Sharp ravines and ledge rock cause trouble especially if the rock is near the proposed house site or in the way of sewer lines. Ledge rock is very expensive to excavate.

18.3D2. LANDSLIDES AND FILLED LAND

In many areas of the country the soil is unstable and is likely to be displaced during heavy rains. There are many places where land has been made by filling in marshes around lakes or wetlands around tidal streams. All of these spots are likely to present unstable foundation conditions and should be avoided. Ask the local building official.

18.3E. Summarizing the Findings

This section is not meant to be prohibitory, only cautionary. There is not much ideal land available at the prices that this book is talking about. The builder must find a piece of land with the most advantages. It must be emphasized here that all the foregoing steps in the process of finding a good building site are necessary to avoid serious error. A good building site may be priced at $10,000 or more. This is important money to a small builder. It is worth his spending several days of his time.

18.4. WHAT TO PAY FOR RESIDENTIAL LAND

Section 17.2 mentions a builder who, for ease of financing, marketability, and other reasons, has decided to build a three-bedroom, two-bath house with a full basement and a two-car garage to be priced at $55,000. It is obvious then that the price of the land is a very important factor in arriving at the final predetermined cost. Following is an example of how the builder can set a limit on the price that he can pay.

1. It is assumed that the builder has a plan and outline specifications (see Chap. 20) which he has adapted for his own use and which meet the building code.

2. From his plans and specifications, he must estimate the cost of the house just as though he were building it for an owner at a fixed contract price. He should obtain tentative bids from subcontractors, obtain current lumber and material prices, and

estimate his own labor costs. Then the bid should be assembled (see Chap. 3).

3. In speculative building, the builder must bear all the carrying costs that are normally paid for by the owner in contract construction. These include mortgage interest during construction, taxes during construction, insurance, permits, and legal fees. The builder should also be prepared to pay a sales commission to a broker (but only if all other sales efforts fail).

A summary sheet can be drawn up as follows:

Estimated construction cost	
(including overhead and profit)	35,000.
Interest on $40,000 mortgage at 12% for 6 months	2,400.
Taxes during construction	
(50 mills on $20,000 for 6 months)	500.
Insurance	500.
Permits	100.
Legal fees (closings on land and house)	500.
Lost interest on own investment	
($10,000 at 7% for 6 months)	350.
	39,350.
Builder's speculative profit,	
(over and above his contractor's profit)	2,500.
	41,850.
The most he should pay for the land	11,000.

It is to be noted that the $2,150* left between estimated total cost and profit will pay for only part of the brokerage commission (if this becomes necessary) and must also pay for advertising and other small expenses. To keep an adequate margin, the work should be closely supervised to cut costs, and the house should have sales appeal so that it moves quickly.

18.5. LOCATING LAND FOR MULTIFAMILY AND BUSINESS USE

The basic principles to be used in finding such land are generally the same as for residential property. The builder will not find as many newspaper advertisements for business property as he will for residential. Most brokers, especially in small towns, handle very little of this kind of property. Brokers for such property are usually located in the larger towns and they carry listings for all surrounding areas.

*$2,150 is difference between total cost of building and land ($52,850) and sales price of $55,000.

But the best way to locate multifamily or business property is by means of the builder's own zoning maps and the accompanying regulations. Zoning laws are now pervasive. Every town or community of any consequence has a zoning code. The zoning map will show the parts of town where multifamily use is allowed and where businesses of various kinds are permitted. The regulations will describe each zone saying what residential density (families per unit of land area) is permitted and what business density (square feet of space and height) is permitted. The small builder should be interested in the low-density areas because first, they allow only smaller buildings, and second, such land is a good deal cheaper than high-density-use land.

The next step is for the builder to decide whether he wants to build a small condominium, a store and office building, or an office building.* Each kind of use requires a different location, and these locations are clearly defined on the zoning maps. And if they are not, they should be clearly defined by the local zoning official (in writing if possible).

Land for a condominium is usually close to low-density business zones. The code in this area allows one family unit per 3500 sq ft of land and a height not exceeding 35 ft. If the builder wishes to build a ten-unit condominium he must look for at least 35,000 sq ft or more to enable him to comply with the parking and yard requirements. All utilities should be in place. A very good way to find such a piece of land is to examine the entire zone. Vacant land is obviously the first target but in every town there are private residences which were built before zoning. Many of these occupy fairly large pieces of property that might easily be for sale. Names of owner can be obtained from tax assessment rolls, which are open to the public. The names of the occupants of a building may also be obtained from voter's lists or the town directory† which is usually available at the local library or town hall. The reason for obtaining the occupant's name is that in some instances the ownership is listed as a real estate trust or a corporate or institutional name. A simple telephone call to the tenant may give the builder the name of the owner and his address. The builder is warned, however, when he is talking to a tenant not to say that he is interested in the purchase of the property. Most tenants would be quite uncooperative in such a case. Most towns also have a "street tax directory," which gives owner's names, assessed valuations, and size of property. These are usually published in a central town. They are available at libraries, real estate offices, or the town hall. Sometimes there may even be a for sale sign on the property.

Desirable land for business use may be found in the same way as multi-

---

*There are, of course, structures for other uses that are built speculatively, but these are mostly special-use buildings such as one- or two-story truck stations or factory space which may be built in industrial parks by large developers.

†Town directories are published in large towns. They cover the entire area on a town-by-town basis and carry much valuable information. The local publisher can be found by contacting the Association of North American Directory Publishers, 50 Orange St., New Haven, Conn. 06509.

family residential land. The location for a building with stores and offices is obviously different from that for a small office building. The brokers and newspapers may have some listings, but again the best way is by the use of the zoning map. Any small town or even the outlying business districts of a large city will probably have a row of two or three-story buildings with shops below and with a number of one-story stores and an occasional nonbusiness building scattered in between. This is the kind of spot the builder should look for. Some of the older houses may be for sale for their land value. Many of these small local retail centers may have streets leading off which are zoned for business back for 100 ft or even more. A building plot on such a side street is likely to cost much less than one on the main street. The builder, however, must make a traffic count and otherwise ascertain that people do walk on these side streets (possibly on the way from a public parking lot) and that a building on such a side street will be visible from the main street.

Land for an office building need not be in the center of town. People come to work or to visit offices by automobile. Such property may be found from broker's listings or by driving around the area. There are many instances where a small area occupied by small houses, but adjoining a business zone, is rezoned for business. Some of the residences are convertible to small professional office buildings, others may have to be purchased for the land value only. It is of course all a matter of the "bottom line" in a projection of initial cost, income, and expense.

18.6. WHAT TO PAY FOR BUSINESS LAND

The rules for the cost of land for condominiums and those for business buildings are quite different. To start with, a condominium is for sale and when the last one is sold the builder's only responsibility is set by the guarantees he gives the new owners and by the legal sales documents (see Chap. 19). A business building, on the other hand, is not primarily built for sale but rather for income. It is for sale (of course), but the price will depend on the income as it is built up (see Chap. 23, Financing a Speculative Venture), and it could very well be to the advantage of the builder to wait. There is also an IRS reason for waiting (long-term capital gain).

It is well to mention here that while the speculative builder can purchase ready-made residential plans and adapt them to his purpose, it is difficult to file plans for multifamily dwellings or any business building without an architect's or engineer's seal. Chapters 20 and 21 on plans and specifications, will go into detail on how plans for residential buildings may be obtained and modified to suit the local building and zoning codes, and how the builder may work with an architect to obtain business plans to suit either his own or a future tenant's requirements.

18.6A. Condominiums

The price that a builder should pay for land for a condominium may be determined somewhat as follows:

1. The builder would like to start with ten units* of a combination of one-, two-, or three-bedroom apartments. These can be in a single structure or in a mixture of town houses and a multifamily building, or a combination of both.

2. The builder has set his price for the two-bedroom, 1½ bath apartments at an average of $35,000 and wants six of these. The price for the four three-bedroom, two-bath apartments is an average of $45,000. This makes a total price of $390,000 that he expects to obtain when all the apartments are sold. One-bedroom units can be priced at $28,000.

3. At this point, the sequence of operations changes because, while in the case of a private residence the plans are inexpensive and a proposed house plan can be altered to suit a building lot, this cannot be done for a condominium, without great expense. The plans must be drawn to suit the building site and, since such plans are drawn to meet many regulations, changing them is a major expense.

4. The builder must therefore acquire at least 35,000 to 38,000 sq ft of land (see Sec. 18.5) and obtain approval to build a condominium before he orders plans and specifications (see Chap. 19). The plans and specifications at this point need only be a plot plan, dimensioned line drawings, and outline specifications. This work is only a small part of an architect's work and therefore should cost only 15 percent of the final total cost of a complete set of working drawings. The builder need not commit himself to plans and specifications at this time.

5. The outline plans and specifications can now be used for estimating purposes, including obtaining estimates from subcontractors.

6. A summary sheet should then be prepared as in Sec. 18.4.

To recapitulate, this summary sheet should contain the following:

- Estimated construction cost (including architects' and engineers' fees, overhead, and profit)

*This number can be scaled up or down depending on the market, the location, and the financial picture.

- Interest on mortgage during construction

- Taxes during construction

- Permits

- Legal fees (closings on land, blanket mortgage, and individual units sales, preparation and filing of legal papers for condominium)

- Insurance during construction

- Lost interest on own investment

- Builder's speculative profit

- Brokerage or other commissions

- Advertising and sales promotion

- Total cost

- Total sales price

- What the land should have cost

The question should arise here, "If the land is already purchased, why go through this exercise to determine what the land should have cost?" The answer is that the purpose of this exercise is to tell the builder what the ideal price of the land should have been to preserve his profit and his equity. If the price he paid is higher or lower he can always adjust his prices for the units. As he becomes more experienced he will be able to "guesstimate" a summary sheet *before* he buys the land.

18.6B. Business Building

The method of determining the cost of land for a business building is comparatively simple. While the builder is negotiating for the purchase of a piece of land for a two- or three-story store or office building, he can employ an architect (or can perform this preliminary step himself) to determine the allowable maximum size of a building which can be on a lot of this size in this zone (including parking).

The cost of construction of a building of this kind is fairly well standardized, as is the rental income that the builder may expect to obtain. The builder can then prepare a summary sheet, which for a business building must include estimated rental income and expense so that he can determine what the return on his investment will be. Following is what a summary sheet should contain:

- Estimated rental income

- Estimated expense (including electricity, cleaning, supplies, taxes, mortgage interest, and amortization)

- Net income allowing 10 percent for vacancy

- Estimated cost
  Land (what is being asked for it)
  Construction cost
  All other expense (See preceding summary sheets)
  Total cost
  Amount of mortgage
  Builder's equity to make up difference between total cost and the mortgage

The net income as a percentage of the builder's equity should be at least 12 percent. If not, the builder is paying too much for the land or the estimated construction cost is too high. More calculations are called for.

18.7. POSSIBLE LEGAL PROBLEMS IN THE PURCHASE OF LAND

When the builder purchases land, there are several legal matters that he should be aware of. He is, of course, advised to retain an attorney but there is no reason why he, himself should not have a basic understanding of the law involved. The builder should understand, for example, the following.

The deed. When title to land is being transferred from one party to another, it must be done in a form prescribed by law so that it may be entered into the land records of the community in which the land is located. A deed must contain certain information such as the name of the seller (grantor) and buyer (grantee). It must contain a description of the land and the consideration involved and it must contain "words of conveyance" such as "the grantor conveys and warrants" the property to the grantee. The deed must also contain information about any restrictions, easements, or reservations on the land. Finally, it must be recorded and given to the purchaser. It is his proof that he owns the land.

Easements. One of the restrictions that a deed should record is easements. An easement is the right of someone other than the owner to enjoy certain privileges pertaining to the land. The most common kind of easement is one which grants a "right of way." Such a "right of way" may be a defined road or a specific piece of land on which someone has the right to build a road to reach a piece of landlocked property. Or a right of way may be for a power line or for a buried gas line. If such an easement goes with the land there is nothing the new owner can do but make up his mind to live with it—or decide not to buy the land. Easements are dangerous for a speculative builder. He may not mind, but his prospective purchasers may object.

Restrictive covenants or deed restrictions. It may be a condition of the deed that only a certain type of house can be built on the land. Some restrictions go so far as to say it must be a two-story brick colonial of a certain square footage. Such restrictions limit the choice of the builder and may be too restrictive to live with. In some cases a land developer for the sake of uniformity may place restrictions on the kinds of houses that can be built on the land. Such restrictions may be filed only when the developer records the entire development. It is up to the builder and his attorney to find out what these restrictions are.

Riparian rights. These pertain to property that fronts on water. There may be fishing rights, or a "right of way" to the water, or, in the case of tidal water, the right of the public to cross the land between the high- and low-water marks. The builder should consult an attorney about the rights that go with the land so that he in turn can reassure his prospective purchasers.

19
CONDOMINIUMS

19.1. WHAT A CONDOMINIUM IS

In a condominium an individual has real estate title to one or more dwelling units in a multiunit project. It may consist of a group of low-rise apartments (garden apartments), a group of attached or detached single-family homes (town houses), or a combination of these. There are also high-rise condominiums as well as business condominiums, but they will not be discussed in this book. The owner of one of these units also has, along with the owners of the other units, an undivided interest in the common areas and facilities serving the project. These common areas include such elements as the land, the roofs, floors, lobbies, halls, parking spaces, main walls, and community facilities.

The condominium method of ownership has become popular for several good reasons. Because of the scarcity and high cost of urban land, condominium ownership is the answer to those who want to own a dwelling near an urban center but cannot afford the cost of the land for a single-family dwelling. Others do not wish to be faced with the maintenance of the building and grounds. It has also (in the past) allowed developer-builders to earn a great deal of money.

19.2. THE MARKET FOR CONDOMINIUMS

One of the largest markets for condominiums has been in areas in which the climate is attractive to older couples who no longer wish to own or maintain private homes in colder areas. There is also a large market, in these regions, for people who wish to use them for vacation purposes and who try to rent them when they (the owners) are not in residence. These units are usually purchased for future retirement.

There are also resort condominiums in recreational areas where there is

271

boating, fishing, skiing, golfing, tennis, and other sports. The ownership of such condominiums is sometimes "pooled" among several families. The builder-owner must be very careful about becoming involved in any "pooling" arrangement which can cause a great deal of legal trouble.

The condominiums that are built in the perimeter areas of population and business centers attract another market. The people who purchase these may be lone males or females who wish to be within commuting distance of their work and at the same time not be at the mercy of a landlord. Many young couples will purchase such a condominium because they cannot afford a single-family house of their own. They plan to keep the condominium until its possible rising value and their savings enable them to purchase a house. For such couples the condominium is just a way station. They do not really want to live in a multiunit dwelling. Other possible purchasers are working couples who have no children and who want to be free of the usual duties of home ownership.

If a condominium builder concentrates on small units, he is very likely to attract young singles who purchase because of certain tax advantages but who may not make the most desirable tenants and certainly cannot be mixed with older couples or couples with children.

There are other markets for condominiums in addition to those mentioned above, and all of these have combined to make the condominium an attractive venture for the builder-owner. In spite of inflation and economic slowdown, these markets are still in existence. The only difference is that now the builder-owner must approach condominium construction with great caution. The condominium can no longer be considered as a simple profit-making venture.

19.3. WHY BUILD A CONDOMINIUM

The speculative builder who has successfully built and sold a number of single-family homes and has possibly built and rented a small office building or a garden apartment building may ask, "Why build a condominium?" He has heard about lawsuits and new laws and unfinished projects and could very well come to the conclusion that it is something he should not become involved in. The fact remains, however, that the condominium still commands the largest housing market* in the country and that the successful condominium builder can obtain a higher profit than for any other kind of speculative building.

The construction of a small condominium presents all the cost savings to the builder that are obtained when building a small apartment project:

1. He builds in "wholesale lots." The usual zoning that allows condominiums (or apartment buildings) calls for less land per

---

*In many areas condominiums account for 30 percent to over 50 percent of all new housing.

unit than does the usual residential code. This is high-density construction, which is always more economical than single-family construction.

2. Because these housing units represent more work, more lumber, and more materials, he can obtain lower prices for materials and lower prices from subcontractors.

3. He can use his own work force to better advantage because he can shift a floorlayer, a trim carpenter, or a framing carpenter from unit to unit as the work progresses.

4. Most important, when the work is completed, he can sell the units and, except for the guarantees and his obligations under the master deed and purchase agreement, he is free and clear. He is not faced with being a landlord of an apartment house and obligated to maintain it, collect rents, pay taxes, etc. And then there is the greatest advantage—the profit.

Let us take a 10-unit condominium as an example. The land cost per unit is normally less than the cost of a minimum lot in a residential zone. The builder has built 10 housing units and has had the material and labor advantage of building wholesale. Instead of four exterior walls for each unit he has one or two at the most. Instead of one stairway per unit he has two stairways (in accordance with the fire code) for 10 units. There is only one roof and one basement. Because of less exposure, the heating and air conditioning plant can be smaller. In such a small project he need not provide any amenities.

His competition is single-family housing on single lots. He can undersell such housing by thousands of dollars and still earn a high profit.

19.4. THE SELLING POINTS IN MARKETING A CONDOMINIUM

In marketing a condominium the developer must stress the points that will appeal to all kinds of possible purchasers:

1. A condominium apartment is generally less expensive than a private residence of the same size, and many condominiums have extra facilities such as a tennis court, etc. These extras of course, are not recommended for a small project.

2. There is an advantage that appeals to everyone. That is the saving in income tax from being able to write off the mortgage interest and the taxes on the unit just as though it were a private home.

3. There is the advantage of ownership as a hedge against infla-

tion. As long as inflation lasts, the unit should go up in value. The owner at the end of any period is left with a valuable housing unit instead of a packet of cancelled rent checks. This, of course, is also true for single-family homes.

4. The monthly maintenance cost (which includes salaries for staff plus their various benefits; legal, accounting, and management fees; maintenance and repair of common property; funds for establishment of a cash reserve for major repairs; etc.) is normally much lower than the rental for comparable quarters even after taxes, mortgage interest, and amortization are added, and it eliminates a landlord's profit.

5. The condominium owner does not have to be concerned with maintenance problems. Keeping the lawn mowed or the driveway plowed, repairing a leaky roof, fixing a kitchen faucet, etc., are taken care of by the monthly maintenance charge.

6. A condominium offers much greater security than a private residence. There are close neighbors, there are workers, there might be a night watchman—and in large condominiums—a security guard.

7. A condominium offers a class of neighbor who owns his unit and is not likely to move precipitously. This neighbor is also financially responsible. This makes for more neighborliness for those who want it.

8. Because condominiums are run by an association of tenants whose duty is to enforce the rules of occupancy, including the financial aspects such as maintenance fees, cash reserves, and other matters. Each unit owner has a vote according to his interest and certainly each owner has a say in how the condominium is run. The unit owner has almost more say here than he would with bad neighbors who live in their own house next door.

19.5. CONDOMINIUMS ARE IN TROUBLE. WHY?

The great surge in condominium construction—which is of fairly recent origin—and which gives every sign of continuing *under the proper safeguards*—has attracted numbers of ill-prepared or borderline builders. As is true in every case where a rising market appears, the condominium surge attracted people who were out for the "quick buck" and did not really care about how they made it. The result has been a number of consumer protective laws, numerous law suits, and wary purchasers. These are some of the abuses that brought on the disrepute into which some condominium construction has fallen:

- *Poor construction.* The borderline builders built cheaply and badly. There were thin walls, poor lumber that shrank as it dried, little or no insulation, no sound deadening, poor plumbing fixtures, undersized heating and air conditioning plants, etc.

- *Misleading advertising.* The unprincipled builder-developer has given the impression that condominium ownership is completely trouble free. He has consistently understated the monthly carrying charge. He has advertised amenities such as clubhouses, pools, and tennis courts, which he has been unable or unwilling to furnish.

- *Ownership of facilities.* Many of these builders have retained ownership of all facilities except for the units themselves and have charged exorbitant rent for their use.

- *Owner association and maintenance.* These builders have packed owners associations* with their own "stooges" and have retained control of the maintenance costs, through secretly held subsidiary maintenance companies.

- *Repairs.* Some builders are deaf to owner complaints. Repairs are made late and with poor materials and incompetent help, if they are made at all.

The preceding list of condominium abuses shows why there has been a rash of newspaper, magazine, and book exposés and why many state legislatures have passed restrictive laws of such severity that it becomes difficult and sometimes almost impossible for a legitimate builder to do business. These laws will be modified if the abuses abate, as they will when the unscrupulous are driven out of the market. It is interesting to note that a legitimate builder who builds a good product, who advertises fairly and who gives proper attention to his unit purchasers usually can still earn a very handsome profit.

19.6. CAUTIONS FOR THE WOULD-BE BUILDER

The list of condominium horrors set forth in Sect. 19.5 can be used as an example of what not to do when a condominium project is designed and built. But there are other matters to be considered before the builder arrives at this stage.

*See Sec. 19.8A regarding owner's associations.

The builder can be in trouble unless he is highly experienced in choosing sites, in the intricacies of multifamily construction with all its strict code requirements, and in "reading" the market to ascertain that condominiums at a given location and price will sell. It is precisely for these reasons that so many builders have "gone broke" and so many half-completed projects dot Florida (as an example).

Condominiums can be built only in comparatively high-density residential zones. These areas may be near highways, railroads, and business zones, and in large population centers they may not be too far from industrial zones. The warning to the builder in his choice of land is obvious. Other cautions to the builder are in order:

- *Poor construction.* This is certainly something that the builder can control. Construction can be sturdy without being expensive. Stairs should not creak, walls between units should be soundproof, the exterior walls and roof should be insulated, the doors and windows should be of good quality, the plumbing fixtures should be of a standard quality, etc. Poor construction goes along with bad architecture. Odd roof lines, unnecessary balconies and protruding bays are expensive gimmicks and add very little to sales appeal. Simple exteriors of wood or masonry or both, a simple peaked roof, a good-looking entrance and entry hall, and well-chosen planting will appeal to the majority of purchasers.

- *Poor views.* The builder must be very careful about how he locates units on the site. Certainly the larger, more expensive units should have the best views. Planting trees for screening poor views is recommended. The architect or site planner should orient the units for the best views—within the limits of the zoning code of course.

- *Choice of unit sizes.* This choice depends on the general area. If the project is located on the outskirts or within commuting distance of a population and business center, the builder should consider the young working couples who may be able to afford only an efficiency unit of one bedroom and bath, a living room, and a kitchen. Such units in "bedroom" communities are eminently saleable. Another popular size is the two-bedroom, 1½-bath unit. This is popular everywhere. It is suitable for a small family anywhere, is fine for resort areas and is especially suitable for part-time leasing. Three-bedroom units are saleable, but they attract only a limited number of people who can afford them and should be built only in selected communities.

- *Ability to finance.* If a piece of land for a single-family house costs $10,000, the builder may have to lay out $60,000 or more for a ten-unit condominium. His construction mortgage could be $300,000 instead of $35,000 or $40,000. The builder is cautioned not to proceed until he can carry the burden of financing costs, mortgage interest, and amortization (until the units are sold), insurance, and heavy legal expenses.

- *Codes.* The builder must be thoroughly familiar with the intricacies of the building code as it refers to multifamily housing, and with the zoning code, which very often takes a rather dim view of high-density condominium construction.

19.7. SOME RECOMMENDATIONS TO PROMOTE SALES

19.7A. Design

- *Cluster units.* Builders have been very successful in selling town houses grouped as a cluster instead of in a long row. This grouping appeals to a great many people who enjoy a sense of neighborliness and community.

- *Playgrounds.* Play areas should be located where parents can see their children but where other unit owners can not hear them.

- *Parking.* If there is sufficient land, the providing of two parking spaces per unit is highly recommended.

- *Recreational storage.* A covered shed with pipe racks for chaining bicycles and other large recreational equipment is a plus.

- *Construction extras.* Good sound insulation in walls and floors, good heat insulation, double-glass windows, weatherstripping, soundproof (and fireproof by code) party-wall construction are all sales promoters.

19.7B. Facilities

There have been many instances of successful projects where the builder has donated the land and the money for the owner's committee to use in accordance with the voted wishes of the unit owners. Thus there are not unused facilities which many unit owners resent because they know they are paying for their upkeep but do not use them.

19.8. THE LEGAL ASPECTS

In 1961 the federal government, through the Federal Housing Administration, enacted a model statute. The purpose of the law was to regulate the conduct of the owner/builder of a condominium from beginning to completion and sale, and then to ensure that all the warranties, guarantees, and covenants in the deeds of sale are carried out. Since then all the 50 states have enacted their own legislation based on this model statute. In the past few years it has become apparent that these laws have not been sufficiently rigorous to bar dishonest promoters. Now, state after state is voting for and enforcing severely restrictive consumer protection laws. Each state law is different but there are some common denominators.

19.8A. How a Condominium is Established

A condominium must be established by the recording of a master deed or enabling declaration that dedicates the property to a condominium plan of ownership. This deed must contain the following:

1. The plans of the project.

2. The by-laws of the association of the owners (prospective).*

3. An accurate description of the various units. Many states require not only a dimensional plan but an air view of the unit in space, a "cube of title."

4. An accurate description of the common areas.

5. The valuation and proportioned interests of each unit. These must be accurately stated, since the extent of interest that the owner of a unit has in the common areas and facilities is governed by the ratio of the value of his unit to the total value of all units. Square-footage ratios can also be used. This ratio represents the individual owner's voting interest in the condominium owners' association and it determines his proportional share of the expenses of the association.

6. No language is permitted in the deed, by-laws, or exhibits that would permit the grantor (owner-builder) to retain ownership of any community facilities or that would restrict the resale rights of the owner of a unit.

Before commencing any work on a condominium project the builder is advised to employ an attorney who is familiar with the statutes governing

---

*The by-laws set forth the rules under which the association of owners is organized and operated.

such projects. (An experienced attorney is *very important*.) Besides the master deed, there are more than 20 additional forms which must be filed and approved before the project can become legally designated as a condominium. For his own information, the builder can obtain sample forms and a listing or the correct procedures from the U.S. Department of Housing and Urban Development (HUD), Washington, D.C. 20410. He can also obtain the state's legal requirement from his own state capital, usually the department of commerce. If there is any difficulty in obtaining this information there is one other source of information—the district congressperson and the district state representative whose names are listed in the telephone book under U.S. government or state government.

19.9. FINANCING A CONDOMINIUM

There are several ways of financing the construction of a condominium.

19.9A. Federal Housing Administration

The FHA has set up rules and regulations for the issuance of mortgage insurance on condominiums. If the owner-builder (sponsor) complies with its requirements for the filing of a proper master deed and other required information, the FHA makes a feasibility analysis. If it finds the proposed project practicable, it will issue a certificate of insurance which will enable the sponsor to borrow money from a financial institution on a blanket mortgage which will cover the entire project. It will also grant mortgage insurance to the individual purchasers of the units. Many financial institutions welcome the FHA insurance, which helps them to recover in case of loss and also assures them that the project has been analyzed and found to be a practical one.

19.9B. Conventional Mortgage

The mortgage departments of banks, building and loan associations, and insurance companies usually welcome applications for a blanket mortgage because such a mortgage gives the institution entree to the individual purchaser. The institution will require all the information as set forth in Sec. 19.8 or as regulated by state law, but may not be quite as strict about some matters as the FHA. For instance, the FHA requires that any down payment by a unit purchaser be placed in escrow and not be released until the unit is completed and title transferred to the new owner. In addition, in many cases FHA requires that 80 percent of the units be sold before any title can be conveyed to the new owners.

Conventional institutional mortgages are usually not that strict. Their commitment papers may state that no part of any down payment may be expended for any purpose until a stated number of units has been sold by a certain date. This requirement protects the builder as well as the final owner because the builder need not go ahead with his program if he finds he cannot sell the requisite number of units. There are also real estate investment trusts (REITs) which will still lend money on very secure risks. Many insurance companies and mortgage bankers maintain such trusts.

19.10. FINANCIAL RISKS FOR HIGH PROFITS

The creation of a condominium is a high-risk business. It requires an experienced, well-financed builder-developer who has the financial ability to employ experienced architects and attorneys. Such an individual or company need not confine itself to the newly constructed residential condominium. There are resort condominiums and commercial condominiums. A builder developer can purchase a multifamily apartment building and convert it to a condominium. Each of these is hedged about with the rules and regulations of federal agencies, with state-enacted consumer protection laws, with the demands and cautions of the lending institution, and with local codes and regulations.

The builder-developer has to purchase land and employ professionals before he can even qualify under the law for approval to seek financing. More and more prospective owners will not purchase until they see what they are buying. If the units do not sell as expected, permanent financing may not be forthcoming.

Nevertheless, the condominium is becoming the most popular form of home ownership in the country. The smaller builder should enter this field cautiously and be sure he is well financed and advised. It is a high-risk business for high profits.

20

THE PLANS AND SPECIFICATIONS FOR A PRIVATE RESIDENCE

20.1. THE BUILDER AS THE OWNER

In Chap. 2 a set of plans and specifications for a single-family residence was analyzed trade by trade. The builder was told what to look for in these documents to make sure that every point was covered and that his estimate did not omit anything needed to make the house ready for occupancy or to fulfill his contractual obligation.

Now the builder is on his own. Until the house is sold he is the owner as well as the builder. He is not bound by a set of written obligations to use certain materials or workmanship and his work will be examined only by the local building inspector for quality and compliance with the local building code. There will also be an occasional "looker" who may be a prospective purchaser, but the majority of these casual visitors know very little about construction. Therefore the builder must become his own critic. He must build a sturdy house with good lines and materials,. He can economize by using good materials that are not necessarily the most expensive but carefully chosen. It would not do for the builder to build a house in which the plumbing leaks, the floors become uneven because of poorly seasoned floor joists, the ceilings develop cracks, the doors bind, etc. It takes only a little care and not a great deal of money to ensure that these things don't happen. The purchasing public will soon learn that this builder's houses are either to be avoided or conversely are well-built houses that give value for the purchase price.

This chapter will outline the choices the builder has in the selection of materials and systems that will produce a house acceptable to the purchasing public and will have added sales appeal. These choices cover a wide range in prices and the builder must be careful to note that the materials and systems he chooses are compatible with his budget.

281

20.2. CHOOSING THE BEST EXTERIOR

20.2A. The Architecture

The exterior design of the house is what every prospective purchaser sees at first. What he sees is what his friends and neighbors will see. It is a first impression and is very important. A good interior layout can be encased in almost any reasonably styled architectural exterior. Styles of architecture vary widely over the country. To a large extent they are adapted to the climate. This book is not concerned with houses built for owners who may want an all-glass house in northern Maine or a peaked-roof wood house in Arizona. This book is for the builder who wishes his house to appeal to a broad spectrum of the public. As such it can have good lines and good proportions but it should conform to the prevailing architectural style of the region and of the surrounding area.

The size of the house is also important. People who purchase large houses do not want them to be located on streets where they are surrounded by small houses and vice versa.

20.2B. The Materials

The material of the exterior should conform to the general look of the surrounding area to some extent. However, it will certainly not harm a possible sale if the builder uses a little imagination and variety. Good exterior doors that close with a satisfying click and good windows that slide or glide easily and close properly are extremely important. A gliding window or a cranked casement window over a kitchen sink has considerable appeal. Above all, the exterior should give an appearance of solidity and sturdy construction.

20.3. CHOOSING THE BEST INTERIOR

There are a number of simple rules concerning the shape and size of the various rooms and their relationship to each other. These arrangements have been proven by time and experience to make daily living more convenient and will certainly have a strong appeal for the homemaker who usually has a great deal to say about the purchase of a house. Following are some of these rules.

20.3A. Entryways

By code there must be two of these and certainly no house is salable without a "front" and "back" door. The "back" door is the service door. In many houses it is practically the only door used. The children coming in or out, tradesmen, and the owners coming home with bags of groceries use this door. It should therefore enter into a working area such as a kitchen, laundry room, mudroom, or pantry. It should also be convenient to the garage, driveway, or carport so that people can go from automobile to house without being inconvenienced by bad weather. This entrance is also convenient for muddy feet or wet clothes. The stairway to the basement (if there is one) should be located in this area. This door should also, if possible, lead through the work areas to the bedrooms (if it is a single-story house). The front door should open into the living room through an entryway hall or an entry space. If it is a two-story house the front door should lead directly to the stairway. This stairway should be in an entry space or in an entry hall alongside the living room.

20.3B. The Living Room

This room is for entertaining, and, if there is no family room or den, it is also the family gathering place. It should be generously sized, even in a small house, not less than 13 × 17 ft. If possible, the living room should not have to serve as a passage to other rooms.

20.3C. Bedrooms and Closets

A bedroom in even a small house should not be less than 9 ft-6 in. in any dimension. A master bedroom can be 12 × 13 ft or 14 ft and a second bedroom 9 ft-6 in. × 12 ft. The builder is urged to provide sufficient closet space. Closets can be used as a sound barrier between bedrooms. With the present cost of construction there are houses being built with a third bedroom 9 ft-6 in. × 9 ft-6 in. The bedrooms should all lead into a central hall which gives access to a bathroom. If it is at all financially possible a master bedroom with its own bath is almost a must. The second bath can be for the other two bedrooms.

20.3D. Baths

If the cost of two full bathrooms is not within the budget, the builder can think about a powder room-lavatory. Such a room contains a water closet and a wash basin and can be as small as 5 ft × 2 ft-6 in. It can be used in a pinch for all bathroom purposes that do not require a shower. Another solution is to provide two such lavatories—one on either side of a tub-shower room. A satisfactory bath can be put in a space that is 6 ft-6 in. × 7 ft and a luxurious one can be in a space 7 ft × 9 ft.

20.3E. Kitchens

The kitchen is probably one of the biggest selling points in a house. Every kitchen is made up of three activity centers—a storage center, cooking center, and cleanup center. The storage center is where the groceries are unpacked and stored and should be convenient to the entry and to the cooking center. The cooking center should have sufficient counter space around it so that food can be served directly from the stove. The cleanup center—sink, dishwasher, and garbage compactor—should have counter space to store used dishes, etc. The dishwasher should be located so that it can be loaded directly from the sink.

There are several generally acceptable kitchen shapes. The U shape is the most efficient and the corridor shape the most economical of floor space. The L shape can provide for a breakfast space, which is always a good sales point.

A satisfactory kitchen can be arranged in a space that is 8 × 12 ft or 10 × 12 ft at most. The kitchen is a work space and need not be any larger than is necessary. The kitchen should not be much larger than this because space is too valuable for the speculative builder of medium-priced houses. Every square foot of space costs an average of $25 or more, and this is very important today when even a small house may cost $35,000 to $50,000.

20.3F. Basements

Traditionally the basement has been the place where the furnace is, and before the use of oil and gas fuel, it was for the storage of coal or coke. It was also the place for the washtubs, and was used for storage or for a workshop.

With present construction costs running so high, the need for a full basement is questionable. The usual basement is almost all below grade with light and air coming through small areaway windows. Such a basement cannot by law be used for sleeping quarters. Its use as a laundry room is limited because most homemakers do not like the poorly lighted, poorly ventilated space. It can be used as a playroom if there is no family room, but the writer has found that such playrooms are not very popular because of the unavoidable feeling of being in a basement.

Water is another problem with below-grade basements. There are many thousands of basements in this country that have sump pumps running constantly except in prolonged dry weather. There are other thousands of basements that are constantly damp, that have trickles of water running down the walls or across the floor. If the floor of the basement is more than a foot or so below the water table during the dry season, let the builder beware. To make such a basement completely waterproof is prohibitively expensive. A test pit will help to determine the height of the water table.

With modern heating and air conditioning plants packaged so that they can fit in an ordinary closet and with packaged washer-dryers that take little space, the use of a basement often does not justify the expense of building it. As for storage, the builder can provide such space at the end of the garage or in an attic.

The entire picture changes, however, when a portion of the basement can be above grade because of the slope of the land. Now a basement can be used for sleeping, recreation, and many other purposes, and it can be an excellent sales point. If the slope is parallel to the frontage it may even be feasible to build a split-level house. Split levels are likely to cost more but they appeal to some people. Here again the builder must be sure that split-level houses are salable in his area.

20.4. WORKING DRAWINGS. HOW TO CHANGE PURCHASED PLANS TO MEET EXISTING CONDITIONS

Before starting to build anything, the builder must have working drawings. These drawings should consist of a plot plan showing the location of the proposed house on the lot, drawings of the foundations, floor plans, and exterior elevations. The drawings and/or a set of accompanying specifications should describe the materials to be used. These documents are necessary for the issuance of a building permit by the town authorities, but they are even more important for the speculative builder. The builder must know in advance exactly what he is going to build and what materials he is going to use. It is only by doing this that he can estimate his own cost and obtain reliable bids from subcontractors.

There are many ways of obtaining working drawings. The services of a registered architect or engineer are usually too expensive for a small builder. Sometimes an arrangement can be made with a designer who is not an architect but who is acceptable in many communities in which a registered architect or engineer is not required for the filing of single-family residences. There are also plan services which will sell a set of working drawings and specifications for a quite reasonable fee.* Although he may want to use the basic layout which may almost meet his needs, the builder need not use these plans just as they are shown. He may have an odd-shaped lot or a narrow lot that will not accommodate the dimensions of the house as shown and which will still comply with local zoning. He may want an unfinished attic or a larger or smaller bedroom. He may want to "flip" the plan over so that the garage is on the opposite side.

Figures 20-1 and 20-2 are two somewhat similar plans for small houses. They are conventional layouts which will appeal to the great majority of the house-buying public. The accompanying suggestions will show how they can be altered to meet the particular requirements of various situations. Figure 20-1 shows the plans of a small three-bedroom house with an attached two-car garage. There are no interior stairways shown, which means that there is no basement and no second floor. The heating plant is shown on the first floor. The house without the garage measures 27 ft-8 in. wide by 50 ft-0

---

*These plan services are available through such magazines as *American Home, Better Homes and Gardens, House and Garden,* and others.

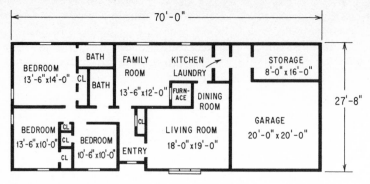

Figure 20-1

in. long or 1380 sq ft. The garage and storage space are 20 ft-0 in. wide by 27 ft-8 in. deep, or 552 sq ft.

The layout is good and complies with the rules for a livable layout. The entryway opens into the living room on one side and the bedrooms on the other and goes straight through to the kitchen. The back door leads through a laundry room to the kitchen. The living room is almost square and a good size. The bedrooms are all above minimum size and there are two baths— one being the master bath.

Structurally the house is simple with a bearing partition in the middle so that 14-ft ceiling joists can be used on either side. The 12 ft space over the living-dining area can be bridged by an I beam supported by two lally columns or three 2 × 8-in. joists on lallies. It will show a beam projecting from the ceiling but this is not considered objectionable.

With this basic plan as a starting point, the speculative builder can now rearrange it or change it to suit his market or his lot:

1. He can reverse the plan so that the garage is on the left.

2. He can make the garage an open carport for one car instead of two.

3. If he has a narrow lot he can reverse the plan and then turn it sideways with the garage/carport in back.

4. If he wants an expansion attic he can make his entryway 2 ft wider and install a stairway 2 × 9 ft long to a second floor. He will then have to raise his roof to accommodate a space as shown here and add two dormers for front bedrooms and one wider dormer for a bath in the rear. If he does this, the attic can be used for storage and he can eliminate the storage space in back of the garage/carport. An expansion attic adds a great deal of space at a very reasonable extra cost if it is done during the

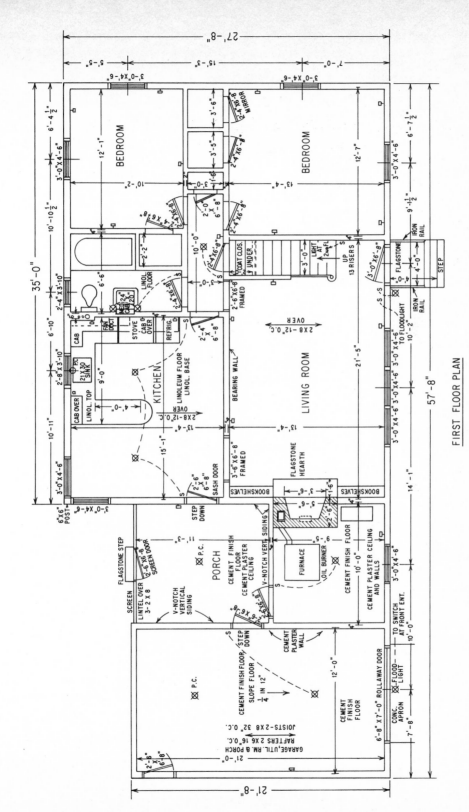

FIRST FLOOR PLAN

Figure 20-2

construction. (It adds the extra length of the rafters and the three dormers.) It has great appeal for a growing family and the builder can more than recover the additional cost in his selling price. (See Figs. 20-3 and 20-4.)

5. He has the choice of building the house on a flat slab or providing a crawl space. This depends on the climate of the area, the character of the land, and the preferences of the buying public.

With all of these changes, the builder can still preserve the inherent good layout and simple exterior of the house.

Figure 20-2 shows the first-floor plans of a small house with one bedroom, a bath, and a family room (or second bedroom) on the first floor and (not shown) two bedrooms, a bath and a storage room on the second floor. The second-floor bedrooms are 11 ft-8 in. × 12 ft-0 in. and 11 ft-8 in. × 14 ft-0 in., with a large storeroom reached through one of the bedrooms. The bath is directly over the first floor bath and is 6 ft-6 in. × 7 ft-0 in. with a stall shower.

This house is 35 ft-0 in. × 27 ft-8 in. with an extension containing a furnace, laundry room, and breezeway porch with dimensions of 21 ft-8 in. × 10 ft-0 in. There is also a one-car garage. The total finished area (if the second floor is left unfinished) is 1360 sq ft. There is no basement but there is a 3 ft-6 in. crawlway. It is a simple house to build with a bearing partition down the middle and with 14 ft-0 in. floor and ceiling joists falling into place without cutting.

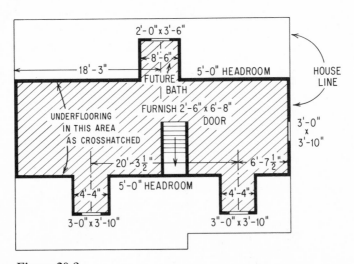

Figure 20-3

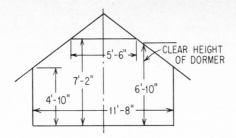

Figure 20-4   Profile of an expansion attic.

This plan can be changed to meet the builder's requirements and the needs of the market:

1. He can reverse the plan so that the garage is on the right.

2. He can make the garage an open carport where the climate permits.

3. He need not finish the second floor; he can leave it for the purchaser to complete.

4. He can build a basement or can put the house on a slab—again where the land and the climate permit.

5. He can make the house longer to make larger bedrooms and a wider bath.

The builder must in all cases assure himself that the plans as drawn or as revised by him meet the building and zoning codes.

20.5. CHOOSING THE BEST PLUMBING AND HEATING SYSTEMS

20.5A. Plumbing

The plumbing and sanitary system of any structure is subject to quite restrictive codes which are designed to ensure potable water and safe drainage and sewage disposal. Codes vary to some extent in the various states and communities, but they all have certain features in common. For instance, the well must be at a certain distance from the septic drain field. The soil must pass a percolation test by the sanitation or building inspector before the size of the drain field can be ascertained. These problems, of course, are of no concern when there is city water or city sewage.

The manner in which a plumbing system is installed with waterseal traps, cleanouts, fresh air vents, prohibition against cross connections into the potable water supply, etc., is the same everywhere in the country. The only difference is in the materials that are allowed to be used. In this instance local codes vary widely as do purchaser's preferences. In some parts of the country where there is "soft" water, galvanized piping corrodes very rapidly and the purchaser has learned that copper hot- and cold-water supply lines are best. In the areas where there is "hard" water, galvanized wrought iron or steel piping will last very well. In the past few years plastic piping has made its appearance and is being used more and more as the local codes allow it. Most codes still require cast iron and galvanized piping for sanitary and drainage piping, but here again plastic piping is starting to invade the field. Plastic piping has many advantages. It is impervious to many corrosive materials; it is lightweight; it is easy to cut, and, if properly connected, the joints are stronger than the pipe itself. Many codes are now allowing its use in residential construction. The builder should obtain comparative prices on the use of any material that is allowed by the code.

The plumbing fixtures that are used in a speculatively built house are of the greatest importance as an aid to sales appeal. There are normally three fixtures in a bathroom and frequently there are shower stalls as well in more expensive houses. Bathtubs can be of solid vitreous china, enameled cast iron, or enameled sheet metal. The first is quite expensive but of course looks the best. The enameled cast iron tub is the kind most frequently used in medium-priced houses. Over a long period, it is subject to staining but it is generally satisfactory and it looks substantial. The enameled sheet metal bathtub is the lightest and easiest to handle. It looks inexpensive. The builder who uses it is advised to pack the underside of the tub solidly with some vermin proof material so that stepping in the tub or running water into it does not make a hollow drumming sound. The wash basin or lavatory should be of vitreous china and the water closet has to be of vitreous china. An attractive feature to most purchasers is the installation of an enclosure under the lavatory. Some of these come assembled with a plastic basin which makes a good appearance and is generally accepted. If there is a stall it should be substantial looking with a glass door and a ceiling light, and it should be lined with tile or one of a number of plastic-coated materials that are waterproof and good looking. There are also cast plastic stalls which include a base. The base of a shower stall, if separate, should be a single piece of waterproof material. Kitchen sinks and washtubs are usually of enameled cast iron or of vitreous china, which is much better (and looks it). Many kitchen sinks are of stainless steel, which can be an appealing sales point.

20.5B. Heating and Air Conditioning

The speculative builder has a choice of heating plants and of the fuel that is used. To a large extent his choice is dictated by the prevailing climate of the area. There are nine (or ten) climatic zones in the country and the heating system can vary from no heat in Key West or southern Florida or southern California to a complete warm-air or hot-water system in Maine or northern Michigan. A discussion of the possible systems and fuels follows.

In warm climates, in which heat is not required constantly but is used on a stand-by basis, an oil-fired or natural-gas-fired underfloor furnace or electrically heated wall panels can be used. The furnaces heat directly through floor registers.

Forced-warm-air heat is widely used in colder climates. Such an installation can be converted to a combination heating and air conditioning plant, which is a very advantageous selling point in climates with hot summers and cold winters. The forced-warm-air system is used extensively in speculatively built houses because it is the least expensive of the central heating systems.

Forced-hot-water heating is, in the opinion of the author, the best heating system available for a private residence and is the most expensive. Because of the substantial materials of the piping and the radiators and the fact that water loses its heat slowly, the system retains heat and therefore furnishes a more even heat. Hot-water heating can be piped by a series system in which the hot water circulates through one radiator after another or by the slightly more expensive one-pipe system which allows the water to flow in a closed loop but diverts it by a special fitting up to each radiator. Almost all heating by hot water is now being done by baseboard radiation, which is unobtrusive and seems to appeal to most home buyers.

Another advantage of forced-hot-water heating in the larger home is the fact that it can be zoned very accurately. This is a large plus in sales appeal. Zoning simply means that various portions of a larger house can be kept at different temperatures. For instance bedrooms on an upper floor can be kept at a lower temperature than a living room or other rooms that are used during the day. This is accomplished by the use of thermostats which are connected to small circulating pumps located on the branch line that heats these zones. When the thermostat calls for heat, the pump drives hot water into that zone.

This is a more positive way of controlling temperatures than through the use of dampers for zoning in hot-air systems. Balancing a damper-controlled system is for an expert, not the ordinary householder.

It should be mentioned here again that all of these suggestions concerning the use of materials and systems are not obligatory. The builder must observe his budget *but* anything he can add to his house over the basics helps his sales and his reputation.

20.5B1. THE VARIOUS FUELS

As mentioned before, heating and air conditioning units are now so packaged that they require very little space. They can be oil-fired or natural-gas-fired, depending on the availability and the cost of the various fuels. In some parts of the country where coal is readily available there are many stoker-fired coal-burning furnaces in use. The builder must use his judgment as to the salability of a new house with this kind of heating system.

The use of electricity for heating was starting to become popular before the advent of the present high cost of electricity. Electricity is really not a fuel. A fuel, such as natural gas, coal, or oil, is used to produce it. It is clean, convenient, and expensive. It is used most often in resistance heating (as in a toaster or a small electric heater). It can be installed as baseboard heat, radiant panels, central furnace heating, or floor furnace heating. The public is very much aware of the cost of electricity and the builder is advised against the use of electricity for heating purposes (unless the builder is willing to install extra-heavy insulation and the electric rates are low).

There are other sources of energy which can be mentioned here but which are only in a primary state of development and are not for the use of a speculative builder at this time. He should, however, be familiar with them.

20.5B2. SOLAR ENERGY

Solar energy is much talked about and has been in use for many years in small installations. This system consists of collector panels that are usually placed on a roof and are positioned so as to be exposed to maximum sunlight. The heat of the sun warms a liquid which circulates through these panels and the warm liquid is stored in insulated tanks for use when the sun is not shining or the weather is cool. The system requires a rather massive installation and can alter the roof line, which may not suit all tastes. At this time it is quite expensive, but the federal government is subsidizing manufacturers of the equipment and may eventually subsidize the builder who uses it. Solar energy use is presently confined mostly to areas of maximum sunshine.

20.5B3. WIND ENERGY

As with solar energy, wind energy is only in a government-sponsored experimental stage, but is not nearly as advanced. Essentially it consists of large wind-driven fans or turbines which in turn drive electric generators to produce electricity for instant use or store it in massive banks of storage batteries for later use.

20.5C. Air Conditioning

Air conditioning has great sales appeal, especially in warmer climates. In the more temperate climates it is an extra that is rarely installed in private residences although it is often installed in condominiums. In the warmer climates it is essential.

There are many ways in which space can be air-conditioned, but the all-air system is the simplest and the least expensive. Even this system has several varieties, but this section will describe only the single-duct variable-volume installation. This system uses a compressor to cool and dehumidify the air, which is forced through the same ducts that supply heat in the cold weather. Dampers on these ducts can modify the volume of the air so that the warmer parts of the house or unit get the most air.

If the house is heated by hot water, then an all-water air conditioning system must be used. In this case both the heat and air conditioning are supplied by fan-coil units which consist of copper fins on a pipe which is either hot or cold and a fan to blow the air into the room—all encased in a radiator enclosure. This is expensive and can be offered only in high-priced houses.

There is a table on page 391 (an Appendix to Part 2), which gives the builder a guide to loads for the areas that he wishes to air-condition. The system design, including pipe sizes, duct sizes, fan sizes, and tonnage, will have to be done by an expert, but all large companies that manufacture air conditioning equipment will render such a service if the builder purchases their equipment.

20.6. THE ELECTRICAL INSTALLATION

Electrical installations are strictly governed by national, state, local, and underwriters' codes. The size of the service, the kind of wiring devices, and the size of the circuit wiring are all spelled out. The builder who wishes to build a minimum house need only follow these minimum codes. The builder who wishes to add a little extra sales appeal can leave room for a couple of spare circuits in the panel box or can add one or more base outlets. An inexpensive but appealing "gadget" is the use of a live wiring strip around the kitchen counter so that the homemaker can plug in a kitchen appliance at any point instead of at fixed outlets.

20.7. INSULATION

In the past few years the cost of energy-producing fuels has increased enormously. In addition there is the constant threat of a shortage of fuel oil and natural gas, which in turn also affects the cost of electricity. To counteract this trend, there has been a trend toward the use of more efficient fuel-burning furnaces, more efficient distribution, and fuller use of insulation. Most home purchasers ask about insulation because it affects their future fuel costs.

The builder is concerned only with the built-in insulation. Other insulation such as storm windows is normally the obligation of the tenant. The insulation that is built-in can do much to save the loss of heat through walls and ceilings. The standard insulation is used between exterior studs and between ceiling joists. If the attic is for future expansion and is not heated the insulation is laid between the ceiling joists of the first floor. If the attic or second floor is to be used, the insulation should be stapled between the roof rafters. The most widely used insulation consists of "bats" of a vermin-proof fibrous material such as rock wool, mineral wool, or glass wool encased in a heavy paperlike material. These bats come in rolls of standard widths to fit between studs or rafters and are of various thickness. The usual thickness that is used in better-built homes is 4 in. for exterior walls and 6 in. for the ceiling or roof. Bats now come with a vapor barrier of aluminum foil or impregnated building paper. The vapor barrier is for the purpose of preventing condensation between the exterior and interior walls, which can occur when there is a large difference in temperature between these walls.

The federal government is taking a great interest in the proper use of insulation to conserve fuel, and there have been several bills proposed in Congress offering rewards to builders for such use. The builder may be doubly rewarded, once by the purchaser of his house and once by the government!

21

PLANS AND SPECIFICATIONS FOR A COMMERCIAL OR MULTIFAMILY BUILDING

21.1. THE BUILDER, ARCHITECT, ENGINEER TEAM

Few smaller communities in this country, even those in the outlying areas of big cities, require that a builder use the services of an architect or engineer before they will issue a building permit or a certificate of occupancy for a private residence. However, these same communities will require a professional seal on any plans for a building that is to be used for business or multifamily purposes.

A speculative builder who wishes to expand his business ventures into this field must therefore be prepared to deal with a licensed architect or engineer, or both. In order to save time and money, it is well for the builder to be prepared before he asks for professional help. Some of the matters he should be familiar with follow.

21.1A. The Zoning Code

The builder should be familiar with the local zoning code. These codes are not difficult to interpret. He should start with a zoning map to find the zone in which his property is located, then look up the requirements of that zone for height, bulk, side and front yards, parking, etc. This should determine the size of his building. An architect who is trained to work with and interpret codes will refine this and, by changing the shape or orientation of a building, may be able to find more area for building than was first evident. This is especially true for multifamily buildings. Nevertheless the builder should do it first.

21.1B. The Building Code

The builder is not expected to master the building code as it applies to commercial or multifamily buildings. He should, however, be familiar with the general requirements as they may relate to his proposed structure. In many states there is a uniform state building code which applies universally. The builder should purchase this.

When a typical building code is examined, the following major points by which the code is administered become apparent.

21.1B1. USE GROUP

Determining the "use group" into which the proposed structure falls is probably the most important part of the code. The use to which the building will be put determines how it should be built. The use groups are determined by the fire hazards inherent in the particular use. These groups vary from high-hazard buildings used for the manufacture of highly flammable products, through warehouses and industrial buildings, to business buildings and residential buildings. The use groups are further divided into "types of buildings" which can vary from those built entirely of noncombustible materials to frame structures, or a combination of both. The kind of structure that a small builder is apt to build can usually do with all-frame construction or a combination of masonry walls and an all-wood-framed interior or light steel joists and wood floors. The choice can depend on the kind of occupancy the builder is aiming for in a business building (for instance, heavy floor loading, a considerable amount of equipment, etc.). In a family building such as a condominium, he should consider the permanence of the structure and the insurance rates for an all-frame building as they compare with a partially fire-retardant structure. A prospective purchaser can be discouraged by an all-frame-building with high fire-insurance rates. For a business building that he plans to rent, the builder is the one who must pay the high rates and maintain the structure.

The use group also determines the size and number of exit facilities, the extent of fire protection, and other provisions that cost money.

All of the above is intended to be a general guide. It is the architect who will interpret the code exactly and in detail. He can also outline several different schemes of code-conforming construction so that the builder can price them. This can be very important for a successful venture.

21.1C. The Program

A program is a set of instructions prepared by the builder for the use of the architect. First it tells the architect what the building is to be used for. Then it tells the architect how the space is to be divided.

21.1C1. COMMERCIAL BUILDING

In a commercial building the builder may require two or three stores on the street floor and office space on the second floor, or he may want professional offices on the first floor and office space on the second floor. There are many combinations. If the builder is fortunate enough to obtain a long-term tenant before he starts to build, he can plan his program accordingly. However, he should not arrange the space so that no one else can ever use it.

In addition to advising the architect on how he wants the general areas divided into stores, offices, and professional offices, the builder should also have an idea of what column spacing he would like, what ceiling height he prefers, whether he wants a hung ceiling with recessed lighting, how he wants the exterior to look, the kind of windows and doors he prefers. These last items are very important. Many thousands of small office buildings have been built in the past few years with metal and glass skins and fixed windows. Fixed windows are less expensive but they also force the builder or landlord to furnish 100 percent of the interior weather, which is becoming more and more expensive to produce.

21.1C2. MULTIFAMILY BUILDING

With a condominium or rental property the builder should outline his requirements for the sizes of apartments that he thinks will sell most readily. From his survey of other condominiums or rental properties he should also have an idea of room sizes, ceiling heights, and general architectural style, remembering to avoid peculiar overdecorated styles. Another important part of a program is the location of the apartments. The most expensive ones should have the best views and the most privacy. The builder must also decide whether he wants townhouses, two- or three-story multiapartment buildings, or a combination of both.

21.1C3. THE MATERIALS OF CONSTRUCTION AND THE FACILITIES

In addition to his program concerning the proposed use of the building, the builder should also outline his preference for certain materials and methods of construction. It is at this point that his knowledge of the building code and the use group into which his building will fall will be of great help to him. In general, of course, the architect should know a great deal more about the application of the code than the builder, but he will not resent and may even welcome the instructions of a well-informed client. There are multiple choices that conform to the code in the case of a small business or multifamily building. This is because this type of structure, when it is built in a zone that restricts the height and bulk, also requires almost the lowest fireproof rating. Here, of course, is where the builder can build smaller buildings. Land in higher-use zones is much more expensive and requires much larger construction for economic reasons.

21.1C3a. Structural Framing

This was discussed in Sec. 21.1C1 under "use group." There are many more combinations than those mentioned. The builder should remember that sturdy soundproof construction is the most salable or rentable.

21.1C3b. Soundproofing and Insulation

All codes require fireproof walls between town houses in condominiums, but the builder has a choice of what to do with the walls between separate office tenants, or separate condominium or rental units, or between these units and the public areas. In all of these cases fire-retardant partitions are called for, but sound insulation is not. The use of a soundproof insulating blanket in such partitions is not expensive and is strongly recommended. Thought should also be given to the sound insulation of floors. In wood-frame or light steel construction a double floor and a fire-retardant wallboard ceiling underneath will usually be sufficient. Some condominiums offer carpeting over subflooring, which is, of course, an excellent sound deadener.

While insulation of walls and ceilings against outside temperature changes has been in use for a long time, in the past few years it has taken on added importance because of the shortage and the subsequent high price of energy. The builder should be aware of this and make sure that the building design allows for sufficient insulation. Some states now have energy codes, and the federal government is constantly publishing new data on this subject. The architect should know about this.

21.1C3c. Heating and Air Conditioning

In a condominium or in any commercial building, the first cost of this installation must be one of the main concerns. The very best system may add enough to the price of a unit or to the rental to discourage purchasers or renters. The cheapest installation may be wasteful of energy and give uneven heating. It may even be one that prospective condominium purchasers have been warned against. A study of the heating and air conditioning systems that are advertised and installed in other successful condominiums in the same price range will be helpful in choosing the right one. The design engineer who is employed by the architect should be familiar with the first costs, the effectiveness, and the economics of the various systems.

The air conditioning and heating of a commercial building presents a different set of rules. The builder can either provide a central heating system with individual air conditioners which can be mounted through the exterior wall and separately controlled by the tenant, or he can provide central heating and air conditioning. Stores can be supplied through the central system.

It is possible to install an inexpensive central heating and air conditioning system in a small building which is to be occupied by only a very few large tenants whose opening and closing times are about the same and whose operations are similar. (Such a system is not very flexible and cannot easily respond to the demands of a widely varied tenancy.) This central system consists of a heating-air conditioning plant, located in the basement or on the first floor, which distributes cold or warm air through ducts and ceiling grilles into the various spaces and collects the return air through a plenum chamber, which is simply the space between the hung ceiling and the floor above (see Fig. 21-1). The system can be zoned for northwest and southeast parts of the building, or for any two zones.

21.1C3d. Electrical

Before the present high cost of electricity many small office buildings were electrically heated and cooled by individual heating and cooling units which the tenant controlled by a thermostat. The cost of installation is cheaper than any central system but the cost of operation, especially for electrical resistance heating, can become prodigious.

Lighting is another factor. Most tenants are looking for recessed fluorescent lighting. A lighting intensity of 50 foot-candles is sufficient for almost all purposes. Stores usually require more lighting, but this can be installed by the store owners at their own expense. The forward-looking builder who intends to own the building should look into the possibility of splitting the feeder lines so that any individual tenant's use of electricity can be metered at any later date. Of course in condominiums and most residential rental units, units are separately metered while the public facilities are jointly metered.

21.2. THE BUSINESS CONSIDERATION

All of the preceding discussion of architecture, materials, and heating, air conditioning, and electrical systems has one major purpose. While the quality of the materials and the systems has not been ignored, the basic goal has been to guide the speculative builder in how best to conduct a profitable business. Profitable business means repeat business, and this is where the quality of the construction comes into play. In making his choices the builder must be constantly aware of his budget.

21.3. THE BUILDER-ARCHITECT RELATIONSHIP

The services of an architect are necessary when the builder expands into the field of commercial or multifamily construction. Architects employ engineers for structural, mechanical, and electrical design and pay them directly.

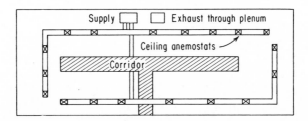

Figure 21-1   Elementary heating and air conditioning.

Professional fees are established by state professional organizations, but there is no law that forbids the builder and the professional from negotiating the fee.

From the schematic line drawings and outline specifications to the finished working drawings and specifications, the builder (owner) and the architect must have a meeting of the minds. The builder as owner must constantly look over the architect's shoulder and be aware of the cost implications of the architectural and mechanical design as it progresses. This is common practice during the design period of any structure. In large projects, owners, builders, architects, and engineers meet constantly and the owner expects the builder* to prepare a running estimate as the design progresses and to sound a warning immediately if any item appears which may raise the cost over budget. However, the speculative builder is the owner. He must protect his budget himself by constant vigilance.

*In many cases the builder is employed as an estimator and consultant on a fee basis. He may not be the final low bidder.

22

THE SHELL HOUSE

22.1. WHAT A SHELL HOUSE IS

In the dictionary a "shell" is defined as "any framework or outside covering of a structure." Because of the rising cost of construction the single-family residence has, in many parts of the country, been priced out of the reach of many people, especially younger couples, who want a home of their own. To meet this challenge and to keep their business going, speculative builders in many parts of the country have built shell houses for their clients. This involves the construction of a weathertight structural frame which can be completed in stages and made livable by the owners.

22.2. THE OPTIONS THAT A BUILDER CAN OFFER

22.2A. The Building Lot

The builder can offer to build the shell on his own land, which he will then sell along with the structure, or he can build it on his client's land. In the latter instance the builder acts as though he were building any house for any owner, except that he does not have to bid the job because he and his client have come to an agreement on a fixed price for a fixed plan. It is up to the owner of the land to produce proof of title and a survey to show that he owns the land free and clear. In some cases the land may be subject to a mortgage. Section 22.8 explains what the builder must do in such circumstances.

22.2B. Size and Style

The builder is advised to confine himself to offering only small houses of conventional design, and the choice should be among not more than four or five designs. The reason for this is twofold. First, the builder must prepare a complete cost estimate for each design for both its basic construction (see Sec. 22.3) and for all the alternates that he is offering with each design. Second, multiplicity of choice tends to confuse the prospective purchaser. People rarely know exactly what they want and experience has shown that a definite choice among a small number of good designs is easier to make. The builder must also be prepared to meet prospects (especially younger couples) who would like much more house than they can afford. Some of the choices might be:

- A one-story colonial with three bedrooms, two baths, a living room–dining room, kitchen, and laundry room. Garage or carport optional.

- A 1½-story Cape Cod with an expansion attic. The first floor could contain two bedrooms, one bath, a kitchen-dining room, a living room, a laundry room, and a breezeway or porch. This house should have a stairway leading to a future second floor. Garage or carport can be optional. The second floor would be large enough for two bedrooms and a bath. Dormers for the future bedrooms and bath are optional.

- A two-story colonial with living room, dining room, kitchen-family room, and lavatory on first floor and three bedrooms with one or two baths on second floor. Garage or carport optional.

The builder can also offer the option of a flat slab foundation, a crawlway, or a full or half basement.

22.3. THE BASIC CONSTRUCTION

The simplest shell house must be weathertight, structurally safe, and secure. This involves:

- Foundations.
- Structural frame and bearing partitions.
- Chimney for heating plant. Fireplace optional.
- Rough flooring.
- Exterior sheathing of roof and walls.
- Windows and doors with hardware for security.
- Flashing at windows, doors, chimney. Leave holes in roof for plumbing stacks.
- Heavy waterproof covering over roof and wall sheathing.

Either during the original negotiations or as the construction progresses, the builder can offer options for advancing the construction further toward completion. This can be quite successful. Most people do not realize the magnitude of the work involved in finishing a house until they actually see it.

22.4. THE OPTIONS FOR WORK BEYOND COMPLETION OF SHELL

The builder can offer to add:

- A fireplace
- Interior stud partitions other than bearing partitions
- Wallboard on walls and ceilings
- Roofing and sheet metal—shingles, gutters, and leaders
- Exterior finish—clapboard, shingle, brick, vertical siding, etc.

The builder can also offer to obtain the services of plumbing, heating, and electrical subcontractors, but should make prior arrangements with them. He should also explain to his clients that it is required by the building code that plumbing and electrical work be done by licensed contractors and that no power company will connect to a house unless there is a proper permit. Installation of a septic tank and drain field must be done before the house is considered habitable.

22.5. THE BUILDER'S OBLIGATIONS

The builder of shell houses is obligated to perform certain services for his client over and above the actual construction.

22.5A. Building Code and Permit

The builder should include in his price the cost of filing a full set of plans and specifications with the local building department, even though he may be building only the shell. Prior to this filing he must, of course, be sure that his plans meet the building code of the locality. The permit that he obtains enables his clients to complete the house without further need to contact the town authorities except for periodic inspection, and to obtain the final certificate of occupancy.

22.5B. Zoning Code

Whether he is building on his own or his client's land, the builder must be sure that the structure is so placed on the land that it will meet the requirements of the zoning code. He should allow for a garage and for later additions to the house if at all possible. A plot plan is usually required and the builder should prepare and file this. If he is building on his own land he should also furnish a survey.

Several copies of the plans, specifications, and the survey should be given to the client for his use. The obligations as mentioned above are really excellent sales points and should certainly give the prospect confidence in the good will of the builder.

22.6. PRICING THE BASIC STRUCTURE

The builder who wishes to pursue the shell house phase of speculative building in a serious way must be prepared to offer his clients very definite choices and fixed prices. If the structure is not to be on his land, he must be sure that the house style and size that his clients choose will fit on their land and will be in compliance with zoning. Then, in order to avoid any misunderstanding or worse, he must spell out in detail exactly what he is going to build and for how many dollars. For instance:

> House style A. Shell only, single story, no basement or habitable attic, three bedrooms, two baths, living-dining room, kitchen, and laundry room, no garage. "The intent of this contract is for the builder to provide a building that is structurally sound and weathertight so that interior finishing work may proceed as desired by the owner. The builder will provide all labor and material to complete the work as outlined below for the sum of $_____."

The plan, as approved by the client, and the outline specifications that follow must be carefully priced by the builder. He should know the foundation conditions on his own land and should carefully investigate them if he is building on his client's land. The builder should have a price list and an outline specification for each style of shell house that he offers. He must also keep aware of price changes in labor, materials, equipment rental, and other construction items so that his price lists are current.

A typical specification might be as follows:

- *Foundation.* Flat slab construction on solid earth to be built as follows: Footings to be of size and depth to be in accordance with town of _____ building code. Flat slab to be of 4 in. of concrete, reinforced with wire mesh, laid over heavy plastic moisture shield which will be laid over 2 in. of crushed stone.

- *Structure.* Sills to be secured to foundation by bolts fastened into foundation. Exterior walls and interior bearing partitions to be of 2 × 4 in. studs 16 in. on center with single 2 × 4-in. sole and double 2 × 4-in. plate. All windows and doors to be framed with double 2 × 4s. Lintels over windows and doors to be as required by code. Structure to be corner-braced. Rafters and ceiling joists to be of size and spacing as required by code.

- *Millwork.* Exterior doors to be of catalog No. _____ for front door and catalog No. _____ for rear door. Windows to be double hung of size as shown on plan and style as shown by catalog No. _____.

- *Exterior.* Exterior walls and roof to be sheathed with whatever material is usually used in the locality. Exterior wall and roof sheathing to be covered with extra-heavy tarred felt, to be securely fastened with roofing nails and furring strips.

- *Masonry.* Front and rear steps to be furnished. Brick chimney to be furnished for heating plant. Chimney to be lined with approved flue lining in accordance with code. (If fireplace is desired, the option must be exercised before construction starts.)

- *Hardware.* All exterior window and door hardware to be furnished and installed. Hardware to be as manufactured by _____ _____ and to be of styles _____.

- *Accessories.* Pull-down attic stairs to be furnished and installed and an area of 6 × 10 ft at head of attic stairs to be rough-floored.

- *Flashing.* Flashing (aluminum, copper, etc.) to be furnished and installed over all exterior openings and around chimney.

- *Provisions for mechanical and electrical work.* The builder will provide the proper openings in the foundation for water and sewer lines and for fuel line for the heating plant. Provision will also be made for future meter pan and panel box for electrical installation.

22.7. PRICING THE OPTIONS

Section 22.4 has mentioned most of the typical options that a builder can offer to his client. Each option for each house must be separately priced.

22.7A. Plumbing, Heating, and Electrical

The builder may be able to make a deal with local plumbing, heating, and electrical contractors for a price that he can quote to his client. However, many subcontractors will be unwilling to go through all the estimating work required to arrive at a fixed price for four or five different styles of houses. It is therefore the builder's responsibility to have a tight set of plans and specifications for these trades. The specifications should list heating capacities, manufacturers' names and catalog sizes, catalog numbers for plumbing fixtures, piping materials, electrical panel box sizes, capacity of electrical service, etc. The builder can obtain such a set of specifications and capacities by conferring with one or more plumbing, heating, and electrical contractors or by approaching the sales representatives of the equipment manufacturers, whose names can be found in the yellow pages of any telephone directory.

With such plans and specifications in hand for the client to approve, the builder can offer to have the work installed at a price *which he must first check with the subcontractor,* and which includes a percentage for his supervision and overhead.

A word of warning to the builder is necessary here. To avoid trouble with his client he must tell the client *exactly* what he is to get and the client must give his approval by, at least, initialing the plan and specification. This is fairly simple for heating and plumbing where catalog numbers of boilers, fixtures, etc., are spelled out, but it is different for electrical work. In this case the builder must state how many base outlets, switches, ceiling outlets, and wall outlets he is providing for each room, the size of the service, the capacity of the panel box, and the provisions for furnace and major appliances. He can make an allowance for fixtures if the client so desires.

22.7B. Other Options

Every option that the builder offers must be as carefully documented as the ones for plumbing, heating, and electrical work. For instance, if the builder is offering a fireplace, he should indicate the width, height, and depth of the opening, the width of the fireplace breast, whether there is to be a mantel, the size and kind of dampers, the size of the hearth. The best way to do this is by a dimensioned drawing. This can be standard for all the houses offered.

Another example is interior wallboarding. In this case the builder can say "All interior wallboard to be installed after plumbing, heating, and electrical roughing is complete. Wallboard to be ⅝-in. thick and to be as manufactured by _____ or equal. All joints to be taped and spackled and the spackling to be brought to a feathered edge. All nail holes and other imperfections to be spackled. All surfaces to be completed ready for painting."

Each one of these and other options should have a fixed price tag. This pricing need not all be done at once but can be done as the sales progress and the options are offered.

22.8. FINANCING A SHELL HOUSE

Banks and other lending institutions will finance a shell house in the same manner that they do any construction. They will grant a construction loan to the owner and make payouts as the work progresses in accordance with their payment schedule. The interest rate on a construction loan to an owner is usually at the going rate, but if the speculative builder wishes to build a shell house on speculation he must be prepared to pay at least two extra points.

The construction loan is changed to a permanent mortgage only when the house is fully completed.

The builder who is building for an owner must be sure that the payouts are arranged so that he is paid in full when his work is completed.

If the land is mortgaged, the bank will insist that the land mortgage be subordinated to its mortgage.

The client or owner should know that he must pay interest on each advance from the day that the money is paid out.

The builder must be sure that he is covered by a builder's risk comprehensive insurance policy to the full extent of his contractual obligation. Lending institutions prefer such policies to be in the amount of the finally completed house.

Lending institutions have also indicated that they will consider construction financing and final financing on shell structures other than single-family residences—for instance, multifamily rental housing.

23

FINANCING A SPECULATIVE VENTURE

23.1. THE FUNDAMENTAL REQUIREMENTS

The financing of a speculative venture can be a great deal more difficult than the financing of a construction business in which the builder confines himself to building for specific owners. (See Part 1, Chap. 11.) When he is building "on order" the builder does not have to concern himself with long-term financing or cash flow because the owner is responsible for the construction loan which provides for specific payments as the work progresses. The builder is also assured that he will be paid on completion and therefore will not have the burden of interest or principal payments on any mortgage or other form of loan. His only concern is short-term financing to bridge the gap between the progress payments and his cash requirements.

In speculative building, the builder is on his own. He must be prepared for long-term financing and for an outlay of his own capital. In some cases he may be able to sell a single-family house or a condominium unit, or rent a commercial building or multifamily dwelling before he has completed construction, but he must be ready for the worst. He must be prepared to complete his venture and carry it for some time before he can sell and get his money out, or before his rental income will at least equal his expenses.

It is hoped that before the builder undertakes speculative ventures, he has a going construction business that gives him some cash flow. The builder should have accumulated some capital of his own and his cash flow should more than cover his personal living expenses.

23.1A. The Builder's Credit Standing

One of the most important requirements for operating a successful speculative building business is the maintenance of a high credit rating. It is interesting to note that the word "credit" means financial or commercial trustworthiness, or esteem or recognition. To obtain a high credit rating it is necessary for the builder to prepare himself for a thorough scrutiny of his business, his borrowings, his promptness in paying back loans, his balance sheet, his record of profitable business, his inventory of equipment, his record of payments for labor and material and, very often, his personal life and reputation. In his day-to-day construction work for clients (as set forth in Part 1, Chap. 11) he should have built up a line of credit with one or more financial institutions, made a number of short-term loans and paid them back promptly, and paid his material dealers and his subcontractors on time. He should have established a reputation for performing good work on time for satisfied customers.

Now if he needs an extension of credit or a deferment of mortgage amortization there is a good chance that it may be granted. This can make the difference between success and failure.

23.2. PRELIMINARY STEPS BEFORE FINANCING

Before the builder can approach a financial institution, a mortgage banker, or any prospective investor, he must be prepared to submit a complete statement showing exactly what he wishes to build, an estimate of its cost, a statement showing his own assets, a market survey showing the possibilities for quick sale or rent at a profit, and other pertinent facts and figures. In short he must prove to the investor, mortgagee, or whomever he proposes to borrow the money from, that the lender will get his money back with interest or otherwise earn a long or short-term profit on his investment. *The profit must be commensurate with the risk.*

23.2A. A Sample Fact Sheet

- *Location.* In town of Scarboro, lot 47 on Jones Ferry Road. Copy of plot attached. Zoned ½-acre residential.

- *Structure.* Two-story, three-bedroom, 1½-bath, single-family residence. Plans and specifications attached.

- *Land.* Purchased for $10,000 from Ferry Properties, Inc. Owned free and clear.

- *Estimated cost of structure.* $35,000 including builder's overhead and profit, and including painting interior and exterior in colors to suit purchaser. House ready for occupancy with certificate of occupancy in hand.

- *Required amount of mortgage.* $35,000.

- *Marketability.* The site is located near the fastest-growing area in the town. Streets are paved and sewers are in place. Houses of this size and character in the immediate area have been selling at an average price of $55,000 and none has been on the market for more than two months before sale. There is a school-bus stop within two streets, and the location is a 20-minute drive from the center of the town and 35 to 40 minutes drive from Large City.

23.2B. Financial Statement

As can be noted from the sample of required information in Table 23-1, the speculative builder who wishes to enter into the credit market must tell all and be prepared to have all of his statements investigated.

23.3. SOURCES OF FINANCING

There are many ways in which a speculative builder may obtain financing for his *first* venture. The word "first" is emphasized because if this one is successful and results in the prompt payoff of a mortgage or its assumption by the purchaser, or in a substantial profit for a private investor, the builder will find that subsequent financing is much easier to obtain.

TABLE 23-1   SAMPLE FINANCIAL STATEMENT

Assets	Liabilities
Cash (show bank)	*Notes payable to:*
Investments—stocks, bonds, etc. (attach schedule)	Installment accounts payable (schedule)
	Other accounts payable
Investment in own business* (attach schedule)	Mortgages on real estate (attach schedule)
Accounts and notes receivable	Unpaid real estate taxes
	Unpaid income taxes
Real estate owned (attach schedule)	Loans on life insurance policies
Auto (make and year)	Other debts (attach schedule)
Life insurance (cash surrender value)	Total liabilities
Personal property	
Other assets	
Total assets	

*Include inventory of tools, equipment, material, office furniture, business property, down payments on equipment, current construction, etc.

23.3A. Financial Institutions

For a small loan such as this, the builder's best source of money is a local bank or a savings and loan association. If the builder has built up a credit standing he should have no trouble in obtaining a construction mortgage, which will pay out as the construction progresses. Chapter 11 of Part 1 shows a typical payment schedule. The builder must also be prepared to pay several percent over the going rate.

There are many other sources of funds among financial institutions such as insurance companies, pension funds, and various trust funds but they will not usually be interested in small loans.

23.3B. Small Business Administration

This organization was formed by the federal government to help finance the formation and the day-to-day need for funds of a small business. There are offices of the SBA in every city in which a federal office center exists. The SBA lends money to state and local development agencies which in turn lend it to small business people. As is the case for any lending agency, the builder must show evidence of good credit standing and good character. A word of caution—the SBA is reluctant to do any financing if the business can obtain funds from any other source at a reasonable rate of interest. Table 23-2 gives the SBA plan in detail.

23.3C. Other Sources of Funds

For many years the private investor has been a source of venture capital for many types of business enterprises. The private investor ventured his capital for one reason—the financial rewards. With the high rates that have recently become available from nonspeculative ventures, private capital is more difficult to obtain.

There are still some small investment trusts that will lend money on a business building, multifamily rental property, or condominium, but they will usually demand a higher rate of interest than a chartered financial institution.

Another source of funds can be the person from whom the builder has purchased the land. The owner of one or two building lots for private residences or for a commercial building may very well be interested in participating in a speculative building venture. He can invest part or all of the cost of the land as his share of the venture and be willing to share in the quick profit from a sale or a long-term profit resulting from the successful renting of a business or multifamily property. The furnishing of such outside capital can reduce the builder's need for borrowing mortgage money, with a resultant saving of interest. He will also find that lenders will be more willing to lend a smaller percentage of the value. There is another side to this coin which will be discussed in Sec. 23.5 under the subject of Leverage.

TABLE 23-2 KEY FEATURES OF SBA'S SMALL BUSINESS LOAN PROGRAMS

(For information about loans to state and local development companies, loans to small business investment companies, and disaster loans, contact the nearest SBA field office or write to the Small Business Administration, Washington, D.C. 20416.)

	Regular Business	Small Loan Program	Simplified Bank Participation Plan	Simplified Early Maturity Plan
Who is eligible?	Most businesses that are independently owned and operated and not dominant in their fields, that cannot obtain private financing on reasonable terms and are not eligible for financing from other government agencies, and that qualify as "small" under SBA's size standards, which generally are based on dollar volume of business or number of employees.	Any business that meets criteria stated under regular business loan plan. Small loan plan is specifically designed to meet the needs of very small firms unable to obtain other financing because of lack of adequate collateral.	Any business that meets criteria for regular business loans, if bank will provide greater of: 25% of total loan, or an amount equal to bank loan to be refinanced.	Same as under regular business loan plan. Major distinction between this plan and simplified bank participation plan is that bank provides at least 50% of loan and is repaid before SBA.
Loan purposes	Business construction, conversion or expansion; purchase of equipment, facilities, machinery, supplies or materials; and working capital.	Same as under regular business loan plan.	Same as under regular business loan plan.	Same as under regular business loan plan.

313

TABLE 23-2 KEY FEATURES OF SBA'S SMALL BUSINESS LOAN PROGRAMS (Continued)

	Regular Business	Small Loan Program	Simplified Bank Participation Plan	Simplified Early Maturity Plan
Maximum amount	$350,000 to any one borrower. This is maximum SBA share of "participation loan" —one made jointly by SBA and private lending institution—and maximum SBA "direct loan"—one made entirely by agency.	$15,000 to any one borrower, as SBA share of participation loan or SBA direct loan.	$350,000 to any one borrower, as SBA share of loan.	Same as under simplified bank participation plan.
Interest rate	Maximum of 5½% per annum on SBA share of "immediate participation loan" (where SBA and private lending institution each put up part of loan funds immediately) and on SBA direct loan. Where SBA guarantees a portion of a loan, lending institution may set "reasonable and legal" rate on entire loan. However, if SBA later provides its share of loan, rate on SBA share then is maximum of 5½%.	Same as under regular business loan plan.	Same as under regular business loan plan.	Same as under regular business loan plan, but on immediate participation basis only.

Maturity	Maximum of 10 years as a rule. However, working capital loans generally are limited to 6 years, while construction loans may have maximum of 10 years plus estimated time required for construction.	Maximum of 6 years, plus time needed for construction if loan is used for building construction.	Same as under regular business loan plan.	Same as under regular business loan plan.
Type of collateral	Real estate or chattel mortgage; assignment of warehouse receipts for marketable merchandise; assignment of certain types of contracts, guarantees or personal endorsements; in some instances assignment of current receivables, and inventories stored in bonded or otherwise acceptable warehouse.	Whatever worthwhile collateral is available, including any fixed assets purchased with the loan.	Same as under regular business loan plan.	Same as under regular business loan plan, except that collateral must be of a type not subject to rapid depreciation or obsolescence.

315

23.3C1. TAX ADVANTAGES IN REAL ESTATE INVESTMENT

The builder must be able to point out to the private investor that there are tax advantages in investing in real estate, some of which are not available in other speculative ventures and none of which are available in bond interest, bank interest, or stock dividends. The first of these is the long-term capital gain. The period of time the investment must be held before realizing a sales profit is longer. However, this does not affect an income-producing property which should be held in any case for a period long enough to produce the best profit. Thus the investor can be participating in these profits until the time has come to sell (if ever). The second of these advantages is the depreciation. The depreciation of investment real estate is one of the most potent factors in the profitability of this type of investment. If properly managed under the guidance of an experienced tax counsel it can result in the builder and his investors being able to take most of their profit on an almost tax-free basis. This is an important point for the builder to keep in mind when he is looking for investment capital.

23.4. THE BUILDER'S RESPONSIBILITY FOR INTERIM FINANCING

The builder must be prepared to carry the financial burden resulting from his ownership of a property until it is sold or until the rental income reaches the level of his carrying costs. The sum of money involved can be considerable. One of the most common causes of failure in any business is the lack of capital to carry on a business during a period of poor sales or other adverse circumstances. Previous chapters of this book have advised the speculative builder about analyzing market conditions so that he will avoid falling into a financial trap. Nevertheless he must still be prepared.

In the case of any structure he must pay mortgage interest and taxes; he must pay for fuel and heating plant maintenance if the structure is vacant during cold weather, and he must pay for maintenance of the grounds of a private residence if it is vacant during the growing season. He may be able to defer the payment of mortgage amortization but he cannot defer for any significant length of time the payment of bills for material or to subcontractors, and of course labor must be paid for immediately. The above items can amount to several thousands of dollars. It may be that after one or two successful ventures the builder may wish to build more than one structure at a time. There is no reason why he cannot do this if he has enough of his own capital to finance the construction between payouts. He is advised not to start them at the same time so that he may deploy his men between them as they reach certain stages of construction. He is warned, however, not to use the payouts for one building to help carry the other nor to use any of the money for any other purpose than that for which it is intended. Banks and other lenders take a dim view of such actions and pyramiding debt can lead to financial disaster. The builder should not bite off more than he can chew.

23.5. THE USE OF LEVERAGE IN REAL ESTATE INVESTMENT

The use of leverage is for the financial sophisticate and really should not be in a book for a beginning speculative builder. However, there may be a time when such a builder can use it and in any case he should know about it for future use. Simply explained, "leverage" consists of the use of other people's money in order to gain a high rate of return on one's own cash investment. As an example:

An income property represents a total investment of $150,000. The builder will be able to obtain a construction loan of at least $112,500, which is 75 percent of the total value. The balance of the cost will be his cash or it will be shared with an investor. At the completion of the project the builder will want to obtain a permanent mortgage. He should ask for $125,000 and will probably get $120,000. This sets up as follows:

Total cost	$150,000
Estimated gross income after all expense except debt service	15,000
Debt service $120,000 @ 9½%	11,400
Net income on builder's equity of $30,000	3,600
Return on builder's equity	12%

If the builder can now obtain a second mortgage as well from the original owner of the land, the return to him would be as follows:

Total cost	$150,000
Estimated gross income, etc.	15,000
Debt service	
First mortgage $120,000 @ 9½%	11,400
Second mortgage 15,000 @ 10%	1,500
Net income after total debt service of $12,900	2,100

The builder's equity is now only $15,000 and his rate of return is now 14%. If he can increase his rents or economize in management, all of the extra income is his because the mortgage interest rates are at fixed percentages, and with only 10 percent of his own cash invested in this property, he maintains freedom of action.

Again a final word of caution. Leverage must be used with great care and on a rising market. In using it the builder is amassing a large debt with very little leeway.

24

SELLING AND RENTING A SPECULATIVE VENTURE

24.1. THE SINGLE-FAMILY RESIDENCE

24.1A. How to Increase Sales Appeal

This section should really be divided into two parts. The first part should be called "How to Produce Sales Appeal." This means that the builder must produce a quality house before he tries to add the extras that he thinks will produce a quick sale. He can have a well-built house without exceeding his budget. He should have a good foundation, solidly nailed bridging between joists, corner bracing, solidly nailed lintels, and an extra nail here and there. This will produce a house with the appearance of sturdiness and solidity for which the purchaser is looking.

The architecture of the house and the layout of the rooms are very important. (See Chap. 20.) People are not very adventurous when it comes to the investment of their savings in a home. They do like some small changes, such as a different material for siding or shingles or a change in a roof line, but generally the house for sale should represent the architecture of the region. The prospective homeowner who wants something startlingly different will usually have it specially designed and built to order.

If the builder has produced a well-built, well-laid-out, and architecturally sound house, his next step is to add whatever extra amenities he can afford, without notably raising the sales price. A good start could be the kitchen. He has access to many magazine articles and illustrations of kitchen layouts. Stove burners can be part of an attractive cabinet and the oven can be built into one side of it. Kitchen cabinets are made in dozens of designs and in many stock sizes. The use of stock sizes is of course recommended both for economy and availability. He should consider an island counter and breakfast area. It would be a good idea to get the advice of a kitchen design service. The bathroom is another place that can have extra appeal. There are attractive shower stalls now on the market that come in one piece, ready for installation. One of these could be considered for a second bathroom. A cabinet sink containing a laundry hamper can be an attractive feature. Many such units come in stock sizes. Some of these are extremely gaudy, and may not appeal to everyone. The builder should strive for simplicity.

There are also such extras as wall-to-wall carpeting instead of finished floors; wall covering in the bath; bathroom and kitchen floor covering; kitchen and bathroom ceiling or cabinet lighting, etc.

24.1B. Pricing for a Quick Sale

There were references to this very important subject in the preceding sections of this book (for example, Sec. 18.4). It will now be explained in detail. To start with, the speculative builder will be better off if he can sell his house before it is completed. If he does this, he will obviously have to set a firm price on an uncompleted house. Setting the price at this time is almost the same as bidding a job from a set of plans and specifications. This is what a builder does when he is building for specific clients. But in speculative building he must pay the taxes, construction loan interest, permit fees, insurance, and financing. On the other hand, the builder has more leeway during the construction. He is not subject to the whims of an architect or a client. He can use his own judgment in the selection of materials.. The steps and the calculations the builder must make before setting a sale price are as follows.

24.1B1. FOR THE HOUSE THAT IS SOLD BEFORE COMPLETION

The builder has carefully estimated his construction costs, which include labor, material, rental of equipment, construction insurance, permits, cost of money used between bank payouts, overhead, and his builder's profit. In these costs he has also included finish grading and some elementary landscaping. He also knows his full land costs.

To this he should now add a sum for contingencies which may arise before he can deliver a completed house to his customer. This contingency allowance can be lowered as the house nears completion.

The last addition to the cost includes the speculative costs. These consist of the interest on his construction loan, builder's risk insurance, interest on his own investment, taxes during construction, and his speculative profit.

The advantage to the builder of a sale before completion is that he has limited his speculative costs, and there is no reason why he cannot offer part of this cost saving to the purchaser in return for a quick contract and a quick closing, subject to final completion and obtaining a certificate of occupancy. As a matter of fact he can even forego a portion of his speculative profit in return for the freeing of his invested capital and his access to a full credit line free of the incumbrance of his construction loan.

In conclusion, the builder should be fully aware that there are not many sellers of real estate who get their first asking price. Overpricing a property may drive prospective purchasers away before they have even looked at it. The builder must be prepared to fall back somewhat from his asking price and still allow himself a reasonable speculative profit. The matter of a broker's fee will be discussed in Sec. 24.1D.

24:1B2. FOR THE HOUSE THAT IS SOLD AFTER COMPLETION

The builder must go through the same steps in pricing the house as he has done in the preceding section. In this case, however, he has not so much to bargain with. It is true that he now does not have to add any contingency for completion, but he is faced with the financial burden of carrying a completed structure with the consequent extra expense. He must set a price at which he is willing to sell. He can only guess at the period of time he will have to hold the house before sale. If he estimates a 6-month period and has priced the house accordingly, and if he sells in 3 months, he has that much more bargaining leeway. The important thing is that when the speculative builder prices his house for sale he must keep his records so clearly that he is constantly aware of the lowest price he can accept and still earn a speculative profit over and above his builder's profit.

24.1B3. THE MORTGAGE

It is very important for the builder making a construction loan to come to an agreement with the lender regarding the amount and the terms of a permanent mortgage. A sale is more apt to occur when immediate mortgage money is available. The purchaser must of course be able to meet all the financial standards that a bank or other lender may set. This qualification applies to FHA or VA guaranteed mortgages as well as to conventional mortgages.

24.1C. Advertising

When a builder has set a price on his finished product, his next step is to bring it to the attention of prospective purchasers. He can start his advertising campaign as soon as he comes into possession of the land.

24.1C1. SIGNS ON THE SITE

The first step in making a project known to the public is to place a sign on the site. As he is clearing the land, digging the foundation, and erecting the structural frame, the builder should display in a prominent place on his property a sign, which could say: "To be built on this site. A 3-bedroom, 2-bath single-story ranch house. For further detail call John Jones, 112-621-4400. Early purchase will give buyer choice of finishing materials." The last statement can be a powerful incentive for a quick sale. The choice is *only* for finishing materials such as lighting fixtures, hardware, interior and exterior wall finishes, kitchen cabinets, but—if the purchase is early enough—could even include the siding material. At this point the builder must be so aware of his costs that he is able to give the purchaser an even exchange or quote the difference between the builder's specifications and the purchaser's choice. The builder is urged not to be too heavy-handed in his quoted extras. He can kill a sale.

The next step comes when the house is nearing completion. The sign on the site should now be changed. "For sale. This 3-bedroom, 2-bath house with ½ acre. Will decorate interior in colors to be chosen. For further details call John Jones, 112-621-4400." The builder is to be careful not to quote any numbers on the telephone but should arrange to meet the prospect at the site. See Sec. 24.1C4 on how to handle telephone calls.

24.1C2. NEWSPAPERS AND MAGAZINES

In advertising single-family homes for sale, the builder should always remember that he is dealing with people who are looking for a new home, a place where they will spend a lot of their time and where they will feel comfortable. The advertisement should therefore be composed with care. The first line should draw immediate attention such as: "Traditional House on Wooded Site," or "View of Rolling Hills," or "Sunny Meadowland," or "Old Stone Walls." The descriptive material can follow these "punch lines." The builder is advised not to give the exact location of the house. He can name the town and the general location.

The advertisements should start as soon as the house is well underway and the builder has set the asking price. A suggestion on timing is publication on Sunday (if there is a Sunday edition) or every other week in a local weekly newspaper. Most areas have one or more "giveaway" newspapers or trade sheets which live on their advertising revenue. These are mostly thrown away, but if the rates are low an occasional advertisement might bring a response. The advertising dollar must be carefully budgeted and watched. There are, of course, the nearest city papers. Advertisements in the Sunday real estate sections are expensive. If the budget allows, the builder should try it once or twice.

24.1C3. RELOCATION SERVICES

All national companies shift key personnel from one location to another. This includes manufacturing and sales organizations, insurance companies, national service agencies, and others. If the builder is within commuting distance of a large or medium company it is suggested that he write to the employee relocation service of that company to offer his house or houses for sale. Large companies are listed in *Fortune Magazine* (1271 Avenue of the Americas, New York, N.Y. 10020). He can then look up any of the names mentioned in *Fortune* in the telephone book for the nearest city. Such a city directory is well worth subscribing to. A call to the company will give him the address of its relocation service.

There are companies that advertise themselves as relocation services in the yellow pages of telephone directories or in other media. The builder must be cautious about listing his property with these services because most of them are simply real estate brokers who charge regular brokerage fees. When writing to a company relocation service the builder must make it clear that his price does not include a brokerage fee. It is a good idea for him to have his attorney look at the form of the letters.

24.1C4. HOW TO HANDLE TELEPHONE CALLS

Since the builder has given his telephone number on his signs and in his advertisements, he will get telephone calls. He should therefore instruct anyone who answers the telephone to give out no more than the information available on the sign or advertisement, and courteously ask for a return telephone number so that the inquirer may be called back for an appointment to view the house. If the builder answers he should try to *arrange to see the caller in person before committing himself to anything.* The caller could be a broker, a curiosity seeker, a competitive builder, or a salesman.

Even when showing the house, the builder is wise to ask for the prospect's address and telephone number so that it can be added to a mailing list. He should identify the person before getting into a serious discussion. He can certainly ask if the person is a broker or represents a broker, or whether he is looking for himself and is the bona fide purchaser or is a "front" for someone else. The builder should try to ascertain whether the person has the financial ability to purchase the house. Sometimes a builder has thought that he has sold a house only to find two weeks later that his prospective purchaser cannot qualify for a mortgage, or again he has sold a house to a "nominee" who unveils the actual purchaser at the closing. Most states will allow a seller to withdraw his house from the market. The builder should consult his attorney.

24.1D. Listing with Brokers

If the house has not sold quickly and he is faced with carrying the financial burden for an unknown time, the builder must make up his mind whether he wishes to list the house with brokers. Brokers always get referrals from other towns and from big cities. They have lists of prospects. They can probably sell the house more quickly than the builder. They also get about $3000 in commission for selling a $50,000 to $60,000 house.

It is a matter of arithmetic and financial stamina. How long can the builder hold the house unsold before he has used up $3000 in carrying charges? Can he rent it unfurnished with permission to show it?

If he does not want to go through all of this and if he has (as he should) allowed for brokerage in his budget, the question then arises as to whether the listing should be an exclusive for 30 days with his favorite broker or whether it should be multiple-listed. If it is an exclusive, the broker is expected to pay for some advertising and to make a special effort.

When a property is listed with a broker there must be a very clear-cut understanding on everyone's part as to the terms and conditions under which the builder will sell. He must clearly state his asking price; he can say that the bank has promised to turn his construction loan into a permanent mortgage to a qualified purchaser for a certain face amount and at a certain rate of interest. This should be in writing—bankers can change their minds and leave builders high and dry. The builder must also state whether the building is to be delivered "as is—where is," or whether he is prepared to perform additional work such as landscaping, seeding, or finish painting of some rooms with a choice of color. Such clearly stated terms will avoid arguments among sellers, brokers, and purchasers.

24.2. THE INCOME PROPERTY (RENTING)

Income property is very often considered by the speculative builder as an investment. However, if the builder wishes to sell such property he is strongly advised to rent it first so that he can show at least one full year's income and expense before putting it on the market.

Unlike selling or renting a private home, renting a commercial property is relatively simple. In the first place, the builder knows who his prospective tenants are. They are presently tenants in other office buildings or have shops in the general area. They may be doctors, dentists, attorneys, insurance brokers, travel agents, or others who require street floor space. It may be a bank that wishes to open a branch.

24.2A. Signs

The first step is to place a sign on the site that will give passers-by the details of what is to be built. Such a sign might read: "To be built on this site. A 2-story store and office building. For rental details call 241-111-2200." The sign can then be changed to: "For rent, 4500 sq ft office space, will divide to suit. 2 stores, each 2100 sq ft. For details call 241-111-2200."

24.2B. Direct Mail

As soon as the builder has concluded his financing and has firmed his plans, he can start a limited direct-mail advertising campaign. A single sheet can show line drawings of the two floors and the area for rent. The sheet should also include the location; what services will be given (such as heating and air conditioning, some tenant parking, lighting and electricity, hall and stair cleaning); and a description of the building (acoustic ceilings, recessed fluorescent lighting, resilient tile floors, etc.). The sheet must also state that there will be only direct rentals from owner to tenant.

The sheet can be reproduced by photo-offset and sent to 500 office tenants and shopkeepers in the area for a quite reasonable expenditure of money.

24.2C. Advertising

Local newspaper advertising can start during the construction of the building. An attention-getting first line might be: "Across from Town Hall" or "Busiest Block on Main St." or "Free Parking around the Corner." The ad can then go on with the detail. The advertisements can be placed for two consecutive weeks in weekly papers and on two consecutive Sundays in daily papers. The builder should wait for results before he spends any more money. As always, he must make sure that his prospective tenants are bona fide.

24.2D. Brokers

The space to be rented can be listed with brokers when the builder feels he is willing to pay the necessary commissions. He must be sure that the brokers understand the terms and conditions under which the space is to be rented.

24.2E. Tenant Work

There are as many ways of performing tenant work and negotiating the financial considerations as there are owners. Some choices follow.

The owner is obligated to construct the boundary partitions for each rented space. He must also construct a fire-retardant passage to all exit ways. He need not construct such passages or corridors until he has leases for space in hand. If he obtains a large tenant, he may be able to cut down substantially on the corridor construction by concentrating the large space at one end or one wing of the building. The owner also furnishes resilient flooring, acoustic ceilings, recessed fluorescent lighting, and sanitary facilities.

Many other facilities and construction items that a tenant requires for comfortable occupancy are negotiable. The landlord can offer to paint the office walls in a choice of light colors. All other decorating, including painting dark colors, wallpapering, and paneling, is paid for by the tenant. Unless the lease is for a period of over 5 years, the owner should ask for a deposit as a restoration charge, especially for paneling and heavy wall coverings. The landlord can offer an allowance for omission of the resilient floor if the tenant desires carpeting, but generally it is advisable to install the initial flooring for the time when a new tenant may want it.

The builder should install the acoustic ceiling and the recessed fluorescent lighting in a planned pattern as he completes the building because, on a piecemeal basis, installation is quite expensive. The question then arises as to who will pay for a possible rearrangement of the lighting to suit the tenant's requirements. This includes not only the cost for the initial rearrangement but the cost for the restoration back to the standard pattern. Again the negotiation will depend on the length of the lease. The owner can also offer a fixed price for performing this work, the cost to be amortized over the period of the lease.

Interior partitions are another factor to be considered. There are many different methods for building such partitions. These range from permanent wallboard partitions on either wood or metal studs to a movable wallboard partition or to a movable metal partition (which is the most expensive and is rarely used in small buildings). Owners of large buildings will give a tenant a certain amount of linear feet of partition for certain amounts of rented space. (Example: 1 lin ft partition for every 12 sq ft of space.)

The negotiation depends on the tenant's requirements, the strength of the rental market, and the length of the lease. The owner can offer to build the required partitioning and amortize its cost over the term of the lease.

The owner in this case is also the builder. Therefore he can perform much of the tenant change work himself, but it is advisable that he obtain some unit prices from subcontractors and material dealers for those portions of the tenant work which he does not do. A prior knowledge of what his costs will be for certain items of construction will help him in his lease negotiations. Unit prices should be obtained for the following:

- Moving a ceiling light up to 6 ft from its present location
- Cost per base outlet or per switch
- Cost per new fluorescent fixture (labor and material)
- Moving an anemostat or installing an extra one, cost to include duct work (an elephant trunk) of up to 10 ft
- Corridor door and hardware (lock set)
- Interior door and hardware (latch set)

One more important matter regarding work for tenants is how its cost is budgeted. It can be a capital expense or an operating expense, and the builder is advised to consult his tax man on how best to do it.

24.2F. Tenant Services and Rent Inclusion

The owner of any rental property is obligated to give certain basic services to the tenant as part of the rent:

Sanitary facilities and water

Cleaning of public spaces

Maintenance of the structure against weather

Heating in the colder climates

Lighting fixtures and the original lamps

Parking spaces

A sample exhibit of services rendered in a large office building is shown in Table 24-1.

Some buildings include electricity as part of the service, the electricity to be used only for lighting and normal business machines. In this case the owner should figure that it will cost him so much per square foot per year for the electricity and then include it in the rent. The same is true for air conditioning. The power and fuel used in a central air conditioning system should be taken into account in the rent.

Many buildings provide for separate electric metering for all tenants. There is no other good way—short of a detailed survey—of arriving at a proper charge for electricity if a tenant uses x-ray machines or a computer, or requires more than average lighting and is open for long hours. Many smaller buildings also provide through-wall air conditioners which can be connected to the tenant's meter circuit.

The one thing the owner-builder must keep in mind is that all services cost money and that he must provide for reimbursement of all of his expenditures by means of the rent.

24.2G. Leases (Escalation Clauses)

A lease in its simplest form is a contract by which one party (the owner) conveys real estate to a second party (the tenant) for a term of years, or terminable at will, for a specified rent. There are numerous standard printed forms that can be used and they vary somewhat from state to state. The builder can obtain the form that is legal in his state and have his attorney read the fine print.

The lease must contain certain essential information such as the date of the lease, the parties entering into the lease agreement, the term of the lease, the rental to be paid, the services the owner will furnish, the work that is to be done for the tenant and how it is to be paid for, and other standard lease clauses. Following is a list of items that the owner may be able to add to a lease as "lease riders." This list applies to rental apartments as well as to business buildings.

- Requirement for a security deposit. At least 1 month's rent to pay for the last month of occupancy. This security should be kept in a separate account. (*List continued at bottom of p. 328.*)

TABLE 24-1   SAMPLE OF SERVICES GIVEN TO TENANTS OF A LARGE OFFICE
BUILDING

2. SERVICE

The Landlord shall provide, at the Landlord's expense except as otherwise provided,

(a) Janitor service in and about the office space, Saturdays, Sundays and holidays excepted.

(b) Heat and, except for basement space, air-conditioning, daily from 8 a.m. to 5 p.m., Saturdays, Sundays and holidays excepted, sufficient to maintain comfortable temperature and humidity on the basis of one person per 100 square feet of space reasonably subdivided.

(c) Hot and cold water for drinking, lavatory and toilet purposes.

(d) Passenger elevator service at all times. Freight elevator service daily from 8 a.m. to 5 p.m., Saturdays, Sundays and holidays excepted. Any or all elevator service may be automatic.

(e) Window washing of all exterior windows, both inside and out, weather permitting.

(f) Painting of interior, during regular business hours, as required, but not more frequently than every 5 years, commencing 5 years after the commencement of the term hereof.

(g) Reasonable amounts of electricity for ordinary lighting and usual small business machines purposes; provided, however, if Tenant uses IBM equipment or other large office machines on the Premises requiring additional electricity, such additional electricity shall be paid for by the Tenant.

Any additional work or service of the character described above and any unusual amount of such work or service, including service furnished outside the stipulated hours, required by the Tenant shall be paid for by the Tenant at cost, plus 15% thereof for the Landlord's overhead. The Landlord does not warrant that any of the services above mentioned will be free from interruptions caused by repairs, renewals, improvements, alterations, strikes, lockouts, accidents, inability of the Landlord to obtain fuel or supplies, or other causes beyond the reasonable control of the Landlord. Any such interruption of service shall never be deemed an eviction or disturbance of the Tenant's use and possession of the Premises or any part thereof, or render the Landlord liable to the Tenant for damages, or relieve the Tenant from performance of the Tenant's obligation under this lease.

- Forbid subletting or assignment without owner's permission.

- Use of automatic renewal clause to be exercised by either party within 90 days or less.

- In apartments—limit number of persons that can occupy an apartment. Reserve right to show apartment for a certain time before termination of lease.

- Require permission to enter premises during lease term for repairs or inspection.

- In business buildings—no tenant should have the grant of an exclusive right to conduct a particular business. For store rentals the owner should fix a basic rent which can be increased by a percentage of the sales above a certain amount. For instance, if a store rents for $6000 per year and there is a percentage clause allowing 10 percent on sales over $60,000, the owner will get $1000 as additional rent if the sales go to $70,000. Percentage leases can vary in different communities and are set to some extent by local real estate boards. Some sample percentages are: shoe stores, 8; restaurants, 5; boutiques, 7; food stores, 5; luncheonettes, 8½.

The owner of commercial property must insist on the inclusion of an escalation clause in the lease. With ongoing inflation in which the prices of everything from soap and water to electricity and taxes keep going up, the owner must protect his investment by asking the tenant to share the burden. There are many types of escalation clauses, but they all are based on the cost of operation of the building. However, it would not be good business for the owner to produce his books for the tenants to inspect. Instead the escalation is calculated from real estate taxes and some readily available index such as the "cost of living." The tenant's rent is increased once a year at a certain fixed time and the tenant's share is based on the area he rents as compared with the total rentable area. Samples of an office building escalation clause are in Table 24-2.

The owner of multifamily housing usually cannot increase the rent by an escalator clause, but he can protect himself by granting only short leases and increasing the rent for a new term. Some states may allow an escalation clause to be placed in a lease to be applied at the time of renewal. The owner's attorney should know.

24.2H. How to Measure Rentable Area

There are three ways of measuring a building. The construction cost is based on the gross square foot area, which is a measure of the entire content of the building from the outside of the walls. The gross rentable area is the space measured from the interior of the glass line and includes corridors and toilet rooms but excludes stair wells, elevator shafts, and utility areas. The tenant pays rent based on his share of the gross area, which means that he pays for a share of the corridors and the toilet rooms in addition to the space he actually occupies within his own four walls.

The ratio of gross rentable space to the gross area of the building is a measure of its efficiency. This varies but is usually from 75 to 85 percent.

TABLE 24-2 SAMPLE OF AN ESCALATION CLAUSE FOR A LARGE OFFICE BUILDING*

(b) It is understood that the Rent specified in Paragraph (a) does not anticipate any increase or decrease in the amount of taxes on the Property or in the cost of operations and maintenance thereof. Therefore, in order that the rental payable throughout the term of the lease shall reflect any such increase or decrease the parties agree as hereinafter in this section set forth. Certain terms are defined as follows:

Building Rentable Area: The total number of square feet of rentable floor area of office and store space in the Building.

Tenant's Share: The amount of the tenant's pro rata share of the increase or decrease, as the case may be, in Taxes and Operating Expenses over the Base Year for Taxes and Base Year for Operating Expenses, all as hereinafter defined. The Tenant's Share is agreed to be ____% of such increase or decrease.

Base Year for Taxes: The first full calendar year of the term of this lease in which at least 50% of the Building Rentable Area is occupied by tenants and real estate taxes have been payable based on an assessment of the Building as complete.

Base Year for Operating Expenses: The first full calendar year of the term of this lease during which at least 50% of the Building Rentable Area is occupied by tenants.

Taxes: (i) All real estate taxes, payable (adjusted after protest or litigation, if any) for any part of the term of this lease, exclusive of penalties or discounts, on the Property, (ii) any taxes which shall be levied in lieu of any such taxes, (iii) any special assessments against the Property.

For this lease, and in the year following the year in which the lease terminates, the Landlord shall deliver to the Tenant a statement setting forth the amount of Taxes payable or paid by the Landlord and Operating Expenses paid or incurred by the Landlord during the immediately preceding calendar year and, except in the case of the statement for the Base Years, comparable figures for the Base Years. Within 30 days after the delivery of such statement, other than the one for the Base Years, the Tenant shall pay to the Landlord as Additional Rent (if the statement indicates an increase in Taxes and Operating Expenses) or the Landlord shall pay to the Tenant (if the statement indicates a decrease) the Tenant's Share. If the Base Year for Taxes and the Base Year for Operating Expenses shall be different, the foregoing provisions of this paragraph shall apply only to the earlier, until the later occurs. If the term of this lease ends on other than the last day of a year, the Tenant's Share shown on the statement delivered after the end of the term shall be reduced proportionately and paid as aforesaid or, at the Landlord's option and upon 30 days notice by the Landlord, at the end of the term the Tenant shall pay as Additional Rent, or receive from the Landlord, an appropriate proportion of the Tenant's Share for the immediately preceding year.

Operating Expenses: Those expenses (including the premiums for all kinds of insurance carried by the Landlord, except insurance against the loss of rents) incurred or paid on behalf of the Landlord in respect of the operation and maintenance of the Property which, in accordance with accepted principles of sound accounting practice used by the Landlord, as applied to the operation and maintenance of first class office buildings, are properly chargeable to the operation and maintenance of the Property, and the cost, as reasonably amortized by the Landlord, with interest at the rate of 5%

TABLE 24-2   SAMPLE OF AN ESCALATION CLAUSE FOR A LARGE OFFICE
BUILDING* (Continued)

___

per annum on the unamortized amount, of any capital improvement made after the Base Year for Operating Expenses which reduces other Operating Expenses, but in an amount not to exceed such reduction for the relevant year. Operating Expenses shall not include (i) franchise or income taxes imposed on the Landlord, (ii) interior painting in tenant spaces, and (iii) the cost of any work or service performed in any instance for any tenant (including the Tenant) at the cost of such tenant.

In determining the amount of Operating Expenses for the purpose of this section, either for the Base Year for Operating Expenses or for any subsequent year, (1) if less than 100% of the Building Rentable Area shall have been occupied by tenants and fully used by them, at any time during the year, Operating Expenses shall be deemed for the purposes of this section to be increased to an amount equal to the like operating expense which would normally be expected to be incurred, had such occupancy been 100% and had such full utilization been made during the entire period, or (2) if the Landlord is not furnishing any particular work or service (the cost of which if performed by the Landlord would constitute an Operating Expense) to a tenant who has undertaken to perform such work or service in lieu of the performance thereof by the Landlord, Operating Expenses shall be deemed for the purposes of this section to be increased by an amount equal to the additional Operating Expense which would reasonably have been incurred during such period by the Landlord if it had at its own expense furnished such work or service to such tenant.

(c) Not later than the 31st day of March (or within a reasonable time thereafter) in the first year following the Base Year for Taxes and the Base Year for Operating Expenses, in each year thereafter during the term of

___

*The clause can be made much simpler for a small building but all the essentials must be adhered to.

24.2I. How to Set the Rental Rate

Setting the rental rate for a commercial or multifamily apartment building is simply a matter of arithmetic and judgment. There are several decisions the builder/owner must make before he starts his calculation. What percent of return would he like on his equity investment? What services is he going to give to the tenants without making a specific charge? How much work will he do for the tenant without making a specific charge?

A sample calculation of the rent to be charged follows.

- The total cost to the builder of land and building, including corridor partitions and boundary partitions to be built later $150,000

- The amount of the mortgage   120,000

- The amount the builder wants in return for his equity of $30,000 at 12%   3,600

The total annual operating cost for a building of 5000 sq ft gross at 85 percent efficiency, with 4250 sq ft rentable is:

Payroll or cost of maintenance service	$ 2,000
Fuel	2,500
Electricity for 4250 sq ft at $0.40 (5 watts/sq ft)	1,700
Repairs and supplies including 5-year decorating	1,000
Water	300
Insurance—fire and extended coverage	500
Taxes	5,000
Cost of broker's commissions	1,000
Mortgage interest and amortization—$120,000 @ 9½%	11,400
Amount builder would like as return on equity	3,600
Total	$29,000

The amount of the total operating cost is divided by the total of the gross rentable area. This gives a per square foot per year rental to be used as a base. Now the owner decides how he will divide this square foot rental so that ground floor stores or professional offices pay more than upper-floor office tenants. In the example the rent per square foot comes to approximately $7.00. With stores and offices occupying equal space, the builder can set the rent at $9.50 for the stores and $4.50 for the upper space. The average per square foot rental will then remain at $7.00 per square foot.

The next step is to add or deduct from the base rent for extra services. The total rate as shown included the full cost of electricity so that the tenants are already paying for this. If tenants are metered separately the owner has some leeway in reducing the rent. If the owner decides to perform some work for the office or store tenants without charge he must calculate the cost per square foot (a suggested figure is $1.00/sq ft) and add this to the rent. If the tenant is paying for work the owner must amortize the cost over the period of the lease (plus interest).

The owner must also allow for vacancies. This can amount to as much as 15 percent or more of the rent roll during the first year and could remain at a constant 5 percent. During the first year the owner must absorb the vacancy loss but certainly he can add 5 percent to his going rental rates for a possible continuing vacancy. This would add up to a rent for office space of $4.50 plus $1.00 plus 5 percent of $4.50 (or $0.25) to make a total of $5.75/sq ft/year. The same additions would be made to the store rental.

One last comment—the owner when setting the rents must allow himself some bargaining power. A large tenant will very often request a reduction in the rental rate or the rental market may take a downturn. The owner should determine the lowest rental rate which will allow him to break even.

The rental rate for apartments can be set in much the same way as it is for commercial buildings. The areas of the various apartments can be measured, and to such areas the builder must add each apartment's share of the entire gross space. After going through the same process as for commercial buildings he will arrive at an annual square foot rent which he can then convert into a gross annual rent or a monthly rent. Apartments with better exposure or better layouts should be higher priced. Efficiency apartments with expensive kitchen and bathroom plumbing should be higher priced.

It is not the custom to give apartment tenants free electricity or, unless there is a central system, air conditioning. Electricity is usually metered separately to each apartment and all equipment such as stove, refrigerator, and window or through-wall air conditioners is on the tenant's meter.

There are sample operating budgets for commercial and multifamily buildings in Chap. 26.

24.3. HOW TO SELL NEW INCOME PROPERTY TO THE BEST ADVANTAGE

24.3A. Before the Property is put on the Market

24.3A1. BUILDING UP THE INCOME

If the owner-builder decides to sell an income property, he must make every effort to build up the income to the point at which it will be attractive to investors. Although income real estate has many advantages over other types of investments, there is still an element of risk which scarcely exists in high interest bonds, selected common stocks, or high-interest bank deposits. The income from real estate must pay at a considerably better rate of return to compensate for the risk factor.

Even if the builder has built for a quick sale, he is ill-advised to attempt to sell the property when it is half rented or before his operating expenses and taxes have been fully established. The price that he can obtain will certainly take into account the extra risk factor of the uncertainty of the ultimate return on the investment.

The builder-owner should therefore make every effort to hold the property until it has an established rent roll and at least a number of months of operating experience. (A full year and at least an 80 percent rent roll are recommended.)

24.3A2. HOW TO SET UP THE OPERATING STATEMENT

When the owner decides that he has enough "hard figures" to show to a purchaser, his next step is to set up an operating statement which can be shown to a prospective purchaser. On the expense side the statement would look like the statement shown in Sec. 24.2I. On the income side, the statement would show the rent roll at the time of the offering and the income from extra charges for extra services. If the building is 85 percent rented, some of the operating costs such as maintenance (if it is on a per square foot basis), electricity, water, repairs, and supplies can be 85 percent of the full budgeted cost. This is only done on an estimated expense basis and not if there is a full year of expense. The owner must also omit his own return on equity. The summary of an operating statement can look like this:

Total annual operating expense (85% of $25,400)	$21,590
Total rent roll at 85% occupancy [85% of $29,750 (gross rent roll)]	25,290
Extra charges to tenants	1,000
Annual operating profit at 85% rental	4,700
Anticipated profit at 95% rental	
Increase rent roll by 10% ($2975) to $29,265	7,675

In addition to the operating statement, the owner should prepare a list of tenants, their lease terms, the escalation clause, the extra charges, and the present amount of the mortgage.

It is also an advantage if the owner has approached the mortgagor to ascertain that the mortgage will be continued at the same rate and at the same terms to a new, duly qualified owner. He should also be sure that the mortgage can be paid off without serious penalty.

The owner must be very careful about disseminating such detailed information to anyone until he is sure that he has a fully qualified prospective purchaser or reliable broker. Casual brokers will use such detailed information to "peddle" the property to anyone they think is even remotely interested.

24.3A3. SETTING THE PRICE

In setting the asking price for his property the owner must take a number of facts into consideration:

How anxious is he to sell the property quickly?
Does he have to sell for financial or personal reasons? How soon?
Is he selling on a rising or falling market?
What are the going rates for other forms of investment?
Is the area stable? Going up? Going down?

Each one of these facts has a bearing on his price. If he does not have to sell quickly he can hold out for a higher price. If interest rates have gone down, he can hold out for a higher price because the rate of return on his property will look more attractive. If his property is in a stable area he can hold his price. If the area seems on the verge of decline he should sell it more quickly.

Consider this particular property in a stable area: It is a little over 2 years old and is in excellent repair. It is 90 percent rented. The operating statement shows that an owner has an earning potential of $7262 or more if the building becomes 100 percent rented. The escalation clauses in the leases protect this income. The new owner would also have the benefit of depreciation.

The income of $7675 is 12% of	$ 64,000
The mortgage is for	120,000
The brokerage fee is approximately	10,000
The asking price	$194,000

The rent roll is $29,750 at full occupancy. Seven times the rent roll (which is a very rough indicator) is $208,000. The land is in a stable area and is appreciating each year. The owner/builder can certainly set the price at $200,000 and be prepared to come down to $195,000, which will give him a $40,000 profit after the broker's commission.

24.3A4. HOW TO FIND A PURCHASER FOR INCOME PROPERTY

24.3A4a. Direct Advertising

It is not a good idea to let the tenants of a commercial or multifamily property know that it is for sale. The owner is strongly advised not to put up for-sale signs. If he advertises in the trade magazines that specialize in real estate, or in the Sunday edition of a nearby large city newspaper, he should give enough particulars to interest a purchaser but not enough to identify either the property or himself:

**FOR SALE—NEW 2-STORY STORE AND OFFICE BUILDING
APPROX. 5000 sq ft EXCELLENT LOCATION. EXCELLENT INCOME
AND DEPRECIATION. MUST SELL. CALL 211-111-1122**

The telephone number should not be readily identifiable. There are many people with sufficient capital who would like to invest in income real estate both for its superior return and the depreciation, but desire to do it privately and hope to get a bargain on a direct sale without having to pay a broker's commission. Every small town and suburban area has such people and they are readily identifiable. They are the local* businessmen—the insurance broker, the supermarket owner, the attorney, the doctor, the large service station owner, the larger contractor, and owners of real estate whose names can be obtained from the tax rolls. A letter to each of these giving more detail than the advertisement and specifically noting that this is for direct sale with no broker's commission involved may bring a surprising number of replies. A sale such as this is obviously very advantageous to both seller and buyer.

24.3A4b. Listing with a Broker

If the owner is really anxious to sell and does not wish to go through the effort of direct sale, then he can list the property with a broker—*but not just any broker.* This should be a broker who specializes in income property and who is well established in this field. It must be a broker who employs full-time professional help. The names of such brokers can be obtained from the local real estate board without the owner revealing his own name. When a broker is chosen the owner should make it very clear as to the terms and conditions under which he is willing to sell. He should also make it very clear that he does not expect to be bothered with "bargain hunters" who offer ridiculously low prices or people who do not have any money but hope to raise it—somehow.

If the owner gives the broker an operating statement, he must be sure that the broker shows it only to responsible prospects and he should also advise the broker that no figures are to be changed unless he gives his prior consent.

24.3A5. HOW TO SELECT A BONA FIDE PURCHASER

The preceding section has told the owner how to deal with a broker about selecting qualified prospective purchasers. However, brokers don't always do this and it becomes part of the seller's business to make sure that the broker does not waste his time or neglect a bona fide prospect because of a prospect who cannot buy the property. The owner must have answers to a number of valid questions. There is no reason why this information cannot be obtained directly from the prospect as long as the broker is present and his sales commission is guaranteed—if a sale results. Some of the questions could be:

- Has the prospect sufficient cash to make the purchase which in this case would be more than $60,000 over the first mortgage?

- If the immediate cash is not available how does the prospect intend to raise it? Has he approached anyone and how much time does he require?

*Local in this case can mean several surrounding towns as well as the one in which the property is located.

- Can the prospect qualify with the present holder of the first mortgage?

- The next question may not be strictly the seller's business, but could be useful to him for future sales. Why is the prospect interested in the property—for the depreciation, for long-term income, for a quick speculative profit? In the case of a multifamily property, is he looking for an apartment which he can occupy on a rent-free basis and make a profit besides?

24.3A6. INCOME TAX ON THE PROFIT

The author is not a tax expert and strongly advises the employment of tax counsel. It is a fact, however, that a long-term capital gain is taxed at a lesser rate than current income. The builder-owner should also be aware that he can deduct the cost of any improvement or major repairs he has made on the property since it was built. A portion of the depreciation can be taken at the time of the sale. The sale of real property is one of the cases where he can defer his profit over a number of years with the consequent saving of tax. Again, tax counsel is recommended.

25

BUILDING AN INCOME-PRODUCING ESTATE

25.1. REAL ESTATE AS AN INVESTMENT

In the opinion of many business people, tax experts, economists, and others, real property in well-located areas is probably the best hedge against inflation. One has only to check the price of land or the price of residential property both old and new to know that real-estate prices have not only kept up with the pace of inflation but in many cases have outstripped it. Real estate (other than vacant land) provides a basic human need—shelter for people, for business, for storage, for manufacturing, for communications, and so on.

The income-producing property provides another incentive which is not usual in most businesses—a tax shelter through depreciation. In the building used as an example in Chap. 24, Sec. 24.2 and 24.3, the income is over $7000. If the building is depreciated at (let us say) 4 percent per year, the depreciation amount is $120,000 (building only) at 4 percent, or $4400 per year. *This amount is tax-free income.*

Besides being a hedge against inflation and a source of tax free income, real estate in a stable or growing area presents the opportunity for a long-term investment with a stable source of income. In towns and suburban communities all over the country, there are many structures, either commercial or multifamily, which have been continuously occupied for over 25 years. These are properties in good repair and in well-located areas which are protected by zoning.

These structures can be modernized from time to time and if they are kept in repair there is no reason why they cannot last another 25 or more years.

25.2. THE BUILDER AS AN INVESTOR

25.2A. He has Built in the Proper Location

The speculative builder of income-producing property is in a unique situation regarding real estate investment. It is assumed that he will build only in selected areas and in selected locations. To summarize Chaps. 16, 17, and 18 of Part 2, he has gone through the following steps to find building sites in places that will remain stable or that will grow in value:

He has ascertained that the general area is economically stable with good prospects for growth.* Its population is growing and it has a good percentage of people under the age of 49. It has a median annual family income of over $12,000. It has good transportation and a diversification of industry. More than 10 percent of the heads of families commute daily to a large city. There is one bank for every 1500 dwelling units. It contains two major universities and more than six junior colleges.

The marketing survey has shown what kinds of buildings are needed in certain localities—apartments, condominiums, office buildings, private residences. It also has indicated the price range which purchasers of private residences or condominiums are willing to pay and the going rents for multifamily dwellings, offices, and stores.

In his search for the proper site for his building, he has investigated the zoning code and zoning maps to determine that the location will not be subject to any adverse influence.

25.2B. The Quality of the Construction

In the planning and construction of income-producing property for sale, the speculative builder should always keep in mind the fact that he may want to keep it. Perhaps he has started out with a quick profit in mind so that his finances may be in a more liquid position, or he may think that he does not want to be bothered with the details of management. It is true that the management of a building with the collecting of rent, the paying of bills, the making of repairs, etc. is time-consuming (see Chap. 26, on management), but the partially tax-free income that is produced by such a property is well worth the effort.

In any event the fact that he may want to keep the building could produce quality construction. This book is all about quality construction, but there is always a little more that can be done when it is for one's own use. For

---

*This is a description of a particular area which is high in educational facilities and in median income. There are hundreds of areas in which the median income is much lower and in which the educational facilities and general amenities are not as good but which are stable prosperous areas.

instance, for a little extra money the builder can incorporate products that require very little maintenance:

- To produce a weathertight building there can be an extra ply of roofing, close inspection of flashing and caulking, and possibly use of corrosion-resistant metal flashing and a slightly better grade of window.

- The mechanical and electrical systems can be upgraded. The heating and cooling plant need not be designed as tightly (if the design engineer agrees). Plumbing piping, accessories, and fixtures can be upgraded. The lenses in fluorescent lighting fixtures are of varying qualities. A good sharp lens gives more light than a cheaper one for the same amount of electricity.

- In the finishing of the building many small improvements can be made such as hardware selection, solid-core instead of hollow-core wood doors, reinforcement at door and window heads to prevent cracking, a better grade of interior finish that will last longer and be washable.

- There is the matter of heat insulation and sound insulation. The proper use of roof and exterior-wall insulation can result in large savings of fuel and electricity for both heating and cooling. The sound insulation of tenants' bounding walls, floors, and corridor walls can result in satisfied tenants—and satisfied tenants do not move and they pay their rent promptly.

- For multifamily dwellings, the kitchen can usually be improved. The quality of the major appliances is a major factor in reducing maintenance costs and tenant complaints. There are also the cabinet work and countertops. Real estate owners claim that the cost of land and construction is so high that the size and quality of the kitchen are the first things to be sacrificed. This may be so for big cities but it is not as true for smaller communities where land costs and construction costs are not as high.

It must be understood by the builder that very little if any of the above mentioned extra work is to be done unless and until *he has definitely made up his mind to keep the building.* All of the extra quality, which costs several thousands of dollars, will be worth nothing to a purchaser who is looking for tax-sheltered income or for a quick speculative turnover. A building that adheres strictly to the building code and nothing more is sufficient for such purposes.

25.3. INVESTING IN OLDER BUILDINGS

Many people have made a great deal of money by purchasing and restoring old buildings. The builder is in an excellent position to do this. He has his own crew which he can use in between jobs or during jobs when some of the workers are not needed. He maintains contact with subcontractors who can also use these restoration jobs as fill-ins and thereby reduce their costs. The builder also maintains constant relations with at least one bank or other financial institution so that he should have no great trouble with financing the purchase and restoration. Every locality has endless opportunities for this kind of investment.

An example of a restoration could be a large old house that is run down and only partly used or not used at all. There are many such houses on the fringe of business or light-manufacturing districts which have been rezoned for light business or commercial use. Many of these buildings can be renovated to be used as multifamily apartments or as offices. The writer has seen examples of such old houses being changed into four or more family units or into offices for many small tenants.

25.3A. The Necessary Investigation

Before starting such work there are certain precautions the builder should take:

- *Zoning.* He must be sure that the area is zoned for his purpose and that it will not be rezoned for adverse uses in the foreseeable future.

- *Building code.* He must study the existing construction to ensure that he will be able to comply with the code with regard to exit facilities, fire retardation, sanitary facilities, light and air, and heat. For this purpose it is best to make a dimensioned sketch of the building and to lay out on this sketch the proposed secondary means of exit, the locations where fire-retarding materials for stair wells and exit corridors must be added, the future sanitary facilities, the riser shafts for plumbing and heating, the electrical panel boxes.

- *Structural soundness.* The builder should thoroughly examine the building for signs of deterioration such as rotted sills, rotted joists caused by water leakage, termite infestation. He should also determine whether any of the plumbing or heating can be salvaged. For instance, cast-iron boilers last for a long time. He should look for cracks or other signs of foundation trouble.

25.3B. The Budget of Cost, Income, and Expense

If he finds that the structure is sound and is capable of being renovated the next step is to make up a budget as follows:

Asking price for building

Estimated cost of renovation including cost of construction loans

Probable amount of permanent mortgage (after discussion with bank)

Builder's equity

Income and expense
   Estimated rental income
   Estimated operating expense (including mortgage interest and taxes)
   Estimated return on builder's equity

With this budget on hand the builder can now make an offer for the property that will assure him of an adequate return on his investment. This entire process need not take more than a few days and most properties will hold for that long a period. If, however, the builder thinks that he has a real "hot" property and a quick inspection and budget process confirms this, he can offer a few hundred dollars for a 10-day option.

The investment in older buildings also carries certain tax advantages which should be carefully explored with tax counsel. It is very possible that an old renovated building can provide a greater net return on capital than a new building. The builder is warned, however, not to put "all his eggs in one basket." New buildings in new or stable neighborhoods have much more potential for growth in value than do these old buildings.

25.4. INVESTING IN VACANT LAND

The builder who is willing to tie up a portion of his capital and to wait for an indeterminate time for any return on his investment can invest in strategically located vacant land. When a builder does this, not only does he tie up capital in a nonliquid form because vacant land does not sell as readily as improved property, but he is put to some expense to maintain it. He must pay taxes and often is forced to eliminate objectionable weeds or to perform other work on his land which is called for by local authority.

There is an old saying in real estate circles about vacant land—"Buy on the fringe and wait." This is all very well for the builder who can spare the capital for an indefinite time, but it is bad advice for the speculative builder who is still living on a month-to-month basis. There have been many cases where a builder has purchased one or more choice pieces of land for future development and has failed because of the consequent tie-up of capital. In some of these instances, the land has not even been held for a long-term increase in value, but for development within a comparatively short time.

Before he invests in "fringe" vacant land, therefore, the builder must clearly define his purpose in his own mind. Is he willing to wait for 10 years or more before either developing or selling the land? Is he buying it for his heirs? Although he has carefully studied the growth pattern of the area, is he willing to take the chance that adverse influences may prevent growth in the direction of his land?

Purchase of vacant land on the fringe is at best a highly speculative venture and should be done only by those who can afford it. The speculative builder should confine himself to the purchase of vacant land that he can develop immediately.

Any builder can look on his real estate investments as his old age pension plan. It is well worth working for.

26

MANAGEMENT OF INCOME PROPERTY

26.1. SETTING UP MANAGEMENT

It has been suggested that speculative builders sometimes sell income property so they do not have to go through the trouble and possible annoyance of dealing with tenants or with the petty repairs necessary to maintain a property. Actually the problems of management need not be a burden to the owner if he sets up a simple system of record keeping and keeps the small details of management at a minimum by using outside help when he can justify the extra expense.

The size of the property is the determining factor in selecting this intermediary. It can be a resident janitor-handyman in a multifamily property who gets an apartment free or a reduction in rent for keeping public spaces clean, changing faucet washers, keeping a watch on the heating plant, etc. This person can also show vacant apartments, and when necessary can collect an occasional rent check. In a small office building an arrangement can be made with a part-time daily cleaner to keep the public spaces clean, renew toilet paper and towels, generally keep an eye on the premises, and notify the owner if there is anything amiss. When the building is small the owner should be prepared to receive telephone calls directly from the tenants if repairs or service are required, to show vacant space and to call about delinquent rent.

If the property is large enough (as an instance—over 50 apartments or over 30,000 sq ft of office space) the owner can employ a full-time janitor-handyman in the apartment building and give him a free apartment and a salary. In an office building he can employ a part-time building manager or employ the kind of good building-management concern which is hard to find in a small town.

345

26.1A. Real Estate Management Firms or Do-it-Yourself

There are some real estate brokerage firms that will manage property for a fee which is usually a percentage of the rent roll. They also charge a brokerage commission for leasing vacant space. Such a firm will collect rent, pay the help, pay the utility bills, etc., and send the owner a monthly statement and a check for the difference between income and expense.

Such an arrangement is fine if the builder-owner is willing to lose at least 5 percent of his rent roll. It is not recommended for at least the first four or five income properties and it need never become necessary if the owner is willing to set up his own part-time management staff which can grow with his assets.

The primary function of property management is to produce the highest net income possible. This obviously is done by making leases at the highest going rates, including escalation, and by keeping a careful watch on expenditures to keep them as low as possible consistent with maintaining the property in good rentable condition and keeping the tenants reasonably content. This requires the constant vigilance that can best be exercised by the owner himself. He must begin by setting up an office and a procedure for management.

26.1B. Establishing an Office and a Management Procedure

The speculative builder who desires to start building an income-producing estate should set up a miniature management office well before the completion of his first commercial or apartment building. He may still be operating his construction business from an office in his home, but he must go to a certain amount of extra expense to start the management procedure in order to keep his construction and management accounts separate for his own financial safety and for tax reasons. The only way in which he can judge which of his projects is exceeding his estimate or is earning a profit is by keeping separate accounts for every construction project and every management project whether commercial or housing. Some of the actions he must take are these:

- Provide a separate space, a work table, a filing cabinet, stationery such as rent bills, letterheads, and leases, and a set of bound ledgers (the builder's accountant should advise), and keep this space free for the management functions.

- Provide a separate telephone with its onw number to be listed under "ABC Management, Inc." This telephone number is the one listed in the rental advertisements and signs. This phone will be answered "ABC Management."

- Provide a separate telephone with its own number to be listed segregate the management accounts from the construction account and from each other. Such an account might be titled "ABC Management—27 Main St."

The builder must himself set aside enough time or must employ some part-time help to keep records and to pay bills, collect rent, make proper entries into the proper books as advised by his accountant, answer calls from tenants and rental prospects, make necessary calls, make up a payroll, etc. For a single small building or even two, this may be possible without extra help, but it is advisable for the builder to start looking for part-time help such as a high-school student who has had some bookkeeping courses or a local housewife who has had experience in this field.

26.1C. Handling Normal Renting, Tenant Relations, and Maintenance

Even with part-time help, the owner must perform the more responsible work himself. Renting space in apartment houses is simple enough because the janitor can show such space and should have a list of vacancies and their rental. The owner need only become involved when a prospect becomes serious about renting. At that time he should see the prospective tenant and come to terms on the lease. It is more difficult to show and rent office space. Unless the building is large enough to support the salary of a part-time manager, the owner must either show it himself or employ a rental broker.

Although the owner of an office building can leave the small details of the everyday cleaning and maintenance to his part-time cleaner, he must set aside enough time to deal with his tenants on more serious matters. In an apartment building, of course, he has someone in the building who can maintain relations with the tenants and involve him only rarely.

So far as maintenance and operations are concerned, the owner will have his accountant set up the correct procedures, but he himself should delegate the responsibility for handling such day-to-day items as:

- Preparation and presentation of rent bills, collection of rents, deposits in bank, follow-up of delinquent tenants.

- Payrolls.

- Ordering of supplies, inventory control.

- Payment of bills for materials, utilities.

- Payment of mortgage interest, taxes, insurance.

- Keeping a day-to-day "tickler" file to be sure that mortgage payments, taxes, and insurance are paid on time and that those bills which allow discounts are paid in the discount period.

- Ordering of repairs by outside contractors when the owner's in-house help cannot make them. There should be bids on any important items.

As soon as the owner has set up the nucleus of a management operation (which he can reinforce as its duties increase), his next important step is to set up a system of records.

26.2. RECORD KEEPING FOR BUILDING MANAGEMENT

The owner should know the financial status of his property at all times and he should be able to find the proper information by looking at the bookkeeping records. There are several kinds of records that will provide this information. Each property is kept separately:

1. A record of the rental income. Who has paid and the amount and the date of payment. This should be checked against the rent roll. Extra payments for extra services or for amortization of tenant work should be noted separately. Any other income from this property should also be noted separately.

2. A record of operating and maintenance expense. Salaries plus insurance, Social Security, and unemployment taxes. Fuel, electricity, and telephone. Repairs including plumbing, heating, electrical, roofing, etc. Painting and decorating of public spaces and for tenants. Services including exterminating, rubbish removal, water. Supplies including soap, towels, cleaning materials, mechanical and electrical supplies, and kitchen and bathroom equipment for apartment tenants. Insurance including comprehensive fire insurance, compensation, and public liability (the insurance broker should be consulted).

3. General expense. Interest and amortization on first mortgage. Interest and amortization on any other loan. Real estate taxes. State or any other taxes. Depreciation on building, equipment, furniture, etc.

All of the accounts and records are entered into various ledgers such as the rental ledger, accounts payable ledger, etc. *These accounts must be set up by the owner's accountant,* who should check them at certain prearranged periods.

26.3. FINANCIAL STATEMENTS

The day-to-day records of income and expense from income real estate and the day-to-day records from his construction business enable the speculative builder-owner to have two very important financial statements prepared. They are the profit-and-loss statement and the balance sheet. These are the records that every lender and investor will inspect before they make any financial commitments. The accounts for every construction job and every property are kept separately so that the builder-owner can see which kind of investment property is most successful and which of his construction projects is showing a profit or loss. But all of these accounts can be consolidated in his balance sheet and profit-and loss statement so that at fixed periods he can examine the complete financial status of his business.

26.4. LANDLORD AND TENANT RELATIONS

In the ownership and management of property there is a contractual relationship between the landlord and tenant which is equivalent to the relationship between the builder and the owner. Each has certain obligations to the other. Many of these obligations are set by law but there are others which are set by the lease.

26.4A. The Lease

A lease should spell out all the terms of the agreement between the landlord and tenant. Most leases are for a fixed term but there are leases, especially in rental housing, which call for tenancy-at-will. This means that the term of the lease is on a month-to-month basis with either party able to terminate on one month's notice in writing. Although many such tenancies are on an oral basis, the landlord is advised that a written lease is much more effective in controlling the tenant's actions. It is also a very good way of getting rid of undesirable tenants. Once a tenant has been given the requisite notice to vacate on a certain day the landlord must not accept any money for rent after this date. All tenancies of course are cancelable for nonpayment of rent. Leases should also contain a clause which prohibits assignment or subletting without the landlord's prior consent.

The terms and conditions of a typical lease including escalation where it applies are shown in Sec. 24.2G.

26.4B. Responsibility for Maintenance of Property

Unless otherwise specifically stated, the tenant is responsible for the maintenance of his own rented quarters. It is assumed by law that the tenant in taking possession of the premises has accepted them "as is" at the time of occupancy and will return them in the same condition at the termination of his occupancy, normal wear and tear excluded. The tenant is liable for any damages.

A tenant cannot sell anything on the premises without consent of the landlord. A tenant cannot make any alterations to his premises or overload the floors or use any mechanical device for business purposes, without the prior consent of the landlord.

The landlord is responsible for that portion of the property outside of the tenant's control. This includes plumbing, heating, air conditioning from a central plant, the exterior walls and windows, the electric system, the roof, and all public spaces. In apartment buildings the replacement or repair of major kitchen appliances or through-wall air conditioners is a matter for lease negotiation.

26.5. INSURANCE

The landlord is generally not responsible for injuries sustained within the leased premises. He is also not responsible for damage to a tenant's personal possessions within these premises—the tenant is presumed to be carrying his own loss insurance or to be "self-insured."

The landlord must carry fire insurance with extended coverage, workmen's compensation insurance (if there are any employees), and public liability insurance. If he uses any vehicles in his business with the property, he should also investigate automobile liability and property damage insurance. He is advised to consult his insurance broker on the limits to be carried. It is recommended here that the small extra cost of higher limits is well worthwhile. Awards for injuries have been reaching astronomical proportions. The owner might look into an overall "umbrella policy."

26.6. RENT COLLECTIONS

The writer cannot overemphasize the importance of collecting rents on time. *Rent is payable on the day when it is due.* At the high rates of interest that landlords pay on the mortgage and on borrowed money, tenant delinquency is money out of pocket. To take a simple example—a $3000 monthly rent roll at 10 percent annually is worth $300 per month in interest. If rents are not paid until the tenth of the month, the landlord is out one-third of $300 or $100 a month or $1200 a year in interest.

The tenants must understand that interest will be charged on delinquent accounts.

26.7. SUMMARY. SUCCESSFUL PROPERTY MANAGEMENT

It will be found, if the chapter is carefully read, that income and expense items amount to only a very few entries on a daily basis. There are only a few basic items to remember.

- Tenants should be chosen carefully. If the owner is not sure, he must give them only a month-to-month lease until he is sure.

- Rents must be collected on time.

- There must be a careful scrutiny of repair and maintenance items before they are undertaken. The owner should be sure that they are his obligation.

- Records must be kept on a daily basis.

- The property should be inspected by the owner at regular intervals.

- The speculative builder-owner can carry on his building business and give it the greater part of his time, and still own and manage income property.

27
ENERGY CONSERVATION IN SPECULATIVE BUILDING

27.1. THE TOTAL ENERGY PICTURE

The United States is the single greatest consumer of energy in the entire world, and the end is not yet in sight. The demand for energy is still growing at a rate of 5 percent per year and domestic production of oil is growing at only 3 percent per year and is falling farther behind every year. The result is that this country is becoming more dependent on foreign oil, which is now our major source of energy. An embargo on oil like the one that happened recently, and the subsequent increase in price, would create a bad dislocation of business and the public habits of the country. It would also serve to drive many small manufacturers out of business. A threat to drastically increase oil prices causes panic in the business and manufacturing community, and a serious increase in price would upset the entire economy of the country.

One way to minimize this threat is through a serious effort to conserve energy. It is estimated that more than 30 percent of all the energy used in this country is wasted, and it is also estimated that 33 percent of the total energy is used by buildings. This could mean that buildings waste 10 percent (33 percent of 30 percent) of the total energy. This figure represents a great challenge to the architect, the engineer, the builder, and the owner of real estate.

27.2. THE ENERGY-SAVING HOUSE AS AN AID TO SALES

Because of constant prodding by the government and the subsequent newspaper and magazine articles, the public has become aware of the need to save energy, and of course the mounting cost of electricity, gas, and oil has helped to convince the public that saving energy is in its own immediate interest. This is especially true of the homeowner. To the homeowner, a possible shortage of heating fuel is more serious than a shortage of gasoline, and he has become much more aware of electric and fuel bills.

It is unfortunate that some speculative builders are more interested in first cost than in energy savings. This is due to some extent to a misconception of the cost involved, and of the sales appeal of energy savings. Some publications for builders which tell him about insulation and other savings devices do not mention the best that can be obtained. There is no reason why the differential in first cost between *reasonable* insulation and *the best* according to government standards cannot be passed on to the purchaser on the basis that this first cost will be amortized in a very few years.

The speculative builder should be aware of public consciousness and take advantage of it to promote his sales. If he can state that his house is fully insulated in accordance with government standards and that his heating and cooling plant is at top efficiency, he will certainly help his sales. As a matter of fact, some government pamphlets suggest that the prospective purchaser make a point of asking about insulation and heating or cooling efficiency. The same point is also valid for condominiums because the condominium owner also pays his own electric and fuel bills.

The writer has very rarely noted any advertising matter or other "sales pitch" which bothers to mention that the seller of a house or condominium has done anything about energy saving. It is about time that this subject be made more important, and the builder who does it will certainly be ahead of the game.

27.3. ENERGY-SAVING INCOME PROPERTY AS AN AID TO PROFITABLE OWNERSHIP

The speculative builder who builds income property for his own investment has even more of a stake in energy-saving construction than the builder and seller of private houses. As the owner of the property, he will always be subject to shortages and price increases of fuel. He must take these into account when he is building and do the best job he can with them: insulation, electric fixtures and major appliances, wiring system, and design and installation of the heating and cooling plant.

During construction, when it is most economical to do it, the builder-owner can afford to spend the money necessary to bring his property up to the prescribed standards for maximum fuel efficiency, because experience has shown that in most instances he will amortize this extra expense in three years. After that he gets a free ride. The saving in energy cost is a major aspect of profitable management.

27.4. BUILDING ENERGY SAVINGS INTO CONSTRUCTION

This section will devote itself to quality insulation as recommended by government and reputable "brand name" manufacturers.

27.4A. Measuring Insulation Efficiency. The Private House

Insulation is used to maintain the highest possible difference in temperature between the interior and the exterior of a structure. In warm weather it keeps the heat out and in cold weather it keeps the heat in. The builder should become familiar with three common terms that are used in measuring the efficiency of insulation or of any other material that keeps heat in or out. One is the overall coefficient of heat transfer, which is signified by the letter U. The second is the Btu (British Thermal Unit), which is the amount of heat required to raise the temperature of one pound of water one degree Fahrenheit. The coefficient U is expressed as a number and it tells the Btu per hour that is transmitted per square foot of surface for every degree Fahrenheit difference between two spaces. As an example:

Outside temperature	20°F
Inside temperature	68°F
Differential	48°F
U^*	.26

This means that every square foot of this surface will transmit .26 × 48 = 12.5 Btu/h.

If we take this one step further to arrive at the cost of such transmission of heat:

1 gal of household heating oil costs $0.42/gal
1 gal of household heating oil = 144,000 Btu
1000 sq ft of the surface transmits 12.5×1000 = 12,500 Btu/hr

This equals 9 percent of 144,000 or 9 percent of 42 cents, or 3.8 cents. Therefore every 1000 sq ft of uninsulated surface between the inside and the outside of this structure costs 3.8 cents/hr or $0.91/day when it is 20°F outside and 68°F inside. Two inches of properly installed insulation would reduce this $0.91 to $0.30 and 4 in. would reduce it to $0.15. An average small house has about 3000 sq ft of surface that is exposed to the weather. The heat loss through uninsulated ceilings, roof, and walls under the weather conditions shown in this example would be $0.91 per 1000 sq ft per day × 3 = $2.73 per day or $81 per month. If the contractor installs 2 in. of insulation, the absolute minimum, he can reduce this heat loss by two-thirds to $27 per month and if he uses 4 in. in the walls and 6 in. in the ceiling, he can reduce this by half again to $13.50 per month. This saving can be used as a good example to a prospective purchaser of what can be saved by optimum

*This value of the coefficient U is for the surface of a wood-framed house, clapboard over plywood sheathing and ½ in. gypsum board inside.

insulation—and the purchaser will be willing to pay for the small extra cost involved.

The third unit of the measure of heat transfer, and the one that the builder will use most often, is R. This expresses the ability of insulation to decrease heat flow. R is $1/U$. For the U of .26 used in the example above, R can be expressed as $1/.26$, or 4. The proper value for R in a northern climate is between 16 and 20,* which is equivalent to the use of 4 in. in the walls and 6 to 8 in. in the ceiling joists or at the roof rafters.

The example shown above is valid only in some portions of the country, and of course the outside temperature varies from day to day. As one goes farther north, the temperature differential becomes greater. In warm climate areas when the insulation is used to keep out heat, the temperature differential might be 22° at 100°F outside and 78°F inside. The calculation steps are the same.

27.4B. Insulation. The Private House

The best and most economical way of installing wall and ceiling insulation is, of course, to do it when a building is under construction. At this time insulating blanket can be stapled to the studs before the inside wall is started, loose insulation or blanket can be placed between ceiling joists before the attic floor is placed, and insulating blanket can be stapled between the rafters. The recommended insulating material is fireproof and verminproof rock wool or glass fiber. The builder should be aware that some insulating materials give off noxious fumes when hot, and others are not fireproof. The blanket should come with a vapor barrier to prevent condensation from wetting the fiber and thereby reducing its efficiency. The vapor barrier, which is usually of foil, should be placed with the foil side nearest the living space. Blanket insulation is also recommended for hot air ducts, and air-cell covering is recommended for hot- and cold-water piping.

27.4C. Insulation. Commercial Property

The savings in fuel cost created by efficient insulation should also be apparent to the speculative builder, especially if he intends to own the property after it is completed. Outside walls in wood-framed structures should be blanketed with fireproof mineral wool. Flat roofs should have 2 in. (or more) of insulating material such as glass fiber or polyurethene rigid blocks laid in pitch under the finished roofing material. Masonry structures should have furring strips to separate the inner from the outer wall. The dead air space created by this furring is an excellent insulator. It is recommended also that the usual wallboard interior walls have foil backing to serve as a vapor barrier.

*An R value of 20 is $1/.05$.

The insulation of piping for hot water heating and of sheet metal ducts for heating and air conditioning is also an important item, especially where the pipes and ducts are in exposed places. If the hot water heating lines are also used to keep a basement warm, they can be exposed but if they run through outside walls or other open spaces, it is recommended that they be covered with 2-in. air-cell insulation. Exposed sheet metal ductwork is responsible for a great deal of energy loss, and the cost of covering it with 2 to 4 in. of insulating blanket will more than pay for itself in a very few years. Double glazing of windows is costly but pays for itself in a few years. It should be considered.

27.4D. Air Leakage

There is no normal construction that can be made airtight without the use of protective material. In a well-insulated house, the transfer of heat through the leakage of air between the inside and the outside (which maintain different temperatures) is the greatest source of energy loss. This of course applies to air conditioning as well as to heating.

These leaks can be stopped by weatherstripping all openings and by caulking. It is interesting to note that a weatherstripped double-hung window will cut down air leakage by one-third and a weatherstripped door will reduce it by one-half. The best kind of weatherstripping to use is the interlocking channel, which can be installed by any skilled carpenter during construction.

Caulking is used when two different materials or pieces of construction meet. Places that need caulking are at joints between window and door drip caps and sills and siding (or masonry, etc.), at joints between window and door frame and siding, etc., at sills where wood structure meets the foundation, at joints where chimney or other masonry meets wood siding, at any break in the exterior wall. All of this caulking can be done with a caulking gun or caulking rope. The work is not very expensive and keeps the structure watertight as well as airtight. Another source of air leakage is the fireplace damper. A good tight damper costs little more than an inefficient one.

Windows are a source of air leakage and have a very low R factor (or a high U factor). A single pane of window glass will, on the average, transmit more than 10 times as much heat as an ordinary wood or masonry wall. Storm windows will cut this in half, and, while it is not usually included in the contractor's work, he can certainly recommend the installation as an extra. In general the agencies which deal in energy conservation have recommended that the glass area of a house be not more than 10 times the floor area. This would mean that a house of 1000 sq ft could have only eight 3 ft-0 in. × 4 ft-6 in. windows. While this is good for energy conservation, it may create buyer or renter resistance. The contractor must use his judgment while keeping as close to this figure as he can.

27.4E. Miscellaneous Energy Savers

The use of fluorescent lighting wherever possible is recommended in private homes and commercial buildings. Many people do not like the blue-white fluorescent lamps, which are certainly not flattering. The use of warm white lamps may counteract this feeling. It is calculated that a single 40-watt fluorescent lamp gives as much light (lumens per watt) as three 60-watt incandescents.

The roofing should be light-colored in warm climates and dark-colored in cold climates.

If possible there should be more windows on the south side in cold climates and more windows on the north side in warm climates.

All of these efforts take some time and some expense. (Optimum insulation may cost over $1500 more than ordinary insulation.) The questions that the speculative builder must ask is "Will the expense be justified by quicker sales?" and "Can I pass off some of this extra cost to the purchaser?" The answer to both is yes.

27.5. ENERGY-SAVING MAINTENANCE OF INCOME PROPERTY

Once the speculative builder has built and sold a single house or a condominium, he is through with it except for his guarantees. But if he has built a commercial building or a multifamily dwelling which he intends to keep as an investment, he cannot be content with having built in insulation and other energy savers. He must maintain his property in order to keep all of his plant and equipment at maximum efficiency. This is not a time-consuming job. It simply means that he must prepare a regular maintenance schedule to which he should adhere. Following are some energy-saving maintenance hints.

- *Air infiltration.* Examine the weatherstripping of windows and doors on an annual basis, preferably just before cold weather or, in warm climates, just before hot weather. Replace and repair where necessary. Repair caulking around all openings. Install good door checks on outside doors. Ask tenants not to open windows when building is being heated or cooled. If there is a closed garage under the building, have its door operated by key or by a radio-frequency device which is given to each authorized parker (on payment of a deposit).

- *Ventilation.* Every cubic foot of air that is brought into a building has to be either heated or cooled, and therefore close control of ventilation (where forced ventilation is required) plays an important part in the saving of energy. Once the air is in the building and has been heated or cooled, it is best to maintain a slight positive pressure in the building so that unwanted air will not infiltrate. Ventilation of toilet rooms should be accomplished by exhaust only—using interior air for the supply—and such exhausts should be run at the minimum rate required by the code. Ventilation in office buildings should be at a minimum or shut off entirely during weekends and holidays.

- *Fans, pumps, and motors.* Keep fan blade clean. Check for excessive vibration. Inspect and lubricate bearings at specified times. Keep fan belts tight. Keep screens clean. Check pump packing for leakage. Check motors for excessive noise or vibration.

- *Air handling equipment.* Inspect ductwork for leakage or loose insulation. Inspect dampers to see that the blade is actually operated by the outside handle. Clean or replace air filters at regular intervals. Inspect heating and cooling coils for cleanliness. Use of a detergent is recommended. Keep all equipment lubricated at regular intervals.

- *Refrigeration equipment.* Check compressor for leakage, excessive starting and stopping, and excessive vibration. Check gauges to see whether readings correspond with manufacturer's instructions. Keep air-cooled condenser clear for maximum efficiency. For self-contained units (window or through-wall) keep evaporator and condenser coils clean. Check to be sure that air flow is unrestricted. Clean or replace air filters at regular intervals.

- *Heating equipment.* Keep boiler clean from scale deposits or sediment. Check for deposits of fly ash or soot. Stacks should be kept clear and should be cleaned at regular intervals. Observe stack discharge—look for heavy smoke which indicates burner adjustment is necessary or that there is insufficient air. Check fuel burner efficiency by analysis of flue gas. (This can be done by any intelligent high-school senior who has the correct kit.) There should be no more than 2 percent of oxygen and no carbon monoxide. If heating is by gas, the carbon dioxide should be 9 or 10 percent and for No. 2 fuel oil it should be 11.5 to 12.8 percent for maximum efficiency. Check stack temperature. (All of this can be done by a service which will also adjust the burner. The fuel supplier or the gas company usually does this.)

The above procedures can be reduced to a simple chart which can be read at a glance. However the chart means nothing if the work is not done when it is called for.

27.6. EXAMPLE OF AN ELEMENTARY CALCULATION TO DETERMINE INSULATION THICKNESS

In the construction of multifamily dwellings or small office buildings, the speculative builder will require the services of an architect who should be familiar with the calculations required to determine the optimum thickness of insulation for a particular area. The architect should also be familiar with the best kind of insulating material to use. In the case of a private house, however, more often than not the builder purchases plans from a plan service or has a "designer" draw plans for him. It is well therefore for the builder himself to become familiar with the simple calculations that should be made.

The United States is usually divided into five heating zones and five cooling zones.* The heating and cooling zones are not necessarily alike because of prevailing winds and other factors. The first step the builder should take is to determine in what heating and cooling zone his construction activities are located.

The next step is to determine the value of the coefficient of heat transfer U (see Sec. 27.4). The value can be found in the *Insulation Manual for Homes and Apartments* issued by the National Association of Home Builders, Washington, D.C., and in handbooks on construction. For instance, a house with $\frac{1}{2} \times 8$-in. lapped siding on building paper over $\frac{1}{2}$-in. plywood sheathing on the exterior and $\frac{1}{2}$-in. gypsum board with a vapor barrier will have an R value of 3.89 or a U value of $1/3.89 = 0.26$. If insulation between the studs is added, an R value of 3.70 may be added for every inch of thickness. R for 2 in. of insulation will therefore be 7.40. Even if only 2 in. of insulation is added, the coefficient U becomes $1/(3.89+7.40)$ or .089. Adding 2 in. of insulation has reduced heat loss through the walls by two-thirds (.089 is approximately one-third of .26).

This heat loss can be translated into dollars by using the formulas shown in Sec. 27.4. The builder will note that these formulas used certain temperatures (20°F outside, 68°F inside) and a fuel oil price of $0.42 per gallon as an example. The temperature zone charts will give the builder the degree-days* or other basic information about the temperatures in his zone. If the average winter temperature in his zone is above or below 20°F (used in the example), he must use this number. If he uses gas instead of oil he must calculate the cost by the therm (100,000 Btu) instead of by the gallon of oil at $0.42 or whatever the going price is in his area.

Putting these figures together will enable the builder to arrive at an independent conclusion as to the amount of insulation he should use in his

---

*See Appendix to this chapter for maps of zones, tabular information, and instructions for calculation of insulation thickness.

*Degree-day—the difference between the mean temperature for that day and 65°F. For example, a mean temperature of 40°F equals 25 degree-days.

speculative house and will enable him to tell prospective purchasers what they will save in fuel costs.

This section is fundamental. It is really an exercise in arithmetic and in judgement—in balancing extra cost against quick sale at a higher price. It is not intended to make the builder an engineer.

27.7. SOME CODE REQUIREMENTS

Although the United States has no uniform requirements for energy saving in any field, the various states have had committees of architects, engineers, and builders study various practical means to change design and construction requirements to encompass energy-saving procedures. The American Society of Heating, Refrigeration and Air Conditioning Engineers (ASHRAE) has published an authoritative handbook on energy savings in design and construction. Some states now have energy-saving requirements in their codes.

27.8. SOLAR ENERGY

Up to the present time, solar energy has been the only source of energy that has given any promise of reducing the reliance on fossil fuels and nuclear energy to any extent. The federal government has spent, and is spending, a great deal of money and effort in an attempt to develop the use of solar energy to the point where it will compare in price and output to the present sources of energy. The branch of government which is involved is the Energy Research and Development Administration (ERDA), and it is engaged in advancing the use of solar energy especially for single-family homes.

ERDA will shortly solicit design proposals for the use of solar energy in residential buildings in certain specific locations. The builder who submits a proposal for the installation of a system which meets with the energy administration's approval will obtain a contract from the government to build it and to use it as a demonstration model.

Information can be obtained from the Department of Housing and Urban Development, Office of Policy Development and Research, Washington, D.C.

APPENDIX TO CHAPTER 27: CALCULATION OF INSULATION THICKNESS

1. Locate your city on the heating zone or cooling zone map, Figs. 27-1 and 27-2. (Our house is located in heating zone III and cooling zone B.)

2. Our house currently uses fuel oil at a cost of 34¢ a gallon to heat. It uses electricity at 4¢ a kilowatt hour to cool. Obtain your unit heating and

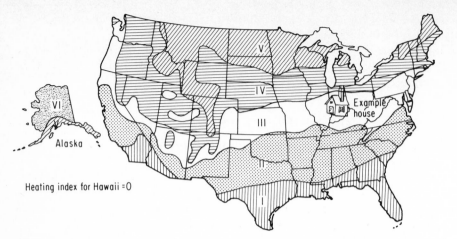

Figure 27-1 Winter heating zones. If your house is on the borderline of two zones, select the zone in which the climate is more typical of your area.

cooling costs from the utility companies as follows: Tell your company how many therms (for gas) or kilowatt hours (for electricity) you use in a typical winter month and summer month (if you have air conditioning). The number of therms or kilowatt hours is on your monthly fuel bill. Ask for the cost of the last therm or kilowatt hour used, including all taxes, surcharges, and fuel adjustments. For oil heating, the unit fuel cost is simply your average cost per gallon plus taxes, surcharges, and fuel adjustments.

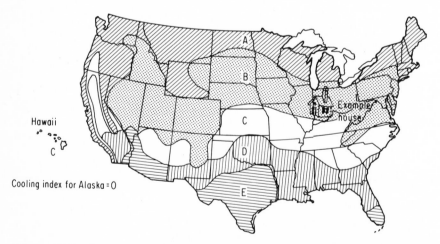

Figure 27-2 Summer cooling zones. If your house is on the borderline of two zones, select the zone in which the climate is more typical of your area.

TABLE 27-1　HEATING INDEX

Type of Fuel	Cost per Unit,* ¢									
Gas (therm)	9	12	15	18	24	30	36	54	72	90
Oil (gallon)	13	17	21	25	34	42	50	75	100	125
Electric (kWh)	1	1.3	1.7	1	1.3	1.6	2	3	4	5
Heat pump (kWh)	1	1.3	1.7	2	2.6	3.3	4	6	8	10
Heating Zone	Index Factor									
I	2	2	3	3	4	5	6	9	12	15
II	5	6	8	9	12	15	18	27	36	45
III	8	10	13	15	20	25	30	45	60	75
IV	11	14	18	21	28	35	42	63	84	105
V	14	18	23	27	36	45	54	81	108	135
VI	22	28	36	42	56	70	84	126	168	210

*Cost of last unit used (for heating and cooling purposes) including all taxes, surcharges, and fuel adjustments.

TABLE 27-2   COOLING INDEX FOR ATTICS

Type of Air Conditioner	Cost per Unit,* ¢						
Gas (therm)	9	12	15	18	24	30	36
Electric (kWh)	1.5	2	2.5	3	4	5	6
Cooling Zone	Index Factor						
A	0	0	0	0	0	0	0
B	2	2	3	4	5	6	7
C	3	5	6	7	9	11	13
D	5	6	8	9	12	15	18
E	7	9	11	14	18	23	27

*See footnote to Table 27-1.

3. Locate your heating index from Table 27-1 by finding the number at the intersection of your heating zone row and heating fuel cost column (to the nearest cost shown). (Our house has a heating index of 20.)
   If your house is air conditioned, or you plan to add air conditioning, find your cooling indexes from steps 5 and 6. If your house is not air conditioned and it is not planned, your cooling indexes are zero.

   Note: In Tables 27-1 through 27-3, if your fuel costs fall midway between two fuel costs listed, you can interpolate. For example, if our fuel oil costs were 38¢ a gallon, our heating index would be 22.5.

4. Locate your Cooling Index for Attics from Table 27-2 by finding your

TABLE 27-3   COOLING INDEX FOR WALLS

Type of Air Conditioner	Cost per Unit,* ¢						
Gas (therm)	9	12	15	18	24	30	36
Electric (kWh)	1.5	2	2.5	3	4	5	6
Cooling Zone	Index Factor						
A	0	0	0	0	0	0	0
B	1	1	2	2	2	3	4
C	2	2	3	4	5	6	7
D	3	3	4	5	7	8	10
E	4	5	6	8	10	13	15

*See footnote to Table 27-1.

TABLE 27-4   ATTIC FLOOR INSULATION AND ATTIC DUCT INSULATION

Index (Heating index plus cooling index for attics)	R Value	Attic Insulation Approximate Thickness, in.			Duct Insulation*	
		Mineral Fiber Batt/Blanket	Mineral Fiber Loose-fill†	Cellulose Loose-fill‡	R Value	Approximate Thickness, in
1–3	R-0	0	0	0	R-8	2
4–9	R-11	4	4–6	2–4	R-8	2
10–15	R-19	6	8–10	4–6	R-8	2
16–27	R-30‡	10	13–15	7–9	R-16	4
28–35	R-33	11	14–16	8–10	R-16	4
36–45	R-38	12	17–19	9–11	R-24	6
46–60	R-44	14	19–21	11–13	R-24	6
61–85	R-49	16	22–24	12–14	R-32	8
86–105	R-57	18	25–27	14–16	R-32	8
106–130	R-60	19	27–29	15–17	R-32	8
131–	R-66	21	29–31	17–19	R-40	10

*Use heating index only if ducts are not used for air conditioning.

†High levels of loose-fill insulation may not be feasible in many attics.

‡Assumes that joists are covered, otherwise use R-22.

cooling zone and cooling cost to the nearest cost shown. (Our house has a cooling index for attics of 5.)

5. Locate your cooling index for walls from Table 27-3 by finding your cooling zone and cooling cost to the nearest cost shown in the table. (Our house has a cooling index for walls of 2.)

TABLE 27-5   INSULATION UNDER FLOORS AND STORM DOORS

Index (heating index only)	Insulation Under Floors*		Storm Doors
	R Value	Mineral Fiber Batt Thickness, in.	
0–7	0†	0†	None
8–15	11†	4†	None
16–30	19	6	Optional
31–65	22	7	Optional
66–	22	7	On all doors

*If your furnace and hot water heater are located in an otherwise unheated basement, cut your heating index in half to find the level of floor insulation.

†In zones I and II R-11 insulation is usually economical under floors over open crawlspaces and over garages; in zone I insulation is not usually economical if crawlspace is closed off.

TABLE 27-6 WALL INSULATION, DUCT INSULATION, AND STORM WINDOWS

Index (heating index plus cooling index for walls)	Wall Insulation (blown in)	Insulation around Ducts, in Crawlspaces, and in other Unheated Areas (except attics),* Resistance and Approximate Thickness, in.	Storm Windows [(triple-track) minimum economical window size], sq ft
0–10	None	R-8 (2)	none
11–12		R-8 (2)	20
13–15		R-16 (4)	15
16–19	Full-	R-16 (4)	12
20–28	wall	R-16 (4)	9
29–35	insulation	R-16 (4)	6
36–45	approximately	R-24 (6)	4
46–65	R-14	R-24 (6)	All windows†
66–		R-32 (8)	All windows†

*Use heating index only if ducts are not used for air conditioning.

†Windows too small for triple-track windows can be fitted with one-piece windows.

6. Find the sum of your heating index and cooling index for attics. (Our sum is 25.)

7. Find the sum of your heating index and cooling index for walls. (Our sum is 22.) Energy saving result from decreasing the heat flow through the exterior shell of the building. The resistance, or R, value of insulation is the measure of its ability to decrease heat flow. Two different kinds of insulation may have the same thickness, but the one with the higher R value will perform better. For that reason, our recommendations are listed in terms of R values with the approximate corresponding thickness. R values for different thicknesses of insulation are generally made available by the manufacturers.

8. Find the resistance value of insulation recommended for your attic and around attic ducts from Table 27-4. (For our house the recommended resistance value is R-30 for attic floors and R-16 for ducts.)

9. Find the recommended level of insulation for floors over unheated areas from Table 27-5. (Our house should have R-19.) Using Table 27-5, check to see whether storm doors are economical for your home. Storm doors listed as optional may be economical if the doorway is heavily used during the heating season.

10. Find the recommended level of insulation for your walls and ducts in unheated areas from Table 27-6. (Our house should have full-wall insulation if none existed previously and R-16 insulation around ducts.) Table 27-6 also shows the minimum economical storm window size in square feet for triple-track storm windows. (Our house should have storm windows on all windows 9 sq ft in size or larger where storm windows can be used.)

11. Weather stripping and caulking. Regardless of where you live or your cost of energy, it is almost always economical to install weather stripping on the inside around doors and windows where possible and to caulk on the outside around doors and window frames—if you do it yourself. This is especially true for windows and doors which have noticeable drafts.

28

COMBINING CONTRACT AND SPECULATIVE BUILDING

28.1. HOW TO DIVIDE ONE'S TIME AS A CONTRACTOR

The contract builder who wishes to go into speculative building is well advised to continue with his contract work at least until he has become established in this new field. As a matter of fact, the builder who wishes to erect a few residences a year, or perhaps a small commercial or apartment building on speculation, need never abandon his contract business. The cash flow provided by his contract business can often help him over rough financial spots.

The problem is time. The builder who is just starting in business for himself must give all of his time to his contract business until he has established a routine. He learns by experience which portions of his business require his attention on a continual basis and which portions can be taken care of at periodic intervals. A conscientious contractor should spend 60 hours a week to carry on his business, especially during the period when he is starting out. The time devoted to the contract part of his business can be reduced, however, if eventually the contractor spends only the time allotted to the profit-making part of his business and delegates the routine to trustworthy persons. These routine matters will take fewer hours a week if he checks on them periodically but does not do them himself.

28.1A. The Profit-Making Activities of the Contract Business

Until the business becomes so big that he cannot do these things himself, the contractor should spend most of the time available to him on the following.

28.1A1. ESTIMATING

A good competitive estimate involves accurate quantity take-offs, a knowledge of the productivity of labor, competitive subcontract bids; and business judgment in arriving at the lowest price possible consistent with earning a reasonable profit over and above the contractor's weekly pay. The contractor must do this himself unless he has a trusted employee. However, he still must go over all the figures carefully and assemble the bid himself.

28.1A2. PURCHASING

Here again it is important for the principal to either do the work himself or at least check the figures before any agreement is closed. This includes conducting the final negotiations with subcontractors and obtaining competitive bids from material dealers, equipment renters, etc.

28.1A3. FIELD SUPERVISION

At the beginning the contractor must do the supervising himself. He can eventually leave some of the supervision to a trusted working foreman during certain stages of the construction (he should decide this). He need not inspect every job every day.

28.1A4. NEW BUSINESS AND CLIENT RELATIONS

The contractor must look for new business himself and spend as much time as necessary to ensure a constant flow of work. He is the one who must visit, call, or write to all the possible sources of new work. He must maintain good client relations so that he will be recommended as a trustworthy and competent builder. A constant flow of work enables the contractor to deploy his work force most advantageously and to keep his competent craftspeople on the payroll. He can also obtain better prices from material dealers and subcontractors if he is regarded as a contractor whose good will it is important to keep.

28.1A5. LABOR RELATIONS

This important matter is related to the constant flow of work that the contractor should strive to attain. A steadily employed laborer will be very careful to be productive, and if he sees other jobs coming he will not be inclined to take all kinds of "breaks." Even if there is a union involved, its business agent will be inclined to be much more friendly with a steady employer. Dealing with the various types of workers is an important duty of the contractor.

28.1A6. RECORD KEEPING, BOOKKEEPING

This work can be done by others *so long as it is done on a daily basis* and with periodic checking by the contractor.

28.1A7. FINANCIAL, LEGAL, INSURANCE, TAXES

In these activities the contractor can combine his speculative business with his contract business, being sure that he keeps separate records of the cost of these services and of his own time.

It is entirely possible that with good planning the principal will have to spend only 30 hours a week on the contract end of his business and be able to spend the remainder of his time on starting and continuing a speculative building business.

28.1B. The Contractor's Time at the Start of Speculative Building

Chapters 16 and 17 describe the research work that is necessary before a contractor decides to start any speculative building. He is about to put his own money on the line and he must choose the proper location, the kind of building, and the price range that makes it most salable or rentable and he must very carefully ascertain his own financial capability.

28.1B1. RESEARCH WORK

This is the builder's first step and it is going to take a considerable portion of his time until he has established some reliable guide posts which show where and what he should build. He must study advertisements and local real estate news, local economic forecasts, and bank forecasts. He must speak to many people and he must drive many miles to see for himself what is going on in his immediate vicinity and in the surrounding area. In fact, that may take most of his spare time for at least several weeks.

28.1B2. LOCATING BUILDING SITES

When he has decided where to build and what to build, the contractor has now to find building lots on which to build what he wants. This involves study of zoning maps, locating the sites that can be purchased, locating the owner, sales negotiations, and financing. This again may take most of his spare time for several weeks after he has finished his research. Up to this point the builder has possibly spent two months or more just to buy a good building site.

28.1B3. PLANS AND SPECIFICATIONS

If the builder's first venture is in single-family houses—and most speculative builders start in this way—then he must have plans and specifications. These can be purchased from several sources and they can be changed by the builder to suit his lot conditions and the zoning (see Chap. 20). He can also change the plans to eliminate costly features or to make the house larger or smaller.

28.1B4. ESTIMATING

When the builder has purchased the building lot and has decided on the plans and specifications, his next step is to prepare a careful estimate of what the house will cost in order to make certain that the combined cost of house, land, and other expense will enable him to price it within the range that he has decided will sell most readily.

28.1B5. FINANCING

Before he starts to purchase materials or subcontracts or starts actual construction, the builder must be sure of his financing. If he has a good record as a contract builder he should have no trouble in obtaining a construction loan, and it is at this point that he can start to build.

Up to now the contractor has for a period of several months spent all of his spare time away from his contract business and has not yet even poured a foundation. But what he has done has laid a solid foundation for the future of his speculative business.

It will be noted that up to this point there has been no mention of the construction of speculative commercial or multifamily buildings or of condominiums. These require the sophistication that comes only from "learning the ropes." They also require an amount of financing that is not normally available to the beginning speculative builder.

28.2. THE ADVANTAGES OF COMBINING BOTH BUSINESSES

28.2A. Scheduling and the Deployment of the Work Force

One of the advantages of the combining of contract and speculative building is the freedom of action the contractor has in deploying his work force in the most efficient manner. Contract work is always on a fixed time schedule. In order to keep architects and clients happy the contractor is strongly advised to adhere to this schedule. On the other hand the speculative part of the business has a more flexible schedule. The contractor should schedule his work so that the speculative construction is staggered with the contract work. He can do this because he controls the speculative part. For instance:

The builder is awarded a contract to build a private residence. The contract gives him 6 months from the start of construction. He also has a building lot on which he wants to erect a speculative private residence.

He starts the excavation and foundation work on the contract work. He starts his framing crew on the contract work. While his framing crew is working he starts the excavation and foundations on his speculative house. When the framing crew is finished on the contract house he can move some of them to his own house. He must leave some crew behind but he need not go so fast on his own house. Right at this point he has provided a continuation of work on excavating, foundations, and framing.

At the later stages of construction he can schedule the trim, wallboarding, plumbing, heating, etc., so that one house follows another. In a pinch he can always take the crew off his own house and send them to the contract house for a day or two or more.

When there is bad weather he may be able to place workers in the weathertight house, and then in fair weather take some of them back to his own house, thus ensuring a continuous flow of work.

28.2B. Deployment of Materials and Equipment

Another advantage to the builder is in the use of his equipment and in his ability to shift material from one job to another (keeping careful records, of course). He can do this if he is building more than one contract house at the same time but there is always the matter of the tightness of the schedule of the contract house. If the contractor has several rotary saws or other power equipment, he can use one on his own house when it is not immediately required. He can also give first choice to the contract house if it suddenly requires a couple of sheets of plywood or an extra ladder. It is the more flexible scheduling of the speculative house that makes this possible.

28.2C. Purchasing

It is not necessary to point out the differential in price a contractor gets from the lumber yard, concrete-mix dealer, or others if he buys for two jobs at once—to follow in sequence. This holds true for the subcontractors as well, who can plan sequential work for their crew.

28.3. RECORD KEEPING

28.3A. Keeping Separate Records

It is absolutely essential that the contractor keep separate records for each of his construction projects and especially between his contract and his speculative building. This can eventually be full-time work for a bookkeeper.

If the time comes when the contractor has built income property which he wishes to manage himself, there will be a third set of records—the management records.

28.4. THE CONTRACTOR'S TIME WHILE OPERATING A SPECULATIVE BUSINESS

In Sec. 28.1A the conclusion was tentatively reached that a contractor need only spend half of his time on his contract business once he has established a routine and has been able to leave many time-consuming duties to trusted subordinates. As for essential duties of the contractor in Secs. 28.2 and 28.3, it is expected that the contractor can combine these with his contract work during his normal work week. The transition in his thinking and work habits should be easy because of the essential similarity of the two kinds of operations.

The contractor is urged to put it down on paper. He should plan and write out his week-by-week progress schedules—his schedule for ordering materials and subcontractors and his own time in performing the two operations. He can certainly do both if he thinks a program through and schedules it correctly. There must be no emergencies. Emergencies cost money.

28.5. FINANCES

28.5A. Cash Flow

A continuity of cash flow is the life blood of any business. Bills must be paid on time; labor must be paid weekly; taxes, insurance, mortgage, interest, etc., must all be paid on time. This is not peculiar to the construction business. Everyone must pay rent, taxes, insurance, grocery bills, etc., on time. Most people get a weekly salary and that is all. The contractor also gets a salary, but in addition he gets a contract or speculative profit, and to get this he must make an extra effort. This extra effort involves many aspects of his business which have been mentioned many times before, and one that is as important as any is the maintenance of a steady cash flow. This is where the combination of contract and speculative building can be very helpful.

25.5A1. CONTRACT BUILDING

In contract building the contractor is paid by a lending institution on a prescribed construction loan schedule that calls for four or five progress payments at certain stages of the work. The owner is responsible for this loan. The money that the contractor receives must first be used to pay for his labor, his material bills, and other charges that are due *on this particular property.* Sometimes (see Sec. 11.2B1, Part 1) he even has to take short-term loans from the bank to carry him over certain periods when his progress payments fall behind his expense. But the fact is that he is sure of being paid at certain times and it is his own money that he gets; not borrowed money. The contractor has a certain amount of leeway. He cannot, of course, use any of the money to pay bills on any other project but he can use the profit and overhead (which is his) for any purpose.

28.5A2. SPECULATIVE BUILDING

In speculative building the contractor also has obtained a construction loan which is paid out in the same manner as the loan on a contract house. This loan is borrowed money. He must use it to pay all the bills due on the particular house and he again will have money left over. But the prudent builder should not spend this as if it were his own money. It is not—until he sells the house. He must put some of it aside to carry the house if it does not sell readily. It is at this point that the contract advances can at least help carry his personal expenses.

In general, the contractor who continues to carry on a flow of contract building with its subsequent constant contact with lenders, architects, owners, subcontractors, and material dealers will find it easier to get into speculative building. He will be able to obtain credit, loans, and good prices. He should also be able to obtain information on vacant land, on price trends, and even about prospective purchasers or renters.

29

THE COMING METRIC SYSTEM IN CONSTRUCTION

29.1. THE HISTORY OF THE METRIC SYSTEM IN THE UNITED STATES

In July 1971, the United States Department of Commerce issued a report concerning the possible conversion of our system of measurements from the one now in use to the metric system. This report was the result of an exhaustive study by the National Bureau of Standards in response to an act of Congress of August 1968.

The Department of Commerce report stated that it would be advantageous to the business efficiency and the general welfare of the country to change to the International Metric System on a gradual basis. The report stated that there was much less dissent on the part of industry to this gradual changeover than had been anticipated.

On January 14, 1975, Congress enacted a law "to declare a national policy of coordinating the increasing use of the metric system in the United States, and to establish a United States Metric Board to coordinate the *voluntary* conversion to the metric system." The law is titled "Metric Conversion Act of 1975."

Until this act was passed the United States was the only industrialized nation which had not committed itself to a national policy of encouraging and coordinating the use of the international metric system. Private industry, however, had not been standing still. Within a year of the enactment of the bill, 37 of our largest corporations, whose total annual sales amount to over $130 billion, had announced plans to convert to metric dimensions.

It is interesting to note that the use of metric measurement standards in the United States has been permitted by law since 1866. The metric system is used extensively in science but has never become popular in this country as a unit of ordinary weights and measures.

377

29.2. THE CURRENT USE OF METRIC IN OTHER COUNTRIES

A study of how the metric system or a national dimensional coordination system was introduced in other English-speaking countries will be of interest. The United States is profiting by their experience in setting up its own dimensional system, which will of course be the same as theirs. Incidentally, the United States is the last of the English-speaking countries to adopt the system.

It is a fact that the new system was not greeted with any great enthusiasm by the construction industry, until the great benefits of the standardization of building materials and of measurements were understood. At this time Canada is well along on the program and has set up dates for the "hard conversion" to metric (or standardization) of a number of strategic building materials. This decision was made by committees composed of material manufacturers, construction contractors, construction unions, architects, engineers, and others. They studied the impact of the various changes and came to agreement before the changes were made. The United States is going through the same process. The changes, when they are made, will still not have the force of law but when wallboard and brick, precast concrete and windows, ductwork and diffusers are manufactured in metric and the plans are in metric, the building contractor will have small choice.

29.3. CURRENT USE OF METRIC IN THE UNITED STATES

There are currently a number of states that are teaching children metric weights and measures along with our customary system. Many food processors are labeling their products in both customary and metric measurements and a number of states have now labeled their road signs in both customary miles and metric kilometers. With the surge of foreign car sales in this country, automobile mechanics in many communities now have tools and gauges in both customary and metric units. Manufacturers of roller bearings have almost completely changed to metric although they still give their sizes in feet or inches.

The present forward surge in metric use is a result of the effort of the government to simplify its system of weights and measurements, as in the use of the meter and its decimals instead of inch, foot, yard, fathom, furlong, rod, mile. Use of metric is also a must for this country's foreign trade. At present almost everything we export must be manufactured in metric, whereas everything we use domestically is manufactured in customary units. The waste of effort is apparent. Currently there is a government-appointed coordination committee for the construction industry. The committee's function is to introduce the new system of measurements with the least possible confusion and at the least possible expense.

29.4. DESCRIPTION OF THE METRIC SYSTEM

The metric system is a decimal system. Its primary units of measurement are the meter, which is 39.37 in. long, and the kilogram which weighs 2.2 lb. These units can be divided or multiplied by 10 to obtain smaller or larger units. For instance, the meter, which is the metric unit of measurement, can be divided by 10 (a decimeter) or by 100 (a centimeter). It can also be multiplied by 10, by 100, or by 1000 (a kilometer). The kilogram can also be divided by 10 (a hectogram) or multiplied by 10 (a miriagram), although these units are rarely used in everyday transactions. Instead one uses a "kilo" (2.2 lb), ½ kilo, or 2 kilos, etc.

Once the public becomes accustomed to its use, the metric system is much easier to use. Instead of 12 in. in a foot, 3 ft in a yard, and 5280 ft in a mile, there would be 1000 millimeters (mm) in a meter (m) and 1000 meters in a kilometer (km). Instead of a cubic yard, which is 27 cubic feet, there would be a cubic meter, which is 1.3 cubic yards and which could be divided by 10 to become a cubic decimeter or 3.5 cubic feet. It can be divided by 1000 to become a liter (1 qt). When one becomes used to it, it will be found much simpler to use than our customary units.

29.5. THE TIMING FOR CONSTRUCTION USE

The construction contractor need not be worried by the use of the metric system in construction. Its use is voluntary and it is not likely that any future act of Congress will make it compulsory. It will come gradually and it need not be expensive—certainly not so far as the small contractor is concerned. If the experience of other countries, and even the United States since 1866 (when the metric system became legal), is taken into account, some units of measurement or weight will not change for a long time. For instance, the acre as a measurement of land will not be changed until it is resurveyed and conveyed to a new owner and may not be changed even then. (There are land records in Texas that are still in varas, a spanish unit.) As a matter of fact, the acre need never be changed if it would mean a major upheaval in land records.

So the time when the contractor will be building in metric is still a number of years away. Many steps (some expensive) must be taken by many people before the use of the metric system filters down to the small builder. His expense will be very little. For instance, hammers, power saws, planes, chisels, surveying instruments, ladders, adjustable wrenches, etc., can do their work in metric or customary units without any change at all. The screws and nuts and bolts that the builder uses may be in metric, but they will be equivalent to the sizes that he knows. Pipes and fitting sizes and wire gauges may change for the plumber and electrician, but again they will be the equivalent of the sizes of material that are familiar to these contractors.

Buildings and land are not export products and the question will arise "Why go metric at all in the construction business?" The speculative builder can still build a house that is 50 ft × 25 ft on one-half acre of land, and his clients will know exactly what they are getting. Why change?

The answer is that construction will eventually go metric because it will be forced to. Manufacturers will find that they can reduce the variety of sizes that they now manufacture. For instance, a nut and bolt manufacturer can stock 200 sizes in metric versus 405 in customary units. A ball bearing manufacturer can stock 30 sizes in metric versus 280 sizes in customary. Multinational corporations who manufacture electrical and plumbing products are now manufacturing in both metric and in customary. Manufacturers of wallboard, insulation, brick, and ceramics will change to all-metric to make the large savings involved in standardization. School children in many states are being taught weights and measures in both metric and customary, and it is found that metric is much easier to learn. In fact some states are preparing to teach only metric within a few years.

29.6. THE PROBABLE SEQUENCE BEFORE THE CONTRACTOR BUILDS IN METRIC

To start with, the contractor will not be expected to convert any dimensions of material from customary to metric. It will all be done for him. Architects and engineers everywhere in the country who have anything to do with

TABLE 29-1   SOME COMMON UNITS

Length	Mass	Volume	Temperature	Electric Current	Time
Metric:					
meter	kilogram	liter	Celsius (Centigrade)	ampere	second
Customary:					
inch	ounce	fluid ounce	Fahrenheit	ampere	second
foot	pound	teaspoon			
yard	ton	tablespoon			
fathom	grain	cup			
rod	dram	pint			
mile		quart			
		gallon			
		barrel			
		peck			
		bushel			

TABLE 29-2 APPROXIMATE CONVERSIONS FROM CUSTOMARY TO METRIC AND VICE VERSA

	When You Know:	You Can Find:	If You Multiply by:
Length:	inches	millimeters	25
	feet	centimeters	30
	yards	meters	0.9
	miles	kilometers	1.6
	millimeters	inches	0.04
	centimeters	inches	0.4
	meters	yards	1.1
	kilometers	miles	0.6
Area:	square inches	square centimeters	6.5
	square feet	square meters	0.09
	square yards	square meters	0.8
	square miles	square kilometers	2.6
	acres	square hectometers (hectares)	0.4
	square centimeters	square inches	0.16
	square meters	square yards	1.2
	square kilometers	square miles	0.4
	square hectometers (hectares)	acres	2.5

TABLE 29-2   APPROXIMATE CONVERSIONS FROM CUSTOMARY TO METRIC AND VICE VERSA
(Continued)

	When You Know:	You Can Find:	If You Multiply by:
Mass:	ounces	grams	28
	pounds	kilograms	0.45
	short tons	megagrams (metric tons)	0.9
	grams	ounces	0.035
	kilograms	pounds	2.2
	megagrams (metric tons)	short tons	1.1
Liquid volume:	ounces	milliliters	30
	pints	liters	0.47
	quarts	liters	0.95
	gallons	liters	3.8
	milliliters	ounces	0.034
	liters	pints	2.1
	liters	quarts	1.06
	liters	gallons	0.26
Temperature:	degrees Fahrenheit	degrees Celsius	$\frac{5}{9}$ (after subtracting 32)
	degrees Celsius	degrees Fahrenheit	$\frac{9}{5}$ (then add 32)

foreign work are now designing that work in metric. Local architects whose only practice is in domestic work are not averse to using metric when the proper time arrives. It will mean the use of metric scales and some use of conversion tables, but the plan that the builder uses will not require any calculations on his part. For instance, instead of stating that studs will be 2 in. × 4 in. (this is now 1½ in. × 3½ in.) on 16-in. centers, the plan may say that studs will be 40 × 90 mm, 400 mm on center. This of course presupposes that lumber mills will have changed to metric. The contractor will probably now have to have a 2-m (2000-mm) rule instead of a 6-ft rule. Each meter will be divided into 1000 mm. The acceptable sizes of every material in the building codes will have to be revised to metric, and a committee is now working on this.

So far as the mechanical equipment is concerned, the manufacturers of boilers, piping, fittings, motors, and fans are now sizing part of their production in metric so that they can change to metric as soon as they convert their production machinery, which is now in customary dimensions, to metric.

However, the builder should be aware that conversion to metric will not be without trouble. It is true that a metric plan, metric rules and tapes, metric lumber, and metric code sizes would entail no trouble to him. But unfortunately all of these changes will not occur at the same time. When metric lumber arrives the builder will still have to complete an unfinished house in customary measurements. He may have to bid on a metric plan while metric lumber is in short supply.

It may take a year or more to convert fully from one system to another, and this could be a time of trouble and delay. This trouble need not be too serious if the builder makes himself familiar with metric measurements before he has to use them. There are books of tables on metric equivalents for our customary measurements.

Tables 29-1 and 29-2 show how much simpler the use of metric can be.

APPENDIXES TO
PART TWO

How to Locate a Building
on a Lot by Taping

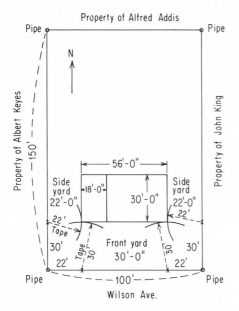

Property of Alfred Addis

Pipe · · · · · · · · · · · · · Pipe

Property of Albert Keyes

Property of John King

N ↑

—150'—

56'-0"

Side yard 22'-0" ←18'-0"→ 30'-0" Side yard 22'-0"

22' Tape

Tape 30'

Front yard 30'-0"

30' 30'

22' 22'

Pipe — — 100' — — Pipe

Wilson Ave.

TO FIND FRONT CORNERS

- Measure 22' from each corner on front line.
- Measure 30' from each front corner on side lines.
- Swing 22' tape and 30' until the arcs intersect.
- Square building by swinging 22' tape from side lines and 30' tape from front corner.
- Drive stakes at corners.
- Tape diagonals (should be equal).

Use of Batter Boards for
Excavation and Foundations

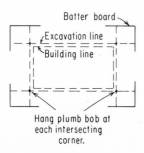

Batter board

Excavation line
Building line

Hang plumb bob at each intersecting corner.

After building lines are staked out then batter boards are put in place and mason lines are hung approximately 2'-0" outside building line to allow for excavation. Plumb bobs are hung at each intersection. When excavation is complete, the lines are moved back to actual building lines and plumb bobs are rehung.

Typical Foundation Details

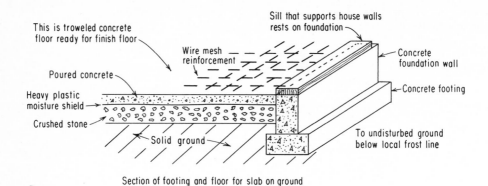

This is troweled concrete floor ready for finish floor

Sill that supports house walls rests on foundation

Wire mesh reinforcement

Poured concrete

Concrete foundation wall

Heavy plastic moisture shield

Concrete footing

Crushed stone

Solid ground

To undisturbed ground below local frost line

Section of footing and floor for slab on ground

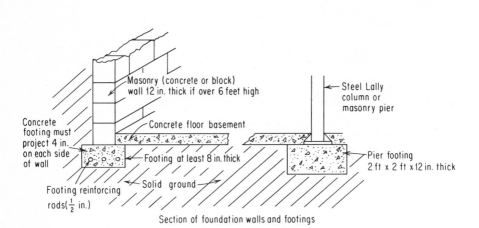

Masonry (concrete or block) wall 12 in. thick if over 6 feet high

Steel Lally column or masonry pier

Concrete footing must project 4 in. on each side of wall

Concrete floor basement

Footing at least 8 in. thick

Pier footing 2 ft x 2 ft x 12 in. thick

Footing reinforcing rods($\frac{1}{2}$ in.)

Solid ground

Section of foundation walls and footings

Typical Framing Details

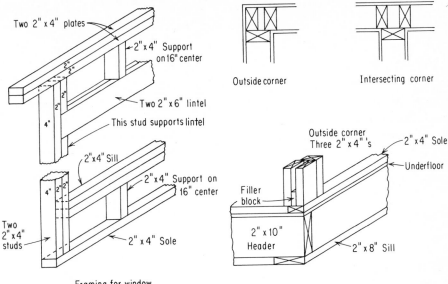

Two 2" x 4" plates

2" x 4" Support on 16" center

2"
2"
4"

Two 2" x 6" lintel

This stud supports lintel

2" x 4" Sill

2" x 4" Support on 16" center

4" 2" 2"

Two 2" x 4" studs

2" x 4" Sole

Framing for window
(other openings interior or exterior same upper framing)

Outside corner

Intersecting corner

Outside corner Three 2" x 4"'s

2" x 4" Sole

Underfloor

Filler block

2" x 10" Header

2" x 8" Sill

Corner of platform framing

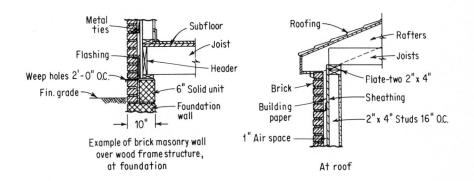

Metal ties

Subfloor

Joist

Flashing

Header

Weep holes 2'-0" O.C.

Fin. grade

6" Solid unit

Foundation wall

10"

Example of brick masonry wall over wood frame structure, at foundation

Roofing

Rafters

Joists

Plate-two 2" x 4"

Brick

Sheathing

Building paper

2" x 4" Studs 16" O.C.

1" Air space

At roof

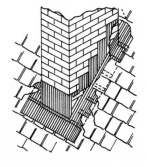

Example of step flashing at chimney

Typical Framing Details

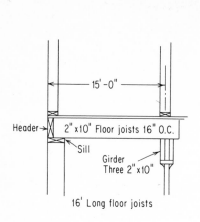

16' Long floor joists

Header→ 2"x10" Floor joists 16" O.C.

Sill

Girder
Three 2"x10"

15'-0"

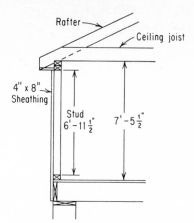

Rafter

Ceiling joist

4" x 8"
Sheathing

Stud
6'-11½"

7'-5½"

Dimensions necessary to use 4" x 8"
sheathing without waste
(Note: This is a low ceiling)

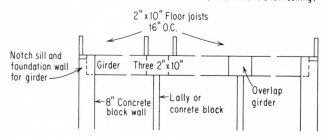

2"x10" Floor joists
16" O.C.

Notch sill and
foundation wall
for girder

Girder   Three 2"x10"

Overlap
girder

←8" Concrete
block wall

←Lally or
conrete block

Girder layout

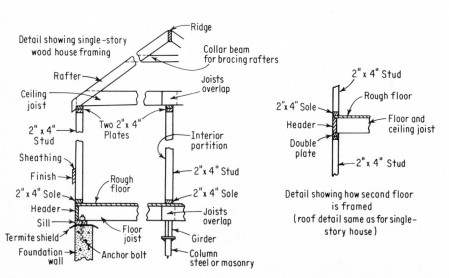

Detail showing single-story
wood house framing

Ridge

Collar beam
for bracing rafters

Rafter

Ceiling
joist

Joists
overlap

Two 2"x 4"
Plates

Interior
partition

2" x 4"
Stud

Sheathing

Finish

Rough
floor

2"x10" Stud

2"x 4" Sole

2"x 4" Sole

Header

Sill

Joists
overlap

Termite shield

Foundation
wall

Floor
joist

Anchor bolt

Girder

Column
steel or masonry

2" x 4" Stud

Rough floor

2"x 4" Sole

Header

Double
plate

Floor and
ceiling joist

2"x 4" Stud

Detail showing how second floor
is framed
(roof detail same as for single-
story house)

390

Rough Guide for Design
of Air Conditioning System

(Not to be Used for Actual Design)

Residential	Average occupancy	400 sq ft per person
	Lighting	2 watts per sq ft
	Refrigeration	1 ton per 500 sq ft
	Air quantities	
	East, South, West elevations	1.2 cu ft per minute per 1 sq ft
	North elevation	0.8 cu ft per minute per 1 sq ft
Office	Average occupancy	125 sq. ft. per person
	Lighting	5.8 watts per sq. ft.
	Refrigeration	1 ton per 300 sq. ft.
	Air quantities	
	East, South, West elevations	0.5 cu ft per minute per 1 sq ft
	North elevation	Same as other elevations
Stores	Average occupancy	30 sq ft per person
	Refrigeration	1 ton per 260 sq ft
	Air quantities	
	All elevations	Average 1.5 cfm per 1 sq ft

Typical Code of Allowable Maximum Spans for Floor Joists and Rafters

(Private Residence)

FLOOR JOISTS

Size of Joist	Spacing in Inches	Maximum Clear Span
2″ × 8″	12	12′-0″
	16	11′-4″
	24	9′-6″
2″ × 10″	12	15′-0″
	16	14′-0″
	24	12′-0″
2″ × 12″	12	18′-6″
	16	16′-6″
	24	14′-6″

RAFTERS

Size of Rafter	Spacing in Inches	Maximum Clear Span 5-in-12 Pitch (or Less)	Over 5-in-12
2″ × 6″	12	12′-6″	14′-2″
	16	10′-9″	12′-6″
	24	9′-0″	
2″ × 8″	12	16′-0″	18′-4″
	16	14′-0″	16′-7″
	24	12′-0″	
2″ × 10″	12	20′-0″	
	16	18′-0″	
	24	15′-0″	

Note: These tables based on use of common structural-grade Douglas fir or No. 1 common Southern pine—40-lb live load for joists, 30-lb roof load for rafters.

A Nailing Schedule
from a Typical Town Code

RECOMMENDED NAILING SCHEDULE

Building Element	Nail Type	Number and Distribution
Stud to sole plate	Common-toe nail	4—8d
Stud to cap plate	Common-end nail	2—16d
Double studs	Common-direct	16d 12″ o. c. or 16d 30″ o. c.
Corner studs	Common-direct	16d 30″ o. c.
Sole plate to joist or blocking	Common	26d 16″ o. c.
Double cap plate	Common-direct	16d 24″ o. c.
Cap plate laps	Common-direct	3—16d
Ribbon strip—6″ or less	Common-direct	2—10d each bearing
Ribbon strip—over 6″	Common-direct	3—10d each bearing
Roof rafter to plate	Common-toe nail	3—16d
Roof rafter to ridge	Common-toe nail	2—16d
Jack rafter to hip	Common-toe nail	3—10d
Floor joists to studs (no ceiling joist)	Common-direct	5—10d or 3—16d
Floor joists to studs (with ceiling joist)	Common-direct	2—10d
Floor joists to sill or girder	Common-toe nail	2—16d
Ledger strip	Common-direct	3—20d at each joist
Ceiling joists to plate	Common-toe nail	2—16d
Ceiling joists to alternate rafters	Common-direct	3—16d
Ceiling joists (laps over partition)	Common-direct	3—16d
Collar beam	Common-direct	4—10d
Bridging to joists	Common-direct	2—8d each end
Diagonal brace (to stud and plate)	Common-direct	2—8d each bearing
Tail beams to headers (when nailing permitted)	Common-end nail	1—20d each 4 sq ft floor
Header beams to trimmers (when nailing permitted)	Common-end nail	1—20d each 8 sq ft floor
(1″) sub-flooring 6″ or less	Common-direct	2—8d each joist
(1″) sub-flooring 8″ or more	Common-direct	3—8d each joist

A Nailing Schedule
from a Typical Town Code (Continued)

(2″) subflooring	Common-direct	2—20d each joist
(1″) sheathing—8″ or less	Common-direct	2—8d each stud or rafter
(1″) sheathing—over 8″	Common-direct	3—8d each stud or rafter
Plywood sheathing	Common-direct	6d 5″ o. c. exterior edges
Plywood sheathing	Corrosion resistive	6d 10″ o. c. intermediate
Roof sheathing—6″ or less	Common-direct	2—8d each rafter
Roof sheathing—over 6″	Common-direct	3—8d each rafter
Fiber board sheathing	Common-direct	8d—6″ o. c. intermediate
		8d—3″ o. c. exterior edges
Gypsum sheathing	Large head	7—No. 11g × 1¾″ per bearing under shingles
		4 per bearing all other cases
Shingles—wood	Corrosion resistive	2—No. 14 B&S each bearing
Weather boarding	Corrosion resistive	2—8d each bearing

Shingle nails shall penetrate not less than ¾ inch into nailing strips, sheathing or supporting construction except attached directly to sheathing less than one (1) inch thick shall be secured by barbed or other mechanically-bonding nails of an approved type.

A Nailing Schedule
from a Typical Town Code

NUMBER OF NAILS TO THE POUND

Size	Length	Common	Finishing
2d	1″	850	
3d	1¼″	550	640
4d	1½″	350	456
5d	1¾″	230	328
6d	2″	180	273
7d	2¼″	140	170
8d	2½″	100	151
9d	2¾″	80	125
10d	3″	65	107
12d	3¼″	50	
16d	3½″	40	
20d	4″	31	
30d	4½″	22	
40d	5″	18	
50d	5½″	14	
60d	6″	12	

Arithmetic Tables for
Numbers 1 to 1000

1-50

No.	Square	Cube	Sq. Root	Cu. Root	Reciprocal
1	1	1	1.0000	1.0000	1.000000000
2	4	8	1.4142	1.2599	.500000000
3	9	27	1.7321	1.4422	.333333333
4	16	64	2.0000	1.5874	.250000000
5	25	125	2.2361	1.7100	.200000000
6	36	216	2.4495	1.8171	.166666667
7	49	343	2.6458	1.9129	.142857143
8	64	512	2.8284	2.0000	.125000000
9	81	729	3.0000	2.0801	.111111111
10	100	1,000	3.1623	2.1544	.100000000
11	121	1,331	3.3166	2.2240	.090909091
12	144	1,728	3.4641	2.2894	.083333333
13	169	2,197	3.6056	2.3513	.076923077
14	196	2,744	3.7417	2.4101	.071428571
15	225	3,375	3.8730	2.4662	.066666667
16	256	4,096	4.0000	2.5198	.062500000
17	289	4,913	4.1231	2.5713	.058823529
18	324	5,832	4.2426	2.6207	.055555556
19	361	6,859	4.3589	2.6684	.052631579
20	400	8,000	4.4721	2.7144	.050000000
21	441	9,261	4.5826	2.7589	.047619048
22	484	10,648	4.6904	2.8020	.045454545
23	529	12,167	4.7958	2.8439	.043478261
24	576	13,824	4.8990	2.8845	.041666667
25	625	15,625	5.0000	2.9240	.040000000
26	676	17,576	5.0990	2.9625	.038461538
27	729	19,683	5.1962	3.0000	.037037037
28	784	21,952	5.2915	3.0366	.035714286
29	841	24,389	5.3852	3.0723	.034482759
30	900	27,000	5.4772	3.1072	.033333333
31	961	29,791	5.5678	3.1414	.032258065
32	1,024	32,768	5.6569	3.1748	.031250000
33	1,089	35,937	5.7446	3.2075	.030303030
34	1,156	39,304	5.8310	3.2396	.029411765
35	1,225	42,875	5.9161	3.2711	.028571429
36	1,296	46,656	6.0000	3.3019	.027777778
37	1,369	50,653	6.0828	3.3322	.027027027
38	1,444	54,872	6.1644	3.3620	.026315789
39	1,521	59,319	6.2450	3.3912	.025641026
40	1,600	64,000	6.3246	3.4200	.025000000
41	1,681	68,921	6.4031	3.4482	.024390244
42	1,764	74,088	6.4807	3.4760	.023809524
43	1,849	79,507	6.5574	3.5034	.023255814
44	1,936	85,184	6.6332	3.5303	.022727273
45	2,025	91,125	6.7082	3.5569	.022222222
46	2,116	97,336	6.7823	3.5830	.021739130
47	2,209	103,823	6.8557	3.6088	.021276596
48	2,304	110,592	6.9282	3.6342	.020833333
49	2,401	117,649	7.0000	3.6593	.020408163
50	2,500	125,000	7.0711	3.6840	.020000000

Arithmetic Tables for
Numbers 1 to 1000 (continued)

50-100

No.	Square	Cube	Sq. Root	Cu. Root	Reciprocal
50	2,500	125,000	7.0711	3.6840	.020000000
51	2,601	132,651	7.1414	3.7084	.019607843
52	2,704	140,608	7.2111	3.7325	.019230769
53	2,809	148,877	7.2801	3.7563	.018867925
54	2,916	157,464	7.3485	3.7798	.018518519
55	3,025	166,375	7.4162	3.8030	.018181818
56	3,136	175,616	7.4833	3.8259	.017857143
57	3,249	185,193	7.5498	3.8485	.017543860
58	3,364	195,112	7.6158	3.8709	.017241379
59	3,481	205,379	7.6811	3.8930	.016949153
60	3,600	216,000	7.7460	3.9149	.016666667
61	3,721	226,981	7.8102	3.9365	.016393443
62	3,844	238,328	7.8740	3.9579	.016129032
63	3,969	250,047	7.9373	3.9791	.015873016
64	4,096	262,144	8.0000	4.0000	.015625000
65	4,225	274,625	8.0623	4.0207	.015384615
66	4,356	287,496	8.1240	4.0412	.015151515
67	4,489	300,763	8.1854	4.0615	.014925373
68	4,624	314,432	8.2462	4.0817	.014705882
69	4,761	328,509	8.3066	4.1016	.014492754
70	4,900	343,000	8.3666	4.1213	.014285714
71	5,041	357,911	8.4261	4.1408	.014084507
72	5,184	373,248	8.4853	4.1602	.013888889
73	5,329	389,017	8.5440	4.1793	.013698630
74	5,476	405,224	8.6023	4.1983	.013513514
75	5,625	421,875	8.6603	4.2172	.013333333
76	5,776	438,976	8.7178	4.2358	.013157895
77	5,929	456,533	8.7750	4.2543	.012987013
78	6,084	474,552	8.8318	4.2727	.012820513
79	6,241	493,039	8.8882	4.2908	.012658228
80	6,400	512,000	8.9443	4.3089	.012500000
81	6,561	531,441	9.0000	4.3267	.012345679
82	6,724	551,368	9.0554	4.3445	.012195122
83	6,889	571,787	9.1104	4.3621	.012048193
84	7,056	592,704	9.1652	4.3795	.011904762
85	7,225	614,125	9.2195	4.3968	.011764706
86	7,396	636,056	9.2736	4.4140	.011627907
87	7,569	658,503	9.3274	4.4310	.011494253
88	7,744	681,472	9.3808	4.4480	.011363636
89	7,921	704,969	9.4340	4.4647	.011235955
90	8,100	729,000	9.4868	4.4814	.011111111
91	8,281	753,571	9.5394	4.4979	.010989011
92	8,464	778,688	9.5917	4.5144	.010869565
93	8,649	804,357	9.6437	4.5307	.010752688
94	8,836	830,584	9.6954	4.5468	.010638298
95	9,025	857,375	9.7468	4.5629	.010526316
96	9,216	884,736	9.7980	4.5789	.010416667
97	9,409	912,673	9.8489	4.5947	.010309278
98	9,604	941,192	9.8995	4.6104	.010204082
99	9,801	970,299	9.9499	4.6261	.010101010
100	10,000	1,000,000	10.0000	4.6416	.010000000

Arithmetic Tables for
Numbers 1 to 1000 (continued)

100-150

No.	Square	Cube	Sq. Root	Cu. Root	Reciprocal
100	10,000	1,000,000	10.0000	4.6416	.010000000
101	10,201	1,030,301	10.0499	4.6570	.009900990
102	10,404	1,061,208	10.0995	4.6723	.009803922
103	10,609	1,092,727	10.1489	4.6875	.009708738
104	10,816	1,124,864	10.1980	4.7027	.009615385
105	11,025	1,157,625	10.2470	4.7177	.009523810
106	11,236	1,191,016	10.2956	4.7326	.009433962
107	11,449	1,225,043	10.3441	4.7475	.009345794
108	11,664	1,259,712	10.3923	4.7622	.009259259
109	11,881	1,295,029	10.4403	4.7769	.009174312
110	12,100	1,331,000	10.4881	4.7914	.009090909
111	12,321	1,367,631	10.5357	4.8059	.009009009
112	12,544	1,404,928	10.5830	4.8203	.008928571
113	12,769	1,442,897	10.6301	4.8346	.008849558
114	12,996	1,481,544	10.6771	4.8488	.008771930
115	13,225	1,520,875	10.7238	4.8629	.008695652
116	13,456	1,560,896	10.7703	4.8770	.008620690
117	13,689	1,601,613	10.8167	4.8910	.008547009
118	13,924	1,643,032	10.8628	4.9049	.008474576
119	14,161	1,685,159	10.9087	4.9187	.008403361
120	14,400	1,728,000	10.9545	4.9324	.008333333
121	14,641	1,771,561	11.0000	4.9461	.008264463
122	14,884	1,815,848	11.0454	4.9597	.008196721
123	15,129	1,860,867	11.0905	4.9732	.008130081
124	15,376	1,906,624	11.1355	4.9866	.008064516
125	15,625	1,953,125	11.1803	5.0000	.008000000
126	15,876	2,000,376	11.2250	5.0133	.007936508
127	16,129	2,048,383	11.2694	5.0265	.007874016
128	16,384	2,097,152	11.3137	5.0397	.007812500
129	16,641	2,146,689	11.3578	5.0528	.007751938
130	16,900	2,197,000	11.4018	5.0658	.007692308
131	17,161	2,248,091	11.4455	5.0788	.007633588
132	17,424	2,299,968	11.4891	5.0916	.007575758
133	17,689	2,352,637	11.5326	5.1045	.007518797
134	17,956	2,406,104	11.5758	5.1172	.007462687
135	18,225	2,460,375	11.6190	5.1299	.007407407
136	18,496	2,515,456	11.6619	5.1426	.007352941
137	18,769	2,571,353	11.7047	5.1551	.007299270
138	19,044	2,628,072	11.7473	5.1676	.007246377
139	19,321	2,685,619	11.7898	5.1801	.007194245
140	19,600	2,744,000	11.8322	5.1925	.007142857
141	19,881	2,803,221	11.8743	5.2048	.007092199
142	20,164	2,863,288	11.9164	5.2171	.007042254
143	20,449	2,924,207	11.9583	5.2293	.006993007
144	20,736	2,985,984	12.0000	5.2415	.006944444
145	21,025	3,048,625	12.0416	5.2536	.006896552
146	21,316	3,112,136	12.0830	5.2656	.006849315
147	21,609	3,176,523	12.1244	5.2776	.006802721
148	21,904	3,241,792	12.1655	5.2896	.006756757
149	22,201	3,307,949	12.2066	5.3015	.006711409
150	22,500	3,375,000	12.2474	5.3133	.006666667

Arithmetic Tables for
Numbers 1 to 1000 (continued)

150-200

No.	Square	Cube	Sq. Root	Cu. Root	Reciprocal
150	22,500	3,375,000	12.2474	5.3133	.006666667
151	22,801	3,442,951	12.2882	5.3251	.006622517
152	23,104	3,511,008	12.3288	5.3368	.006578947
153	23,409	3,581,577	12.3693	5.3485	.006535948
154	23,716	3,652,264	12.4097	5.3601	.006493506
155	24,025	3,723,875	12.4499	5.3717	.006451613
156	24,336	3,796,416	12.4900	5.3832	.006410256
157	24,649	3,869,893	12.5300	5.3947	.006369427
158	24,964	3,944,312	12.5698	5.4061	.006329114
159	25,281	4,019,679	12.6095	5.4175	.006289308
160	25,600	4,096,000	12.6491	5.4288	.006250000
161	25,921	4,173,281	12.6886	5.4401	.006211180
162	26,244	4,251,528	12.7279	5.4514	.006172840
163	26,569	4,330,747	12.7671	5.4626	.006134969
164	26,896	4,410,944	12.8062	5.4737	.006097561
165	27,225	4,492,125	12.8452	5.4848	.006060606
166	27,556	4,574,296	12.8841	5.4959	.006024096
167	27,889	4,657,463	12.9228	5.5069	.005988024
168	28,224	4,741,632	12.9615	5.5178	.005952381
169	28,561	4,826,809	13.0000	5.5288	.005917160
170	28,900	4,913,000	13.0384	5.5397	.005882353
171	29,241	5,000,211	13.0767	5.5505	.005847953
172	29,584	5,088,448	13.1149	5.5613	.005813953
173	29,929	5,177,717	13.1529	5.5721	.005780347
174	30,276	5,268,024	13.1909	5.5828	.005747126
175	30,625	5,359,375	13.2288	5.5934	.005714286
176	30,976	5,451,776	13.2665	5.6041	.005681818
177	31,329	5,545,233	13.3041	5.6147	.005649718
178	31,684	5,639,752	13.3417	5.6252	.005617978
179	32,041	5,735,339	13.3791	5.6357	.005586592
180	32,400	5,832,000	13.4164	5.6462	.005555556
181	32,761	5,929,741	13.4536	5.6567	.005524862
182	33,124	6,028,568	13.4907	5.6671	.005494505
183	33,489	6,128,487	13.5277	5.6774	.005464481
184	33,856	6,229,504	13.5647	5.6877	.005434783
185	34,225	6,331,625	13.6015	5.6980	.005405405
186	34,596	6,434,856	13.6382	5.7083	.005376344
187	34,969	6,539,203	13.6748	5.7185	.005347594
188	35,344	6,644,672	13.7113	5.7287	.005319149
189	35,721	6,751,269	13.7477	5.7388	.005291005
190	36,100	6,859,000	13.7840	5.7489	.005263158
191	36,481	6,967,871	13.8203	5.7590	.005235602
192	36,864	7,077,888	13.8564	5.7690	.005208333
193	37,249	7,189,057	13.8924	5.7790	.005181347
194	37,636	7,301,384	13.9284	5.7890	.005154639
195	38,025	7,414,875	13.9642	5.7989	.005128205
196	38,416	7,529,536	14.0000	5.8088	.005102041
197	38,809	7,645,373	14.0357	5.8186	.005076142
198	39,204	7,762,392	14.0712	5.8285	.005050505
199	39,601	7,880,599	14.1067	5.8383	.005025126
200	40,000	8,000,000	14.1421	5.8480	.005000000

Arithmetic Tables for
Numbers 1 to 1000 (continued)

200-250

No.	Square	Cube	Sq. Root	Cu. Root	Reciprocal
200	40,000	8,000,000	14.1421	5.8480	.005000000
201	40,401	8,120,601	14.1774	5.8578	.004975124
202	40,804	8,242,408	14.2127	5.8675	.004950495
203	41,209	8,365,427	14.2478	5.8771	.004926108
204	41,616	8,489,664	14.2829	5.8868	.004901961
205	42,025	8,615,125	14.3178	5.8964	.004878049
206	42,436	8,741,816	14.3527	5.9059	.004854369
207	42,849	8,869,743	14.3875	5.9155	.004830918
208	43,264	8,998,912	14.4222	5.9250	.004807692
209	43,681	9,129,329	14.4568	5.9345	.004784689
210	44,100	9,261,000	14.4914	5.9439	.004761905
211	44,521	9,393,931	14.5258	5.9533	.004739336
212	44,944	9,528,128	14.5602	5.9627	.004716981
213	45,369	9,663,597	14.5945	5.9721	.004694836
214	45,796	9,800,344	14.6287	5.9814	.004672897
215	46,225	9,938,375	14.6629	5.9907	.004651163
216	46,656	10,077,696	14.6969	6.0000	.004629630
217	47,089	10,218,313	14.7309	6.0092	.004608295
218	47,524	10,360,232	14.7648	6.0185	.004587156
219	47,961	10,503,459	14.7986	6.0277	.004566210
220	48,400	10,648,000	14.8324	6.0368	.004545455
221	48,841	10,793,861	14.8661	6.0459	.004524887
222	49,284	10,941,048	14.8997	6.0550	.004504505
223	49,729	11,089,567	14.9332	6.0641	.004484305
224	50,176	11,239,424	14.9666	6.0732	.004464286
225	50,625	11,390,625	15.0000	6.0822	.004444444
226	51,076	11,543,176	15.0333	6.0912	.004424779
227	51,529	11,697,083	15.0665	6.1002	.004405286
228	51,984	11,852,352	15.0997	6.1091	.004385965
229	52,441	12,008,989	15.1327	6.1180	.004366812
230	52,900	12,167,000	15.1658	6.1269	.004347826
231	53,361	12,326,391	15.1987	6.1358	.004329004
232	53,824	12,487,168	15.2315	6.1446	.004310345
233	54,289	12,649,337	15.2643	6.1534	.004291845
234	54,756	12,812,904	15.2971	6.1622	.004273504
235	55,225	12,977,875	15.3297	6.1710	.004255319
236	55,696	13,144,256	15.3623	6.1797	.004237288
237	56,169	13,312,053	15.3948	6.1885	.004219409
238	56,644	13,481,272	15.4272	6.1972	.004201681
239	57,121	13,651,919	15.4596	6.2058	.004184100
240	57,600	13,824,000	15.4919	6.2145	.004166667
241	58,081	13,997,521	15.5242	6.2231	.004149378
242	58,564	14,172,488	15.5563	6.2317	.004132231
243	59,049	14,348,907	15.5885	6.2403	.004115226
244	59,536	14,526,784	15.6205	6.2488	.004098361
245	60,025	14,706,125	15.6525	6.2573	.004081633
246	60,516	14,886,936	15.6844	6.2658	.004065041
247	61,009	15,069,223	15.7162	6.2743	.004048583
248	61,504	15,252,992	15.7480	6.2828	.004032258
249	62,001	15,438,249	15.7797	6.2912	.004016064
250	62,500	15,625,000	15.8114	6.2996	.004000000

Arithmetic Tables for
Numbers 1 to 1000 (continued)

250-300

No.	Square	Cube	Sq. Root	Cu. Root	Reciprocal
250	62,500	15,625,000	15.8114	6.2996	.004000000
251	63,001	15,813,251	15.8430	6.3080	.003984064
252	63,504	16,003,008	15.8745	6.3164	.003968254
253	64,009	16,194,277	15.9060	6.3247	.003952569
254	64,516	16,387,064	15.9374	6.3330	.003937008
255	65,025	16,581,375	15.9687	6.3413	.003921569
256	65,536	16,777,216	16.0000	6.3496	.003906250
257	66,049	16,974,593	16.0312	6.3579	.003891051
258	66,564	17,173,512	16.0624	6.3661	.003875969
259	67,081	17,373,979	16.0935	6.3743	.003861004
260	67,600	17,576,000	16.1245	6.3825	.003846154
261	68,121	17,779,581	16.1555	6.3907	.003831418
262	68,644	17,984,728	16.1864	6.3988	.003816794
263	69,169	18,191,447	16.2173	6.4070	.003802281
264	69,696	18,399,744	16.2481	6.4151	.003787879
265	70,225	18,609,625	16.2788	6.4232	.003773585
266	70,756	18,821,096	16.3095	6.4312	.003759398
267	71,289	19,034,163	16.3401	6.4393	.003745318
268	71,824	19,248,832	16.3707	6.4473	.003731343
269	72,361	19,465,109	16.4012	6.4553	.003717472
270	72,900	19,683,000	16.4317	6.4633	.003703704
271	73,441	19,902,511	16.4621	6.4713	.003690037
272	73,984	20,123,648	16.4924	6.4792	.003676471
273	74,529	20,346,417	16.5227	6.4872	.003663004
274	75,076	20,570,824	16.5529	6.4951	.003649635
275	75,625	20,796,875	16.5831	6.5030	.003636364
276	76,176	21,024,576	16.6132	6.5108	.003623188
277	76,729	21,253,933	16.6433	6.5187	.003610108
278	77,284	21,484,952	16.6733	6.5265	.003597122
279	77,841	21,717,639	16.7033	6.5343	.003584229
280	78,400	21,952,000	16.7332	6.5421	.003571429
281	78,961	22,188,041	16.7631	6.5499	.003558719
282	79,524	22,425,768	16.7929	6.5577	.003546099
283	80,089	22,665,187	16.8226	6.5654	.003533569
284	80,656	22,906,304	16.8523	6.5731	.003521127
285	81,225	23,149,125	16.8819	6.5808	.003508772
286	81,796	23,393,656	16.9115	6.5885	.003496503
287	82,369	23,639,903	16.9411	6.5962	.003484321
288	82,944	23,887,872	16.9706	6.6039	.003472222
289	83,521	24,137,569	17.0000	6.6115	.003460208
290	84,100	24,389,000	17.0294	6.6191	.003448276
291	84,681	24,642,171	17.0587	6.6267	.003436426
292	85,264	24,897,088	17.0880	6.6343	.003424658
293	85,849	25,153,757	17.1172	6.6419	.003412969
294	86,436	25,412,184	17.1464	6.6494	.003401361
295	87,025	25,672,375	17.1756	6.6569	.003389831
296	87,616	25,934,336	17.2047	6.6644	.003378378
297	88,209	26,198,073	17.2337	6.6719	.003367003
298	88,804	26,463,592	17.2627	6.6794	.003355705
299	89,401	26,730,899	17.2916	6.6869	.003344482
300	90,000	27,000,000	17.3205	6.6943	.003333333

Arithmetic Tables for
Numbers 1 to 1000 (continued)

300–350

No.	Square	Cube	Sq. Root	Cu. Root	Reciprocal
300	90,000	27,000,000	17.3205	6.6943	.003333333
301	90,601	27,270,901	17.3494	6.7018	.003322259
302	91,204	27,543,608	17.3781	6.7092	.003311258
303	91,809	27,818,127	17.4069	6.7166	.003300330
304	92,416	28,094,464	17.4356	6.7240	.003289474
305	93,025	28,372,625	17.4642	6.7313	.003278689
306	93,636	28,652,616	17.4929	6.7387	.003267974
307	94,249	28,934,443	17.5214	6.7460	.003257329
308	94,864	29,218,112	17.5499	6.7533	.003246753
309	95,481	29,503,629	17.5784	6.7606	.003236246
310	96,100	29,791,000	17.6068	6.7679	.003225806
311	96,721	30,080,231	17.6352	6.7752	.003215434
312	97,344	30,371,328	17.6635	6.7824	.003205128
313	97,969	30,664,297	17.6918	6.7897	.003194888
314	98,596	30,959,144	17.7200	6.7969	.003184713
315	99,225	31,255,875	17.7482	6.8041	.003174603
316	99,856	31,554,496	17.7764	6.8113	.003164557
317	100,489	31,855,013	17.8045	6.8185	.003154574
318	101,124	32,157,432	17.8326	6.8256	.003144654
319	101,761	32,461,759	17.8606	6.8328	.003134796
320	102,400	32,768,000	17.8885	6.8399	.003125000
321	103,041	33,076,161	17.9165	6.8470	.003115265
322	103,684	33,386,248	17.9444	6.8541	.003105590
323	104,329	33,698,267	17.9722	6.8612	.003095975
324	104,976	34,012,224	18.0000	6.8683	.003086420
325	105,625	34,328,125	18.0278	6.8753	.003076923
326	106,276	34,645,976	18.0555	6.8824	.003067485
327	106,929	34,965,783	18.0831	6.8894	.003058104
328	107,584	35,287,552	18.1108	6.8964	.003048780
329	108,241	35,611,289	18.1384	6.9034	.003039514
330	108,900	35,937,000	18.1659	6.9104	.003030303
331	109,561	36,264,691	18.1934	6.9174	.003021148
332	110,224	36,594,368	18.2209	6.9244	.003012048
333	110,889	36,926,037	18.2483	6.9313	.003003003
334	111,556	37,259,704	18.2757	6.9382	.002994012
335	112,225	37,595,375	18.3030	6.9451	.002985075
336	112,896	37,933,056	18.3303	6.9521	.002976190
337	113,569	38,272,753	18.3576	6.9589	.002967359
338	114,244	38,614,472	18.3848	6.9658	.002958580
339	114,921	38,958,219	18.4120	6.9727	.002949853
340	115,600	39,304,000	18.4391	6.9795	.002941176
341	116,281	39,651,821	18.4662	6.9864	.002932551
342	116,964	40,001,688	18.4932	6.9932	.002923977
343	117,649	40,353,607	18.5203	7.0000	.002915452
344	118,336	40,707,584	18.5472	7.0068	.002906977
345	119,025	41,063,625	18.5742	7.0136	.002898551
346	119,716	41,421,736	18.6011	7.0203	.002890173
347	120,409	41,781,923	18.6279	7.0271	.002881844
348	121,104	42,144,192	18.6548	7.0338	.002873563
349	121,801	42,508,549	18.6815	7.0406	.002865330
350	122,500	42,875,000	18.7083	7.0473	.002857143

Arithmetic Tables for
Numbers 1 to 1000 (continued)

350-400

No.	Square	Cube	Sq. Root	Cu. Root	Reciprocal
350	122,500	42,875,000	18.7083	7.0473	.002857143
351	123,201	43,243,551	18.7350	7.0540	.002849003
352	123,904	43,614,208	18.7617	7.0607	.002840909
353	124,609	43,986,977	18.7883	7.0674	.002832861
354	125,316	44,361,864	18.8149	7.0740	.002824859
355	126,025	44,738,875	18.8414	7.0807	.002816901
356	126,736	45,118,016	18.8680	7.0873	.002808989
357	127,449	45,499,293	18.8944	7.0940	.002801120
358	128,164	45,882,712	18.9209	7.1006	.002793296
359	128,881	46,268,279	18.9473	7.1072	.002785515
360	129,600	46,656,000	18.9737	7.1138	.002777778
361	130,321	47,045,881	19.0000	7.1204	.002770083
362	131,044	47,437,928	19.0263	7.1269	.002762431
363	131,769	47,832,147	19.0526	7.1335	.002754821
364	132,496	48,228,544	19.0788	7.1400	.002747253
365	133,225	48,627,125	19.1050	7.1466	.002739726
366	133,956	49,027,896	19.1311	7.1531	.002732240
367	134,689	49,430,863	19.1572	7.1596	.002724796
368	135,424	49,836,032	19.1833	7.1661	.002717391
369	136,161	50,243,409	19.2094	7.1726	.002710027
370	136,900	50,653,000	19.2354	7.1791	.002702703
371	137,641	51,064,811	19.2614	7.1855	.002695418
372	138,384	51,478,848	19.2873	7.1920	.002688172
373	139,129	51,895,117	19.3132	7.1984	.002680965
374	139,876	52,313,624	19.3391	7.2048	.002673797
375	140,625	52,734,375	19.3649	7.2112	.002666667
376	141,376	53,157,376	19.3907	7.2177	.002659574
377	142,129	53,582,633	19.4165	7.2240	.002652520
378	142,884	54,010,152	19.4422	7.2304	.002645503
379	143,641	54,439,939	19.4679	7.2368	.002638522
380	144,400	54,872,000	19.4936	7.2432	.002631579
381	145,161	55,306,341	19.5192	7.2495	.002624672
382	145,924	55,742,968	19.5448	7.2558	.002617801
383	146,689	56,181,887	19.5704	7.2622	.002610966
384	147,456	56,623,104	19.5959	7.2685	.002604167
385	148,225	57,066,625	19.6214	7.2748	.002597403
386	148,996	57,512,456	19.6469	7.2811	.002590674
387	149,769	57,960,603	19.6723	7.2874	.002583979
388	150,544	58,411,072	19.6977	7.2936	.002577320
389	151,321	58,863,869	19.7231	7.2999	.002570694
390	152,100	59,319,000	19.7484	7.3061	.002564103
391	152,881	59,776,471	19.7737	7.3124	.002557545
392	153,664	60,236,288	19.7990	7.3186	.002551020
393	154,449	60,698,457	19.8242	7.3248	.002544529
394	155,236	61,162,984	19.8494	7.3310	.002538071
395	156,025	61,629,875	19.8746	7.3372	.002531646
396	156,816	62,099,136	19.8997	7.3434	.002525253
397	157,609	62,570,773	19.9249	7.3496	.002518892
398	158,404	63,044,792	19.9499	7.3558	.002512563
399	159,201	63,521,199	19.9750	7.3619	.002506266
400	160,000	64,000,000	20.0000	7.3681	.002500000

Arithmetic Tables for
Numbers 1 to 1000 (continued)

400–450

No.	Square	Cube	Sq. Root	Cu. Root	Reciprocal
400	160,000	64,000,000	20.0000	7.3681	.002500000
401	160,801	64,481,201	20.0250	7.3742	.002493766
402	161,604	64,964,808	20.0499	7.3803	.002487562
403	162,409	65,450,827	20.0749	7.3864	.002481390
404	163,216	65,939,264	20.0998	7.3925	.002475248
405	164,025	66,430,125	20.1246	7.3986	.002469136
406	164,836	66,923,416	20.1494	7.4047	.002463054
407	165,649	67,419,143	20.1742	7.4108	.002457002
408	166,464	67,917,312	20.1990	7.4169	.002450980
409	167,281	68,417,929	20.2237	7.4229	.002444988
410	168,100	68,921,000	20.2485	7.4290	.002439024
411	168,921	69,426,531	20.2731	7.4350	.002433090
412	169,744	69,934,528	20.2978	7.4410	.002427184
413	170,569	70,444,997	20.3224	7.4470	.002421308
414	171,396	70,957,944	20.3470	7.4530	.002415459
415	172,225	71,473,375	20.3715	7.4590	.002409639
416	173,056	71,991,296	20.3961	7.4650	.002403846
417	173,889	72,511,713	20.4206	7.4710	.002398082
418	174,724	73,034,632	20.4450	7.4770	.002392344
419	175,561	73,560,059	20.4695	7.4829	.002386635
420	176,400	74,088,000	20.4939	7.4889	.002380952
421	177,241	74,618,461	20.5183	7.4943	.002375297
422	178,084	75,151,448	20.5426	7.5007	.002369668
423	178,929	75,686,967	20.5670	7.5067	.002364066
424	179,776	76,225,024	20.5913	7.5126	.002358491
425	180,625	76,765,625	20.6155	7.5185	.002352941
426	181,476	77,308,776	20.6398	7.5244	.002347418
427	182,329	77,854,483	20.6640	7.5302	.002341920
428	183,184	78,402,752	20.6882	7.5361	.002336449
429	184,041	78,953,589	20.7123	7.5420	.002331002
430	184,900	79,507,000	20.7364	7.5478	.002325581
431	185,761	80,062,991	20.7605	7.5537	.002320186
432	186,624	80,621,568	20.7846	7.5595	.002314815
433	187,489	81,182,737	20.8087	7.5654	.002309469
434	188,356	81,746,504	20.8327	7.5712	.002304147
435	189,225	82,312,875	20.8567	7.5770	.002298851
436	190,096	82,881,856	20.8806	7.5828	.002293578
437	190,969	83,453,453	20.9045	7.5886	.002288330
438	191,844	84,027,672	20.9284	7.5944	.002283105
439	192,721	84,604,519	20.9523	7.6001	.002277904
440	193,600	85,184,000	20.9762	7.6059	.002272727
441	194,481	85,766,121	21.0000	7.6117	.002267574
442	195,364	86,350,888	21.0238	7.6174	.002262443
443	196,249	86,938,307	21.0476	7.6232	.002257336
444	197,136	87,528,384	21.0713	7.6289	.002252252
445	198,025	88,121,125	21.0950	7.6346	.002247191
446	198,916	88,716,536	21.1187	7.6403	.002242152
447	199,809	89,314,623	21.1424	7.6460	.002237136
448	200,704	89,915,392	21.1660	7.6517	.002232143
449	201,601	90,518,849	21.1896	7.6574	.002227171
450	202,500	91,125,000	21.2132	7.6631	.002222222

Arithmetic Tables for
Numbers 1 to 1000 (continued)

450-500

No.	Square	Cube	Sq. Root	Cu. Root	Reciprocal
450	202,500	91,125,000	21.2132	7.6631	.002222222
451	203,401	91,733,851	21.2368	7.6688	.002217295
452	204,304	92,345,408	21.2603	7.6744	.002212389
453	205,209	92,959,677	21.2838	7.6801	.002207506
454	206,116	93,576,664	21.3073	7.6857	.002202643
455	207,025	94,196,375	21.3307	7.6914	.002197802
456	207,936	94,818,816	21.3542	7.6970	.002192982
457	208,849	95,443,993	21.3776	7.7026	.002188184
458	209,764	96,071,912	21.4009	7.7082	.002183406
459	210,681	96,702,579	21.4243	7.7138	.002178649
460	211,600	97,336,000	21.4476	7.7194	.002173913
461	212,521	97,972,181	21.4709	7.7250	.002169197
462	213,444	98,611,128	21.4942	7.7306	.002164502
463	214,369	99,252,847	21.5174	7.7362	.002159827
464	215,296	99,897,344	21.5407	7.7418	.002155172
465	216,225	100,544,625	21.5639	7.7473	.002150538
466	217,156	101,194,696	21.5870	7.7529	.002145923
467	218,089	101,847,563	21.6102	7.7584	.002141328
468	219,024	102,503,232	21.6333	7.7639	.002136752
469	219,961	103,161,709	21.6564	7.7695	.002132196
470	220,900	103,823,000	21.6795	7.7750	.002127660
471	221,841	104,487,111	21.7025	7.7805	.002123142
472	222,784	105,154,048	21.7256	7.7860	.002118644
473	223,729	105,823,817	21.7486	7.7915	.002114165
474	224,676	106,496,424	21.7715	7.7970	.002109705
475	225,625	107,171,875	21.7945	7.8025	.002105263
476	226,576	107,850,176	21.8174	7.8079	.002100840
477	227,529	108,531,333	21.8403	7.8134	.002096436
478	228,484	109,215,352	21.8632	7.8188	.002092050
479	229,441	109,902,239	21.8861	7.8243	.002087683
480	230,400	110,592,000	21.9089	7.8297	.002083333
481	231,361	111,284,641	21.9317	7.8352	.002079002
482	232,324	111,980,168	21.9545	7.8406	.002074689
483	233,289	112,678,587	21.9773	7.8460	.002070393
484	234,256	113,379,904	22.0000	7.8514	.002066116
485	235,225	114,084,125	22.0227	7.8568	.002061856
486	236,196	114,791,256	22.0454	7.8622	.002057613
487	237,169	115,501,303	22.0681	7.8676	.002053388
488	238,144	116,214,272	22.0907	7.8730	.002049180
489	239,121	116,930,169	22.1133	7.8784	.002044990
490	240,100	117,649,000	22.1359	7.8837	.002040816
491	241,081	118,370,771	22.1585	7.8891	.002036660
492	242,064	119,095,488	22.1811	7.8944	.002032520
493	243,049	119,823,157	22.2036	7.8998	.002028398
494	244,036	120,553,784	22.2261	7.9051	.002024291
495	245,025	121,287,375	22.2486	7.9105	.002020202
496	246,016	122,023,936	22.2711	7.9158	.002016129
497	247,009	122,763,473	22.2935	7.9211	.002012072
498	248,004	123,505,992	22.3159	7.9264	.002008032
499	249,001	124,251,499	22.3383	7.9317	.002004008
500	250,000	125,000,000	22.3607	7.9370	.002000000

Arithmetic Tables for
Numbers 1 to 1000 (continued)

500-550

No.	Square	Cube	Sq. Root	Cu. Root	Reciprocal
500	250,000	125,000,000	22.3607	7.9370	.002000000
501	251,001	125,751,501	22.3830	7.9423	.001996008
502	252,004	126,506,008	22.4054	7.9476	.001992032
503	253,009	127,263,527	22.4277	7.9528	.001988072
504	254,016	128,024,064	22.4499	7.9581	.001984127
505	255,025	128,787,625	22.4722	7.9634	.001980198
506	256,036	129,554,216	22.4944	7.9686	.001976285
507	257,049	130,323,843	22.5167	7.9739	.001972387
508	258,064	131,096,512	22.5389	7.9791	.001968504
509	259,081	131,872,229	22.5610	7.9843	.001964637
510	260,100	132,651,000	22.5832	7.9896	.001960784
511	261,121	133,432,831	22.6053	7.9948	.001956947
512	262,144	134,217,728	22.6274	8.0000	.001953125
513	263,169	135,005,697	22.6495	8.0052	.001949318
514	264,196	135,796,744	22.6716	8.0104	.001945525
515	265,225	136,590,875	22.6936	8.0156	.001941748
516	266,256	137,388,096	22.7156	8.0208	.001937984
517	267,289	138,188,413	22.7376	8.0260	.001934236
518	268,324	138,991,832	22.7596	8.0311	.001930502
519	269,361	139,798,359	22.7816	8.0363	.001926782
520	270,400	140,608,000	22.8035	8.0415	.001923077
521	271,441	141,420,761	22.8254	8.0466	.001919386
522	272,484	142,236,648	22.8473	8.0517	.001915709
523	273,529	143,055,667	22.8692	8.0569	.001912046
524	274,576	143,877,824	22.8910	8.0620	.001908397
525	275,625	144,703,125	22.9129	8.0671	.001904762
526	276,676	145,531,576	22.9347	8.0723	.001901141
527	277,729	146,363,183	22.9565	8.0774	.001897533
528	278,784	147,197,952	22.9783	8.0825	.001893939
529	279,841	148,035,889	23.0000	8.0876	.001890359
530	280,900	148,877,000	23.0217	8.0927	.001886792
531	281,961	149,721,291	23.0434	8.0978	.001883239
532	283,024	150,568,768	23.0651	8.1028	.001879699
533	284,089	151,419,437	23.0868	8.1079	.001876173
534	285,156	152,273,304	23.1084	8.1130	.001872659
535	286,225	153,130,375	23.1301	8.1180	.001869159
536	287,296	153,990,656	23.1517	8.1231	.001865672
537	288,369	154,854,153	23.1733	8.1281	.001862197
538	289,444	155,720,872	23.1948	8.1332	.001858736
539	290,521	156,590,819	23.2164	8.1382	.001855288
540	291,600	157,464,000	23.2379	8.1433	.001851852
541	292,681	158,340,421	23.2594	8.1483	.001848429
542	293,764	159,220,088	23.2809	8.1533	.001845018
543	294,849	160,103,007	23.3024	8.1583	.001841621
544	295,936	160,989,184	23.3238	8.1633	.001838235
545	297,025	161,878,625	23.3452	8.1683	.001834862
546	298,116	162,771,336	23.3666	8.1733	.001831502
547	299,209	163,667,323	23.3880	8.1783	.001828154
548	300,304	164,566,592	23.4094	8.1833	.001824818
549	301,401	165,469,149	23.4307	8.1882	.001821494
550	302,500	166,375,000	23.4521	8.1932	.001818182

Arithmetic Tables for
Numbers 1 to 1000 (continued)

550-600

No.	Square	Cube	Sq. Root	Cu. Root	Reciprocal
550	302,500	166,375,000	23.4521	8.1932	.001818182
551	303,601	167,284,151	23.4734	8.1982	.001814882
552	304,704	168,196,608	23.4947	8.2031	.001811594
553	305,809	169,112,377	23.5160	8.2081	.001808318
554	306,916	170,031,464	23.5372	8.2130	.001805054
555	308,025	170,953,875	23.5584	8.2180	.001801802
556	309,136	171,879,616	23.5797	8.2229	.001798561
557	310,249	172,808,693	23.6008	8.2278	.001795332
558	311,364	173,741,112	23.6220	8.2327	.001792115
559	312,481	174,676,879	23.6432	8.2377	.001788909
560	313,600	175,616,000	23.6643	8.2426	.001785714
561	314,721	176,558,481	23.6854	8.2475	.001782531
562	315,844	177,504,328	23.7065	8.2524	.001779359
563	316,969	178,453,547	23.7276	8.2573	.001776199
564	318,096	179,406,144	23.7487	8.2621	.001773050
565	319,225	180,362,125	23.7697	8.2670	.001769912
566	320,356	181,321,496	23.7908	8.2719	.001766784
567	321,489	182,284,263	23.8118	8.2768	.001763668
568	322,624	183,250,432	23.8328	8.2816	.001760563
569	323,761	184,220,009	23.8537	8.2865	.001757469
570	324,900	185,193,000	23.8747	8.2913	.001754386
571	326,041	186,169,411	23.8956	8.2962	.001751313
572	327,184	187,149,248	23.9165	8.3010	.001748252
573	328,329	188,132,517	23.9374	8.3059	.001745201
574	329,476	189,119,224	23.9583	8.3107	.001742160
575	330,625	190,109,375	23.9792	8.3155	.001739130
576	331,776	191,102,976	24.0000	8.3203	.001736111
577	332,929	192,100,033	24.0208	8.3251	.001733102
578	334,084	193,100,552	24.0416	8.3300	.001730104
579	335,241	194,104,539	24.0624	8.3348	.001727116
580	336,400	195,112,000	24.0832	8.3396	.001724138
581	337,561	196,122,941	24.1039	8.3443	.001721170
582	338,724	197,137,368	24.1247	8.3491	.001718213
583	339,889	198,155,287	24.1454	8.3539	.001715266
584	341,056	199,176,704	24.1661	8.3587	.001712329
585	342,225	200,201,625	24.1868	8.3634	.001709402
586	343,396	201,230,056	24.2074	8.3682	.001706485
587	344,569	202,262,003	24.2281	8.3730	.001703578
588	345,744	203,297,472	24.2487	8.3777	.001700680
589	346,921	204,336,469	24.2693	8.3825	.001697793
590	348,100	205,379,000	24.2899	8.3872	.001694915
591	349,281	206,425,071	24.3105	8.3919	.001692047
592	350,464	207,474,688	24.3311	8.3967	.001689189
593	351,649	208,527,857	24.3516	8.4014	.001686341
594	352,836	209,584,584	24.3721	8.4061	.001683502
595	354,025	210,644,875	24.3926	8.4108	.001680672
596	355,216	211,708,736	24.4131	8.4155	001677852
597	356,409	212,776,173	24.4336	8.4202	.001675042
598	357,604	213,847,192	24.4540	8.4249	.001672241
599	358,801	214,921,799	24.4745	8.4296	.001669449
600	360,000	216,000,000	24.4949	8.4343	.001666667

Arithmetic Tables for
Numbers 1 to 1000 (continued)

600-650

No.	Square	Cube	Sq. Root	Cu. Root	Reciprocal
600	360,000	216,000,000	24.4949	8.4343	.001666667
601	361,201	217,081,801	24.5153	8.4390	.001663894
602	362,404	218,167,208	24.5357	8.4437	.001661130
603	363,609	219,256,227	24.5561	8.4484	.001658375
604	364,816	220,348,864	24.5764	8.4530	.001655629
605	366,025	221,445,125	24.5967	8.4577	.001652893
606	367,236	222,545,016	24.6171	8.4623	.001650165
607	368,449	223,648,543	24.6374	8.4670	.001647446
608	369,664	224,755,712	24.6577	8.4716	.001644737
609	370,881	225,866,529	24.6779	8.4763	.001642036
610	372,100	226,981,000	24.6982	8.4809	.001639344
611	373,321	228,099,131	24.7184	8.4856	.001636661
612	374,544	229,220,928	24.7386	8.4902	.001633987
613	375,769	230,346,397	24.7588	8.4948	.001631321
614	376,996	231,475,544	24.7790	8.4994	.001628664
615	378,225	232,608,375	24.7992	8.5040	.001626016
616	379,456	233,744,896	24.8193	8.5086	.001623377
617	380,689	234,885,113	24.8395	8.5132	.001620746
618	381,924	236,029,032	24.8596	8.5178	.001618123
619	383,161	237,176,659	24.8797	8.5224	.001615509
620	384,400	238,328,000	24.8998	8.5270	.001612903
621	385,641	239,483,061	24.9199	8.5316	.001610306
622	386,884	240,641,848	24.9399	8.5362	.001607717
623	388,129	241,804,367	24.9600	8.5408	.001605136
624	389,376	242,970,624	24.9800	8.5453	.001602564
625	390,625	244,140,625	25.0000	8.5499	.001600000
626	391,876	245,314,376	25.0200	8.5544	.001597444
627	393,129	246,491,883	25.0400	8.5590	.001594896
628	394,384	247,673,152	25.0599	8.5635	.001592357
629	395,641	248,858,189	25.0799	8.5681	.001589825
630	396,900	250,047,000	25.0998	8.5726	.001587302
631	398,161	251,239,591	25.1197	8.5772	.001584786
632	399,424	252,435,968	25.1396	8.5817	.001582278
633	400,689	253,636,137	25.1595	8.5862	.001579779
634	401,956	254,840,104	25.1794	8.5907	.001577287
635	403,225	256,047,875	25.1992	8.5952	.001574803
636	404,496	257,259,456	25.2190	8.5997	.001572327
637	405,769	258,474,853	25.2389	8.6043	.001569859
638	407,044	259,694,072	25.2587	8.6088	.001567398
639	408,321	260,917,119	25.2784	8.6132	.001564945
640	409,600	262,144,000	25.2982	8.6177	.001562500
641	410,881	263,374,721	25.3180	8.6222	.001560062
642	412,164	264,609,288	25.3377	8.6267	.001557632
643	413,449	265,847,707	25.3574	8.6312	.001555210
644	414,736	267,089,984	25.3772	8.6357	.001552795
645	416,025	268,336,125	25.3969	8.6401	.001550388
646	417,316	269,586,136	25.4165	8.6446	.001547988
647	418,609	270,840,023	25.4362	8.6490	.001545595
648	419,904	272,097,792	25.4558	8.6535	.001543210
649	421,201	273,359,449	25.4755	8.6579	.001540832
650	422,500	274,625,000	25.4951	8.6624	.001538462

Arithmetic Tables for
Numbers 1 to 1000 (continued)

650-700

No.	Square	Cube	Sq. Root	Cu. Root	Reciprocal
650	422,500	274,625,000	25.4951	8.6624	.001538462
651	423,801	275,894,451	25.5147	8.6668	.001536098
652	425,104	277,167,808	25.5343	8.6713	.001533742
653	426,409	278,445,077	25.5539	8.6757	.001531394
654	427,716	279,726,264	25.5734	8.6801	.001529052
655	429,025	281,011,375	25.5930	8.6845	.001526718
656	430,336	282,300,416	25.6125	8.6890	.001524390
657	431,649	283,593,393	25.6320	8.6934	.001522070
658	432,964	284,890,312	25.6515	8.6978	.001519757
659	434,281	286,191,179	25.6710	8.7022	.001517451
660	435,600	287,496,000	25.6905	8.7066	.001515152
661	436,921	288,804,781	25.7099	8.7110	.001512859
662	438,244	290,117,528	25.7294	8.7154	.001510574
663	439,569	291,434,247	25.7488	8.7198	.001508296
664	440,896	292,754,944	25.7682	8.7241	.001506024
665	442,225	294,079,625	25.7876	8.7285	.001503759
666	443,556	295,408,296	25.8070	8.7329	.001501502
667	444,889	296,740,963	25.8263	8.7373	.001499250
668	446,224	298,077,632	25.8457	8.7416	.001497006
669	447,561	299,418,309	25.8650	8.7460	.001494768
670	448,900	300,763,000	25.8844	8.7503	.001492537
671	450,241	302,111,711	25.9037	8.7547	.001490313
672	451,584	303,464,448	25.9230	8.7590	.001488095
673	452,929	304,821,217	25.9422	8.7634	.001485884
674	454,276	306,182,024	25.9615	8.7677	.001483680
675	455,625	307,546,875	25.9808	8.7721	.001481481
676	456,976	308,915,776	26.0000	8.7764	.001479290
677	458,329	310,288,733	26.0192	8.7807	.001477105
678	459,684	311,665,752	26.0384	8.7850	.001474926
679	461,041	313,046,839	26.0576	8.7893	.001472754
680	462,400	314,432,000	26.0768	8.7937	.001470588
681	463,761	315,821,241	26.0960	8.7980	.001468429
682	465,124	317,214,568	26.1151	8.8023	.001466276
683	466,489	318,611,987	26.1343	8.8066	.001464129
684	467,856	320,013,504	26.1534	8.8109	.001461988
685	469,225	321,419,125	26.1725	8.8152	.001459854
686	470,596	322,828,856	26.1916	8.8194	.001457726
687	471,969	324,242,703	26.2107	8.8237	.001455604
688	473,344	325,660,672	26.2298	8.8280	.001453488
689	474,721	327,082,769	26.2488	8.8323	.001451379
690	476,100	328,509,000	26.2679	8.8366	.001449275
691	477,481	329,939,371	26.2869	8.8408	.001447178
692	478,864	331,373,888	26.3059	8.8451	.001445087
693	480,249	332,812,557	26.3249	8.8493	.001443001
694	481,636	334,255,384	26.3439	8.8536	.001440922
695	483,025	335,702,375	26.3629	8.8578	.001438849
696	484,416	337,153,536	26.3818	8.8621	.001436782
697	485,809	338,608,873	26.4008	8.8663	.001434720
698	487,204	340,068,392	26.4197	8.8706	.001432665
699	488,601	341,532,099	26.4386	8.8748	.001430615
700	490,000	343,000,000	26.4575	8.8790	.001428571

Arithmetic Tables for
Numbers 1 to 1000 (continued)

700-750

No.	Square	Cube	Sq. Root	Cu. Root	Reciprocal
700	490,000	343,000,000	26.4575	8.8790	.001428571
701	491,401	344,472,101	26.4764	8.8833	.001426534
702	492,804	345,948,408	26.4953	8.8875	.001424501
703	494,209	347,428,927	26.5141	8.8917	.001422475
704	495,616	348,913,664	26.5330	8.8959	.001420455
705	497,025	350,402,625	26.5518	8.9001	.001418440
706	498,436	351,895,816	26.5707	8.9043	.001416431
707	499,849	353,393,243	26.5895	8.9085	.001414427
708	501,264	354,894,912	26.6083	8.9127	.001412429
709	502,681	356,400,829	26.6271	8.9169	.001410437
710	504,100	357,911,000	26.6458	8.9211	.001408451
711	505,521	359,425,431	26.6646	8.9253	.001406470
712	506,944	360,944,128	26.6833	8.9295	.001404494
713	508,369	362,467,097	26.7021	8.9337	.001402525
714	509,796	363,994,344	26.7208	8.9378	.001400560
715	511,225	365,525,875	26.7395	8.9420	.001398601
716	512,656	367,061,696	26.7582	8.9462	.001396648
717	514,089	368,601,813	26.7769	8.9503	.001394700
718	515,524	370,146,232	26.7955	8.9545	.001392758
719	516,961	371,694,959	26.8142	8.9587	.001390821
720	518,400	373,248,000	26.8328	8.9628	.001388889
721	519,841	374,805,361	26.8514	8.9670	.001386963
722	521,284	376,367,048	26.8701	8.9711	.001385042
723	522,729	377,933,067	26.8887	8.9752	.001383126
724	524,176	379,503,424	26.9072	8.9794	.001381215
725	525,625	381,078,125	26.9258	8.9835	.001379310
726	527,076	382,657,176	26.9444	8.9876	.001377410
727	528,529	384,240,583	26.9629	8.9918	.001375516
728	529,984	385,828,352	26.9815	8.9959	.001373626
729	531,441	387,420,489	27.0000	9.0000	.001371742
730	532,900	389,017,000	27.0185	9.0041	.001369863
731	534,361	390,617,891	27.0370	9.0082	.001367989
732	535,824	392,223,168	27.0555	9.0123	.001366120
733	537,289	393,832,837	27.0740	9.0164	.001364256
734	538,756	395,446,904	27.0924	9.0205	.001362398
735	540,225	397,065,375	27.1109	9.0246	.001360544
736	541,696	398,688,256	27.1293	9.0287	.001358696
737	543,169	400,315,553	27.1477	9.0328	.001356852
738	544,644	401,947,272	27.1662	9.0369	.001355014
739	546,121	403,583,419	27.1846	9.0410	.001353180
740	547,600	405,224,000	27.2029	9.0450	.001351351
741	549,081	406,869,021	27.2213	9.0491	.001349528
742	550,564	408,518,488	27.2397	9.0532	.001347709
743	552,049	410,172,407	27.2580	9.0572	.001345895
744	553,536	411,830,784	27.2764	9.0613	.001344086
745	555,025	413,493,625	27.2947	9.0654	.001342282
746	556,516	415,160,936	27.3130	9.0694	.001340483
747	558,009	416,832,723	27.3313	9.0735	.001338688
748	559,504	418,508,992	27.3496	9.0775	.001336898
749	561,001	420,189,749	27.3679	9.0816	.001335113
750	562,500	421,875,000	27.3861	9.0856	.001333333

Arithmetic Tables for
Numbers 1 to 1000 (continued)

750–800

No.	Square	Cube	Sq. Root	Cu. Root	Reciprocal
750	562,500	421,875,000	27.3861	9.0856	.001333333
751	564,001	423,564,751	27.4044	9.0896	.001331558
752	565,504	425,259,008	27.4226	9.0937	.001329787
753	567,009	426,957,777	27.4408	9.0977	.001328021
754	568,516	428,661,064	27.4591	9.1017	.001326260
755	570,025	430,368,875	27.4773	9.1057	.001324503
756	571,536	432,081,216	27.4955	9.1098	.001322751
757	573,049	433,798,093	27.5136	9.1138	.001321004
758	574,564	435,519,512	27.5318	9.1178	.001319261
759	576,081	437,245,479	27.5500	9.1218	.001317523
760	577,600	438,976,000	27.5681	9.1258	.001315789
761	579,121	440,711,081	27.5862	9.1298	.001314060
762	580,644	442,450,728	27.6043	9.1338	.001312336
763	582,169	444,194,947	27.6225	9.1378	.001310616
764	583,696	445,943,744	27.6405	9.1418	.001308901
765	585,225	447,697,125	27.6586	9.1458	.001307190
766	586,756	449,455,096	27.6767	9.1498	.001305483
767	588,289	451,217,663	27.6948	9.1537	.001303781
768	589,824	452,984,832	27.7128	9.1577	.001302083
769	591,361	454,756,609	27.7308	9.1617	.001300390
770	592,900	456,533,000	27.7489	9.1657	.001298701
771	594,441	458,314,011	27.7669	9.1696	.001297017
772	595,984	460,099,648	27.7849	9.1736	.001295337
773	597,529	461,889,917	27.8029	9.1775	.001293661
774	599,076	463,684,824	27.8209	9.1815	.001291990
775	600,625	465,484,375	27.8388	9.1855	.001290323
776	602,176	467,288,576	27.8568	9.1894	.001288660
777	603,729	469,097,433	27.8747	9.1933	.001287001
778	605,284	470,910,952	27.8927	9.1973	.001285347
779	606,841	472,729,139	27.9106	9.2012	.001283697
780	608,400	474,552,000	27.9285	9.2052	.001282051
781	609,961	476,379,541	27.9464	9.2091	.001280410
782	611,524	478,211,768	27.9643	9.2130	.001278772
783	613,089	480,048,687	27.9821	9.2170	.001277139
784	614,656	481,890,304	28.0000	9.2209	.001275510
785	616,225	483,736,625	28.0179	9.2248	.001273885
786	617,796	485,587,656	28.0357	9.2287	.001272265
787	619,369	487,443,403	28.0535	9.2326	.001270648
788	620,944	489,303,872	28.0713	9.2365	.001269036
789	622,521	491,169,069	28.0891	9.2404	.001267427
790	624,100	493,039,000	28.1069	9.2443	.001265823
791	625,681	494,913,671	28.1247	9.2482	.001264223
792	627,264	496,793,088	28.1425	9.2521	.001262626
793	628,849	498,677,257	28.1603	9.2560	.001261034
794	630,436	500,566,184	28.1780	9.2599	.001259446
795	632,025	502,459,875	28.1957	9.2638	.001257862
796	633,616	504,358,336	28.2135	9.2677	.001256281
797	635,209	506,261,573	28.2312	9.2716	.001254705
798	636,804	508,169,592	28.2489	9.2754	.001253133
799	638,401	510,082,399	28.2666	9.2793	.001251564
800	640,000	512,000,000	28.2843	9.2832	.001250000

Arithmetic Tables for
Numbers 1 to 1000 (continued)

800-850

No.	Square	Cube	Sq. Root	Cu. Root	Reciprocal
800	640,000	512,000,000	28.2843	9.2832	.001250000
801	641,601	513,922,401	28.3019	9.2870	.001248439
802	643,204	515,849,608	28.3196	9.2909	.001246883
803	644,809	517,781,627	28.3373	9.2948	.001245330
804	646,416	519,718,464	28.3549	9.2986	.001243781
805	648,025	521,660,125	28.3725	9.3025	.001242236
806	649,636	523,606,616	28.3901	9.3063	.001240695
807	651,249	525,557,943	28.4077	9.3102	.001239157
808	652,864	527,514,112	28.4253	9.3140	.001237624
809	654,481	529,475,129	28.4429	9.3179	.001236094
810	656,100	531,441,000	28.4605	9.3217	.001234568
811	657,721	533,411,731	28.4781	9.3255	.001233046
812	659,344	535,387,328	28.4956	9.3294	.001231527
813	660,969	537,367,797	28.5132	9.3332	.001230012
814	662,596	539,353,144	28.5307	9.3370	.001228501
815	664,225	541,343,375	28.5482	9.3408	.001226994
816	665,856	543,338,496	28.5657	9.3447	.001225490
817	667,489	545,338,513	28.5832	9.3485	.001223990
818	669,124	547,343,432	28.6007	9.3523	.001222494
819	670,761	549,353,259	28.6182	9.3561	.001221001
820	672,400	551,368,000	28.6356	9.3599	.001219512
821	674,041	553,387,661	28.6531	9.3637	.001218027
822	675,684	555,412,248	28.6705	9.3675	.001216545
823	677,329	557,441,767	28.6880	9.3713	.001215067
824	678,976	559,476,224	28.7054	9.3751	.001213592
825	680,625	561,515,625	28.7228	9.3789	.001212121
826	682,276	563,559,976	28.7402	9.3827	.001210654
827	683,929	565,609,283	28.7576	9.3865	.001209190
828	685,584	567,663,552	28.7750	9.3902	.001207729
829	687,241	569,722,789	28.7924	9.3940	.001206273
830	688,900	571,787,000	28.8097	9.3978	.001204819
831	690,561	573,856,191	28.8271	9.4016	.001203369
832	692,224	575,930,368	28.8444	9.4053	.001201923
833	693,889	578,009,537	28.8617	9.4091	.001200480
834	695,556	580,093,704	28.8791	9.4129	.001199041
835	697,225	582,182,875	28.8964	9.4166	.001197605
836	698,896	584,277,056	28.9137	9.4204	.001196172
837	700,569	586,376,253	28.9310	9.4241	.001194743
838	702,244	588,480,472	28.9482	9.4279	.001193317
839	703,921	590,589,719	28.9655	9.4316	.001191895
840	705,600	592,704,000	28.9828	9.4354	.001190476
841	707,281	594,823,321	29.0000	9.4391	.001189061
842	708,964	596,947,688	29.0172	9.4429	.001187648
843	710,649	599,077,107	29.0345	9.4466	.001186240
844	712,336	601,211,584	29.0517	9.4503	.001184834
845	714,025	603,351,125	29.0689	9.4541	.001183432
846	715,716	605,495,736	29.0861	9.4578	.001182033
847	717,409	607,645,423	29.1033	9.4615	.001180638
848	719,104	609,800,192	29.1204	9.4652	.001179245
849	720,801	611,960,049	29.1376	9.4690	.001177856
850	722,500	614,125,000	29.1548	9.4727	.001176471

Arithmetic Tables for
Numbers 1 to 1000 (continued)

850–900

No.	Square	Cube	Sq. Root	Cu. Root	Reciprocal
850	722,500	614,125,000	29.1548	9.4727	.001176471
851	724,201	616,295,051	29.1719	9.4764	.001175088
852	725,904	618,470,208	29.1890	9.4801	.001173709
853	727,609	620,650,477	29.2062	9.4838	.001172333
854	729,316	622,835,864	29.2233	9.4875	.001170960
855	731,025	625,026,375	29.2404	9.4912	.001169591
856	732,736	627,222,016	29.2575	9.4949	.001168224
857	734,449	629,422,793	29.2746	9.4986	.001166861
858	736,164	631,628,712	29.2916	9.5023	.001165501
859	737,881	633,839,779	29.3087	9.5060	.001164144
860	739,600	636,056,000	29.3258	9.5097	.001162791
861	741,321	638,277,381	29.3428	9.5134	.001161440
862	743,044	640,503,928	29.3598	9.5171	.001160093
863	744,769	642,735,647	29.3769	9.5207	.001158749
864	746,496	644,972,544	29.3939	9.5244	.001157407
865	748,225	647,214,625	29.4109	9.5281	.001156069
866	749,956	649,461,896	29.4279	9.5317	.001154734
867	751,689	651,714,363	29.4449	9.5354	.001153403
868	753,424	653,972,032	29.4618	9.5391	.001152074
869	755,161	656,234,909	29.4788	9.5427	.001150748
870	756,900	658,503,000	29.4958	9.5464	.001149425
871	758,641	660,776,311	29.5127	9.5501	.001148106
872	760,384	663,054,848	29.5296	9.5537	.001146789
873	762,129	665,338,617	29.5466	9.5574	.001145475
874	763,876	667,627,624	29.5635	9.5610	.001144165
875	765,625	669,921,875	29.5804	9.5647	.001142857
876	767,376	672,221,376	29.5973	9.5683	.001141553
877	769,129	674,526,133	29.6142	9.5719	.001140251
878	770,884	676,836,152	29.6311	9.5756	.001138952
879	772,641	679,151,439	29.6479	9.5792	.001137656
880	774,400	681,472,000	29.6648	9.5828	.001136364
881	776,161	683,797,841	29.6816	9.5865	.001135074
882	777,924	686,128,968	29.6985	9.5901	.001133787
883	779,689	688,465,387	29.7153	9.5937	.001132503
884	781,456	690,807,104	29.7321	9.5973	.001131222
885	783,225	693,154,125	29.7489	9.6010	.001129944
886	784,996	695,506,456	29.7658	9.6046	.001128668
887	786,769	697,864,103	29.7825	9.6082	.001127396
888	788,544	700,227,072	29.7993	9.6118	.001126126
889	790,321	702,595,369	29.8161	9.6154	.001124859
890	792,100	704,969,000	29.8329	9.6190	.001123596
891	793,881	707,347,971	29.8496	9.6226	.001122334
892	795,664	709,932,288	29.8664	9.6262	.001121076
893	797,449	712,121,957	29.8831	9.6298	.001119821
894	799,236	714,516,984	29.8998	9.6334	.001118568
895	801,025	716,917,375	29.9166	9.6370	.001117318
896	802,816	719,323,136	29.9333	9.6406	.001116071
897	804,609	721,734,273	29.9500	9.6442	.001114827
898	806,404	724,150,792	29.9666	9.6477	.001113586
899	808,201	726,572,699	29.9833	9.6513	.001112347
900	810,000	729,000,000	30.0000	9.6549	.001111111

Arithmetic Tables for
Numbers 1 to 1000 (continued)

900-950

No.	Square	Cube	Sq. Root	Cu. Root	Reciprocal
900	810,000	729,000,000	30.0000	9.6549	.001111111
901	811,801	731,432,701	30.0167	9.6585	.001109878
902	813,604	733,870,808	30.0333	9.6620	.001108647
903	815,409	736,314,327	30.0500	9.6656	.001107420
904	817,216	738,763,264	30.0666	9.6692	.001106195
905	819,025	741,217,625	30.0832	9.6727	.001104972
906	820,836	743,677,416	30.0998	9.6763	.001103753
907	822,649	746,142,643	30.1164	9.6799	.001102536
908	824,464	748,613,312	30.1330	9.6834	.001101322
909	826,281	751,089,429	30.1496	9.6870	.001100110
910	828,100	753,571,000	30.1662	9.6905	.001098901
911	829,921	756,058,031	30.1828	9.6941	.001097695
912	831,744	758,550,528	30.1993	9.6976	.001096491
913	833,569	761,048,497	30.2159	9.7012	.001095290
914	835,396	763,551,944	30.2324	9.7047	.001094092
915	837,225	766,060,875	30.2490	9.7082	.001092896
916	839,056	768,575,296	30.2655	9.7118	.001091703
917	840,889	771,095,213	30.2820	9.7153	.001090513
918	842,724	773,620,632	30.2985	9.7188	.001089325
919	844,561	776,151,559	30.3150	9.7224	.001088139
920	846,400	778,688,000	30.3315	9.7259	.001086957
921	848,241	781,229,961	30.3480	9.7294	.001085776
922	850,084	783,777,448	30.3645	9.7329	.001084599
923	851,929	786,330,467	30.3809	9.7364	.001083424
924	853,776	788,889,024	30.3974	9.7400	.001082251
925	855,625	791,453,125	30.4138	9.7435	.001081081
926	857,476	794,022,776	30.4302	9.7470	.001079914
927	859,329	796,597,983	30.4467	9.7505	.001078749
928	861,184	799,178,752	30.4631	9.7540	.001077586
929	863,041	801,765,089	30.4795	9.7575	.001076426
930	864,900	804,357,000	30.4959	9.7610	.001075269
931	866,761	806,954,491	30.5123	9.7645	.001074114
932	868,624	809,557,568	30.5287	9.7680	.001072961
933	870,489	812,166,237	30.5450	9.7715	.001071811
934	872,356	814,780,504	30.5614	9.7750	.001070664
935	874,225	817,400,375	30.5778	9.7785	.001069519
936	876,096	820,025,856	30.5941	9.7819	.001068376
937	877,969	822,656,953	30.6105	9.7854	.001067236
938	879,844	825,293,672	30.6268	9.7889	.001066098
939	881,721	827,936,019	30.6431	9.7924	.001064963
940	883,600	830,584,000	30.6594	9.7959	.001063830
941	885,481	833,237,621	30.6757	9.7993	.001062699
942	887,364	835,896,888	30.6920	9.8028	.001061571
943	889,249	838,561,807	30.7083	9.8063	.001060445
944	891,136	841,232,384	30.7246	9.8097	.001059322
945	893,025	843,908,625	30.7409	9.8132	.001058201
946	894,916	846,590,536	30.7571	9.8167	.001057082
947	896,809	849,278,123	30.7734	9.8201	.001055966
948	898,704	851,971,392	30.7896	9.8236	.001054852
949	900,601	854,670,349	30.8058	9.8270	.001053741
950	902,500	857,375,000	30.8221	9.8305	.001052632

Arithmetic Tables for
Numbers 1 to 1000 (continued)

950-1000

No.	Square	Cube	Sq. Root	Cu. Root	Reciprocal
950	902,500	857,375,000	30.8221	9.8305	.001052632
951	904,401	860,085,351	30.8383	9.8339	.001051525
952	906,304	862,801,408	30.8545	9.8374	.001050420
953	908,209	865,523,177	30.8707	9.8408	.001049318
954	910,116	868,250,664	30.8869	9.8443	.001048218
955	912,025	870,983,875	30.9031	9.8477	.001047120
956	913,936	873,722,816	30.9192	9.8511	.001046025
957	915,849	876,467,493	30.9354	9.8546	.001044932
958	917,764	879,217,912	30.9516	9.8580	.001043841
959	919,681	881,974,079	30.9677	9.8614	.001042753
960	921,600	884,736,000	30.9839	9.8648	.001041667
961	923,521	887,503,681	31.0000	9.8683	.001040583
962	925,444	890,277,128	31.0161	9.8717	.001039501
963	927,369	893,056,347	31.0322	9.8751	.001038422
964	929,296	895,841,344	31.0483	9.8785	.001037344
965	931,225	898,632,125	31.0644	9.8819	.001036269
966	933,156	901,428,696	31.0805	9.8854	.001035197
967	935,089	904,231,063	31.0966	9.8888	.001034126
968	937,024	907,039,232	31.1127	9.8922	.001033058
969	938,961	909,853,209	31.1288	9.8956	.001031992
970	940,900	912,673,000	31.1448	9.8990	.001030928
971	942,841	915,498,611	31.1609	9.9024	.001029866
972	944,784	918,330,048	31.1769	9.9058	.001028807
973	946,729	921,167,317	31.1929	9.9092	.001027749
974	948,676	924,010,424	31.2090	9.9126	.001026694
975	950,625	926,859,375	31.2250	9.9160	.001025641
976	952,576	929,714,176	31.2410	9.9194	.001024590
977	954,529	932,574,833	31.2570	9.9227	.001023541
978	956,484	935,441,352	31.2730	9.9261	.001022495
979	958,441	938,313,739	31.2890	9.9295	.001021450
980	960,400	941,192,000	31.3050	9.9329	.001020408
981	962,361	944,076,141	31.3209	9.9363	.001019368
982	964,324	946,966,168	31.3369	9.9396	.001018330
983	966,289	949,862,087	31.3528	9.9430	.001017294
984	968,256	952,763,904	31.3688	9.9464	.001016260
985	970,225	955,671,625	31.3847	9.9497	.001015228
986	972,196	958,585,256	31.4006	9.9531	.001014199
987	974,169	961,504,803	31.4166	9.9565	.001013171
988	976,144	964,430,272	31.4325	9.9598	.001012146
989	978,121	967,361,669	31.4484	9.9632	.001011122
990	980,100	970,299,000	31.4643	9.9666	.001010101
991	982,081	973,242,271	31.4802	9.9699	.001009082
992	984,064	976,191,488	31.4960	9.9733	.001008065
993	986,049	979,146,657	31.5119	9.9766	.001007049
994	988,036	982,107,784	31.5278	9.9800	.001006036
995	990,025	985,074,875	31.5436	9.9833	.001005025
996	992,016	988,047,936	31.5595	9.9866	.001004016
997	994,009	991,026,973	31.5753	9.9900	.001003009
998	996,004	994,011,992	31.5911	9.9933	.001002004
999	998,001	997,002,999	31.6070	9.9967	.001001001
1000	1,000,000	1,000,000,000	31.6228	10.0000	.001000000

INDEX